CONCEPTS AND CHALLENGES IN PHYSICAL SCIENCE

CONCEPTS AND CHALLENGES IN

Physical Science

SECOND EDITION

LEONARD BERNSTEIN

MARTIN SCHACHTER

ALAN WINKLER

STANLEY WOLFE

STANLEY WOLFE
Project Coordinator

Globe Book Company, Inc.
A CEBCO BOOK
New York/Cleveland/Toronto

ALAN WINKLER

Alan Winkler has taught science in the New York City Public Schools for more than twenty-five years. He has served on several science curriculum committees for the New York City Board of Education, was a writer of the science course of study for Grades 6, 7, and 9, and prepared a special-purpose laboratory program for earth science in Grade 9. Mr. Winkler has also been a consultant in the preparation of filmstrip series in earth science.

LEONARD BERNSTEIN

Leonard Bernstein is the Director of the Isaac Newton School for Mathematics and Science in New York City. His success in science teaching was nationally featured in an article published in the *Wall Street Journal.* Mr. Bernstein is an author of science textbooks and serves as a consultant and lecturer on science teaching methods for college classes, National Science Foundation Institutes, and in-service workshops. He has been a member of the New York City Science Curriculum Revision Committee and has served as consulting editor to the New York City Division of Curriculum Development.

MARTIN SCHACHTER

Martin Schachter is Assistant Principal, Supervision of Science, at Frederick Douglass Intermediate School in New York City. He is a member of the Science Standing Committee of the Bureau of Science for the New York City Board of Education, an instructor in Teacher-Training Workshops in Science sponsored by the New York City Board of Education, and an author of many of the science courses of study in use in the New York City Junior High and Intermediate Schools. Mr. Schachter is a Past President of the Junior High School-Intermediate School Chairmen's Association; a member of American Mensa Ltd.; a consultant for Mississippi Educational Television; an instructor in Science Update, sponsored by the New York City Board of Education; and a lecturer in science education.

STANLEY WOLFE
Project Coordinator

Stanley Wolfe is Assistant Principal supervising science and mathematics at Peter Rouget Intermediate School in New York City. He has had wide experience in the development and implementation of middle-school science curricula and has participated in the writing of the current New York City Science Curriculum for Grades 6, 7, 8, and 9. He has also written an eighth-grade career guidance course of study. Mr. Wolfe is a past Coordinator of the New York City Science Fair.

ISBN 0-87065-466-7

Printed in the United States of America

9 8 7 6 5 4 3

CONTENTS

Why do we measure?

SEEDLESS
raisins
NET WT. 15 OZ.   425 GRAMS

PITTED
PRUNES

NET WT. 12 OUNCES
340 GRAMS

How much? When you shop, you want to get the most for your money. When you buy chopped meat, you want to know how much meat is in the package. The label on the package tells you how much it weighs. Weight is one way of describing the amount of something. Weight is one of the properties of matter that can be measured. Length, area, and volume are also properties we can measure. To find out things about matter, we must describe its properties. Many properties can be measured.

▶ **What are some properties of matter that we can measure?**

Units of mass. We buy chopped meat by the pound. The pound is a <u>unit</u> (YOU-nit) of weight. Scientists do not use weight to mean the amount of something. They use the word mass. They measure mass in grams. The gram is a unit of mass in the <u>metric system</u> (MEH-tric SIS-tem). A nickel has a mass of about 5 grams. Weight and mass are related, but they are not the same. You will learn more about weight and mass in another lesson.

▶ **What unit is used to measure mass in the metric system?**

Too much is too many. The gram is sometimes too small for certain measurements. The mass in grams comes out in large numbers. A person may have a mass of 75,000 grams. The mass of a car may be as much as 1,500,000 grams. It would help to have a larger unit of mass. Then the numbers would be smaller.

▶ **Why is the gram sometimes too small for measuring masses?**

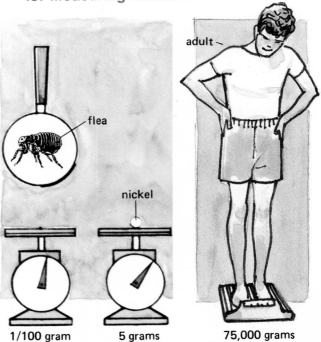

flea

nickel

adult

1/100 gram   5 grams   75,000 grams

Cutting it to size. For large objects, the gram may be too small. For small objects, the gram may be too big. The mass of an insect may be only 1/100 of a gram. The metric system can solve this problem.

PREFIX		MEANING
mega-	(MEG-uh)	one million (1,000,000)
kilo-	(KILL-uh)	one thousand (1,000)
hecto-	(HEC-tuh)	one hundred (100)
deca-	(DEC-uh)	ten (10)
deci-	(DESS-ih)	one tenth (1/10)
centi-	(SEN-tih)	one hundredth (1/100)
milli-	(MILL-ih)	one thousandth (1/1,000)
micro-	(MIKE-roh)	one millionth (1/1,000,000)

Look at the table. A prefix (PREE-fix) can be used to change the size of a unit. It can make the unit larger or smaller. "Kilo-" (KILL-uh) is a prefix that means 1,000. A kilogram (KILL-uh-gram) is 1,000 grams. The mass of large objects is measured in kilograms. A person with a mass of 75,000 grams has a mass of 75 kilograms. "Centi-" (SEN-tih) is a prefix meaning 1/100. An insect with a mass of 1/100 of a gram has a mass of 1 centigram.

▶ **What is a kilogram?**

Just a minute! You have a date at 8:00. How long must you wait? Scientists say that the earth is 5 billion years old. How old are you? Time is not matter. But time matters! It is important to measure time. In daily life, we use many different units to measure time. The second, the minute, the hour, the day, the year, and the century (100 years) are units of time. The second is the main unit of time in the metric system.

▶ **What is the unit for measuring time in the metric system?**

WHAT YOU LEARNED

1. The amount of matter is called its mass.
2. In the metric system, mass is measured in grams.
3. Prefixes are used to make units larger or smaller.
4. Time is measured in seconds.

SCIENCE WORDS

unit (YOU-nit)
  an amount that is used to measure things
gram
  a unit of mass in the metric system
metric system (MEH-trick SIS-tem)
  the units of measurement used by scientists
kilogram (KILL-uh-gram)
  1,000 grams

ANSWER THESE

1. Write the following masses in order from the smallest to the largest.
   milligram
   kilogram
   microgram
   hectogram
   centigram
   gram
2. Use the table of prefixes to find the meaning of each of these:
   microsecond
   millisecond
   megaton

NOW TRY THESE

1. How many seconds are there in a century? Give your answer in megaseconds.
2. Scientists sometimes measure the cost of scientific equipment in "megabucks." A large atom-smasher may cost 500 megabucks to build. What do you think that means?

FINDING OUT MORE

The International Bureau of Weights and Measures is located near Paris, France. The standard unit of mass is kept there. This mass is exactly 1,000 grams or 1 kilogram. Each nation keeps a copy of this mass in its own national laboratory. This is done so that scientists all over the world can be sure they are measuring mass in the same units. The standard kilogram is made of a platinum-iridium alloy that will not rust. It is carefully protected against damage. What might happen if this standard mass became scratched?

How do we measure size?

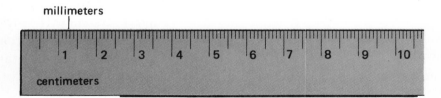

millimeters

centimeters

The long and the short of it. In the metric system, we measure length and distance in a unit called the <u>meter</u> (MEE-ter). We use prefixes to make larger and smaller units of length. A <u>kilometer</u> (KILL-uh-mee-ter) is 1,000 meters. A <u>centimeter</u> (SEN-tih-mee-ter) is 1/100 of a meter. A <u>millimeter</u> (MILL-ih-mee-ter) is 1/1000 of a meter. The table compares the units of length.

▶ **What is the unit of length in the metric system?**

10 millimeters	= 1 centimeter
1000 millimeters	= 1 meter
100 centimeters	= 1 meter
1000 meters	= 1 kilometer

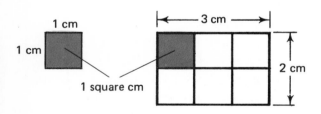

Length x Width = Area

$$\underset{cm}{3} \times \underset{cm}{2} = \underset{\substack{square \\ centimeters}}{6}$$

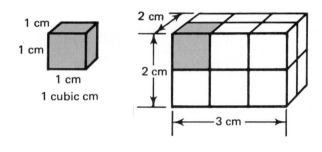

Length x Width x Height = Volume

$$\underset{cm}{3} \times \underset{cm}{2} \times \underset{cm}{2} = \underset{\substack{cubic \\ centimeters}}{12}$$

Measuring area. Look at the drawing of the square. Each side of the square is 1 centimeter long. The area of the square is 1 square centimeter. Now look at the drawing of the rectangle. Its length is 3 centimeters. Its width is 2 centimeters. You can see that the rectangle contains 6 square centimeters. Its area is 6 square centimeters. You can find the area of a rectangle by multiplying its length by its width.

▶ **How can we find the area of a rectangle?**

Measuring volume. Look at the drawing of the cube. Each edge of the cube is 1 centimeter long. The volume of the cube is 1 cubic centimeter. Now look at the drawing of the box. Its length is 3 centimeters. Its width is 2 centimeters. Its height is 2 centimeters. Its volume is 12 cubic centimeters. The volume of a box can be found by multiplying its length by its width by its height.

▶ **How can we find the volume of a box?**

Volume of liquids. Volume is measured in cubic centimeters. Volume can also be measured in units called <u>liters</u> (LEE-ters). The volume of liquids is often measured in liters. A liter is the same as 1,000 cubic centimeters. A box that is 10 centimeters on each side has a volume of 1,000 cubic centimeters (10 x 10 x 10 = 1,000). One liter of a liquid will exactly fill the box. A milliliter (MILL-ih-lee-ter) is 1/1000 of a liter. A milliliter is the same as 1 cubic centimeter.

▶ **How many cubic centimeters are there in 1 liter?**

Abbreviating units. Milligram, kilometer, and cubic centimeter are long words. It takes a lot of space and a lot of time to write them out. We abbreviate (uh-BREE-vee-ate), or shorten, the names of units. For example, km is the abbreviation for kilometer. To abbreviate units of area and volume, we use a small 2 to show square units and a small 3 to show cubic units. To abbreviate square centimeters, we write cm^2. To abbreviate cubic centimeters, we write cm^3. The table shows the abbreviations for units in the metric system.

▶ **How would we abbreviate 100 cubic centimeters?**

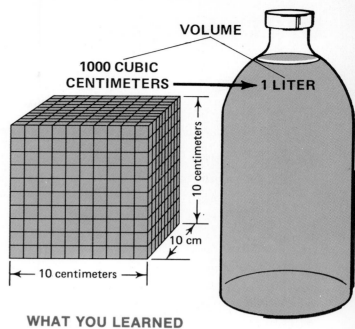

NAME OF UNIT	ABBREVIATION
gram	g
kilogram	kg
milligram	mg
meter	m
kilometer	km
centimeter	cm
millimeter	mm
square centimeters	cm^2
cubic centimeters	cm^3
liter	L
milliliter	mL

WHAT YOU LEARNED

1. The unit of length is the meter.
2. Area is measured in square units.
3. Volume is measured in cubic units.
4. A liter is the same as 1,000 cubic centimeters.
5. Units can be abbreviated.

SCIENCE WORDS

meter (MEE-ter)
the unit of length in the metric system
kilometer (KILL-uh-mee-ter)
1,000 meters
centimeter (SEN-tih-mee-ter)
1/100 of a meter
millimeter (MILL-ih-mee-ter)
1/1000 of a meter
liter (LEE-ter)
1,000 cubic centimeters

ANSWER THESE

1. The unit of length is the
   a. meter
   b. liter
   c. kilogram
2. The volume of liquids is measured in
   a. square centimeters
   b. cubic liters
   c. liters
3. Width X height X length of a box equals its
   a. area
   b. weight
   c. volume

UNIT REVIEW

Do the following questions on a separate sheet of paper.

Matching   *Write down the statements in Column I. Next to each measurement from Column I write the measurement from Column II that is the same.*

Column I	Column II
Group A	
1. 1000 milligrams	10 mg
2. 10,000 grams	100 mg
3. 0.1 gram	1 g
4. 0.1 kilogram	100 g
5. 0.01 gram	10 kg
Group B	
6. 10 centimeters	1 km
7. 1000 centimeters	10 m
8. 1000 millimeters	100 mm
9. 0.1 kilometer	100 m
10. 1000 meters	100 cm

Multiple Choice   *Write the letter of the choice that best completes the statement or answers the question.*

1. The gram is a unit of
   a. mass
   b. weight
   c. volume
2. The prefix for 1000 is
   a. milli-
   b. kilo-
   c. micro-
3. A rectangle 4 cm x 6 cm has an area of
   a. 10 square centimeters
   b. 24 square centimeters
   c. 24 cubic centimeters

4. A bottle marked 1.5 liters has a volume of
   a. 500 cm
   b. 1.5 cubic liters
   c. 150 milliliters
5. A box that is 10 cm x 5 cm has a volume of
   a. 500 cm
   b. 500 cm^2
   c. 500 cm^3

1

Work and Energy

Unit Lessons

1. What are the different forms of energy?
2. How can energy change its form?
3. What happens to energy after it is used?
4. What is conservation of energy?
5. What are the two basic kinds of energy?
6. What is work?
7. How can work be measured?

Goals and Objectives

After completing this unit, you should be able to:
- describe the different forms of energy.
- give examples of energy changing its form.
- define thermal pollution.
- explain the theory of conservation of energy.
- differentiate between potential and kinetic energy.
- define work and the units it is measured by.

What are the different forms of energy?

MECHANICAL ENERGY

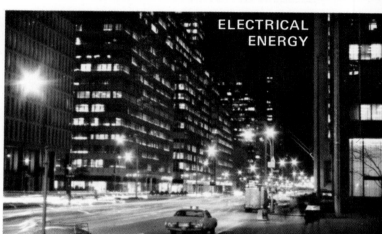

ELECTRICAL ENERGY

Energy and movement. Energy (EN-ur-jee) can make things move. Your body gets energy from the foods you eat. Every time you move, your body uses energy. Automobiles use the energy in gasoline to make them move. Energy is needed to make things move.

▶ What can energy do?

Forms of energy. There are many different forms of energy. These are some of the important forms of energy:

1. *Mechanical Energy.* Energy in moving things is mechanical (muh-CAN-ih-cul) energy. Wind, moving water, falling rocks, and machines that are working all have mechanical energy.

2. *Electrical Energy.* Electrical (ih-LEC-trih-cul) energy is the energy in moving electrons. Radios, television sets, refrigerators, and light bulbs all use electrical energy.

3. *Heat Energy.* Heat energy is the energy in moving molecules. Rub your hands together, and they become warm. Heat energy makes them warm. All things contain some heat energy.

4. *Light Energy.* Light is a form of energy. Some energy comes from the sun to the earth as light energy.

HEAT ENERGY

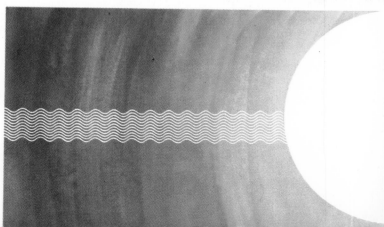

LIGHT ENERGY

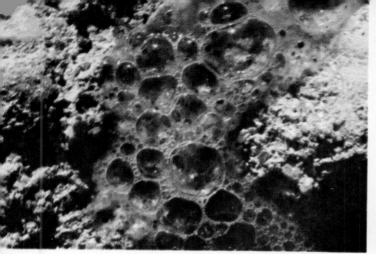

CHEMICAL ENERGY

ATOMIC ENERGY

SOUND ENERGY

5. *Chemical Energy.* Chemical energy is energy stored in chemicals. Add some dilute acid to limestone. It will bubble and fizz. Chemical energy is being released.

6. *Atomic Energy.* Atomic energy is the energy stored in the nucleus of the atom. The light and heat from the sun are produced from atomic energy. The sun will give off light and heat for millions of years. Atomic energy is used on earth to make electricity.

7. *Sound Energy.* During a storm, loud claps of thunder are sometimes heard. These loud sounds can cause houses to shake. Sound energy can make things move.

▶ What are the different forms of energy?

WHAT YOU LEARNED

1. Energy can make things move.
2. Different forms of energy are: electrical energy, heat energy, light energy, chemical energy, mechanical energy, sound energy, and atomic energy.

ANSWER THESE

1. The sun gives off _____ and _____ energy.
2. The noise that a jet makes is _____ energy.
3. Make a list of all the kinds of energy a car uses.

NOW TRY THIS

Match the object in the first column with the energy it contains in the second column. Some things may contain more than one form of energy.

gasoline	sound energy
river	atomic energy
the sun	chemical energy
burning wood	light energy
lightning	heat energy
explosions	electrical energy
	mechanical energy

How can energy change its form?

MECHANICAL ENERGY

SOUND ENERGY

Changing mechanical energy. Mechanical energy can become sound energy. Blow up a balloon. Stick a pin in it. It bursts with a bang. Mechanical energy is used to blow up the balloon. When the balloon breaks, sound energy is produced. Drive a nail into a piece of wood. Part of the mechanical energy from the hammer is changed into sound energy. Pull the nail out of the wood. Feel how hot the nail is. Part of the mechanical energy used to pull the nail out of the wood has been changed into heat energy.

▶ What energy change takes place when a balloon bursts?

Changing chemical energy. Strike a match. Many different energy changes take place. You use mechanical energy to move the match. The mechanical energy is changed into heat energy. The heat energy makes the match start to burn. Burning changes the chemical energy in the match into heat and light energy.

▶ What happens to the chemical energy in a burning match?

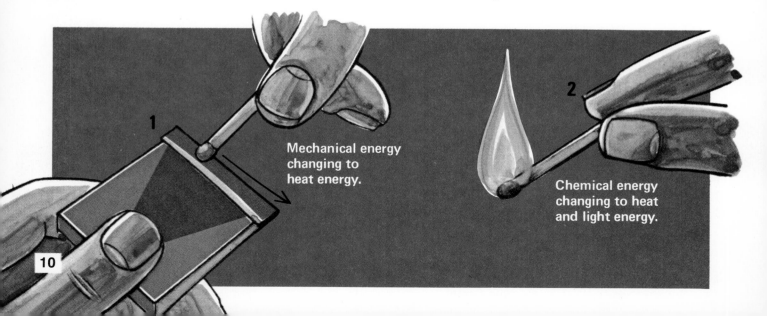

1 Mechanical energy changing to heat energy.

2 Chemical energy changing to heat and light energy.

HEAT ENERGY

LIGHT ENERGY

ELECTRICAL ENERGY

Energy can change form. Many examples of changing forms of energy are around us. When you turn on an electric light, electrical energy is changed into light and heat. When an automobile runs, it changes the chemical energy in gasoline into mechanical energy. Some power plants change atomic energy to electrical energy. Our muscles change the chemical energy in food into mechanical energy. This makes us able to move and to lift things. When we talk, mechanical energy of air moving in our throat is changed to sound energy. Look around you. Where can you see examples of energy changes?

▶ Give two examples of energy changes that take place in your body.

WHAT YOU LEARNED

1. Energy can change from one form to another.
2. Energy changes are going on all around us.

ANSWER THESE

What kinds of energy changes take place in the following examples?
1. The wind slams a door shut with a bang.
2. Lightning strikes a tree and sets it on fire.

DO THIS AT HOME

Each experiment listed below shows energy changing form. Try each experiment. List the changes of energy that take place.

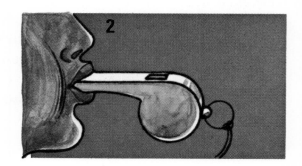

Pull out the nail and feel it.

What happens to energy after it is used?

Where does energy go? During a basketball game the players use a lot of energy. What happens to the energy that has been used? Where does it go? As the players run, their bodies get warmer. This makes the air in the gym warmer. Much of the energy used by the players is changed into heat.

▶ **What happens to the energy basketball players use during a game?**

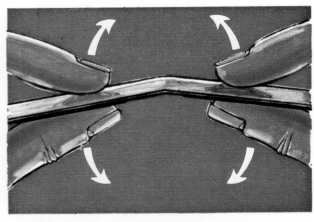

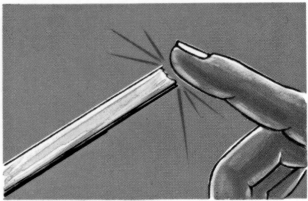

Bending metal. Bend a strip of metal back and forth until it breaks. Mechanical energy is used to bend the metal. What happens to the energy after it is used? Feel the broken ends of the metal strip. They are hot. The mechanical energy has been changed to heat energy.

▶ **What happens to the mechanical energy used to bend a metal strip?**

Wasted heat energy. When energy changes form, some of it is always changed into heat. Most of the time this heat energy is wasted. Scientists and engineers try to find ways to avoid wasting heat energy. They try to build machines that do not give

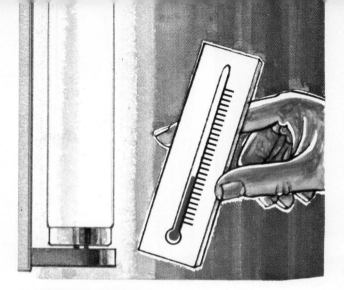

off too much waste heat energy. Place your hand near an ordinary light bulb that is turned on. Do the same thing to a lighted fluorescent bulb. The regular light bulb is much hotter than the fluorescent bulb. The fluorescent bulb can give off just as much light as the regular bulb. But the fluorescent bulb gives off less heat. It does not waste as much energy as the regular bulb. It stays cool.

▶ **What always happens when energy changes form?**

Thermal pollution. When waste heat energy affects the environment, it causes thermal (THUR-mul) pollution. Thermal pollution is causing the air and waters of the earth to become warmer. Water from lakes and rivers is used to remove waste heat energy from power plants. This makes the water warmer. This warm water is poured back into the lakes and rivers. The rivers and lakes become too warm for some living things. Fish may die. Too much heat energy can change the environment.

▶ **What kind of pollution can be caused by waste heat?**

WHAT YOU LEARNED

1. Much energy is changed into heat energy after it is used.
2. When energy changes form, some heat energy is always produced.
3. Wasted heat energy is causing thermal pollution.

SCIENCE WORDS

thermal (THUR-mul) **pollution**
wasted heat that warms the air and waters of the earth

ANSWER THESE

1. Mechanical energy used to break a metal strip becomes
   a. heat energy
   b. chemical energy
   c. mechanical energy
2. Most wasted energy from machines is given off as
   a. light energy
   b. heat energy
   c. sound energy

NOW TRY THIS

1. Explain how energy is wasted in each of the following:
   a. automobiles
   b. television sets
   c. electric lights
2. Unscramble the words below. Each one is the name of something that is used to produce heat energy.
   VOETS
   VEON
   RNAECUF
   BLIOER

DO THIS AT HOME

Look around your house. Try to find things that waste heat energy. Make a list of these things. Can the wasted heat energy from these things cause any problems in your home environment?

What is conservation of energy?

Conservation of energy. We know that energy can change from one form to another. It can move from place to place. But energy can never be lost. Energy can never be made or destroyed. It can only be changed in form. This is called <u>conservation</u> (con-ser-VAY-shun) of energy.

▶ What is conservation of energy?

Energy from the sun. The sun gives off great amounts of heat and light. This energy spreads out all through space. Some of it reaches the earth. Without the light and heat energy from the sun, there could be no life on earth. The energy from the sun goes through many changes on earth. In the end, it all changes to heat energy, and goes back out to space. Energy moves from place to place. Energy changes form. But energy is never lost. Energy is conserved.

▶ What happens to the sun's energy that reaches the earth?

What is a theory? Scientists have studied energy for many years. They have done many experiments with energy and made many observations about it. With the results of these experiments and observations, scientists have formed many ideas about energy. A scientific idea that is

This picture shows coal being delivered to a power plant. Energy from the sun was stored in the coal millions of years ago. In the power plant, the energy will be changed to heat, mechanical energy, and electrical energy.

based on observations and experiments is called a <u>theory</u> (THEE-uh-ree). A theory is an idea based on scientific experiments or observations. Conservation of energy is a theory about energy.

▶ **What is a theory?**

WHAT YOU LEARNED

1. Energy cannot be created or destroyed. It can only be changed from one form to another.
2. A theory is an idea based on scientific experiments or observations.

SCIENCE WORDS

conservation (con-ser-VAY-shun)
   saving
theory (THEE-uh-ree)
   an idea based on scientific experiments or observations

ANSWER THESE

1. Energy cannot be
   a. made or changed
   b. destroyed or changed
   c. made or destroyed
2. A theory is based on
   a. a guess
   b. what you think should happen
   c. observations and experiments
3. Energy comes from
   a. theories
   b. other forms of energy
   c. experiments
4. Energy from the sun is
   a. never changed in form
   b. always conserved
   c. destroyed in space

PEOPLE IN SCIENCE

Albert Einstein (1879-1955)

Albert Einstein was one of the greatest scientists who ever lived. His ideas changed man's thinking about the universe. Before Einstein, scientists thought that matter and energy were different things. Albert Einstein proved that they are different forms of the same thing. Energy can become matter. Matter can become energy. Conservation of energy is still true. Matter and energy cannot be made or destroyed. They can only be changed in form or changed into each other.

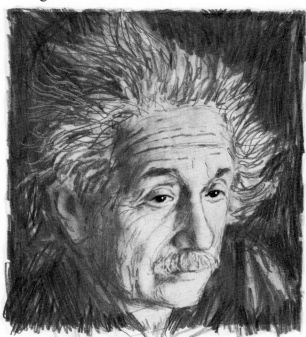

What are the two basic kinds of energy?

Potential energy. <u>Potential</u> (puh-TEN-shul) <u>energy</u> is stored energy. A match has potential energy. Some of the potential energy in a match is stored in the chemicals in the match head. When you strike a match, you release this potential energy. The match burns, giving off heat and light. Potential energy stored in chemicals is called potential chemical energy.

▶ What is potential chemical energy?

Potential mechanical energy. Mechanical energy can be stored. Wind a clock. The clock spring stores mechanical energy. Stored mechanical energy is called potential mechanical energy. As the clock runs, the stored energy is released. This energy makes the clock work.

▶ What is potential mechanical energy?

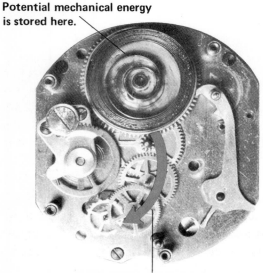

Potential mechanical energy is stored here.

Released mechanical energy runs the clock.

CHEMICAL ENERGY STORED

CHEMICAL ENERGY RELEASED

Energy from gravity. Things that are raised off the ground have potential energy. When they fall, the energy is released. When a falling object hits the earth, it releases energy as sound and heat. Falling water can turn a water wheel and produce mechanical energy. The earth's <u>gravity</u> (GRAV-uh-tee) pulls down

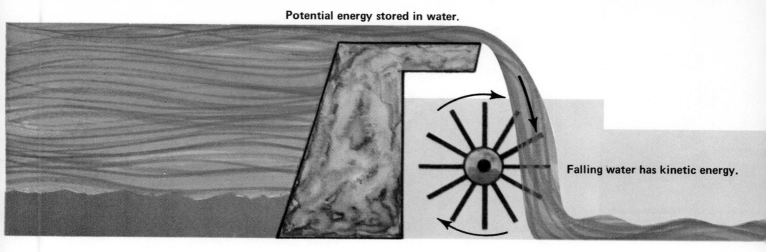

Potential energy stored in water.

Falling water has kinetic energy.

on things and makes them fall. Things that can fall have potential gravitational (grav-uh-TAY-shun-ul) energy.

▶ **What things have potential gravitational energy?**

Kinetic energy. Moving things have energy. The energy in moving things is called kinetic (kuh-NET-ic) energy. When moving things are stopped, their kinetic energy is changed. When you catch a ball, the kinetic energy of the ball is changed into heat and sound. The faster things move, the more kinetic energy they have. A line drive has more kinetic energy than a pop fly. Things that are not moving have no kinetic energy.

▶ **What is kinetic energy?**

WHAT YOU LEARNED

1. Stored energy is potential energy.
2. Energy of movement is kinetic energy.

SCIENCE WORDS

potential (puh-TEN-shul) **energy**
   stored energy
gravity (GRAV-uh-tee)
   the force that pulls things down toward the center of the earth
kinetic (kuh-NET-ic) **energy**
   energy in moving things

ANSWER THESE

Copy these sentences and fill in the missing words. The first letter of each missing word is shown.

1. Match heads store energy as p_____ c_____ energy.
2. Watches and clocks store energy as p_____ m_____ energy.
3. Things that can fall have p_____ g_____ energy.
4. Moving things have k_____ energy.
5. The faster things move, the more k_____ e_____ they have.

NOW TRY THIS

Find the science word.

FINDING OUT MORE

Kinetic and potential energy are conserved. Kinetic and potential energy follow the laws of conservation of energy. To understand this, imagine a large rock on top of a cliff. The rock can fall. It has potential gravitational energy. As the rock falls, it loses its potential energy. The potential energy is being changed into kinetic energy. When the moving rock hits the ground, its kinetic energy is changed into sound and heat. Energy has not been created or destroyed. Energy has been changed in form.

What is work?

Work. Two boys pushed a car stuck in the mud. They were not able to move the car. They were very tired afterwards. The next day in school their teacher told them that they had not done any work when they pushed the car. The boys were very surprised. The teacher explained that for work to be done something must be moved. The boys used a great deal of force, but the car did not move. Work was not done. Work is done when a force makes something move.

▶ **When is work done?**

Work and energy. When a force moves an object, work is done. Energy is the ability to do work. Anything that can make something else move has energy. A moving baseball bat has energy. It can do work. When it hits the ball, the ball moves. A dry cell has energy. It can do work. Electrical energy can turn an electric motor. The energy stored in gasoline can make a car move.

▶ **What is energy?**

ENERGY DOING WORK

Using energy without doing work. Work is not done unless an object moves. The boys pushing the car used a great deal of energy. But no work was done. Energy does not have to do work. Energy may be used without doing any work.

▶ How can energy be used without doing work?

Motion without work. Objects can move without work. Once a rocketship escapes the earth's gravity, its engines can be shut off. It will continue to move through space on a straight course. But no work is being done to keep it moving. It is not being moved by a force. If there is no force pushing or pulling the object, there is no work done.

▶ Why is no work being done when a rocketship moves through space?

WHAT YOU LEARNED

1. Work is done when a force moves an object.
2. Energy is the ability to do work.
3. Energy can be used without doing work.

SCIENCE WORD

energy
   the ability to do work

ENERGY
DOING
NO WORK

ANSWER THESE

1. A boy holds a heavy package for one hour. He is very tired but has not done any work. Explain why he did not do any work.
2. A girl is coasting on a bicycle. She is moving very fast. But she is not doing any work. Explain why no work is being done.
3. A football player kicks a field goal. When is work being done on the football? When is no work being done on the football?

NOW TRY THIS

Which of the following pictures show work being done? Explain your answer.

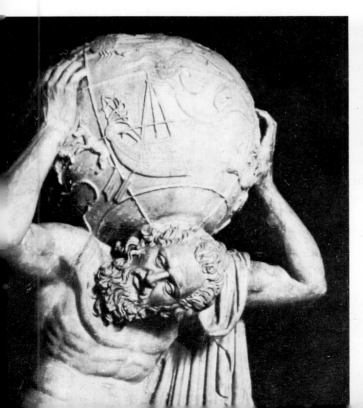

How can work be measured?

FORCE = 10 newtons

mass weighing 10 newtons

DISTANCE = 2 meters

Work = Force used x Distance moved
Work = 10 newtons x 2 meters
Work = 20 newton-meters

Work has two parts. To do work, two things are needed. There has to be a force, and the force has to make an object move. To measure the amount of work, you need to know two things. You need to know the amount of the force used. You need to know the distance the object moves. To find the amount of work, multiply the force by the distance.

▶ **What two things must be known to measure work?**

Measuring work. Lift a mass weighing 10 newtons. (A quart of milk weighs about 9 newtons.) Lift the mass 2 meters. The force of 10 newtons made the mass move 2 meters. To find the amount of work done, multiply the force by the distance.

▶ **How do we find the amount of work done?**

Units of work. A newton is a unit of force. We can measure force in newtons. A meter is a unit of distance. We can measure distance in meters. A newton-meter is a unit of work. It is made of two units multiplied

together. One unit is a unit of force. The other is a unit of distance. We can measure work in newton-meters.

▶ **What can we measure in newton-meters?**

Direction counts. Use a spring scale to pull a mass weighing 10 newtons along a table top. The scale will show less than 10 newtons of force. It may show 4 newtons of force while you

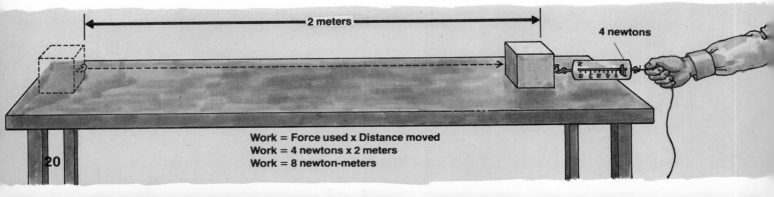

2 meters

4 newtons

Work = Force used x Distance moved
Work = 4 newtons x 2 meters
Work = 8 newton-meters

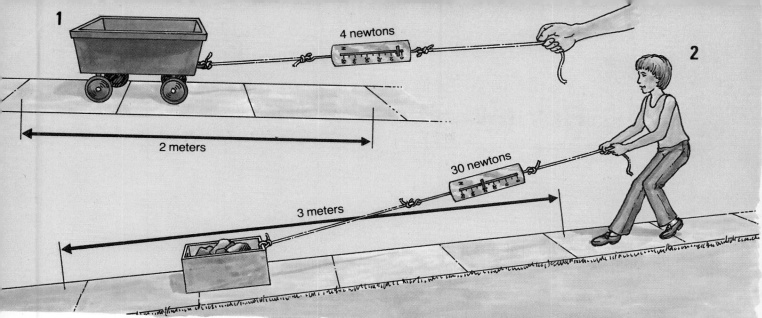

are pulling the mass. Move the mass 2 meters along the table. How much work is done? Multiply the force used by the distance moved. The weight of 10 newtons doesn't count in this case. What counts is the force used to make the object move. The force must be in the same direction as the movement.

▶ **What force do we need to know in order to measure work?**

A special unit of work. If a force of 1 newton moves an object 1 meter, 1 newton-meter of work is done. The newton-meter is a unit of work. Scientists have a shorter name for a newton-meter. They call it a joule (JOOL). One joule equals one newton-meter. A joule is a unit of work.

▶ **If you do 5 newton-meters of work, how many joules is that?**

WHAT YOU LEARNED

1. Work equals force used times distance moved.
2. When force is measured in newtons and distance is measured in meters, work is measured in newton-meters.
3. One newton-meter of work is called one joule.

SCIENCE WORDS

newton-meter
a unit of work
joule (JOOL)
one newton-meter of work

ANSWER THESE
Look at the pictures above. Find the work done. The scale shows the force used.

FINDING OUT MORE

Two men wanted to move a heavy package upstairs. They could not decide if they should carry it up step-by-step or pull it up with a rope. They sat down to figure out which was more work. This is what they discovered. It didn't matter whether the package was lifted step-by-step or pulled up with a rope. The same amount of work is done.

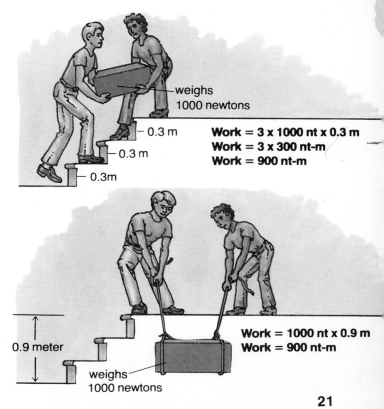

weighs 1000 newtons

—0.3 m
—0.3 m
—0.3m

Work = 3 x 1000 nt x 0.3 m
Work = 3 x 300 nt-m
Work = 900 nt-m

0.9 meter

weighs 1000 newtons

Work = 1000 nt x 0.9 m
Work = 900 nt-m

21

Do the following questions on a separate sheet of paper.

Fill in the Blank   *Write down the statements in Column I. Where there is a blank line in each statement, write the word or phrase from Column II that best completes the meaning of the statement.*

Column I	Column II

Column I

1. The earth's pull on objects is _____.
2. One newton-meter of work is called a _____ .
3. The ability to do work is _____ .
4. Work is done when a force makes something _____ .
5. The energy in moving things is _____ .
6. Stored energy is called _____ .
7. Things that can fall have _____ .
8. The theory that energy cannot be made or destroyed is called the _____ .
9. Atomic energy is stored in the _____ of an atom.
10. Heat energy is the energy of _____ .

Column II

joule
nucleus
gravity
potential energy
moving molecules
energy
kinetic energy
conservation of energy
    theory
move
potential gravitational
    energy

Multiple Choice   *Write the letter of the choice that best completes the statement or answers the question.*

1. Electrical energy is the energy of
   a. chemicals
   b. moving electrons
   c. light
2. Energy cannot be destroyed, but it can
   a. change form
   b. be made
   c. turn into non-energy
3. The faster things move, the more
   a. light energy they have
   b. chemical energy they have
   c. kinetic energy they have
4. A clock spring stores
   a. chemical energy
   b. gravity
   c. potential mechanical energy

5. Work has been done when
   a. energy is used
   b. a force moves an object
   c. energy is conserved
6. If no force is applied to an object,
   a. work is being done
   b. no work is being done
   c. it gains energy
7. A newton is a unit of
   a. force
   b. energy
   c. gravity
8. Work is equal to the force used times
   a. one newton
   b. the weight of the object
   c. the distance moved

UNIT 2

Machines

Unit Lessons

1. How do machines help us?
2. What is a lever?
3. How does a lever work?
4. How do ramps help us do work?
5. How do pulleys help us do work?
6. Why do things turn?

Goals and Objectives

After completing this unit, you should be able to:
- list the ways in which machines make our lives easier.
- name and describe some simple machines.
- explain what a moment of force is.

UNIT 2
Machines
1

How do machines help us?

Jobs for a machine. Machines make work easier for us. The pictures show machines that help people do work. A motor moves a boat. A crane lifts large amounts of material. A pencil sharpener grinds a smooth point on a pencil.

▶ **What do machines do?**

Putting force where you want it. Push down on the key of a typewriter. The letter pops up and hits the paper. Turn the handle of an egg beater. The blades whiz around. Push on the end of a jar opener. The lid comes off the jar. Each of these machines puts a force where you want it. You push down on the typewriter key. The letter hits the paper. You turn the handle of the egg beater. The blades at the other end whip the eggs. Machines help you put force where you want it.

▶ **What is one thing that machines can do to a force?**

Making forces larger. Did you ever try to get the lid off a jar with your bare hand? The lid is on too tight. Your fingers cannot push hard enough to get the lid off. You can do it with a jar opener. The opener multiplies the force you use and makes it larger. It makes the force large enough to get the lid off. Many machines help us do work by making forces larger.

▶ **How does a jar opener help us take the lid off a jar?**

A machine helps you to put a force where you want it.

useful force comes out here

force put in here

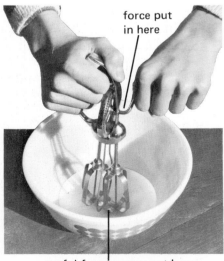

force put in here

useful force comes out here

small force here

large force here

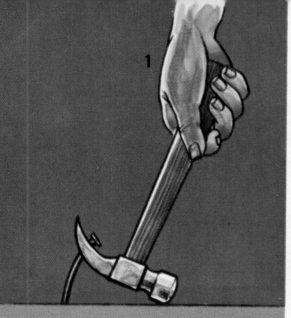

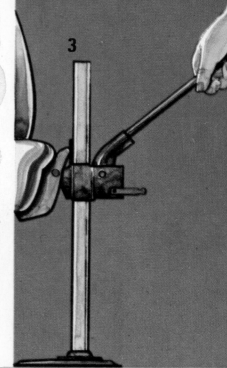

Making things move faster. Turn the handle of an egg beater. The blades spin around much faster than the handle. You could not move your hand that fast. The egg beater helps you beat the eggs quickly. On a bicycle, your feet push the pedals slowly. The bicycle races along the street. The bicycle moves faster than you could run. Many machines are used to make things move faster.

▶ **What can a machine do to the speed of a moving object?**

WHAT YOU LEARNED

1. Machines make work easier for us.
2. Machines can put a force where we want it.
3. Machines can make a force larger.
4. Machines can make things move faster.

ANSWER THESE

Look at these pictures of machines. Explain how each machine puts force where we want it.

WHAT'S HAPPENING

Rube Goldberg was a cartoonist famous for his drawings of funny machines. His machines did very simple things in the hardest possible way. You may have seen pictures of his machines. Most of them had many parts. They would take many steps to do something like turning on a light. The picture shows one machine invented by Rube Goldberg. Can you understand how it works?

PROFESSOR BUTTS STEPS INTO AN OPEN ELEVATOR SHAFT AND WHEN HE LANDS AT THE BOTTOM HE FINDS A SIMPLE ORANGE SQUEEZING MACHINE. MILK MAN TAKES EMPTY MILK BOTTLE(A)PULLING STRING(B) WHICH CAUSES SWORD(C)TO SEVER CORD(D) AND ALLOW GUILLOTINE BLADE(E)TO DROP AND CUT ROPE(F)WHICH RELEASES BATTERING RAM(G).RAM BUMPS AGAINST OPEN DOOR(H)CAUSING IT TO CLOSE. GRASS SICKLE(I)CUTS A SLICE OFF END OF ORANGE(J)AT THE SAME TIME SPIKE(K)STABS PRUNE HAWK(L)HE OPENS HIS MOUTH TO YELL IN AGONY, THEREBY RELEASING PRUNE AND ALLOWING DIVER'S BOOT(M)TO DROP AND STEP ON SLEEPING OCTOPUS(N). OCTOPUS AWAKENS IN A RAGE AND SEEING DIVER'S FACE WHICH IS PAINTED ON ORANGE, ATTACKS IT AND CRUSHES IT WITH TENTACLES, THEREBY CAUSING ALL THE JUICE IN THE ORANGE TO RUN INTO GLASS(O).
LATER ON YOU CAN USE THE LOG TO BUILD A LOG CABIN WHERE YOU CAN RAISE YOUR SON TO BE PRESIDENT LIKE ABRAHAM LINCOLN.

What is a lever?

Moving heavy objects. Many large buildings were built before modern machines were invented. These buildings were made of heavy stone. How were these stones moved? One way these stones were moved was with long sticks. These long sticks were used as levers (LEV-ers). Levers are a kind of machine. They change force and make work easier. Levers can increase force. Levers are still used to move heavy objects.

▶ **What can levers be used for?**

The fulcrum. A lever has different parts. One of the parts of the lever is the fulcrum (FULL-crum). The fulcrum is the point where the lever is supported. When the lever is used, it moves around the fulcrum.

▶ **Where is a lever supported?**

The effort arm. The side of the lever that you push on is called the effort (EFF-ert) arm. The force that you push with is called the effort. The length of the effort arm is the distance from the effort to the fulcrum.

▶ **What is the effort arm?**

The resistance arm. The object moved by a lever is called the resistance (rih-ZIS-tense). The end of the lever that moves the resistance is called the resistance arm. The length of the resistance arm is the distance from the resistance to the fulcrum.

▶ **What is the resistance arm?**

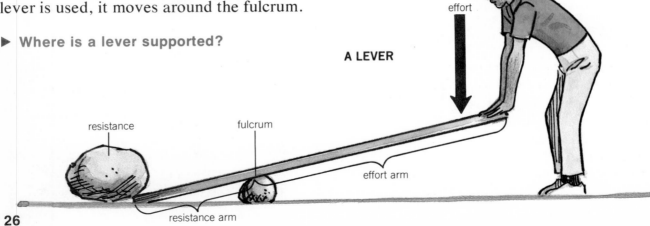

A LEVER

effort

resistance

fulcrum

effort arm

resistance arm

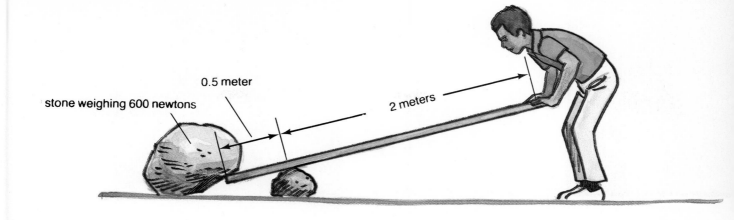

stone weighing 600 newtons

0.5 meter

2 meters

Simple machines. The lever is a simple machine. Many machines have parts that are levers. Automobile engines, clocks, and bicycles all have parts that are levers. Levers are called simple machines because they are often parts of other machines. Simple machines are parts of other machines.

▶ **Why is a lever called a simple machine?**

WHAT YOU LEARNED

1. Levers can increase force.
2. The parts of a lever are
   a. the fulcrum
   b. the effort arm
   c. the resistance arm
3. A lever is a simple machine.
4. Simple machines are parts of other machines.

SCIENCE WORDS

lever (LEV-er)
   a simple machine with a fulcrum, an effort arm, and a resistance arm
fulcrum (FULL-crum)
   the point where a lever is supported
effort arm
   the side of a lever you use a force on
effort (EFF-ert)
   the force used on a lever
resistance (rih-ZIS-tense)
   the object moved by a lever
resistance arm
   the end of the lever that moves the resistance

ANSWER THESE

Use the diagram to answer the questions.
1. How long is the whole lever?
2. How long is the effort arm?
3. How long is the resistance arm?
4. How much is the resistance?
5. How far is the fulcrum from the boy?

DO THIS AT HOME

The lever is the most common simple machine. Most people use levers without even noticing it. You can find out how a lever helps do work. Place several books on your desk. Try lifting them with your little finger. Now try lifting them using a pencil as a lever. Which way is easier?

How does a lever work?

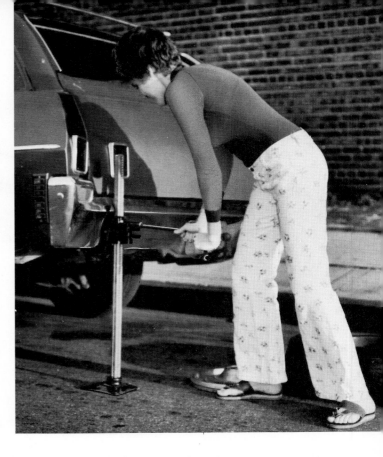

Changing a flat tire. Did you ever change a tire on a car? You have to lift one end of the car off the ground to do it. It may take a force of 5000 newtons to lift the car. You don't have to be Superman to lift the car. You can do it easily if you have a jack. You push down on the jack handle with a force of 100 newtons. The jack pushes up on the car with a force of 5000 newtons. The jack multiplies the force, or effort, that you use.

▶ **What does a jack do to the force you use on it?**

Help from a machine. Most machines help you do work by multiplying your effort. Mechanical advantage (muh-CAN-i-cul ad-VAN-tij) is a number that tells you how many times a machine multiplies the effort used. A machine with a mechanical advantage of 5 multiplies the effort by 5. Suppose you use 100 newtons of effort on a machine with a mechanical advantage of 5. The machine will give a force of 100 newtons x 5, or 500 newtons.

▶ **What is mechanical advantage?**

The mechanical advantage of a lever. A short way to write mechanical advantage is M.A. A lever is a simple machine. It can multiply your effort. To find the M.A. of a lever, divide the length of the effort arm by the length of the resistance arm. If the effort arm is 100 centimeters and the resistance arm is 20 centimeters, the M.A. is 100 divided by 20, or 5.

▶ **How can you find the M.A. of a lever?**

$$M.A. = \frac{\text{length of effort arm}}{\text{length of resistance arm}}$$

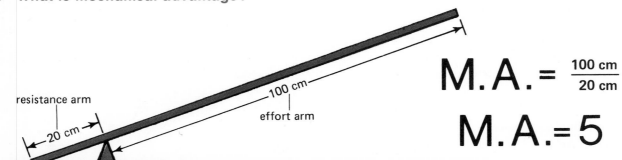

resistance arm

20 cm

100 cm

effort arm

$$M.A. = \frac{100 \text{ cm}}{20 \text{ cm}}$$

$$M.A. = 5$$

Increasing the M.A. of a lever. A crowbar is a lever. You can use it to pull nails out of wood. The M.A. of a crowbar depends on how you use it. First put your hand on the crowbar near the nail. Feel how hard you have to push to get the nail out. Then put your hand near the end of the crowbar. You need less effort when you hold the crowbar near the end. Its M.A. is greater this way. Holding the crowbar at its end makes its effort arm longer. That makes its M.A. greater. When the effort arm of a lever is made longer, its M.A. increases.

▶ **How can the M.A. of a lever be increased?**

How hard must you push? Suppose you want to lift a log weighing 2000 newtons with a lever. You have a lever with an M.A. of 10. How much effort will you have to use? To find out, divide the resistance by the M.A.

$$\text{EFFORT} = \frac{\text{RESISTANCE}}{\text{M.A.}}$$

$$\text{EFFORT} = \frac{2000 \text{ nt}}{10} = 200 \text{ nt}$$

Your effort has to be 200 newtons.

▶ **How can you find the effort if you know the resistance and the M.A.?**

WHAT YOU LEARNED

1. Mechanical advantage tells how many times an effort is multiplied.
2. $\text{M.A.} = \dfrac{\text{length of effort arm}}{\text{length of resistance arm}}$
3. Making the effort arm longer increases the mechanical advantage.

SCIENCE WORDS

mechanical advantage (muh-CAN-i-cul ad-VAN-tij)
   the number of times a machine multiplies the effort

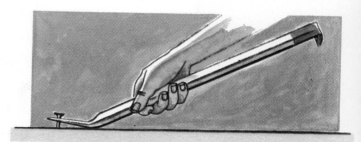

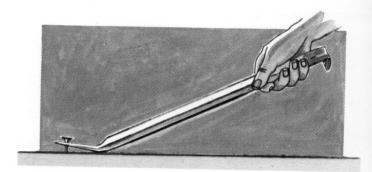

ANSWER THESE

1. A lever triples the effort used. Its M.A. is
   a. 1
   b. 2
   c. 3

2. To increase the M.A. of a lever,
   a. make the resistance arm longer
   b. make the effort arm longer
   c. use a larger force

3. Use the diagram to answer the questions.
   a. What is the M.A. of this lever?
   b. How much effort is needed to move the 300-newton resistance?

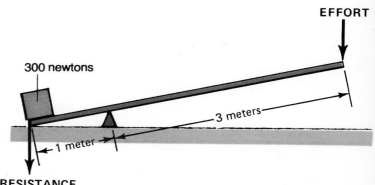

EFFORT

300 newtons

3 meters

1 meter

RESISTANCE

How do ramps help us do work?

100 newtons

300 newtons

3 meters

1 meter

Ramps. Have you ever seen barrels being loaded onto a truck? A long, tilted board may be used to help load the barrels. The barrels are rolled up the board onto the truck. The long, tilted board is an <u>inclined</u> (in-CLINED) <u>plane</u>. Inclined means tilted. A plane is a flat surface, like a board. An inclined plane is a flat surface that is tilted. An inclined plane is also called a ramp. An inclined plane is a simple machine. It helps make work easier.

▶ **What is an inclined plane?**

How much help does a ramp give? Look at the picture of the man rolling the barrel up the ramp. He is moving a 300-newton barrel with only 100 newtons of effort. The ramp has multiplied the effort by 3. The M.A. of this ramp is 3. You can find the M.A. of a ramp by dividing its length by its height.

$$\text{M.A. of a ramp} = \frac{\text{LENGTH}}{\text{HEIGHT}}$$

▶ **How can you find the M.A. of a ramp?**

Where are ramps used? Many times we use ramps without noticing them. If you walk up a hill, you are using a ramp. Often ramps are used in place of stairs. It takes less effort to go up a ramp than to go up stairs.

▶ **Why are ramps better than stairs for lifting things up?**

WHAT YOU LEARNED

1. A ramp is an inclined plane.
2. An inclined plane is a simple machine. It is a flat surface that is tilted.
3. The mechanical advantage of an inclined plane is equal to its length divided by its height.

SCIENCE WORD

inclined (in-CLINED) **plane**
a flat surface that is tilted

ANSWER THESE

1. Find the M.A. of each of the ramps.

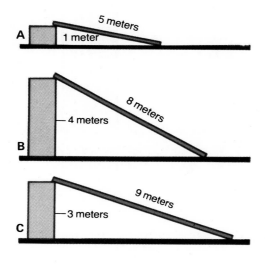

2. Which of these ramps has the smallest mechanical advantage? Explain your answer.

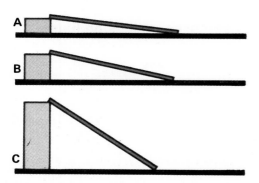

NOW TRY THIS

A car is at the bottom of a hill. The car weighs 10,000 newtons. The hill is 2,000 meters long and 40 meters high. How much effort (force) would be needed to push the car up the hill if there were no friction? HINT: First find the M.A. of the hill. The hill is like a ramp.

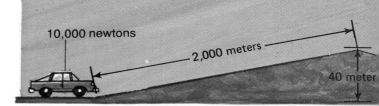

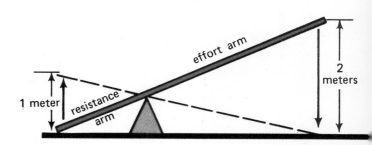

FINDING OUT MORE

Simple machines seem to be giving us something for nothing. A ramp or lever can multiply effort. Where does this extra force come from? Look again at the picture of the truck and barrel. To lift the barrel into the truck we would use 300 newtons of force for a distance of 1 meter. To load the barrel into the truck using the ramp, we would need only 100 newtons of force. But now the barrel has to be moved 3 meters. We use less force, but have to move a longer distance. Simple machines lose in distance what they gain in force.

Look at the picture of the lever. When the effort arm is moved down 2 meters, the resistance arm moves up only 1 meter. What you gain in force, you lose in distance.

How do pulleys help us do work?

What is a pulley? Look at the picture. A pulley is being used to raise a load of bricks. A pulley is a wheel that turns on an axle (AX-ul). A rope runs over the wheel. Pull down on the rope. The load of bricks is pulled up. A pulley is used to change the direction of a force. A pulley is a simple machine that can change the direction of a force.

▶ What is a pulley?

Fixed pulleys. A pulley that stays in the same place is called a fixed pulley. The pulley at the top of a flagpole is a fixed pulley.

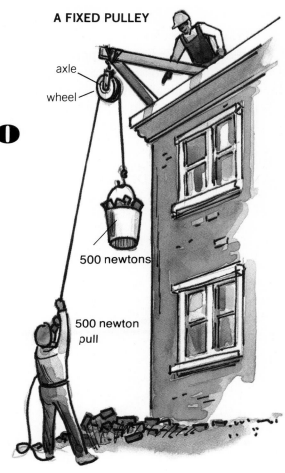

A FIXED PULLEY

axle
wheel

500 newtons

500 newton pull

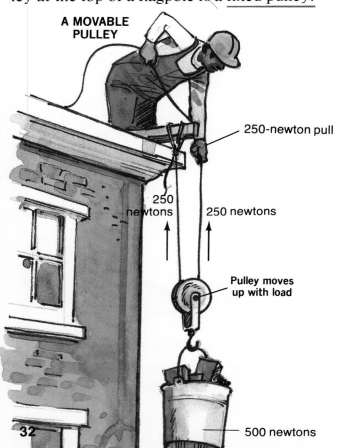

A MOVABLE PULLEY

250-newton pull

250 newtons

250 newtons

Pulley moves up with load

500 newtons

The two pulleys at the ends of a clothesline are both fixed pulleys. Fixed pulleys help you move something from one place to another. With a fixed pulley you can raise a flag. With a clothesline on two pulleys, you can hang the clothes at one end of the clothesline and then move them along to the other end.

▶ How can fixed pulleys be helpful?

Movable pulleys. A fixed pulley can change the direction of a force. But a fixed pulley cannot multiply the effort. To lift 500 newtons of bricks with a fixed pulley takes 500 newtons of effort. There is another kind of pulley that can move. It is called a movable (MOOV-uh-bul) pulley. When the rope is pulled up, the load and the pulley both move up.

▶ What is a movable pulley?

How a movable pulley helps. Look at the drawing of the movable pulley. The load of bricks weighs 500 newtons. There are 2 ropes holding the pulley. So each rope has to pull only 250 newtons. If you pull up on one rope with an effort of 250 newtons, the pulley will lift the 500 newtons of bricks. A movable pulley multiplies the effort by 2. It has an M.A. of 2.

▶ **What is the M.A. of a movable pulley?**

Getting more M.A. with pulleys. Fixed and movable pulleys can be used together to give a large M.A. Look at the drawing of pulleys used to lift a heavy engine out of a car. There are 6 ropes attached to the movable pulleys. These pulleys together have an M.A. of 6. They multiply the effort by 6. Pulleys used together like this are called a block and tackle. A block and tackle can be used to lift heavy cargo out of ships. It can be used to lift a piano to the window of an apartment on a high floor.

▶ **How can we use pulleys to get a large M.A.?**

WHAT YOU LEARNED

1. A pulley is a simple machine with a wheel and an axle.
2. A fixed pulley can change the direction of a force.
3. A movable pulley has a mechanical advantage of 2.
4. Movable pulleys can be used together to get a large M.A.

SCIENCE WORDS

pulley
a simple machine made of a wheel and an axle

axle (AX-ul)
a rod that a wheel turns on

fixed pulley
a pulley that does not move

movable (MOOV-uh-bul) **pulley**
a pulley that moves

A BLOCK AND TACKLE

ANSWER THESE

1. A pulley is
   a. a wheel
   b. a wheel on an axle
   c. an axle
2. A fixed pulley can
   a. make a force larger
   b. make a force smaller
   c. change the direction of a force
3. A movable pulley
   a. has no mechanical advantage
   b. cannot move
   c. has a mechanical advantage of 2
4. A clothesline uses
   a. a single fixed pulley
   b. a single movable pulley
   c. two fixed pulleys

FINDING OUT MORE

You can find the M.A. of any number of pulleys working together. Count the number of ropes holding up the pulleys. That number is the M.A. If the free end of the rope is pulled down, don't count it.

Why do things turn?

Two on a seesaw. Did you ever have fun on a seesaw? When the two people on the ends of the seesaw have the same weight, the seesaw is balanced. What happens when one person is much heavier than the other? If they both sit at the ends of the seesaw, it is not balanced. The end with the heavier person stays down.

▶ **If a seesaw is not balanced, which end stays down?**

Making it balance. Two children with different weights can make a seesaw balance. How can they do it? Try this experiment to find out. Use a meter stick for the seesaw. Use metal weights for the children. Hang the seesaw by a string tied around its middle. The seesaw is like a lever. The place where the seesaw is held up is its fulcrum. The seesaw turns around the fulcrum.

Hang a 50-gram weight at one end of the seesaw. Hang a 100-gram weight at the other end. The seesaw does not balance. The 100-gram weight goes down. Now move the 100-gram weight closer to the fulcrum. There will be one place where the seesaw balances. A real seesaw works the same way. A heavier child has to sit closer to the fulcrum to make the seesaw balance.

▶ **How can a heavy child balance a light child on a seesaw?**

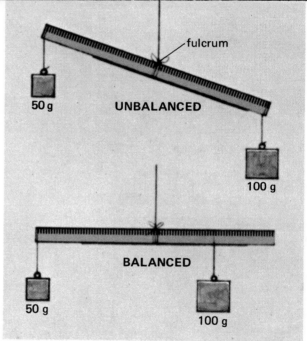

fulcrum

50 g UNBALANCED

100 g

BALANCED

50 g

100 g

Just a moment. You can predict when a seesaw will balance. You must know the forces on the seesaw. You must also know the distance of each force from the fulcrum. Multiply each force by its distance from the fulcrum. The number you get is called the <u>moment</u> (MOH-ment) of the force. The moment of a force is the same as its turning effect. A seesaw balances when the moment of the force on one side equals the moment of the force on the other side. This is called the law of moments.

▶ **When will a seesaw balance?**

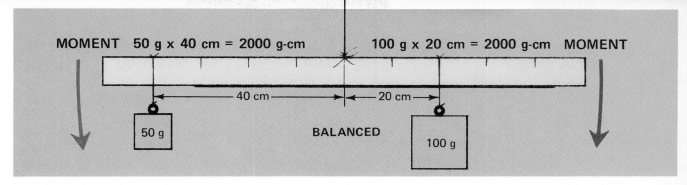

MOMENT 50 g × 40 cm = 2000 g-cm   100 g × 20 cm = 2000 g-cm MOMENT

40 cm   20 cm

50 g   BALANCED   100 g

Try it and see. Use the meter-stick seesaw to prove the law of moments. Put the fulcrum at the 50-centimeter mark. Hang the 50-gram mass 40 centimeters from the fulcrum. Move the 100-gram mass until the seesaw balances. The 100-gram mass will be 20 centimeters from the fulcrum. Are the two moments equal?

50 grams × 40 centimeters =
2000 gram-centimeters
100 grams × 20 centimeters =
2000 gram-centimeters

Try other positions for the masses. Try other masses, too. The seesaw will always balance when the moments are equal. It will not balance when the moments are not equal. An unbalanced seesaw will turn in the direction of the larger moment.

▶ **When a seesaw is not balanced, which way does it turn?**

The moments in your life. Most people know about moments of force even though they never studied them. If you want to carry a tray with one hand, the tray must be balanced. You know you should put heavy dishes near the center of the tray. Then they have the least moment or turning effect. If you must put a heavy dish near the edge of the tray, you put another dish on the other side to balance it. The moments of force must be equal, or the tray will tip.

▶ **Where will a heavy object have the least moment of force?**

WHAT YOU LEARNED

1. The moment of a force is its turning effect around a fulcrum.

2. The moment of a force equals the force times its distance from the fulcrum.

3. An object is balanced when the moments of force on both sides of the fulcrum are equal.

4. A large force has a small moment when it is near the fulcrum.

SCIENCE WORD

moment (MOH-ment)
the turning effect of a force

NOW TRY THIS

Where should Ted sit to balance the seesaw?

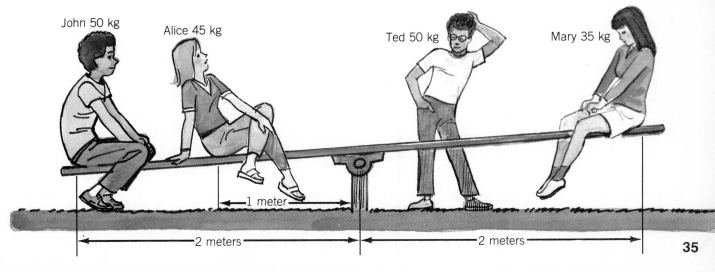

John 50 kg   Alice 45 kg   Ted 50 kg   Mary 35 kg

1 meter

2 meters   2 meters

2 Review

Do the following questions on a separate sheet of paper.

Matching   Write down each of the statements in Column I leaving one line of space after each statement. On the blank line following each statement, write the word or phrase from Column II that is described by that statement.

Column I

1. The point where a lever is supported.
2. The object moved by a lever.
3. The force used on a lever.
4. A flat, tilted surface.
5. A rod that a wheel turns on.
6. A pulley that turns but does not move.
7. A pulley that moves.
8. The turning effect of a force.
9. The distance from the effort to the fulcrum.
10. A lever, ramp, or pulley.

Column II

effort arm
inclined plane
moment
simple machine
fulcrum
effort
resistance
axle
movable pulley
fixed pulley

Multiple Choice   Write the letter of the choice that best completes the statement or answers the question.

1. The side of a lever you use force on is
   a. the handle
   b. the right side
   c. the effort arm
2. The longer the effort arm of a lever, the
   a. greater the M.A.
   b. smaller the M.A.
   c. smaller the resistance
3. The M.A. of a ramp is equal to its length
   a. times its height
   b. divided by its height
   c. minus its height
4. A ramp is also called
   a. an inclined plane
   b. a curved plane
   c. a staircase

5. Several pulleys used together are
   a. a block and tackle
   b. less helpful than one
   c. not helpful at all
6. The moment of a force equals the force
   a. divided by its distance from the fulcrum
   b. times it difference from the fulcrum
   c. plus its distance from the fulcrum
7. When a force moves nearer the fulcrum, it has
   a. a larger moment
   b. the same moment
   c. a smaller moment
8. We use machines to make work
   a. simpler
   b. harder to do
   c. easier to do

3 Force

Unit Lessons

1. What is a force?
2. Why do things fall?
3. How fast do things fall?
4. How does a spring scale work?
5. What is the difference between weight and mass?
6. What is friction?
7. How can friction be reduced?
8. How does friction affect machines?
9. What makes an object tip over?
10. What is pressure?
11. How is pressure measured?

Goals and Objectives

After completing this unit, you should be able to:
- define weight as a force.
- explain the law of gravity.
- describe a spring scale and what it is used for.
- understand the difference between weight and mass.
- give examples of friction in our daily lives.
- define pressure as a force applied over an area.

What is a force?

Pulling. Lift a package from the floor. You pull on the package to lift it. The young man and the donkey in the picture above are pulling in opposite directions. The north pole of a magnet attracts the south pole of another magnet. They pull on each other. All pulls are examples of forces.

▶ Give some examples of pulling forces.

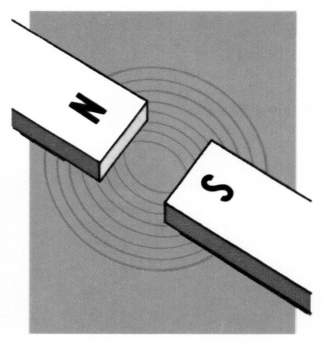

Pushing. The man in the picture is pushing a car. He is using force. When you sit in a chair, you push down on the chair. There is a pushing force on the chair. All pushes are examples of forces.

▶ Give some examples of pushing forces.

All forces are pushes or pulls. Try to think of a force that is not a push or a pull. Is turning a doorknob a push or a pull?

Yes. Your fingers push along the outside of the knob to make it turn. If you cannot think of a force that is not a push or a pull, do not be upset. Scientists have not been able to think of one either. All forces are pushes or pulls.

▶ **What is a force?**

Weight is a force. The earth's gravity pulls every object toward the center of the earth. This pull is a force. It is called the weight of the object. Lift a heavy bag of groceries. You can feel its weight. The weight of an object is the pull of the earth's gravity on it.

▶ **What is the force of the earth's gravity on an object called?**

1. A force is a push or a pull.
2. The weight of an object is the force of the earth's gravity on it.

ANSWER THESE

1. A force is
   a. energy
   b. a push or a pull in any direction
   c. always a downward push or pull

2. In a tug of war, there is
   a. no force
   b. a force at each end of the rope
   c. a force only at one end

3. Weight is
   a. a force
   b. a kind of energy
   c. the opposite of gravity

FINDING OUT MORE

There are different kinds of forces. These are some examples.

1. The force of gravity. All objects pull on other objects with a force called gravity. The sun pulls on the earth and all the planets. The sun's gravity holds the earth and the planets in their orbits around the sun.

2. The electromagnetic force. Electric charges push and pull each other. These pushes and pulls are called electric forces. When electric charges move, they produce magnetic forces. Electric and magnetic forces together are called electromagnetic forces. Electromagnetic forces hold atoms and molecules together. It is this kind of force that makes an iron bar hard to bend or break.

3. Nuclear force. At the center of every atom there is a very small part called the nucleus. The nucleus is made of protons and neutrons. The protons and neutrons are held together by the nuclear force. The nuclear force is the strongest force known. It is millions of times stronger than gravity. But we never notice it because it acts only inside the nucleus of the atom.

Why do things fall?

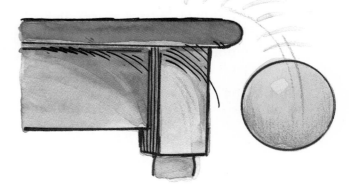

Isaac Newton. Isaac Newton was a scientist who lived in England about 300 years ago. There is a story about him. The story says that he was sitting under an apple tree one day. An apple fell from the tree and hit Newton on the head. He began to wonder why things fall. We don't know whether this story is true. But we do know that Isaac Newton discovered the law of gravity. The law of gravity explains why things fall.

▶ What scientific law did Newton discover that explains why things fall?

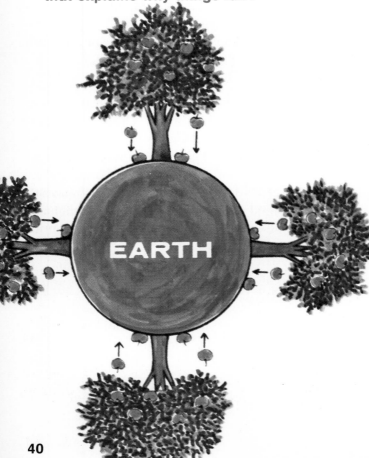

Which way do things fall? When an apple comes loose from a tree, it falls down to the ground. When a ball rolls off a table, it falls down. Look at the picture of the earth. All things fall toward the center of the earth.

▶ In which direction do objects fall?

Why do things fall? Things fall because the force of gravity pulls them down. When an object drops, it is pulled toward the center of the earth. If there were nothing in the way, it would reach the center of the earth. The earth's gravity pulls things down. Gravity is a force that pulls things toward the center of the earth.

▶ Why do things fall toward the center of the earth?

What things have gravity? People did not need Isaac Newton to tell them that things fall to the ground when they are dropped. But Newton's law of gravity told them other things that they did not know.

According to Newton, the earth was not the only thing that has a force of gravity. His law says that every object pulls on every other object. The earth pulls on a falling apple. But the apple also pulls on the earth. All objects pull on all other objects. All objects have a force of gravity.

▶ **What objects have a force of gravity?**

Gravity and size. The strength of gravity of an object depends on two things. First, it depends on the size of the object. Second, it depends on how far away it is.

Large things have large forces of gravity. Small things have small forces of gravity. The earth is large, and its gravity produces a strong pull. Your body has a force of gravity, but it is very small. It is small because your body is very small compared to the earth. Things must be very large before the effects of their gravity can be noticed.

▶ **What kinds of things have strong forces of gravity?**

Gravity and distance. The pull of an object's gravity depends on how far away it is. Near the earth's surface, the earth's gravity is strongest. As a spaceship travels away from the earth, the pull of the earth's gravity gets weaker. But no matter how far away the ship goes, the earth's gravity never disappears. The earth pulls on the moon, the sun, and even the stars. The moon, the sun, and the stars also pull on the earth.

▶ **What happens to the pull of the earth's gravity as you travel far into space?**

WHAT YOU LEARNED

1. All objects fall toward the center of the earth.
2. Every object pulls on every other object.
3. Large things have large forces of gravity. Small things have small forces of gravity.
4. The farther apart two objects are, the smaller the pull of gravity is between them.

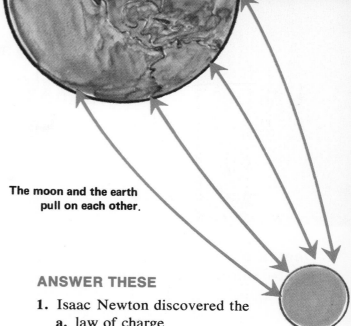

The moon and the earth pull on each other.

ANSWER THESE

1. Isaac Newton discovered the
   a. law of charge
   b. law of gravity
   c. apple tree
2. All objects fall toward the
   a. North Pole
   b. Equator
   c. center of the earth
3. The earth is much larger than the moon. The force of gravity on the earth is
   a. less than on the moon
   b. greater than on the moon
   c. the same as on the moon
4. As you move away from an object, the force of its gravity
   a. becomes larger
   b. becomes smaller
   c. does not change

PEOPLE IN SCIENCE

Isaac Newton (1642—1727)

Isaac Newton was one of the greatest geniuses who ever lived. His law of gravity explained why things fall. It also explained the movement of the moon around the earth, and the movement of the earth and the planets around the sun. The law of gravity was only one of Newton's great discoveries in science. Newton once said this about himself: "If I have seen farther than others, it is because I have stood on the shoulders of giants." What do you think Newton meant by this? Was he using the word "giant" to mean other great thinkers whose ideas helped him?

How fast do things fall?

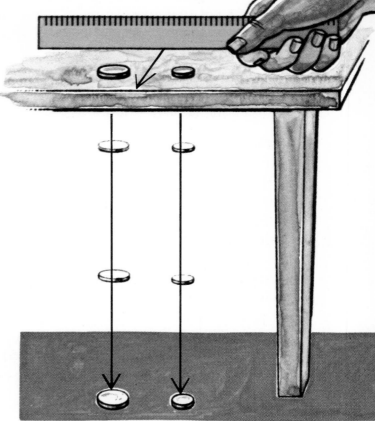

Does a heavy object fall faster than a lighter one? Many people think that heavy objects fall faster than light ones. A quarter is heavier than a dime. Put a quarter and a dime near the edge of a table. Use a ruler to push them off at the same time. The quarter and the dime hit the floor together. They both fell at the same speed. Their weights made no difference. Heavy objects and light objects fall at the same speed.

▶ Which falls faster, a quarter or a dime?

Air slows things down. Take two sheets of paper exactly alike. Crumple one into a ball. Drop both pieces at the same time.

The ball of paper hits the floor first. It has the same weight as the flat sheet, but it falls faster. The reason is that the air slows down the sheet of paper. The air causes more friction on the flat sheet than on the round ball. Friction always acts against motion. So the sheet falls more slowly.

▶ Why does a sheet of paper fall more slowly than a ball of paper of the same weight?

Air friction. The flat sheet of paper falls more slowly than the ball of paper. The sheet has more surface to rub against the air. The sheet of paper is slowed more than the ball because of its shape. Streamlined shapes have the least amount of air friction. Many birds have streamlined bodies. Racing cars are streamlined to cut down air friction.

▶ What kind of shape has the least amount of air friction?

Take away the air. With a pump you can take the air out of a container. You will have a <u>vacuum</u> (VAC-yoom) in the container. In a vacuum, there is only empty space. Scientists have found that in a vacuum all objects fall at the same speed. In a vacuum, a feather falls as fast as a stone. A sheet of paper falls as fast as a ball of paper. There is no air friction to slow them down.

▶ **Which falls faster in a vacuum, a feather or a ball of paper?**

Faster and faster. Because of the earth's gravity, all objects fall toward the center of the earth. As they fall, they move faster and faster. But objects that start to fall together, stay together. They fall at the same speed as each other, unless air friction slows one of them more than the other.

▶ **What happens to the speed of a falling object?**

WHAT YOU LEARNED

1. Friction of the air slows falling objects.
2. Streamlining reduces friction with the air.
3. All objects fall at the same speed in a vacuum.

SCIENCE WORD

vacuum (VAC-yoom)
an empty space

ANSWER THESE

Copy these sentences. If the sentence is true, mark it true. If it is false, change the underlined word to make it true.

1. Heavy objects fall at the <u>same</u> speed as light ones in a vacuum.
2. Friction with the air <u>speeds</u> falling.
3. An object's <u>shape</u> affects its speed of falling.

NOW TRY THIS

Unscramble the words in capital letters.

1. A dime and a penny fall at the same DEPES.
2. IAR IICTONFR slows falling objects.
3. Falling objects obey the law of A VIRTGY.

PEOPLE IN SCIENCE

Galileo Galilei (1564—1642)

Galileo was one of the first scientists to do experiments with moving objects. Before him, most scientists made guesses about how things moved, but did not test their guesses. Galileo rolled balls of different weights down an inclined plane. He measured how long it took for the balls to roll down. He found that the weight of the ball didn't matter. All the balls rolled down the plane in the same time. There is also a story about Galileo that may be true. It says that Galileo dropped stones of different weights from the Leaning Tower of Pisa. He showed by these experiments that all objects fall the same distance in the same time.

How does a spring scale work?

Spring scales. A spring scale has a spring inside it. A pointer is attached to the spring. When the end of the spring is pulled by a force, the spring stretches. The pointer moves. The amount of the force is shown by the pointer.

▶ What happens to the spring in a spring scale when it is pulled by a force?

Making a spring scale. Hang a spring from an iron stand. Attach a pointer to the spring. Hang different weights from the spring. Use a meter stick to measure how much the spring stretches for each weight. For each unit of force that is added, the spring stretches a certain amount. Suppose the weight of a 1-gram mass stretches the spring 1 cm. The weight of a 5-gram mass would stretch this spring 5 cm. How much would a 7-gram mass stretch this spring? 7 grams would stretch this spring 7 cm.

▶ A spring stretches 1 centimeter for each gram. How many grams would stretch it 5 centimeters?

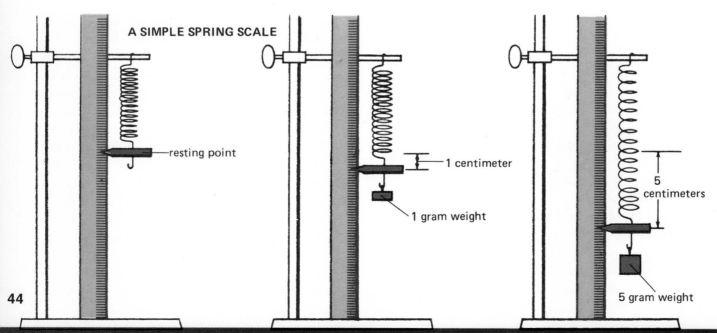

A SIMPLE SPRING SCALE

resting point

1 centimeter

1 gram weight

5 centimeters

5 gram weight

The spring constant. A spring stretches the same amount for each unit of force added to it. The amount that each unit of force stretches the spring is called the spring constant. Different springs may have different spring constants. Some spring scales have a spring constant of 1 centimeter for the weight of a 1-gram mass. These springs stretch 1 cm for each gram added. By measuring how much this spring stretches, we can measure the force used. Suppose you add an unknown weight to this spring, and it stretches 10 cm. Since this spring stretches 1 cm for each gram, you would know that the weight was that of a 10-gram mass.

▶ What is the spring constant of a spring if 1 gram stretches it 1 centimeter?

WHAT YOU LEARNED

1. The stretching of a spring can be used to measure force.
2. The spring constant shows how much each unit of force stretches the spring.
3. Different springs have different spring constants.

SCIENCE WORD

spring constant
   the amount a spring will stretch for each unit of force added

ANSWER THESE

1. Inside every spring scale there is a
   a. weight
   b. spring
   c. force
2. The weight of a 6-gram mass stretches a spring 2 cm. How much will the weight of a 12-gram mass stretch this spring?
   a. 1 centimeter
   b. 2 centimeters
   c. 4 centimeters
3. The spring constant shows
   a. how much a spring will stretch for each unit of force added
   b. when a spring will break
   c. what a spring is made of

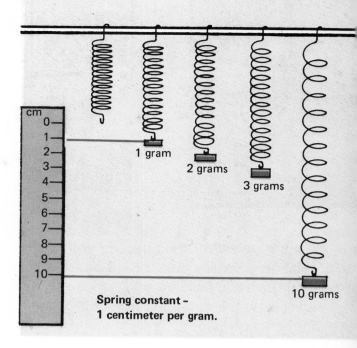

Spring constant –
1 centimeter per gram.

FINDING OUT MORE

Attach a small spring to an iron stand. Add several weights to the spring. The spring stretches. Take the weights off. The spring goes back to its original size. Now attach a large weight, say that of a 1000-gram mass. When you remove the 1000-gram mass, the spring does not return to its normal size. When a spring is stretched too much, it will not return to its original size. We say that the spring has been stretched past its elastic limit. All materials that stretch have elastic limits. If you stretch them past their elastic limit, they do not return to their original size.

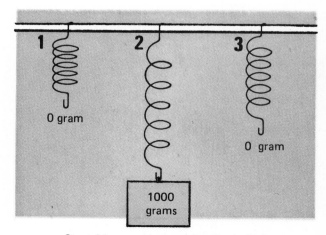

Stretching a spring past its elastic limit.

What is the difference between weight and mass?

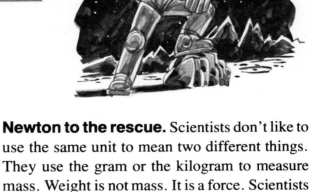

Weight can change. Suppose you hang a weight on a spring, and the spring stretches 6 centimeters. What would happen if you did this on the moon? The force of gravity on the moon is only $1/6$ as much as on the earth. So the spring will stretch only $1/6$ as much. It will stretch only 1 centimeter. The weight of an object is the pull of gravity on it. Objects weigh less on the moon than on the earth. Weight changes when gravity changes.

▶ **Why do things weigh less on the moon than on the earth?**

What is mass? The amount of matter in an object is its mass. Wherever you take an object, its mass does not change. You would weigh less on the moon than you do on earth. But your mass would stay the same. Scientists measure mass in grams. The gram is a unit of mass.

▶ **What is mass?**

Newton to the rescue. Scientists don't like to use the same unit to mean two different things. They use the gram or the kilogram to measure mass. Weight is not mass. It is a force. Scientists want a different unit to measure force. The unit they use is called the newton (NOO-tun).

▶ **What unit do scientists use to measure force and weight?**

Watch your weight. Suppose your mass is 49 kilograms. You stand on a spring scale to measure your weight. The scale reads 480 newtons. You would say that your weight is 480 newtons. On the moon, you would weight only 1/6 as much. The scale would read only 80 newtons. On the moon, you would say your weight is 80

480 newtons

80 newtons

EARTH

MOON

480

08

newtons. But your mass would still be 49 kilograms.

One newton is about the weight of 100 grams on the earth. It is about the same as the weight of 600 grams on the moon.

▶ **If an object weighs 96 newtons on the moon, how much will it weigh on the earth?**

Grams of force. A gram is not a unit of weight or force. But sometimes it is handy to measure forces in terms of the weight of a gram. A gram of force means the weight that a gram of anything has on the earth. For example, suppose we hang a 10-gram mass on a spring scale. We can say that the mass is pulling on the scale with 10 grams of force. In this book, we will sometimes measure force in newtons. At other times we will use grams or kilograms of force. Remember that a newton is the scientific unit of force.

▶ **What do you mean by a gram of force?**

WHAT YOU LEARNED

1. The weight of an object changes when gravity changes.
2. The mass of an object is the amount of matter in it. The mass of an object does not change.
3. The newton is the scientific unit of force.

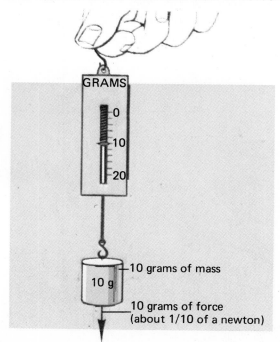

GRAMS

0

10

20

10 grams of mass

10 g

10 grams of force
(about 1/10 of a newton)

What is friction?

The force of friction. Suppose you are sitting in a wagon on a level stretch of sidewalk. Someone gives you a good push, and the wagon starts rolling. But gradually it slows down and stops. Why doesn't the wagon keep moving? Why does it stop? It stops because of <u>friction</u> (FRICK-shun). Friction is a force that acts when one surface moves over another surface. The movement of one surface over another causes friction.

▶ **What happens when one surface moves over another surface?**

Friction acts against motion. Friction is a force. A force is a push or a pull. The force of friction always pushes against you. Push a book across the table. Friction between the book and the table pushes against you. Try to move the table. Friction between the table and the floor pushes against you. The force of friction can be very large. The lid of a jar may be on very tight. A large force of friction makes it hard to unscrew it. A large force of friction makes it hard to pull the cork from a bottle. Whenever we try to make something move, the force of friction pushes against us.

▶ **What does friction do when you push a book across the table?**

Air can cause friction. The rubbing together of two objects always causes friction. As airplanes move through the air, they rub against it. This causes friction. To cut down the friction between planes and the air, planes have a special shape. We say they are <u>streamlined</u> (STREEM-lined).

▶ **Why do airplanes have a streamlined shape?**

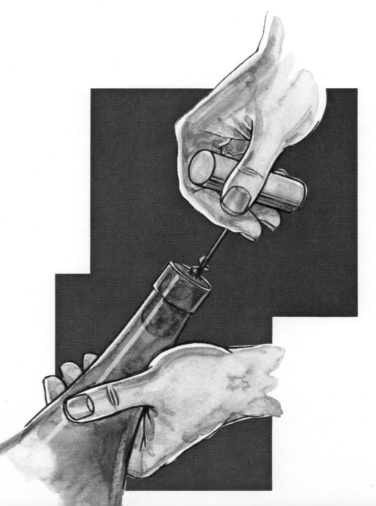

Friction produces heat. Rub the palms of your hands together. They get warm. Feel the blade of a saw right after you have cut something. It is warm. The outer "skin" of a moving plane gets warm from friction. Friction produces heat. Whenever two surfaces rub together, heat is produced.

► **What causes two surfaces to get warmer when they are rubbed together?**

Friction helps us. Try walking on an icy street. It is very hard to keep from falling. Ice is very slippery. There is not much friction when things move over ice. When we try to walk on ice, our feet move too easily and we slip. If there were no friction at all, we would not be able to keep our footing on the ground.

► **Why is it hard to keep your footing on ice?**

Putting friction to use. A traffic light turns red. The driver of a car steps on the brake. Friction stops the car. When the driver steps on the brake, asbestos (as-BES-tus) pads press against the car's wheels. The rubbing of the pads on the wheels stops the car. The brakes on a bicycle work the same way. Our world would be very different without friction.

► **How is friction used in a bicycle?**

WHAT YOU LEARNED

1. Things that move cause friction.

2. Friction produces heat.

3. Friction can be used to stop things from moving.

SCIENCE WORDS

friction (FRICK-shun)
    a force that interferes with the movement of one surface over another
streamlined (STREEM-lined)
    shaped to have little air friction
asbestos (as-BES-tus)
    a material used to make brakes

ANSWER THESE

Copy these sentences into your notebook. If the sentence is true, mark it true. If it is false, change the underlined word to make the sentence true.

1. Friction makes things cooler.
2. To reduce friction, jet planes have a special color.
3. It would be harder to walk without friction.
4. Bike brakes use friction to stop the bike.
5. There is a lot of friction when we move over ice.

49

How can friction be reduced?

Friction can make us do more work.
Moving furniture across a carpet is harder than moving it across a smooth floor. The rough carpet causes more friction than the smooth floor. We can measure how much more friction there is on a rough surface. Tie a weight to a spring scale. Drag the weight across some sandpaper. How much force is needed? Now drag the weight across a smooth table top. How much force is needed now? Much more force is needed on the sandpaper. It takes more work to move the weight over the sandpaper. Friction makes us do more work.

▶ **Why does it take more work to move something over a rough surface than over a smooth surface?**

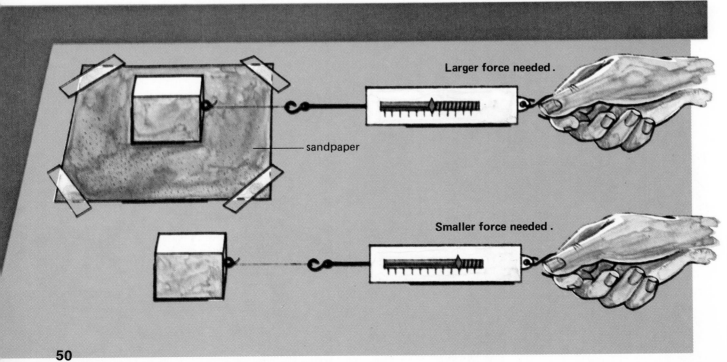

Larger force needed.

sandpaper

Smaller force needed.

SLIDING

ROLLING

Roll it or drag it? The wheels on a wagon are stuck. They cannot turn. When the delivery boy pulls the wagon, the wheels slide along the ground. It is very hard to move the wagon. The boy fixes the wheels so they can turn. The wagon moves very easily now. Things that roll cause less friction than things that are dragged. The wheel was man's greatest invention for cutting down friction and reducing work.

▶ **How does the wheel reduce work?**

Oil it. Things that move cause friction. If your ring gets stuck on your finger, friction is holding it there. Put a drop of oil or a little soap on your finger. The ring slips right off. Oil or soap reduces friction. We put oil on machines to make them run with less friction.

▶ **What can we use to reduce friction?**

WHAT YOU LEARNED

1. There is more friction on rough surfaces than on smooth surfaces.
2. Things that roll cause less friction than things that are dragged.
3. Oil can be used to reduce friction.

ANSWER THESE

1. One wagon has its wheels stuck. Another has good wheels. Which one will be easier to pull?
2. To make a wagon easier to pull, put oil on
   a. the tires
   b. the handle
   c. the axles of the wheels

NOW TRY THIS

Make a list of ten things that work better when they are oiled.

FINDING OUT MORE

Wheels reduce friction and save work. But there is still some friction where the wheel slides on the axle. This friction can be reduced. Look at one of the wheels on a roller skate. You will see small balls inside the wheel. This is called a ball bearing. When the wheel turns, the little balls roll. The friction of the rolling balls is very small. It is much less than the friction of a wheel that slides on an axle. The wheels of automobiles have ball bearings. Anything that reduces friction saves work and saves energy.

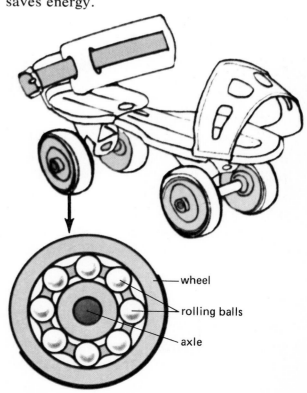

wheel
rolling balls
axle

How does friction affect machines?

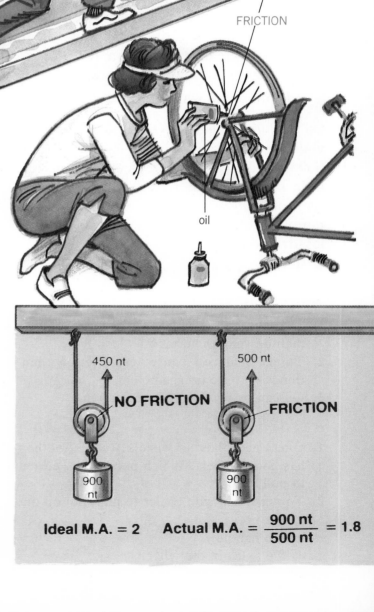

Friction in machines. All machines have parts that move. The parts rub against one another. When things rub, there is friction. The friction wastes energy by changing it to heat. To cut down on friction, machines are oiled.

▶ Why do machines have friction?

Ideal M.A. Because of friction, the actual mechanical advantage of a machine is always less than it should be. Friction reduces the M.A. of a machine. A movable pulley has two ropes holding it up. It should have a mechanical advantage of 2. The ideal (eye-DEEL) mechanical advantage of this pulley is 2. The mechanical advantage that a machine should have is its ideal M.A.

▶ What is the ideal M.A.?

Actual M.A. The picture shows a moveable pulley being moved. It takes 500 newtons of effort to lift a 900-newton load. Divide the

Ideal M.A. = 2   Actual M.A. = $\dfrac{900 \text{ nt}}{500 \text{ nt}}$ = 1.8

resistance by the effort. This gives you the real, or <u>actual M.A.</u> The actual M.A. of this pulley is 900 divided by 500, or 1.8. The ideal M.A. of a moveable pulley is 2. A machine's actual M.A. is always less than its ideal M.A. This is because some effort is wasted by friction.

▶ **How does friction affect the M.A. of a machine?**

How much useful work does a machine do? We use a machine to help us do work. We put work into the machine, and useful work comes out. In an ideal machine, there would be no friction. In a real machine, there is always some friction. The friction causes the machine to waste work. We get less work out than we put in. The wasted work is turned into heat.

▶ **What causes machines to waste work?**

The efficiency of a machine. If a machine wastes only a little work, we say it has a high <u>efficiency</u> (eh-FISH-un-see). This means that the amount of work we get out of the machine is almost as much as we put in. You can find the efficiency of a machine by dividing its actual M.A. by its ideal M.A. Here is an example:

A movable pulley has an ideal M.A. of 2. It has an actual M.A. of 1.8. Its efficiency is 1.8 divided by 2.

$$\text{Efficiency} = \frac{\text{Actual M.A.}}{\text{Ideal M.A.}} = \frac{1.8}{2} = 0.9$$

$$0.9 = 90\%$$

Efficiency is usually shown as a percent. The efficiency of this pulley is 90%. This means that its useful work output is 90% of the work put into it. Only 10% of the work is wasted.

▶ **If a machine does not waste much work, what can we say about its efficiency?**

WHAT YOU LEARNED

1. All machines have friction.
2. Friction reduces the M.A. of machines.
3. Friction causes a machine to waste work.
4. A machine that wastes only a little work has a high efficiency.

SCIENCE WORDS

ideal (eye-DEEL) **M.A.**
   the M.A. a machine would have if there were no friction
actual M.A.
   the M.A. a machine really has
efficiency (eh-FISH-un-see)
   the percent of useful work obtained from a machine

ANSWER THESE

1. A machine puts out
   a. more work than you put in
   b. less work than you put in
   c. the same amount of work that you put in
2. All machines waste some work because of
   a. friction
   b. mechanical advantage
   c. the ideal M.A.
3. The ideal M.A. of a machine is 3. Its actual M.A. could be
   a. 2.5
   b. 3
   c. 4
4. Machines with high efficiency
   a. waste a lot of work
   b. waste little work
   c. waste no work

What makes an object tip over?

center of gravity

Center of gravity. Balance a ruler on one of your fingers. Where is the point of balance? It is at the middle of the ruler. The weight of the ruler is divided equally on both sides of your finger. Your finger is

holding the ruler under a point called its center of gravity. The ruler acts as though all its weight is at its center of gravity. An object will always balance when it is held at or under its center of gravity. The point in an object where all its weight seems to be concentrated is its center of gravity.

▶ **Where should you hold an object to make it balance?**

Turning objects. The girl leading the band is twirling a baton. Try twirling a yardstick. Hold it at one end. It is very hard to twirl the stick when you hold it at one end. Try holding it in the middle. Now it is much easier to twirl. An object turns most easily around its center of gravity. Where do you think the center of gravity of a wheel is? It is at the center of the wheel.

▶ **If you want to twirl a baton, where should you hold it?**

Tipping over. Stand with your heels against the wall. Have a friend place a pencil at your feet. Try to bend over and pick up the pencil without bending your knees. You cannot do it. You tip over. Your body has a center of gravity. As long as your center of gravity is over your feet, you are balanced. When you bend away from the

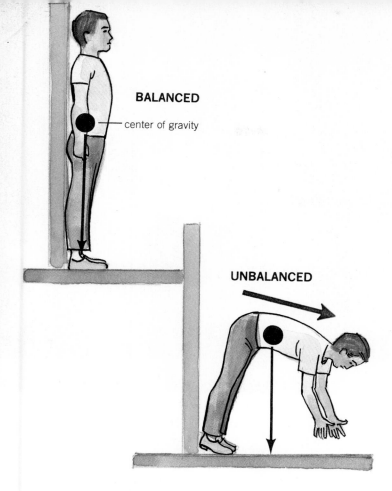

BALANCED

— center of gravity

UNBALANCED

wall, your center of gravity is no longer over your feet. You tip over. Any object will tip over if its center of gravity is not over its base.

▶ **When do things tip over?**

WHAT YOU LEARNED

1. An object acts as though its weight is all at one point called its center of gravity.
2. An object turns most easily about its center of gravity.
3. An object tips over when its center of gravity is not over its base.

ANSWER THESE

1. An object turns best about its
   a. ends
   b. center of gravity
   c. base
2. An object tips over when its center of gravity is
   a. very small
   b. not over its base
   c. over its base

NOW TRY THIS

What's wrong with this picture?

FINDING OUT MORE

An object tips over when its center of gravity is not over its base. Some things are specially made so that they do not tip over easily. These things are designed so that their centers of gravity are as low as possible and their bases as broad as possible.

The center of gravity of an automobile is very low. Its base is very wide. A car could tilt way over, but its center of gravity would still be over its base. Cars do not tip over easily.

Many traffic signs have heavy bases. Their centers of gravity are very low. If you push a traffic sign over, it stands up again. It does not tip over easily because its center of gravity stays over its base.

STREET CLOSED

STREET CLOSED

base

What is pressure?

Pressure. Firemen use high-pressure hoses. Skin divers must not go too deep because of water pressure. Mountain climbers must not go too high because of low air pressure. What is <u>pressure</u>? Pressure is the force on a certain amount of surface. For example, pressure can be the force on one square centimeter of an object's surface.

▶ What is pressure?

Pressure is not the same as force. Hold a book on the palm of one hand. Suppose the book weighs 10 newtons. It presses down on your hand with 10 newtons of force. But this force is spread out over your hand. Suppose your hand has an area of 100 square centimeters. The force on each square centimeter of your hand is only 0.10 newton, as shown in the box. The pressure caused by the weight of the book is 0.10 newton per square centimeter. To find pressure, you have to know the total force and the area it is spread over.

▶ If you know the force on a surface, what else do you need to know to find the pressure?

Matter and pressure. Your books are solids. They cause pressure on your hand as you hold them. Water is a liquid. As you swim under water you can feel the pressure of the water in

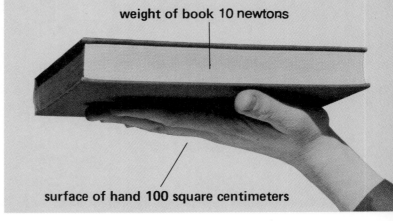

weight of book 10 newtons

surface of hand 100 square centimeters

$$PRESSURE = \frac{FORCE}{AREA}$$

$$PRESSURE = \frac{10\ newtons}{100\ sq.\ centimeters}$$

$$PRESSURE = 0.10\ newtons\ per\ square\ centimeters$$

your ears. Air is all around us. It also causes pressure. Air pressure is about 10 newtons of force per square centimeter at sea level. All matter on earth has weight and causes pressure.

▶ What is the air pressure at sea level?

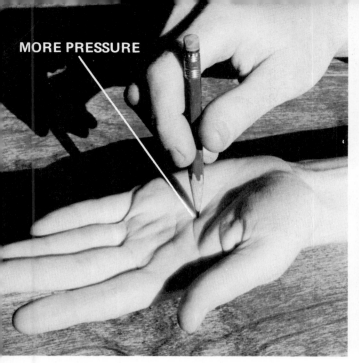

MORE PRESSURE

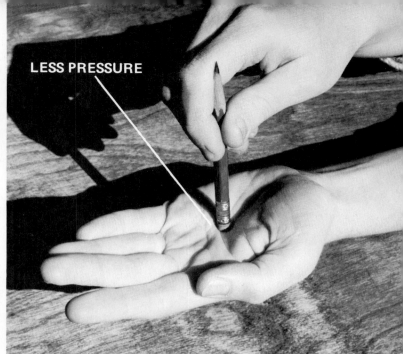

LESS PRESSURE

Pressure and force. Press the point of a pencil gently against your hand. Feel the pressure. Press the point a little harder. Use more force. You can feel the increase in pressure. When the force on an object is increased, the pressure is increased.

▶ How can pressure be increased?

Pressure and area. Pressure can be increased by increasing the force used. Pressure can also be increased by putting the same force on a smaller area. Press the eraser end of a pencil against your hand. Use the same force and press the pointed end against your hand. You can feel that the pointed end causes more pressure. The pointed end has less area than the eraser end. The same force pressing on a smaller area causes more pressure.

▶ What are two ways of increasing pressure?

WHAT YOU LEARNED

1. Pressure is the force on a certain amount of surface; for example, 10 newtons per square centimeter.
2. All matter on earth causes pressure.
3. Increasing force increases pressure.
4. Putting a force on a smaller area increases pressure.

SCIENCE WORD

pressure
force on a certain amount of surface

ANSWER THESE

1. Pressure is
   a. the force on an object
   b. the force on one square centimeter of an object
   c. the surface of an object

2. Pressure on an object can be increased by
   a. increasing the force
   b. decreasing the force
   c. removing the force

3. Pressure on an object can be increased by
   a. putting the force on a larger area
   b. putting the force on a smaller area
   c. putting the force on another area of the same size

FINDING OUT MORE

Why does a knife cut more easily when you sharpen it? When you sharpen a knife, you make the edge of the blade very thin. The edge of the thin blade has a very small area. When the edge is pressed against an object, a force is exerted on a very small area. Because of this, the knife exerts great pressure. This great pressure makes the knife cut.

How is pressure measured?

Manometers. A <u>manometer</u> (muh-NOM-uh-ter) is an instrument used to measure pressure. The manometer in the drawing has a U-shaped tube. The U tube is connected by rubber tubing to a thistle tube. The end of the thistle tube is covered with a thin rubber sheet. The thistle tube and the rubber tubing are filled with air. The U tube is filled with colored water.

Press the rubber sheet on the thistle tube. The pressure from your finger increases the pressure on the air in the tube. The increased pressure makes the water rise in the open end of the U tube. The height of the water shows changes in pressure.

▶ What is a manometer?

Measuring pressure. You can use the manometer to measure the pressure under water. Dip the covered end of the thistle tube into a large jar of water. The colored water moves up the open end of the U tube. This shows rising pressure. Move the thistle tube deeper into the jar of water. The colored water rises higher in the U tube. Move the thistle tube to the bottom of the jar. The water in the U tube moves still higher. As you go deeper into the water, the pressure becomes higher and higher. The pressure comes from the weight of water above pressing down. The pressure of the water increases with depth.

▶ What happens to the pressure as you go deeper into water?

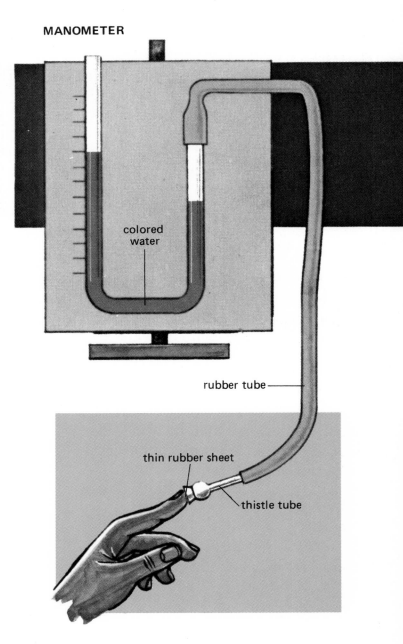

MANOMETER

colored water

rubber tube

thin rubber sheet

thistle tube

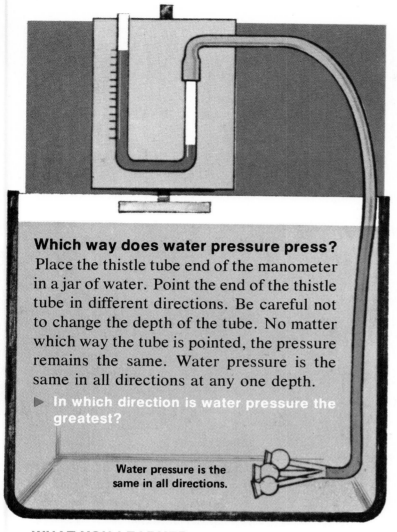

Which way does water pressure press?

Place the thistle tube end of the manometer in a jar of water. Point the end of the thistle tube in different directions. Be careful not to change the depth of the tube. No matter which way the tube is pointed, the pressure remains the same. Water pressure is the same in all directions at any one depth.

▶ **In which direction is water pressure the greatest?**

Water pressure is the same in all directions.

WHAT YOU LEARNED

1. Pressure can be measured with a manometer.
2. Pressure in water comes from the weight of the water pressing down.
3. In water, the pressure increases with depth.
4. In water, the pressure at a given depth is the same in all directions.

SCIENCE WORD

manometer (muh-NOM-uh-ter)
an instrument used to measure pressure

ANSWER THESE

1. As pressure is increased, the liquid in the open end of a manometer
   a. moves up
   b. moves down
   c. does not move

2. Water pressure comes from
   a. the air
   b. a manometer
   c. the weight of the water
3. Pressure in water
   a. decreases with depth
   b. increases with depth
   c. is the same at any depth
4. Pressure in water at a given depth is
   a. the same in all directions
   b. greatest in an upward direction
   c. greatest in a downward direction

NOW TRY THIS

There are ten science words hidden in the block below. Can you find them?

```
E W E I G H T B R P
F X L E W L P G D S
F A Y J W J R T F G
I M A N O M E T E R
C A X V R V S B L A
I S L C K F S K M V
E S E A E H U D Q I
N H Z C G K R O N T
C L P U L L E Y M Y
Y F R I C T I O N N
```

FINDING OUT MORE

Many treasures lie at the bottom of the sea. Deep-sea divers go to the ocean bottom to try to bring these treasures back. The divers face many dangers. One of these is a disease called the bends. The very high pressure at the ocean bottom causes nitrogen to dissolve in the divers' blood. Nitrogen is a part of the air we breathe. If a diver comes up to the surface too fast, the dissolved nitrogen forms bubbles in the blood. These bubbles cause severe pain and can also cause death. To prevent the bends, divers rise to the surface slowly. The dissolved nitrogen then has a chance to leave the body gradually. It does not form bubbles. It is exhaled from the lungs.

UNIT 3 Review

Do the following review questions on a separate sheet of paper.

Modified True/False *Write down each of the following statements, leaving a blank line between each line you write. Before the number for each statement, write T if the statement is true and F if the statement is false. For the false statements, cross out the word written in capital letters and write above it a word that will make the statement true.*

1. A FORCE is a push or pull.
2. The law of MOTION explains why things fall.
3. Empty space is called a VACUUM.
4. WEIGHT is the amount of matter in an object.
5. Friction is REDUCED by a brake.
6. We use the wheel to INCREASE friction.
7. GRAVITY is a force.
8. PRESSURE is the force acting on a certain area.
9. Water pressure increases with DEPTH.
10. MASS is the same on the earth as on the moon.

Multiple Choice *Write the letter of the choice that best completes the statement or answers the question.*

1. The weight of an object is the
   a. mass of the object
   b. pull of the earth's gravity on it
   c. resistance of the earth's gravity to it
2. All objects pull on all other objects according to
   a. the law of push and pull
   b. the law of gravity
   c. the law of force
3. In a vacuum, all objects fall
   a. at their own speed
   b. at the same speed
   c. more slowly than in air
4. The mass of an object
   a. becomes less on the moon
   b. becomes greater on the moon
   c. remains the same on the moon
5. Cars and planes are streamlined to reduce
   a. friction
   b. speed
   c. size
6. The amount of pressure caused by force depends upon
   a. the direction of the force
   b. the type of force
   c. the size of the area it acts upon
7. An instrument used to measure pressure is called
   a. a thermometer
   b. a manometer
   c. a scale
8. Every machine has an actual M.A. that is
   a. less than its ideal M.A.
   b. the same as its ideal M.A.
   c. greater than its ideal M.A.

UNIT 4

Motion

Unit Lessons

1. What are speed and velocity?
2. What is acceleration?
3. What are balanced and unbalanced forces?
4. What is Newton's First Law?
5. What is Newton's Second Law?
6. What is Newton's Third Law?

Goals and Objectives

After completing this unit, you should be able to:

- differentiate between speed and velocity.
- differentiate between instantaneous and average speed.
- define acceleration as a change in velocity.
- describe how unbalanced forces cause motion.
- tell what Newton's three laws of motion are.

What are speed and velocity?

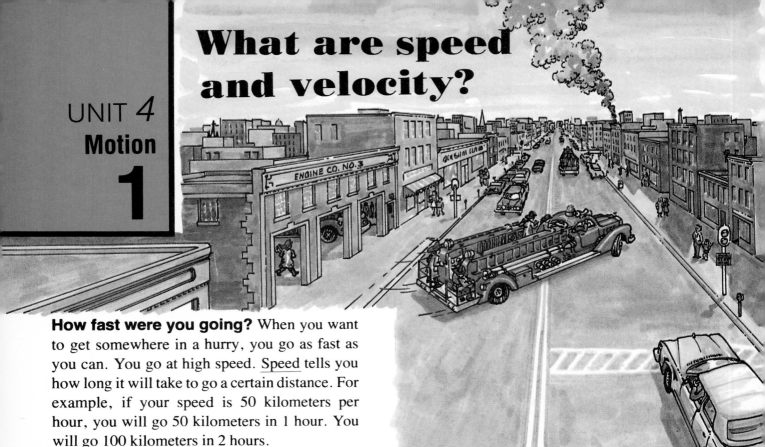

How fast were you going? When you want to get somewhere in a hurry, you go as fast as you can. You go at high speed. Speed tells you how long it will take to go a certain distance. For example, if your speed is 50 kilometers per hour, you will go 50 kilometers in 1 hour. You will go 100 kilometers in 2 hours.

There is a simple formula for finding the distance traveled if you know the speed and the time. Just multiply the speed by the time:

$$\text{Distance} = \text{Speed} \times \text{Time}$$

▶ **If you are moving at 60 km/hr, how far will you go in 3 hours?**

Speed up, slow down, stop. When you travel, you never go at the same speed all the time. If you are going by car or bus, you go faster on the open highway and slower in heavy traffic. You stop for red lights. You may even stop to have lunch.

When your trip is over, you can find your *average speed* for the trip. To do this, divide the distance you traveled by the time used for the whole trip. The formula for finding average speed is:

$$\text{Average Speed} = \frac{\text{Total Distance}}{\text{Total Time}}$$

If you travel 300 kilometers in 6 hours, what is your average speed?

$$\text{Average Speed} = \frac{\text{Total Distance}}{\text{Total Time}}$$
$$= \frac{300 \text{ Kilometers}}{6 \text{ Hours}}$$
$$= 50 \text{ Kilometers/hour}$$

Sometimes during your trip you went faster than your average speed. Sometimes you went slower. But your average speed for the trip was 50 km/hr.

▶ **How can you find the average speed for a trip?**

Keep your eye on the speedometer. Average speed is speed figured over a period of time. Your actual speed at any instant may be more or less than the average. The speedometer of a car shows the actual speed at every instant. This speed is called your <u>instantaneous</u> (in-stun-TAY-nee-us) <u>speed</u>. When we talk about speed, we usually mean instantaneous speed. When a sign reads "Speed Limit 75 km/hr," it means instantaneous speed.

▶ **What is meant by instantaneous speed?**

Velocity. <u>Velocity</u> (vuh-LAHS-uh-tee) tells two things about an object. First, it tells how fast the object is moving. This is its speed. Second, it tells the direction the object is moving. In the drawing below, when the ball is at point A, its velocity is 20 meters per second *upward*. When it is at point B, its velocity is 20 meters per second *downward*.

Velocity is sometimes used to mean speed. We do this when the direction of movement is not important. But strictly speaking, velocity should tell both speed and direction.

▶ **What two things does velocity tell us about an object's motion?**

WHAT YOU LEARNED

1. Speed tells you how long it will take to go a certain distance.
2. Average speed is equal to the total distance traveled divided by the total time used.
3. Instantaneous speed is the actual speed at any given instant.
4. Velocity indicates speed and direction.

SCIENCE WORDS

speed
    how long it takes to go a certain distance
instantaneous speed
    actual speed at any given instant
velocity
    speed and direction of travel

ANSWER THESE

1. Moving at a speed of 40 km/hr, the distance you will travel in 4 hours is
    a. 44 km
    b. 160 km
    c. 10 km
2. If you travel 90 kilometers in 2 hours, your average speed is
    a. 180 km/hr
    b. 92 km/hr
    c. 45 km/hr
3. The actual speed you are traveling at a given moment is called
    a. instantaneous speed
    b. velocity
    c. average speed

FINDING OUT MORE

How fast is fast? The fastest speed ever attained by a piloted plane is almost 1.0 kilometer per second (3 600 km/hr). Traveling at such a speed, the plane could travel from Washington, D.C. to California in slightly more than an hour. It could circle the earth in less than 12 hours. However, as fast as this plane can travel, it moves at a snail's pace compared with the speed of light. Light travels 300 000 kilometers in one second! An object moving at the speed of light could circle the earth almost 8 times in 1 second.

What is acceleration?

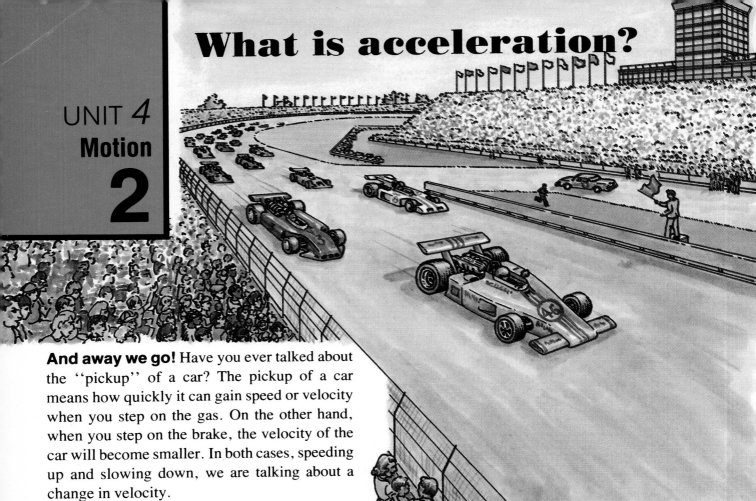

And away we go! Have you ever talked about the "pickup" of a car? The pickup of a car means how quickly it can gain speed or velocity when you step on the gas. On the other hand, when you step on the brake, the velocity of the car will become smaller. In both cases, speeding up and slowing down, we are talking about a change in velocity.

To find the change in velocity of an object, we subtract its velocity at one time from its velocity at a later time. For example, suppose a car has a velocity of 4 meters per second. A few seconds later, its velocity is 9 meters per second. The change in velocity would be 5 meters per second.

velocity later = 9 meters per second
velocity at start = 4 meters per second
change in velocity = 5 meters per second

▶ **How do we find the change in velocity of an object?**

Acceleration. Acceleration (ak-SELL-er-AY-shun) is the science word that tells how fast an object changes its velocity. When a car is speeding up, it is accelerating. A car is also accelerating when it is slowing down. Slowing down is sometimes called negative acceleration, or deceleration (DEE-cel-er-AY-shun). A car is NOT accelerating when it travels in a straight line at constant speed or when it sits at rest.

▶ **When is an object accelerating?**

Is this drag racer accelerating?

Measuring acceleration. Two cars are sitting at a red light. When the light turns green both cars accelerate to a speed of 150 meters per second. One car takes 10 seconds to do this. The other car takes 20 seconds. The first car has a greater acceleration than the second. It speeds up faster.

Acceleration is more than just a change in velocity. It also includes the time taken for the change. To find the amount of acceleration, we divide the change in velocity by the time taken. The formula for acceleration is:

$$\text{Acceleration} = \frac{\text{Change in velocity}}{\text{Time for change to occur}}$$

For example, one of the cars discussed above changed its speed from 0 meters per second to 150 meters per second in 10 seconds. Its acceleration was:

$$\text{Acceleration} = \frac{150 \text{ meters per second}}{10 \text{ Seconds}}$$

$$= \frac{15 \text{ meters per second}}{1 \text{ Second}}$$

This answer is read as ''15 meters per second per second.'' This means that the velocity of the car changed by 15 meters per second every second.

▶ **How do we find the acceleration of an object?**

WHAT YOU LEARNED

1. Any moving object that is changing speed is accelerating.
2. An object moving in a straight line at constant speed is not accelerating.

3. The acceleration of an object can be found from its change in velocity and the time taken for the change.

SCIENCE WORDS

acceleration
how fast an object changes its velocity
deceleration
negative acceleration; ''slowing down''

ANSWER THESE

1. A train sitting in the station (is/is not) accelerating.
2. A train pulling out of the station (is/is not) accelerating.
3. A train traveling at 100 km/hr on a straight stretch of track (is/is not) accelerating.
4. A train slowing down as it pulls into a station (is/is not) accelerating.

NOW TRY THIS

Find the science words.

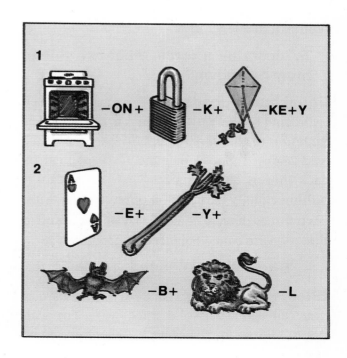

What are balanced and unbalanced forces?

A tug of forces. To describe any force, we must know two things. We must know how large the force is and in what direction it acts. Look at the picture of the tug-of-war. How can we describe the force being applied to the iron ring by the Red team? The size of the force can be read from the spring balance. It is a force of 900 newtons. The direction of the force is to the left. That is, the members of the Red team are pulling to the left.

▶ **To describe a force, what two things must be known?**

Equal but opposite. The force being applied to the ring by the Yellow team is to the right. The direction of this force is opposite to that of the Red team. Suppose that the force applied by each time is equal in size. Then, each team is pulling equally hard, but in opposite directions. Two forces that are equal in size and opposite in direction are called <u>balanced</u> <u>forces</u>.

▶ **What are balanced forces?**

Effects of balanced forces. Push as hard as you can against a solid brick wall. The wall doesn't move. It pushes back with a force equal in size and opposite in direction to your push. Sit on a chair. Your weight (gravity) exerts a downward force on the seat of the chair. The legs of the chair push upward on the seat with an equal force. In both cases described here, the forces are balanced. Notice that there is no motion. The wall doesn't move. The chair doesn't move. You don't move. In the tug-of-war discussed earlier, as long as the two teams exert equal forces in opposite directions, the iron ring will not move. When balanced forces act on an object, the object does not move.

▶ **What effect do two balanced forces have on the motion of an object?**

Unbalanced forces. In the tug-of-war, what would happen if two members of the Yellow team fell down and let go of the rope? Then, the forces acting on the iron ring would not be balanced. The size of the force applied by the Red team would be greater than that of the Yellow team. In this case, the total force being applied to the ring is called an unbalanced force.

An <u>unbalanced force</u> is any force that changes the motion of the object it acts upon. While you are sitting on a chair, there is no motion. Your

66

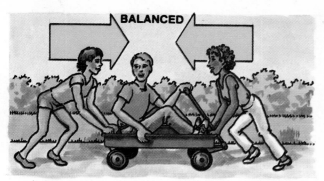

weight pushes down on the seat of the chair. This force is balanced by an upward force on the chair seat exerted by the legs of the chair. If a friend sits on your lap, the downward force on the seat is increased. If the chair legs are strong enough, the upward force is also increased. The forces remain balanced. You do not move. On the other hand, suppose the chair legs are *not* strong enough to balance the added force of your friend's weight. Then, the forces acting on the chair seat become unbalanced. The unbalanced force changes your motion. You and your friend and the chair seat go crashing to the floor!

▶ **What is an unbalanced force?**

Force and motion. An unbalanced force changes the motion of an object in one of four ways:

(1) An unbalanced force can make a stationary object move. This happens when the unbalanced force overcomes the balanced forces that were making the object remain at rest.

(2) An unbalanced force can make the object speed up. This happens when the force is acting in the same direction that the object is moving. A skater gliding forward speeds up when pushed from behind.

(3) An unbalanced force can make an object slow down. This happens when the force is opposite to the direction the object is moving. A skater slows down when pulled from behind.

(4) An unbalanced force can change the direction in which an object is moving. This happens when an object moving in a straight line is pushed or pulled from the side.

▶ **What happens to the motion of an object if an unbalanced force acts on it?**

WHAT YOU LEARNED

1. To describe a force, you must know the size of the force and the direction in which it acts.
2. Balanced forces are equal in size and opposite in direction.
3. An unbalanced force changes the motion of the object it acts upon.

SCIENCE WORDS

balanced forces
 forces that are equal in size but opposite in direction
unbalanced force
 any force that changes the motion of the object it acts upon

ANSWER THESE

Use the correct words to fill in the blank spaces. Write the words on a blank sheet of paper.

1. To describe a force, you must know its _____ and the _____ in which it acts.
2. Forces that are _____ in size and _____ in direction are called balanced forces.
3. _____ forces can cause an object to change its motion.
4. When an unbalanced force acts on an object in the same direction that it is moving, the object will _____ _____.
5. When pushed or pulled from the side, a moving object will change _____.

NOW TRY THESE

A skater is gliding in a northerly direction at a speed of 4 meters per second. Someone gives her a push, causing her speed to change to 6 meters per second in the same direction.

1. Is the push a balanced or unbalanced force? Explain how you know.
2. In what direction is the push applied? Explain how you know.

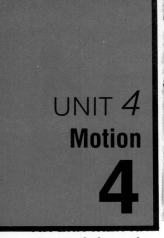

UNIT 4
Motion
4

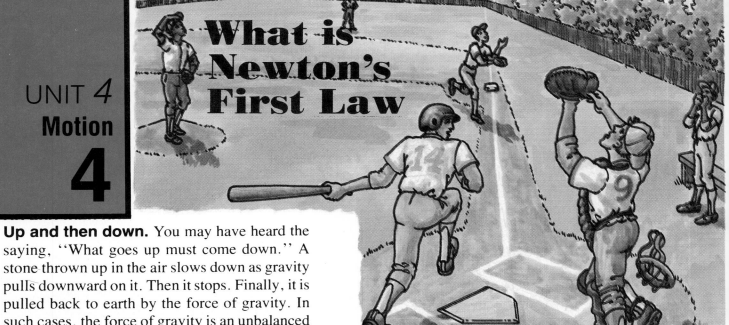

What is Newton's First Law

Up and then down. You may have heard the saying, "What goes up must come down." A stone thrown up in the air slows down as gravity pulls downward on it. Then it stops. Finally, it is pulled back to earth by the force of gravity. In such cases, the force of gravity is an unbalanced force. Do you see why?

▶ **What force pulls downward on objects?**

Breaking away. Not everything that goes up has to come down. As you travel away from the earth, the earth's pull of gravity gets weaker. A spaceship launched by a rocket engine can break away from the earth's gravity. Once in outer space, its engines can be turned off. With no unbalanced force acting on it, its speed and direction will not change. It will coast along at the same speed and in the same direction until it gets near another large object, such as another planet. The force of gravity of the large object may then cause the spaceship's speed or direction to change.

▶ **Why doesn't the velocity of a spaceship change in outer space?**

Newton's First Law. Isaac Newton, the brilliant English scientist, used his knowledge of forces of gravity to study the motion of objects. He studied the motions of objects on earth and those in outer space. From these studies, he developed three basic laws of motion. Although Newton lived long before there were spaceships, he described how spaceships would behave in one of his laws of motion. The law, called **Newton's First Law,** says: If no unbalanced force acts on it, an object at rest will remain at rest, and an object in motion will keep moving at the same speed and in the same direction. This law holds true for all objects on earth as well as for those in outer space.

▶ **What does Newton's First Law say?**

Inertia. According to Newton's First Law, an object will not change its motion unless an unbalanced force acts on it. This tendency of an object to keep its same motion is called inertia (in-ER-shuh). Newton's First Law is often called the law of inertia.

Place a roller skate on a level surface. The skate will stay where you put it. It will not move, because no unbalanced force is acting on it. Give the skate a push. This unbalanced force will start the skate rolling. Even after you stop pushing, the skate will keep on rolling. Its inertia keeps it moving. But another unbalanced force, *friction*, is acting on the skate. This force makes the skate slow down and then stop.

▶ **What is inertia?**

WHAT YOU LEARNED

1. The earth's force of gravity acts as an unbalanced force on objects near the earth's surface.
2. In outer space, the velocity of a spaceship remains unchanged because no unbalanced force acts on it.
3. Newton's First Law says that an object at rest remains at rest and an object in motion keeps moving at the same speed and in the same direction unless an unbalanced force acts on it.
4. The tendency of an object to keep its same motion is canned inertia. Newton's First Law is also called the law of inertia.

SCIENCE WORD

inertia

the tendency of an object to keep its same motion

ANSWER THESE

1. If you throw a ball straight up in the air, the earth's gravity will cause the ball to
   (a) continue moving in a straight line
   (b) slow down
   (c) remain at rest
2. Newton's First Law is also called the law of
   (a) acceleration
   (b) gravity
   (c) inertia
3. According to Newton's First Law, unless acted on by an unbalanced force, an object at rest will
   (a) speed up
   (b) remain at rest
   (c) change direction

NOW TRY THIS

Copy the diagram and fill in the spaces.

Across

1. Force that pulls downward on objects
3. Type of force that changes the motion of objects

Down

2. The tendency of an object to keep its same motion
4. Scientist who developed the laws of motion

FINDING OUT MORE

"Anti-inertia" belts. A moving car has inertia. It tends to keep moving in a straight line, even after the driver's foot is taken off the gas pedal. If the driver is forced to slam on the brakes, friction makes the car slow down very quickly.

Everyone inside the car is traveling at the same speed as the car. They, too, have inertia. However, the brakes don't work on the people. Their inertia tends to keep them moving ahead at the same speed. They keep moving until something stops them. All too often, that "something" turns out to be some solid part of the car, such as the steering wheel, dashboard, or windshield. Unless, of course, the people are wearing seat belts. Seat belts stop their inertia before they can smash into parts of the car. Seat belts could be called "anti-inertia" belts. Whatever you call them, use them! Seat belts can prevent serious injuries.

What is Newton's Second Law?

An unbalanced force acts. When an object has an unbalanced force applied to it, its motion is changed. If the object is at rest, the unbalanced force makes it move. If the object is in motion, the unbalanced force changes its velocity. A change in velocity is an acceleration. Thus, unbalanced forces cause objects to accelerate. When the unbalanced force acts in the same direction in which an object is moving, the object speeds up. When the force is in the opposite direction, the object slows down. When an unbalanced force acts sideways to the direction of motion, the object changes direction.

▶ **What effect does an unbalanced force have on the motion of an object?**

Force, mass, and acceleration. The amount by which an object accelerates depends on two things. These are: (1) the size of the unbalanced force, and (2) the mass of the object to which the unbalanced force is applied.

When applied to the same object, a larger force will give the object a greater acceleration than will a smaller force. For example, if you push a skater, the harder you push, the faster the skater will gain speed. On the other hand, if you apply the same amount of force to two objects having different masses, the object with the larger mass will accelerate more slowly than the one with the smaller mass. If you push equally hard on two skaters, an adult and a small child, the skater with the larger mass (the adult) will speed up more slowly than the skater with the smaller mass.

▶ **What two things affect the acceleration of an object?**

Equal masses; unequal forces

Unequal masses; equal forces

Newton's Second Law.

The relationship between force, mass, and acceleration is summed up in **Newton's Second Law.** Newton's Second Law says: The unbalanced force acting on an object is equal to the mass of the object multiplied by its acceleration. This law can be expressed by this formula:

$$F = m \times a$$

In this formula, F stands for the unbalanced force. The letter m is the mass of the object. The letter a is the acceleration of the object.

▶ **What is Newton's Second Law?**

Using Newton's Second Law.

You can use the formula for Newton's Second Law to find out how much force you need to accelerate an object of known mass. For example, suppose you wanted to know how hard you would have to push a 50-kilogram skater to increase her velocity by 2 meters per second per second (per second squared). Using the formula, we have:

$$F = 50 \text{ kg} \times 2 \text{ m/sec}^2$$
$$= 100 \text{ kg-m/sec}^2$$

This answer is read "100 kilogram-meters per second squared." One kilogram-meter per second squared is the scientific definition for a force of one newton. So, the answer to the problem is 100 newtons.

▶ **How can you find the force needed to accelerate an object of known mass?**

WHAT YOU LEARNED

1. Unbalanced forces cause objects to accelerate.
2. Acceleration of an object depends on two things — the mass of the object and the size of the unbalanced force acting upon it.
3. Newton's Second Law says that the unbalanced force acting on an object is equal to the mass of the object multiplied by its acceleration.

4. One newton is equal to one kilogram-meter per second squared.

ANSWER THESE

If a sentence is true, mark it true. If it is false, change the underlined words to make it true.

1. When acted upon by an unbalanced force, an object at rest will <u>accelerate.</u>
2. If unbalanced forces of equal size act on two objects of different mass, the object of greater mass will speed up <u>faster</u> than the object of smaller mass.
3. According to Newton's Second Law, the unbalanced force acting on an object is equal to the mass of the object times its <u>velocity.</u>
4. The acceleration of an object depends on the size of the unbalanced force acting on it and the <u>mass</u> of the object.

NOW TRY THIS

In the drawings below, decide which object, A or B, has the greater acceleration. Use Newton's Second Law to explain how you decided on your answer.

What is Newton's Third Law?

I can't help pushing back. Stand facing a friend. Push on your friend's hands while your friend keeps his or her hands from moving. Do this three times. The first time push gently. Next, push a little harder. Finally, push harder still. You cannot push on your friend's hands unless your friend pushes back. Also, the harder you push, the harder your friend pushes back. In fact, you both push with the same force.

▶ **If you push against someone with a certain force, how much does that person push back?**

Action and reaction. You cannot push anything unless it pushes back. You cannot push the air, because it doesn't push back. The particles (molecules) of air are too far apart. However, if you fill a balloon with air, you can ''push'' the air. If you squeeze the sides of the balloon, you can feel the air pushing back.

An airplane propeller is designed to push air. The rapidly spinning blades pull air from in front of them and push it out behind the plane. The air pushes back and causes the plane to move forward. You can also push water. When you swim, your hands push on the water. The water pushes back, and you go forward.

Scientists call the force with which you push on something an *action*. The force with which the object pushes back is called a *reaction*. **Newton's Third Law** states that, for every action, there is an equal and opposite reaction. This means that for every force exerted, an equal force will be exerted in the opposite direction. Each of the drawings below show an action and a reaction.

▶ **What is Newton's Third Law?**

5 Density

Unit Lessons

1. What is density?
2. How can we find the density of a liquid?
3. How can we find the density of a solid?
4. What happens to the weight of objects in water?
5. What is Archimedes' Principle?

Goals and Objectives

After completing this unit, you should be able to:
- define density.
- use density to help identify a material.
- find the density of a liquid or a solid.
- understand the principle of water displacement.

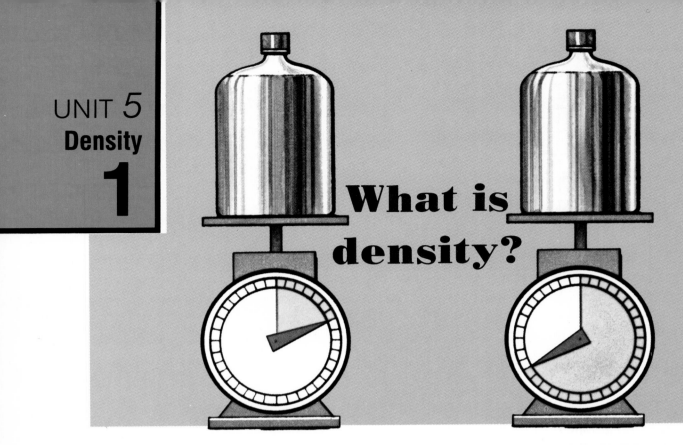

What is density?

Dense materials. You can be fooled by unexpected weight. Two bottles of the same volume are on a table. One is filled with silver paint. The other is filled with mercury, a heavy liquid metal. The bottle of paint is light. The bottle of mercury is much heavier. A small volume of mercury weighs a lot. Materials that are very heavy for their volume are called <u>dense</u> materials. When small objects are heavier than large ones, it is because the small objects are made of denser materials.

▶ **Which is more dense, silver paint or mercury?**

Density. <u>Density</u> (DEN-suh-tee) is the amount of mass of a material in a certain volume. You can find the density of a material by finding the mass of a certain volume of it. For example, the mass of 1 cubic centimeter of water is 1 gram. There is 1 gram of mass in 1 cubic centimeter of water. The density of water is 1 gram per cubic centimeter. One cubic centimeter of mercury has a mass of 13.6 grams. The density of mercury is 13.6 grams per cubic

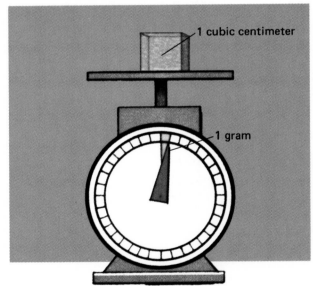

DENSITY = 1 gram per cubic centimeter

centimeter. Mercury is more dense than water. Look at the table of densities on the next page. The table tells how much mass there is in 1 cubic centimeter of each material.

▶ **Which material in the table is the most dense? Which is the least dense?**

MATERIAL	DENSITY (grams per cubic centimeter)
cork	.2
alcohol	.8
water	1
aluminum	2.7
iron	7.9
lead	11.3
mercury	13.6
gold	19.3

Using density. Density is a physical property of matter. We can use density to help identify a material. Suppose we have a piece of metal, and we want to find out what metal it is. We can measure its mass and its volume, and find its density. This will help us identify the metal. If the density is 2.7 grams per cubic centimeter, the metal is probably aluminum. If the density is 11.3 grams per cubic centimeter, the metal is probably lead. Each material has its own density. This helps to identify it.

▶ **Why can density help to identify a material?**

WHAT YOU LEARNED

1. The density of a material is the mass of a certain volume of it.
2. Density can be measured in grams per cubic centimeter.
3. Density can be used to help identify a material.

SCIENCE WORDS

dense
   heavy for its volume
density (DEN-suh-tee)
   mass of a certain volume of a material

ANSWER THESE

1. Which of the following materials is more dense than iron?
   a. water
   b. aluminum
   c. mercury

2. Which of the following is a cubic centimeter?

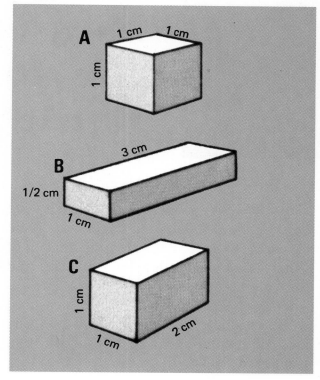

3. The density of water is
   a. 1 gram
   b. 1 gram per square centimeter
   c. 1 gram per cubic centimeter

NOW TRY THESE

1. Which is lightest, a cup of water, a cup of alcohol, or a cup of mercury?
2. What is the mass of 10 cubic centimeters of water?
3. Which is heavier, 1 kilogram of mercury or 1 kilogram of water?

FINDING OUT MORE

Astronomers have learned that as stars get older, they go through certain changes. Some stars become hotter and hotter, and then explode. After the explosion, the matter that is left contracts. The weight of the matter produces so much pressure that the atoms in the star are crushed. All the matter gets squeezed into a very small volume. This is called a neutron star. A neutron star is so dense that it is hard to imagine. Here is what the mass of a single cubic centimeter of a neutron star would be: 1,000,000,000,000,000,000 kilograms.

How can we find the density of a liquid?

Finding density. How can the density of a liquid be found? The most common liquid on earth is water. Let's find the density of water. To find the density, the mass and the volume of a material must be known. The volume of a liquid can be measured with a graduated cylinder or graduate. The mass of a material can be measured with a balance scale.

▶ **What things must we know to find the density of a material?**

Density of water. You can find the density of water using a graduate, a scale, and water. First, take the clean, dry graduate

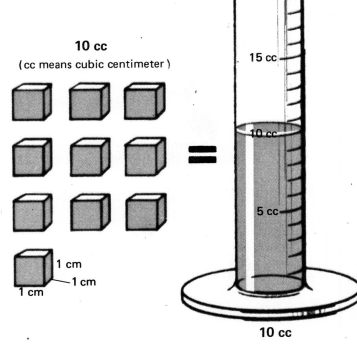

10 cc
(cc means cubic centimeter)

1 cm
1 cm
1 cm

10 cc

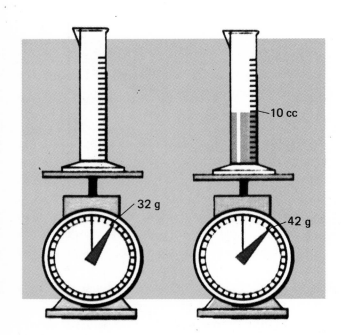

—10 cc

32 g

42 g

and find its mass. Write down the mass. For example:

Mass of graduate = 32 grams

Put exactly 10 cc of water in the graduate. Carefully find the mass of the graduate with 10 cc of water in it. Write down the mass of the graduate with water.

Mass of graduate plus water = 42 grams

To find the mass of the water, subtract the mass of the empty graduate from the mass of the graduate with water.

Mass of 10 cc water = 42 grams — 32 grams = 10 grams

The formula for finding density is:

$$\text{DENSITY} = \frac{\text{MASS}}{\text{VOLUME}}$$

We know the mass of the water is 10 grams and its volume is 10 cc.

$$\text{Density of water} = \frac{\text{Mass of water}}{\text{Volume of water}}$$

$$\text{Density of water} = \frac{10 \text{ grams}}{10 \text{ cc}}$$

Density of water = 1 gram per cubic centimeter

The density of any liquid can be found using this method.

▶ **What is the formula for finding density?**

WHAT YOU LEARNED

The density of a substance is equal to its mass divided by its volume.

ANSWER THESE

1. Different liquids have
   a. the same density
   b. different densities
   c. a density of 1 gram per cubic centimeter
2. To find the volume of a liquid, you could use a
   a. graduated cylinder
   b. balance scale
   c. thistle tube
3. 5 cc of a liquid has a mass of 10 grams. The density of the liquid is
   a. 2 grams per cubic centimeter
   b. 5 grams per cubic centimeter
   c. ½ gram per cubic centimeter

NOW TRY THIS

A beaker with mercury in it has a mass of 50 grams. The beaker alone has a mass of 9.2 grams. Can you figure out how many cubic centimeters of mercury are in the beaker? (Density of mercury = 13.6 grams per cubic centimeter.)

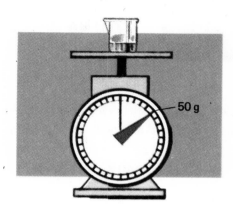

FINDING OUT MORE

In 1848 gold was discovered in California. Many people went West to try to find gold and become rich. One problem with hunting for gold is fool's gold. Fool's gold looks like gold but is really a compound of iron and sulfur and sometimes copper. The density of real gold is 19.3 grams per cc. The density of fool's gold is about 5 grams per cc. How could you tell whether a material is real gold or fool's gold?

How can we find the density of a solid?

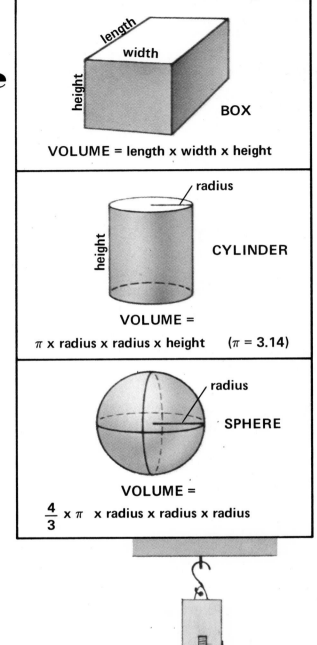

BOX

VOLUME = length x width x height

CYLINDER

VOLUME =
π x radius x radius x height   (π = 3.14)

SPHERE

VOLUME =
$\frac{4}{3}$ x π x radius x radius x radius

Measuring the densities of solids. Some solids have regular shapes. Some have irregular shapes. The regular solids may be cubes, boxes, cylinders, or spheres. Irregular solids may have any shape. You can find the density of any solid if you know its mass and volume.

▶ **What must you know to find the density of a solid?**

Finding volume. Mathematical formulas can be used to find the volumes of solids with regular shapes. The drawings show some of the formulas.

▶ **What is the formula for the volume of a box?**

Finding the density of a regularly shaped object. A bar of aluminum is shown in the picture. You can read its mass from the scale. Can you find its density? Here is how to do it:

Step 1.   Find the mass: **MASS = 2700 grams**

Step 2.   Find the volume: VOLUME = length x width x height

VOLUME = 50 cm x 10 cm x 2 cm = 1000 cubic cm

Step 3.   Find the density: DENSITY = $\frac{MASS}{VOLUME}$

DENSITY = $\frac{2700 \text{ grams}}{1000 \text{ cubic cm}}$

= 2.7 grams per cubic cm

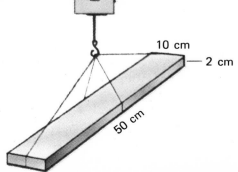

2700 grams

10 cm

2 cm

50 cm

Now find the density of the aluminum cylinder shown in the picture. Here is how to do it:

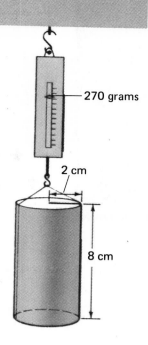
270 grams
2 cm
8 cm

Step 1. Find the mass: **MASS = 270 grams**

Step 2. Find the volume: VOLUME = π x radius x radius x height

VOLUME = 3.14 x 2 x 2 x 8 = 100 cubic cm

Step 3. Find the density: DENSITY = $\dfrac{\text{MASS}}{\text{VOLUME}}$

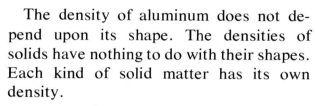

DENSITY = $\dfrac{\textbf{270 grams}}{\textbf{100 cubic cm}}$ = **2.7 grams per cubic cm**

The density of aluminum does not depend upon its shape. The densities of solids have nothing to do with their shapes. Each kind of solid matter has its own density.

▶ **What is the density of aluminum?**

WHAT YOU LEARNED

1. Different materials have different densities.
2. The density of a material can be found from its mass and volume.

ANSWER THESE

1. Aluminum is
   a. more dense than iron
   b. less dense than iron
   c. the same density as iron
2. To find the density of a solid, you must know its
   a. size and shape
   b. size and volume
   c. mass and volume
3. To find the volume of a solid with a regular shape, you could use a
   a. pulley
   b. spring scale
   c. ruler
4. When a metal rod is cut in half, the density of each half
   a. is doubled
   b. is cut in half
   c. remains the same

NOW TRY THIS

Pure materials can be identified by their densities. The densities of some materials are listed below. Find out what each material is.

DENSITY	PURE MATERIAL
1 gram per cubic centimeter	
2.7 grams per cubic centimeter	
19.3 grams per cubic centimeter	
7.9 grams per cubic centimeter	
13.6 grams per cubic centimeter	
11.3 grams per cubic centimeter	

FINDING OUT MORE

Many objects do not have a regular shape. You may want to find the density of an object with an irregular shape. Rocks are irregularly shaped. It is easy to find the mass of a rock with a balance. You can find the volume of the rock by sinking it in water. When the rock sinks, it pushes some of the water out of the way. We say it displaces (dis-PLAY-sez) the water. The volume of the water displaced is equal to the volume of the rock. A large graduated cylinder can be used to measure how much water is displaced. The amount the water rises when the rock is added shows the volume of the rock.

What happens to the weight of objects in water?

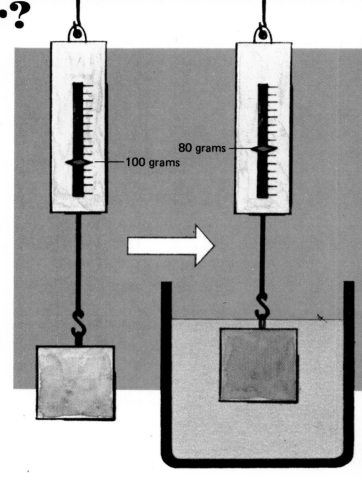

100 grams

80 grams

Weight in water. Things seem to weigh less in water. Have you ever noticed how easy it is to hold up heavy objects when they are in water? At the beach or in a swimming pool have you ever tried to lift someone up? Try to measure the weight an object loses in water. Hang a 100-gram weight from a spring scale. Lower the weight into a glass of water. Notice the reading on the scale when the weight is in the water. The 100-gram weight seems to weigh less in water. All things seem to weigh less in water.

▶ What happens to the weight of objects in water?

Floating. Some things float in water. How can you tell whether or not an object will float? To know whether an object will float, you first must find its density. Materials less dense than water float in water. The density of water is 1 gram per cubic centimeter. The density of most woods is about 0.7 grams per cubic centimeter. These woods float on water. However, there is a wood more dense than water. This wood is ebony. Ebony does not float. It sinks. Most metals are more dense than water. They sink in water. Materials that are less dense than water float. Materials that are more dense than water sink.

▶ What materials will float in water?

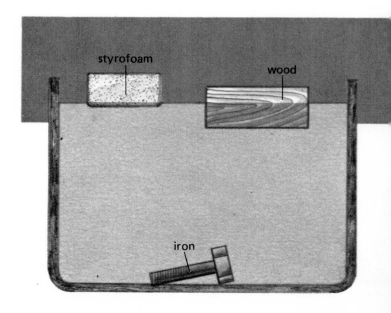

styrofoam

wood

iron

82

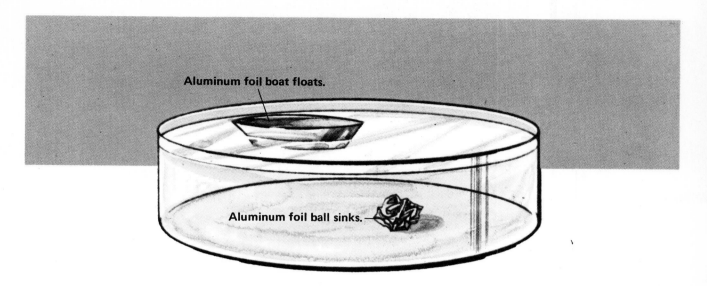

Aluminum foil boat floats.

Aluminum foil ball sinks.

Metal ships can float. Even though ships are made of dense materials, they float on water. You can make a model of a ship with aluminum foil. It will float on water. Crumple the foil into a ball, and it will sink in water. A metal ship floats because it is hollow. When the density of the ship is figured, its volume includes all the hollow space inside. This space has air in it, which doesn't have much mass. So the density of the ship, including the hollow space, is less than 1 gram per cubic centimeter. That's why it floats.

▶ **Why is the density of a metal ship less than 1 gram per cubic centimeter?**

WHAT YOU LEARNED

1. Materials seem to weigh less in water.
2. Materials less dense than water float in water.
3. Materials more dense than water sink in water.

ANSWER THESE

1. Objects in water seem to be
   a. lighter than in air
   b. heavier than in air
   c. the same weight as in air
2. The density of a material is 0.9 grams per cubic centimeter. It will
   a. float in water
   b. sink in water
   c. gain weight in water

3. When you find the volume of a ship, you
   a. count only the metal parts
   b. count only the hollow spaces
   c. count the whole space taken up by the ship

FINDING OUT MORE

Less dense materials float on more dense materials. Mercury, oil, and water are liquids with different densities. Pour them slowly one at a time into a graduated cylinder. Pour them in any order. They will form three separate layers. The most dense liquid is on the bottom. The least dense liquid is on the top. Ice floats on water. What does this tell you about the density of ice?

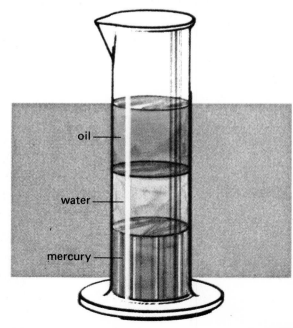

oil

water

mercury

What is Archimedes' Principle?

Archimedes takes a bath. Archimedes (ar-kuh-MEED-eez) was a Greek scientist who lived about 2,000 years ago. One day he stepped into a bathtub filled with water. The water rose up and spilled over the edge as he got in. Archimedes began to think about this. He also noticed that he felt lighter in the water than out of the water. He thought that the rising of the water in the tub and his loss of weight might be connected.

▶ **What did Archimedes notice about his weight when he took a bath?**

Archimedes loses weight. Archimedes was right about his loss of weight in the bathtub. All objects seem to lose weight in water. When objects are put into water, they make the water rise. The water that rises is pushed out of the way by the object. It is called displaced (dis-PLACED) water. Archimedes found that the loss of weight of an object in water is equal to the weight of the displaced water. This is called Archimedes' Principle (PRIN-sih-pull).

Study the drawing. The stone weighs 1000 grams in air. In water, it weighs 800 grams. Its loss of weight in water is 200 grams.

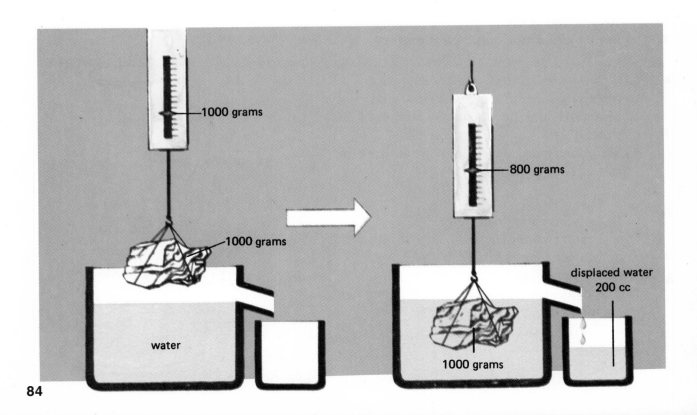

1000 grams

1000 grams

800 grams

displaced water 200 cc

water

1000 grams

The volume of the displaced water is 200 cc. Water weighs 1 gram per cc. The weight of 200 cc of water is about 200 grams. This is the same as the loss of weight of the stone.

▶ **What is Archimedes' Principle?**

Ships float. The weight of a ship in water seems to be zero. According to Archimedes' Principle, the ship displaces an amount of water equal to its loss of weight. A ship that weighs 10 million newtons seems to weigh zero in water. It has lost 10 million newtons of weight. It has displaced 10 million newtons of water. The weight of a ship is called its displacement (dis-PLACE-ment). Displacement tells both the weight of a ship and how much water it displaces.

▶ **What can we tell from the displacement of a ship?**

WHAT YOU LEARNED

1. Objects seem to lose weight in water. The loss of weight is equal to the weight of the displaced water.
2. A ship's displacement tells its weight and the amount of water it displaces.

SCIENCE WORDS

Archimedes' Principle (ar-kuh-MEED-eez PRIN-sih-pull)
the fact that the loss of weight of an object in water is equal to the weight of the displaced water

displaced (dis-PLACED) **water**
the amount of water pushed out of the way by an object

ANSWER THESE

1. What happens to the water level when you get into the tub?
2. What seems to happen to your weight when you get into the tub?
3. How is your loss of weight in the tub related to the amount of water displaced?
4. A ship displaces 2 million kilograms of water. How much does the ship weigh?

NOW TRY THIS

In the letters below are ten important science words. See if you can find them. Read from left to right and from top to bottom.

```
M W H G A S X E D R
A R C H I M E D E S
S I H F W D W D N A
S O L I D O E V S N
V S I N R S I A I U
O M Q O C B G L T Y
L E U Y U S H R Y B
U Z I P M L T N O T
M A D I S P L A C E
E P R I N C I P L E
```

UNIT 5 Review

Do the following review questions on a separate sheet of paper.

Modified True/False   Write down each of the following statements, leaving a blank line between each line you write. Before the number for each statement, write T if the statement is true and F if the statement is false. For the false statements, cross out the word written in capital letters and write above it a word that will make the statement true.

1. Density can be used to WEIGH a material.
2. Gold is very LIGHT for its volume.
3. Density equals mass divided by LENGTH.
4. The density of water is one KILOGRAM per cubic centimeter.
5. Aluminum is MORE dense than iron.
6. The VOLUME of a box is length x width x height.
7. Materials that are LESS dense than water float in water.
8. Most metals are LESS dense than water.
9. Archimedes explained why objects seem to GAIN weight in water.
10. You can determine a solid's density if you know its WEIGHT.

Multiple Choice   Write the letter of the choice that best completes the statement or answers the question.

1. The mass of a certain volume of a material is its
   a. weight
   b. density
   c. cubic volume
2. Gold is nearly twenty times denser than
   a. water
   b. mercury
   c. lead
3. Density is equal to mass
   a. divided by volume
   b. times volume
   c. plus volume
4. To find the mass of an object, you can use a
   a. graduate
   b. cylinder
   c. scale

5. Most wood floats in water because
   a. it is waterproof
   b. it is less dense than water
   c. it is more dense than water
6. A metal ship floats in water because
   a. the metal is less dense than water
   b. it is coated with oil
   c. it has hollow spaces filled with air
7. The loss of weight of an object in water is equal to
   a. the total weight of the object
   b. half the weight of the object
   c. the weight of the water displaced by the object
8. The fact referred to in question 7 is known as
   a. the water bath principle
   b. the volume principle
   c. Archimedes' principle

UNIT 6

Heat

Unit Lessons

1. What is heat?
2. How does heat travel through solids?
3. How does heat travel through gases and solids?
4. How does heat travel through space?
5. What happens when matter is heated?
6. What is temperature?
7. How is temperature measured?
8. How is heat measured?

Goals and Objectives

After completing this unit, you should be able to:
- recognize heat as a form of energy.
- differentiate between insulators and conductors.
- describe a convection current.
- explain how heat reaches us from the sun.
- differentiate between heat and temperature.
- use the Celsius scale.

What is heat?

Keeping warm. Some birds fly south in the winter. Some people do that, too. If we can't go south, we have other ways to keep warm. When your hands are cold, you may rub them together. <u>Friction</u> (FRIC-shun) is another word for rubbing. Friction produces heat. You may run or jump up and down when you are cold. This motion produces heat. To keep our house warm, we burn <u>fuels</u> (FEWLS). A burning fuel produces heat. <u>Heat</u> is a form of energy that we can feel.

▶ What is heat?

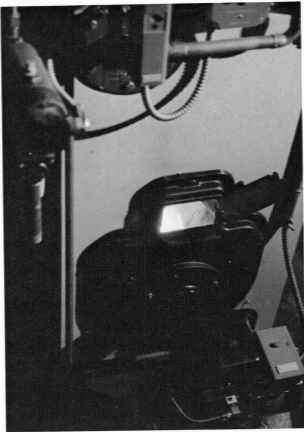

Oil burning inside this furnace produces enough heat to warm an entire house.

Heat is a form of energy. Heat keeps us warm. How do we know that heat is a form of energy? Energy can make things move. You can do an experiment to show how heat can make things move. Heat some water until it boils. You can see the water bubbling and moving around in its container. Heat is making the water move.

Hold a pinwheel over a hot light bulb. You will see the pinwheel turn. Heat is making the air around the pinwheel move. The moving air is turning the pinwheel. Heat is a form of energy. Heat can make things move.

▶ Why do we say that heat is a form of energy?

Moving molecules. You know that matter is made up of tiny particles called molecules. These molecules are always in motion. Heat energy makes molecules move faster. When you boil water, you make the water molecules move faster. The molecules move so fast that they leave the container. If you keep the heat turned on, the water boils away.

▶ **What does heat energy do to molecules?**

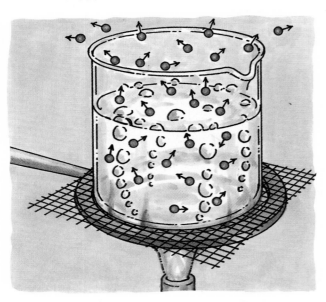

Making things hot. Hit a piece of metal several times with a hammer. Then feel the metal. It feels warmer. The moving hammer has energy. When the hammer hits the metal, its energy goes into the metal. The energy makes the molecules in the metal move

faster. The energy of the hammer was turned into heat energy in the metal. When you touch the metal, you feel the extra heat that it has.

▶ **When you hit a piece of metal with a hammer, does the metal feel warmer or cooler?**

WHAT YOU LEARNED

1. Heat is a form of energy.
2. Heat makes molecules move faster.

SCIENCE WORDS

friction (FRIC-shun)
    rubbing
fuel (FEWL)
    material that is burned to produce heat energy
heat
    a form of energy that we can feel

ANSWER THESE

1. Heating makes molecules move
    a. faster
    b. slower
    c. in circles
2. Heat is a form of
    a. mineral
    b. chemical
    c. energy
3. Hitting a piece of metal makes it
    a. cooler
    b. warmer
    c. heavier

DO THIS AT HOME

Straighten the wire of a coat hanger. Bend the wire back and forth quickly, until it breaks. Then feel the broken ends of the wire. What do you feel?

When you bend the wire, your muscles do work. The energy of this work goes into the wire and heats it. Any form of energy, not just heat, can be used to make things hotter.

How does heat travel through solids?

Metals carry heat. Hold a strip of copper in a flame. The strip quickly becomes too hot to hold. Heat energy from the flame has traveled through the copper strip. Heat travels through solids by <u>conduction</u> (con-DUCK-shun).

▶ **How does heat travel through solids?**

How heat travels by conduction. When you held the copper strip in the flame, it became hot. The part of the strip in the flame became hot first. The molecules in this part of the strip began to move faster. They bumped into molecules around them. The fast-moving molecules made other molecules move faster. Molecules began bumping into each other all along the copper strip. Molecules all along the strip began to move faster. This is how the heat energy traveled through the strip of copper. Heat travels by conduction when moving molecules bump into each other.

▶ **How does heat travel by conduction?**

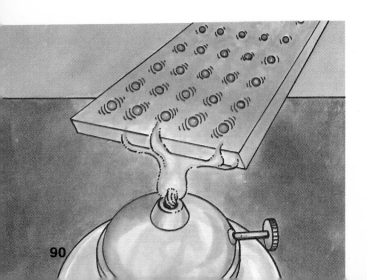

Good conductors of heat. Hold different kinds of metal strips in a flame. You could use copper, silver, iron, and steel. All of the metal strips will soon become too hot to hold. All metals are good conductors of heat. Copper and silver will get hot faster than iron or steel. Copper and silver are two of the best conductors of heat. These metals are also two of the best conductors of electricity. Good conductors of electricity are usually good conductors of heat also.

▶ **What materials are good conductors of heat?**

Poor conductors of heat. Many materials do not conduct heat well. Hold a lighted kitchen match. Hold a burning candle. Can you feel the heat at the end you are holding? Wood, wax, paper, and air are poor conductors of heat. They are insulators. These materials are also poor conductors of electricity. Most poor conductors of electricity are also poor conductors of heat.

▶ **What materials are poor conductors of heat?**

Using insulators. Fuel is burned to heat a house in winter. Houses are insulated to keep the heat in and save fuel. Spaces are left between the inside and outside walls of the house. The spaces are filled with an insulating material. This helps keep heat from getting out of the house. In summer, the insulating material helps keep heat from getting into the house.

▶ **Why are insulating materials used in houses?**

WHAT YOU LEARNED

1. Moving molecules make heat travel through solids by conduction.
2. Most good electrical conductors are good heat conductors.
3. Most poor electrical conductors are poor heat conductors.

SCIENCE WORD

conduction (con-DUCK-shun)
  movement of heat energy by molecules bumping into each other

ANSWER THESE

1. Heat travels by conduction when molecules
   a. are insulated
   b. stop moving around
   c. bump into each other
2. Two of the best conductors of heat are
   a. paper and air
   b. wood and wax
   c. copper and silver
3. Poor conductors of heat are usually
   a. poor conductors of electricity
   b. good conductors of electricity
   c. metals
4. Homes are insulated to
   a. keep them cooler in winter and warmer in summer
   b. keep them warmer in winter and cooler in summer
   c. make them roomier inside

WHAT'S HAPPENING

Polystyrene (POL-ee-STY-reen) is a kind of plastic that can be made with tiny air bubbles in it. This is called polystyrene foam. Polystyrene is a good insulator. Air is also a good insulator. The air and polystyrene together make polystyrene foam an especially good insulator. Polystyrene foam is also very light in weight. It is used to make picnic baskets and jugs. These things will keep hot foods hot and cold foods cold. A jug made of polystyrene foam will keep lemonade cold for hours.

polystyrene foam

How does heat travel through gases and liquids?

WARM AIR

COLD AIR

COLD AIR

Heat travels through air. Cold air is heavier than warm air. When cold and warm air meet, the cold air sinks below the warm air. It forces the warm air to move upward. The smoke coming out of a chimney is warm. It is pushed up through the chimney by cooler air. The warm air carries its heat upward as it rises. This is one way heat travels through air. It is called underline{convection} (con-VEC-shun).

▶ **What happens when cold and warm air meet?**

Moving air. Sinking cool air and rising warm air move heat through the air. These up-and-down movements of the air are called convection currents. Heat travels through the air in convection currents.

▶ **How does heat travel through the air?**

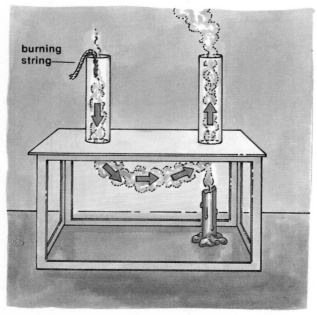

burning string

Seeing convection currents. The box with two chimneys shown in the picture is a convection box. A convection box helps you see convection currents in air. The candle flame heats the air over it. The warm air rises through the chimney over the candle. Cooler air comes down the other chimney and flows through the box. Then it is warmed by the candle and rises out of the box again. A convection current flows through the box. The burning string helps you to see the current. Smoke from the string is moved along by the current of air. The smoke shows you the convection current moving through the box.

▶ **What does the smoke in a convection box show you?**

Convection currents in liquids. Convection takes place in liquids as well as in gases. Cold water is heavier than warm water. Cold water moves down and warm water moves up just as cold and warm air do. Fill a large beaker with water. Put some sawdust in the water. Let the sawdust sink to the bottom of the beaker. Then heat the beaker gently. Convection currents in the water will make the sawdust move. The moving sawdust will show you the convection currents in the water.

▶ **How can sawdust help you see convection currents in water?**

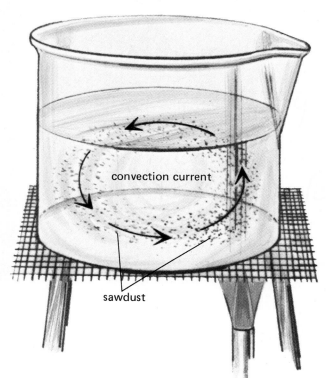
convection current

sawdust

WHAT YOU LEARNED

1. Heat travels through gases and liquids by convection.
2. Convection causes up-and-down movements of a gas or liquid, called convection currents.

SCIENCE WORDS

convection (con-VEC-shun)
the way that heat travels through gases and liquids

convection currents
up-and-down movements of gases or liquids caused by convection

If a sentence is true, mark it T. If it is false, change the underlined word to make it true.
1. Hot air <u>sinks</u>.
2. <u>Cold</u> air rises.
3. Convection currents move through <u>solids</u>.
4. Hot water <u>rises</u> through cold water.
5. Heat travels through liquids by <u>convection</u>.

DO THIS AT HOME

Often you want to have a lot of fresh air in a room. What is the best way to get it? You can find out by making a model of a room. You will need a cigar box, some corks, a candle, and a piece of glass. Make some holes in the box, as shown in the picture. Put the corks in the holes. Stand the box up, and remove the cover. Put the candle in the box and light it. Cover the front of the box with the glass.

The candle will burn best when it has a good supply of fresh air. Try taking different corks out while you watch the candle flame. Find out which holes must be open to make the candle burn best. Does this tell you anything about how to get fresh air into a room? How should you open the windows to get fresh air into a room at home?

glass cover

93

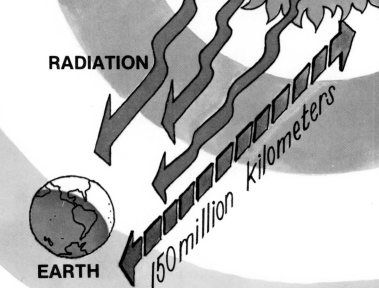

How does heat travel through space?

RADIATION

150 million kilometers

EARTH

SUN

Heat from the sun. The sun is 150 million kilometers from the earth. How does the heat from the sun get to us? Conduction carries heat through solid matter. But there is not enough solid matter between the earth and the sun for heat to travel through. Conduction cannot bring us heat from the sun. There is no air in space. Heat from the sun cannot reach us by convection, either. Heat cannot travel through space by conduction or convection.

▶ **Why can't the sun's heat reach us by conduction or convection?**

How heat travels through space. Heat from the sun reaches us by radiation (ray-dee-AY-shun). Matter is not needed to carry radiation. Radiation can carry heat across space. Heat from other places besides the sun can also travel by radiation. The heat from an electric heater reaches us partly by radiation.

▶ **How can heat travel through space?**

Radiation at work. Radiation is energy. It can make things move. Place a radiometer (ray-dee-OM-uh-ter) in sunlight. Watch the radiometer paddles turn. Now block the light from the radiometer. The paddles stop turning. Radiation coming from 150 million kilometers away makes the radiometer turn. The radiometer works on energy from the sun.

▶ **What makes a radiometer turn?**

Electricity and radiation. Spacecraft can use energy from the sun. Some spacecraft have solar (SOH-ler) cells in them. The solar cells change radiation from the sun into electrical energy. They produce electricity when the sun shines on them. Electricity from the solar cells can run motors on board the spacecraft.

▶ **How do solar cells produce electricity?**

WHAT YOU LEARNED

1. Heat travels through space by radiation.
2. Solar cells can change radiation into electrical energy.

SCIENCE WORDS

radiation (ray-dee-AY-shun)
the way that heat energy travels through space
radiometer (ray-dee-OM-uh-ter)
a device that turns when sunlight shines on it
solar (SOH-ler) **cell**
a device that produces electricity when sunlight shines on it

ANSWER THESE

1. Heat from the sun reaches us by
   a. conduction
   b. convection
   c. radiation
2. Solar cells turn radiation from the sun into
   a. heat
   b. electricity
   c. light
3. There are no convection currents in space because
   a. the sun is too weak to make them
   b. there is no energy in space
   c. there is no air in space to carry them
4. Radiation from the sun supplies the earth with
   a. magnetism
   b. heat
   c. matter

DO THIS AT HOME

Heat from the sun can make a piece of paper burn. Put a piece of paper on a concrete sidewalk. Hold a magnifying glass over the paper. Move the magnifying glass up and down slowly. Find the place to hold it so that it makes a bright spot of sunlight on the paper. Hold the magnifying glass steady. Soon the paper will turn brown and start smoking. Then it will burst into flame. Radiation from the sun makes the paper burn.

The radiation from the sun can be reflected by a mirror. Use the magnifying glass to focus the sunlight onto a mirror. Hold the mirror so it reflects the bright spot of light onto a piece of paper. Again the paper will start burning. Heat that travels by radiation can be reflected.

What happens when matter is heated?

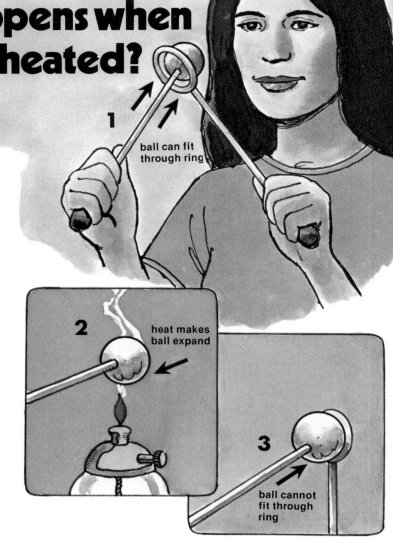

1 ball can fit through ring

2 heat makes ball expand

3 ball cannot fit through ring

What happens when a solid is heated?

The picture shows an iron ball and ring. The ball just fits through the ring. But something happens if the ball is heated. It no longer fits through the ring. Heat makes the iron ball expand (eck-SPAND), or get larger. It becomes too big to fit through the ring. Most solids expand when they are heated.

► **What happens to solids when they are heated?**

What happens when a solid is cooled?

The iron ball can be made to fit through the ring again. It just has to cool off. After the iron ball cools, it will fit through the ring. Cooling makes the iron ball contract (con-TRACT), or get smaller. Most solids contract when they are cooled.

► **What happens to solids when they are cooled?**

1. 2. 3.

water expands   water contracts

HEATING   COOLING

What happens when a liquid is heated and cooled?

Fill a test tube nearly to the top with colored water. Push a glass tube into a one-hole rubber stopper. Place the stopper in the test tube. Now heat the test tube over a flame. You will see the water rise in the tube. The water expands as it is heated. Take the test tube away from the flame and let it cool. You will see the water move back down the tube. The water contracts as it cools. Liquids expand when they are heated, and contract when they are cooled.

► **When do liquids expand and contract?**

What happens when gases are heated and cooled? Stretch a balloon over the mouth of a flask. Heat the flask very gently. You will see the balloon getting larger. Heat makes the air in the flask expand. The expanding air stretches the balloon. Now let the flask cool. The balloon will get smaller again. The air contracts as it cools. Gases expand when they are heated, and contract when they are cooled.

▶ **What happens to gases when they are heated and cooled?**

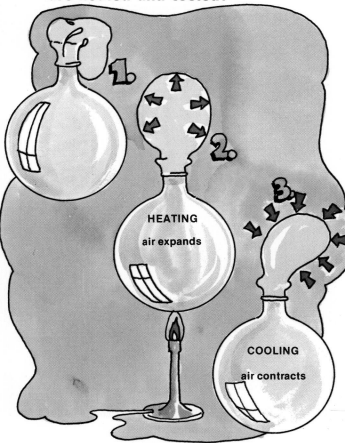

HEATING
air expands

COOLING
air contracts

Expanding and contracting matter. Heat energy makes molecules move faster. As the molecules move faster, they move farther apart. The more they spread out, the more space they take up. Heating matter makes it take up more space. It expands. When the matter is cooled, its molecules slow down. They move closer together. Cooling matter makes it take up less space. It contracts.

▶ **Why does matter expand when it is heated?**

WHAT YOU LEARNED

1. Matter expands when it is heated.
2. Matter contracts when it is cooled.
3. Molecules moving faster or slower make matter expand or contract.

SCIENCE WORDS

expand (eck-SPAND)
  get larger; take up more space
contract (con-TRACT)
  get smaller; take up less space

ANSWER THESE

1. When iron is heated, it
   a. expands
   b. contracts
   c. changes to lead
2. When water is heated, it
   a. expands
   b. contracts
   c. stays the same
3. When air is heated, it
   a. expands
   b. contracts
   c. explodes
4. Matter expands when it is heated because
   a. its molecules get larger
   b. its molecules move farther apart
   c. its molecules break into pieces

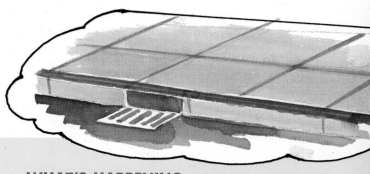

WHAT'S HAPPENING

Have you ever wondered why sidewalks are made with cracks in them? The cracks are there for a good reason. On a very hot day, a concrete sidewalk expands. If the concrete has no space to expand sideways, it will move upward. The sidewalk will buckle and break up. Cracks in the sidewalk help prevent this. The cracks are spaces for the concrete to expand in. The sidewalk can expand sideways, instead of breaking up.

What is temperature?

Changing the temperature of a material.
When heat energy is added to something, it becomes warmer. Its temperature (TEM-pruh-chur) gets higher. When heat energy is taken away from something, it becomes cooler. Its temperature gets lower. The temperature of a material changes when the amount of heat in it changes.

▶ **What causes the temperature of a material to change?**

Making heat move. Heat energy moves from place to place. It moves from a warmer place to a cooler place. Heat some water. Then pour it into a cool pot. Heat energy moves from the hot water to the cool pot. The pot gets warmer. Its temperature rises. The water gets cooler. Its temperature falls. Temperatures change as heat energy moves from warmer places to cooler places.

▶ **Which way does heat energy move?**

Measuring temperatures. Temperature can be measured with a thermometer (ther-MOM-uh-ter). A thermometer may be made with many different materials. Many contain alcohol or mercury in a tube. The liquid goes up the tube when it is warmed, and down when it is cooled. Marks along the tube tell the temperature. Alcohol is the red liquid used in outdoor thermometers. Mercury is the silver liquid in the thermometer you use when you are sick.

▶ **What liquids are used in thermometers?**

OUTDOOR THERMOMETER (alcohol)

FEVER THERMOMETER (mercury)

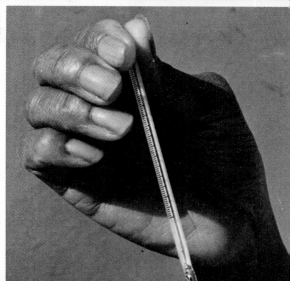

Solid thermometers. A liquid such as alcohol or mercury could not be used in an oven thermometer. The temperatures in the oven would be too high. The liquid would boil, or break the tube. An oven thermometer uses a double metal coil. Heating makes the coil expand. Cooling makes it contract. As the coil expands and contracts, it moves a needle along a dial. Markings on the dial show the temperature.

▶ **Why can't a liquid be used in an oven thermometer?**

OVEN THERMOMETER
(metal coil)

WHAT YOU LEARNED

1. The temperature of a material changes when the amount of heat in it changes.
2. Heat energy travels from warmer places to cooler places.
3. Thermometers use expanding and contracting materials to measure temperature.

SCIENCE WORDS

temperature (TEM-pruh-chur)
  a measure of how hot a material is
thermometer (ther-MOM-uh-ter)
  a tool used to measure temperature

ANSWER THESE

1. When heat is added to a material, its temperature
   a. rises
   b. falls
   c. remains the same
2. Heat energy moves
   a. from cooler places to warmer places
   b. from warmer places to cooler places
   c. only when there is a flame
3. Thermometers may be made
   a. with liquids only
   b. with solids as well as liquids
   c. with anything that will not expand or contract
4. Thermometers used to measure very high temperatures are usually made with
   a. alcohol
   b. mercury
   c. metal coils

DO THIS AT HOME

You have a sense of temperature. You can tell when things feel warm or cool. But sometimes your sense of temperature can be fooled. Here is a trick you can play on yourself:

Fill a pan with very cold water. Put warm water in another pan. Fill a third pan with water as hot as you can touch. Put both your hands in the warm water. Does the temperature of the water feel the same to both hands? Dry your hands. Now put one hand into the cold water, and the other hand into the hot water. Leave them there for about a minute. Then put both hands directly into the warm water again. How does the water feel now? Does the temperature of the water feel the same to both hands? Why do you think your sense of temperature is fooled when you do this?

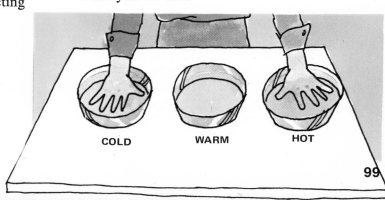

COLD   WARM   HOT

How is temperature measured?

Boiling hot. Half fill a large pot with cold water. Heat it over a low flame while stirring the water with your finger. Soon you feel the water getting warmer. The heat going into the water is making its temperature go up. Take your finger out of the water. Keep heating the water. After a while, the water gets hot enough to boil. Its temperature now is called the boiling point of water.

▶ **What do we call the temperature at which water boils?**

Freeze it. Put a tray of water in the freezer. The water is warmer than the air in the freezer. Heat energy leaves the water, and the water gets colder. After a while, the water gets cold enough to freeze. Its temperature now is called the freezing point of water.

▶ **What do we call the temperature at which water freezes?**

Temperature is not heat. Heat a spoonful of water over a low flame. In a minute or two the water reaches the boiling point. It does not take much heat to boil a spoonful of water. It takes much more heat to boil a pot of water. But the boiling water has the same temperature in both cases. Temperature and heat are not the same thing.

▶ **How does the temperature of a small amount of boiling water compare with the temperature of a large amount?**

Units of temperature. Temperature is measured in units called <u>degrees</u> (duh-GREES). We can use the freezing and boil-

32°F — 0°C

FREEZING WATER

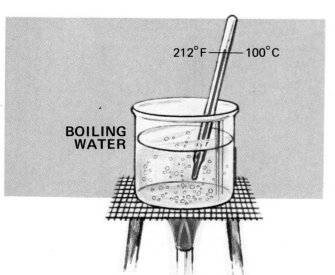

212°F — 100°C

BOILING WATER

ing points of water to mark the degrees on a thermometer scale. On the Fahrenheit (FAR-en-hite) scale, the freezing point of water is marked 32 degrees. This is written 32°F. The boiling point of water is marked 212°F. Temperatures can go below zero. Temperatures below zero are written with a minus sign. A temperature of 10 degrees below zero is written −10°F.

▶ **What is the freezing point of water on the Fahrenheit scale?**

The Celsius scale. Scientists use the Celsius (SEL-see-us) scale for measuring temperatures. On this scale, the freezing point of water is marked zero degrees. This is written 0°C. The boiling point of water is 100°C. There are 100 Celsius degrees between these two points. There are 180 Fahrenheit degrees between these two points (212° − 32° = 180°). A change of one Celsius degree is almost twice as much as a change of one Fahrenheit degree. The picture compares the two temperature scales.

▶ **Which is a bigger change, a temperature drop of 10°C or a drop of 10°F?**

WHAT YOU LEARNED

1. On the Fahrenheit scale, water freezes at 32° and boils at 212°.
2. On the Celsius scale, water freezes at 0° and boils at 100°.
3. A change of 1°C is bigger than a change of 1°F.

SCIENCE WORDS

degree (duh-GREE)
a unit of temperature

Fahrenheit (FAR-en-hite) **scale**
the temperature scale in which the freezing point of water is 32° and the boiling point is 212°

Celsius (SEL-see-us) **scale**
the temperature scale in which the freezing point of water is 0° and the boiling point is 100°

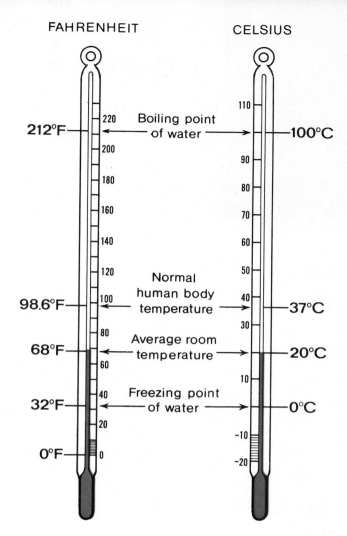

FAHRENHEIT   CELSIUS

212°F — Boiling point of water → 100°C

98.6°F — Normal human body temperature → 37°C

68°F — Average room temperature → 20°C

32°F — Freezing point of water → 0°C

0°F

ANSWER THESE

1. Water freezes at
   a. 32°F
   b. 0°C
   c. both of the above
2. The temperature of 100°C is the same as
   a. 212°F
   b. 100°F
   c. 132°F
3. Celsius degrees are
   a. larger than Fahrenheit degrees
   b. smaller than Fahrenheit degrees
   c. the same as Fahrenheit degrees

NOW TRY THESE

Which temperature is higher?
1. 0°F or 0°C
2. 32°F or 32°C
3. 100°F or 50°C
4. 68°F or 20°C

How is heat measured?

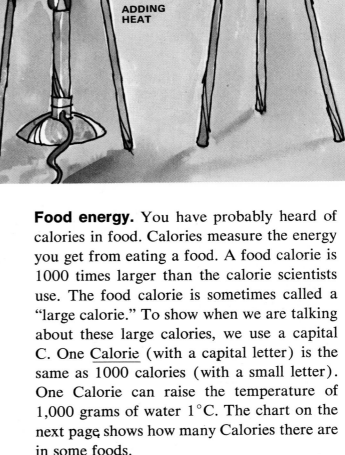

temperature rises

REMOVING HEAT

temperature falls

ADDING HEAT

Adding and taking away heat. Adding heat changes the temperature of a material. When heat is added, the temperature of a material rises. When heat is removed from the material, its temperature falls. The changing temperature tells you whether heat is being added or taken away. How much the temperature changes depends on how much heat is added or removed.

▶ **How can you tell when heat is being added to a material?**

Measuring heat. We can measure heat by the temperature change it causes. Suppose you heat a gram of water until its temperature rises 1°C. The amount of heat you have added to the water is 1 calorie (CAL-o-ree). A calorie is a unit of heat. It is the amount of heat that will raise the temperature of 1 gram of water 1°C. Two calories could raise the temperature of 2 grams of water 1°C. Or they could raise the temperature of 1 gram of water 2°C. A gram of water is just a few drops. A calorie is a small amount of heat.

▶ **What is a calorie?**

10°C + 1calorie → 11°C

1 gram of water   1 gram of water

Food energy. You have probably heard of calories in food. Calories measure the energy you get from eating a food. A food calorie is 1000 times larger than the calorie scientists use. The food calorie is sometimes called a "large calorie." To show when we are talking about these large calories, we use a capital C. One Calorie (with a capital letter) is the same as 1000 calories (with a small letter). One Calorie can raise the temperature of 1,000 grams of water 1°C. The chart on the next page shows how many Calories there are in some foods.

▶ **What do Calories tell us about foods?**

FOOD	AMOUNT	CALORIES
Orange juice, frozen	3½ oz.	45
Corn flakes	1 cup	95
Egg, fried	1	110
Bread, white	1 slice	60
Butter	1 pat	50
Coffee, no sugar with 1 tbsp. hvy. cream	6 oz.	½ 50
Milk	8 oz.	160
Hamburger, with roll	¼ lb.	320
Chili con carne, with beans	8 oz.	290
Pizza	1 slice (3½ oz.)	240
Club sandwich, triple-decker	1	590
Potatoes, french fried	10 pieces	150
Potato chips	1	13
Green beans	½ cup	15
Celery	1 5″ stalk	3
Apple	1	70

FOOD	AMOUNT	CALORIES
Banana	1 large	200
Jelly doughnut	1	225
Macaroon cookie	1	110
Oreo cookie	1	40
Ry-Krisp	1	21
Boston cream pie	1 portion	200
Chocolate cake, with icing	1 portion	350
Apple pie a la mode	1 portion	500
Strawberry shortcake	1 portion	400
Cola drink	8 oz.	110
Chocolate milkshake	10 oz.	420
Chocolate ice-cream soda	8 oz.	250
Chocolate-covered raisins	1 oz.	120
Chocolate bar, with almonds	1	300
Jelly beans	10	70
Peanut brittle	1 oz.	110

WHAT YOU LEARNED

1. Heat energy is measured in calories.
2. One calorie can raise the temperature of 1 gram of water 1°C.
3. A Calorie is equal to 1000 calories.

SCIENCE WORDS

calorie (CAL-o-ree)
   a unit of heat; the amount of heat needed to raise the temperature of 1 gram of water 1°C.
Calorie
   a large calorie; 1000 calories

ANSWER THESE

1. Adding heat to a substance
   a. raises its temperature
   b. lowers its temperature
   c. can do either

2. One calorie of heat energy will raise the temperature of 1 gram of water
   a. 1°F.
   b. 1°C.
   c. 1000°C.
3. Energy in foods is measured in
   a. degrees
   b. small calories
   c. large calories

FINDING OUT MORE

When heat is taken away from a material, its temperature goes down. When all of the available heat has been removed from something, its temperature cannot go down any farther. This temperature is called absolute zero. Absolute zero is the lowest possible temperature for anything. At this temperature, a material would have no available heat at all. Absolute zero is −273°C, or −459°F. It is not possible to lower the temperature of anything all the way to absolute zero. But scientists have come within .01°C of absolute zero. The study of very low temperatures is called cryogenics (cry-oh-JEN-ics).

UNIT 6 Review

Do the following questions on a separate sheet of paper.

Matching   *Write each of the statements in Column I, leaving one line of space after each statement. On the blank line following each statement, write the word or phrase from Column II that is described by that statement.*

Column I	Column II
1. Heat transfer in liquids and gases.	thermometer
2. A unit of heat.	degree
3. A unit of temperature.	Celsius scale
4. Scientist's temperature scale.	convection
5. A measure of how hot a material is.	friction
6. An instrument used to measure temperature.	contract
7. Get larger; take up more space.	heat
8. Get smaller; take up less space.	expand
9. A form of energy we can feel.	temperature
10. Rubbing.	calorie

Multiple Choice   *Write the letter of the choice that best completes the statement or answers the question.*

1. Molecules of matter are always
   a. very still
   b. still until heated above 100°
   c. in motion
2. Good conductors of heat are usually
   a. good conductors of electricity
   b. poor conductors of electricity
   c. unable to conduct electricity
3. A radiometer is a device that turns when
   a. sunlight shines on it
   b. it is exposed to electricity
   c. it is left in the dark
4. Convection currents occur in
   a. liquids and gases
   b. gases only
   c. all materials

5. Radiation can carry heat
   a. only a short distance
   b. only in a circular path
   c. long distances through space
6. Heat usually causes matter to
   a. contract, then expand
   b. expand
   c. contract
7. The boiling point of water is
   a. 100°F
   b. 100°C
   c. 212°C
8. To measure temperature, scientists use
   a. the Celsius scale
   b. the Fahrenheit scale
   c. the Einstein scale

7 Sound

Unit Lessons

1. What is sound?
2. Why are some sounds louder than others?
3. How do sounds differ in pitch?
4. How does sound move through air?
5. What materials can carry sound?
6. How fast does sound travel?
7. What is a sound's quality?
8. What are echoes?
9. How can pitch be changed?
10. What is music?
11. What are the different kinds of musical instruments?
12. How do musical instruments work?

Goals and Objectives

After completing this unit, you should be able to:

- recognize sound as a vibration.
- define pitch in terms of frequency.
- describe sound waves.
- explain how we can use echoes to judge distance.
- give examples of string, percussion, and wind instruments.
- understand how each group of instruments creates sounds.

What is sound?

Sounds fill the world. There are always sounds around us. In a quiet room, we may hear the sound of a watch ticking. We may hear the wind blowing outside. When there are no other sounds, we may hear the sounds of our bodies.

▶ **What sounds may we hear in a quiet room?**

tuning fork

What causes sounds? Sounds are caused by objects moving quickly back and forth. This rapid back-and-forth motion is called vibration (vy-BRAY-shun). Touch your fingers to your throat while you hum. You can feel your throat vibrate. Some vibrations can be seen. Stretch a rubber band. Pluck it. The rubber band vibrates. Listen to the sound.

Some things make sounds even though you can't see them vibrate. Strike a tuning (TOON-ing) fork. Can you see it vibrate? Listen to the sound it makes. Strike the tuning fork again. Put one end of the tuning fork into a glass full of water. Water splashes out of the glass. This shows that the tuning fork is vibrating. Sounds are made by vibrating objects.

▶ **What causes sounds?**

Where do sounds come from? Strum a guitar. The strings vibrate to make sounds. Slap a desk with a ruler. Both the desk and the ruler vibrate and make sounds. Tear a piece of paper. The vibrating paper makes a sound when you tear it. For every sound that is made, some object is vibrating.

▶ **What makes the sounds from a guitar?**

WHAT YOU LEARNED

1. Sounds are caused by vibrating objects.
2. For every sound there is a vibrating object.

SCIENCE WORDS

vibration (vy-BRAY-shun)
 a quickly repeated back-and-forth motion
tuning (TOON-ing) **fork**
 a Y-shaped metal instrument that vibrates to make musical sounds

Fill in the correct words on a separate sheet of paper.
1. In a quiet room you may hear the sounds of your _____.
2. A quickly repeated back-and-forth motion is called _____.
3. Sounds are made when objects _____.
4. The sound of paper tearing is made by the vibrating _____.

NOW TRY THIS

Explain what is vibrating to make a sound in each of the pictures.

WHAT'S HAPPENING

Sounds can come from phonograph records. Look at a record with a magnifying glass. Notice the wavy grooves in the record. As the record turns, the grooves make the needle vibrate. Electricity is used to make the sounds from these vibrations louder.

Why are some sounds louder than others?

Good vibrations. All sounds are made by vibrating objects. Energy is needed to make objects vibrate. You use energy when you talk. Some of this energy is used to make your vocal cords vibrate. Strike the keys of a piano. Sounds are produced. This takes energy. Energy is needed to make sound.

▶ **What is needed to make objects vibrate?**

KIND OF SOUND	DECIBELS
Softest sound we can hear	0
Whisper	15
Soft music	30
Ordinary home	45
Conversation	65
Heavy street traffic	75
Elevated trains, riveters	95
Thunder	110
Painful sounds	120

There are different kinds of sounds. Some sounds are loud. Others are soft. Sound is a form of energy. Loud sounds have more energy than soft sounds. A bus gives off more sound energy than a car. The bus makes a louder noise than the car. A bass drum gives off more sound energy than a toy drum. It makes a louder sound. Sounds also seem louder when you are close to the vibrating object. More sound energy reaches your ears when you are closer to the vibrating object.

▶ **What makes loud sounds different from soft sounds?**

Measuring loudness. The loudness of sounds is measured in decibels (DESS-uh-bells). The loudness of people talking is about 65 decibels. The softest sound a person can hear is zero decibels. A train going by may make a noise of about 95 decibels. Sounds louder than 120 decibels are dangerous. They can damage the human ear.

▶ **How is the loudness of sound measured?**

Making a picture of sound. Tape a pin to one part of a tuning fork. Use tongs to hold a glass plate in a candle flame until the plate is covered with carbon. Clamp the tuning fork to a ring stand. Lower the tuning fork until the pin just touches the glass plate. Strike the tuning fork gently to make a soft sound. Slide the glass plate away in a straight line as the tuning fork vibrates. Then look at the pattern on the glass.

Now strike the tuning fork harder, to make a louder sound. Make a picture of this sound. The louder sound makes a wider pattern. The width of the pattern is called the <u>amplitude</u> (AMP-lih-tood). Louder sounds make patterns with larger amplitudes.

▶ How are the patterns of loud sounds different from the patterns of soft sounds?

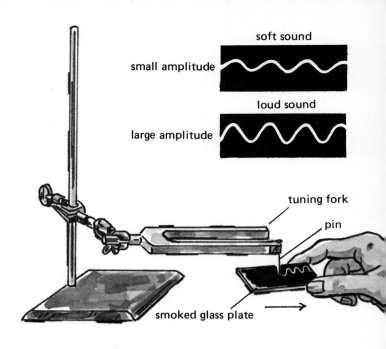

soft sound
small amplitude

loud sound
large amplitude

tuning fork
pin
smoked glass plate

WHAT YOU LEARNED

1. Energy is needed to make sounds.
2. Loud sounds have more energy than soft sounds.
3. The loudness of a sound is measured in decibels.
4. Loud sounds make patterns with large amplitudes.

SCIENCE WORDS

decibel (DESS-uh-bell)
   a measurement of the loudness of sound
amplitude (AMP-lih-tood)
   the width of a sound's pattern

ANSWER THESE

Copy these sentences. If the sentence is true, do not change it. If it is false, change the word in capital letters to make it true.

1. To make objects vibrate, SOUND must be used.
2. ENERGY has the ability to make sounds.
3. Objects giving off a lot of sound energy make SOFT noises.
4. Sounds seem to be SOFTER when you are nearer where they are coming from.
5. When you are close to a vibrating object, MORE sound energy reaches your ear.
6. The loudness of a sound can be measured in DEGREES.
7. Sounds LOUDER than 120 decibels can hurt your ear.

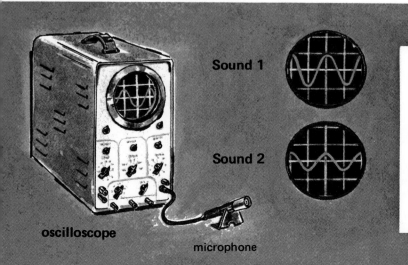

Sound 1

Sound 2

oscilloscope

microphone

FINDING OUT MORE

The Oscilloscope

The oscilloscope (uh-SILL-uh-scope) looks like a complicated television set. It can show a picture of a sound's amplitude. A microphone is attached to the oscilloscope to pick up sounds. Look at the oscilloscope pictures of two sounds. Which sound is louder?

How do sounds differ in pitch?

Sounds can be high or low. A lion roars. A mouse squeaks. How are these sounds different? A lion's roar is louder than a mouse's squeak. The lion's roar also sounds lower or deeper than the mouse's squeak. We say that the sounds are different in pitch, as well as loudness. The lion's roar is lower in pitch than the mouse's squeak. Sounds may be different in loudness. They may also be different in pitch.

▶ **What are two ways that sounds may be different?**

What's the pitch? Sounds are made by vibrations. One vibration is a single back-and-forth movement. The number of times an object vibrates in one second can be counted. The number of vibrations per second is called the frequency (FREE-kwun-see) of the sound. The higher the frequency, the higher the pitch of the sound. The lower the frequency, the lower the pitch. We can hear sounds that have frequencies between 20 and 20,000 vibrations per second. This is called the range of human hearing.

▶ **What is the range of human hearing?**

High-low. The frequency of a tuning fork is stamped on it. A tuning fork marked "128" will vibrate 128 times each second. Its frequency is 128 vibrations per second. It makes a low-pitched sound. A tuning fork marked "256" vibrates 256 times each second. It makes a higher-pitched sound. A tuning fork marked "512" makes the highest-pitched sound of the three. Low-frequency sounds have low pitch. Higher-frequency sounds have higher pitch.

▶ **What kind of pitch do low-frequency sounds have?**

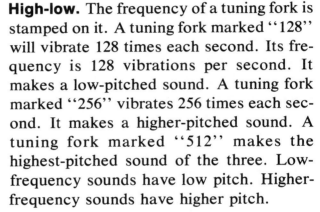

highest pitch — frequency

512

256

128

lowest pitch

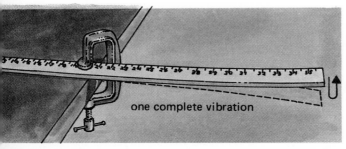

one complete vibration

Sound "hertz." Frequency is measured in vibrations per second. This measurement has been given a special name. Vibrations per second are called <u>hertz</u> (HURTS), after Heinrich Hertz. Hertz was a scientist whose work helped lead to the invention of radio. When you see "10 hertz," it means "10 vibrations per second."

▶ What does "hertz" mean?

WHAT YOU LEARNED

1. Pitch tells how high or low a sound is.
2. Sounds may be different in pitch and loudness.
3. Low-frequency sounds have low pitch. High-frequency sounds have high pitch.

SCIENCE WORDS

pitch
   how high or low a sound is
frequency (FREE-kwun-see)
   the number of vibrations per second
hertz (HURTS)
   the unit used for measuring frequency

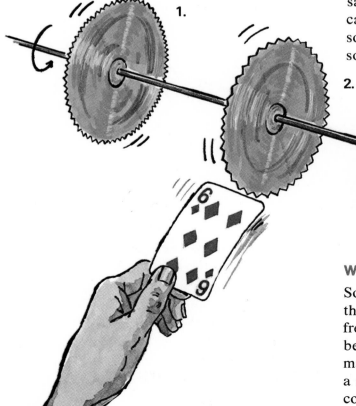

ANSWER THESE

1. Sounds may be different in
   a. loudness only
   b. pitch only
   c. pitch and loudness
2. Compared to a lion's roar, a mouse's squeak
   a. has no pitch
   b. has a higher pitch
   c. has a lower pitch
3. The range of human hearing is
   a. 20-200 hertz
   b. 200-2,000 hertz
   c. 20-20,000 hertz
4. 300 hertz is the same as
   a. 300 vibrations per second
   b. 300 frequencies per second
   c. 300 sounds per second
5. High-frequency sounds have
   a. no pitch
   b. low pitch
   c. high pitch

NOW TRY THIS

The three disks in the picture will all turn at the same speed when the rod is turned. When the card is held against the teeth of each disk, a sound will be heard. Which disk will make the sound with the highest pitch?

WHAT'S HAPPENING

Some sounds have such high frequency that they cannot be heard by humans. Sounds with frequencies too high for people to hear may still be heard by other animals. A dog whistle makes a sound too high for people to hear. But a dog can hear the sound. A dog can learn to come when it hears the high-pitched sound.

How does sound move through air?

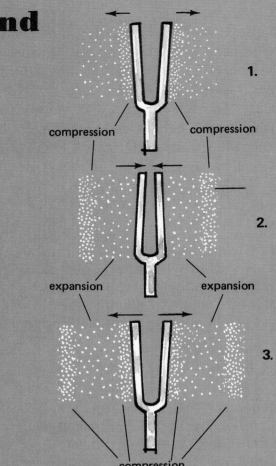

1.

compression   compression

2.

expansion   expansion

3.

compression

How is a sound made? A vibrating tuning fork makes a sound. How does it do this? When the tuning fork vibrates, its tip moves outward. It pushes on the air in front of it. The air is squeezed together, or compressed (kum-PREST). When the tip moves back inward, the air left behind expands (eck-SPANDZ). As the tuning fork keeps vibrating, the air is compressed and expanded many times.

The compressions and expansions move away from the tuning fork. They form a sound wave. A sound wave made in the air cannot be seen. But a Slinky spring can show how it might look.

▶ **What happens as a tuning fork keeps vibrating?**

compression

expansion

compression

expansion

compression

Back and forth. When a wave goes along a Slinky spring, the coils move back and forth along the spring. Waves that move back and forth are called longitudinal (lon-jih-TOO-dih-nul) waves. In a sound wave, compressions and expansions move back and forth. All sound waves are longitudinal waves.

▶ **What kind of wave is a sound wave?**

112

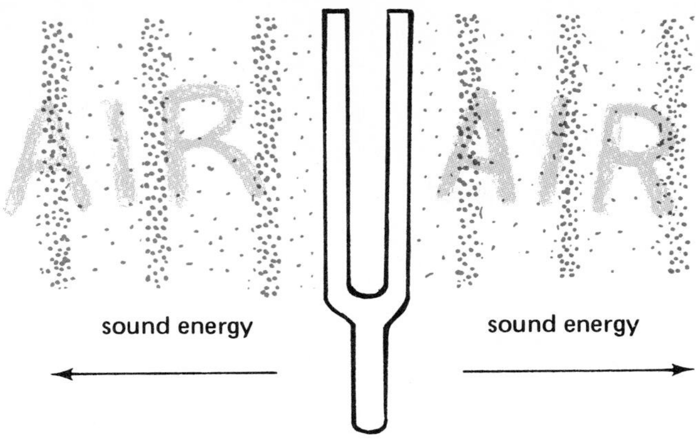

SOUND WAVE

Sound waves carry energy through a medium.

sound energy

sound energy

The medium carries the message.

Sound waves carry energy. As sound waves move, energy is carried with them. Something is needed to carry a sound wave. The material that carries a sound wave is called a medium (MEE-dee-um). Sound waves can be carried by air. Air is a medium for sound waves.

▶ **What is a medium?**

WHAT YOU LEARNED

1. Sound waves are made up of compressions and expansions.
2. Sound waves carry energy through the air.
3. The material that a wave moves through is called a medium.
4. Sound waves are longitudinal waves.

ANSWER THESE

1. Sound waves are made up of
   a. compressions only
   b. expansions only
   c. compressions and expansions
2. To get an idea of what a sound wave is like, you can look at
   a. an ocean wave
   b. a Slinky spring
   c. a waving flag
3. Sound waves are carried by
   a. energy
   b. a medium
   c. gremlins
4. Compressions and expansions in sound waves move
   a. up and down
   b. back and forth
   c. in circles

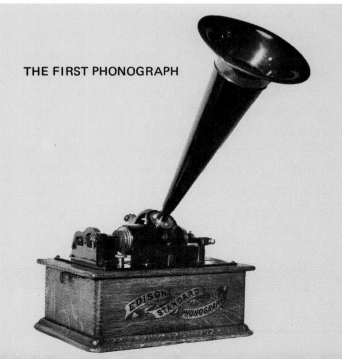

THE FIRST PHONOGRAPH

PEOPLE IN SCIENCE
Thomas Alva Edison (1847-1931)

Thomas Edison is among the most famous of American inventors. You may remember that he invented the electric light. He also invented the first phonograph. The first phonographs were called "talking machines." The first records were shaped like cylinders. But they worked very much like today's records. A needle moved along a wavy groove. The waves in the groove made the needle vibrate. The vibrating needle made sounds that could be heard.

What materials can carry sounds?

Moving waves. Sound waves are in motion. They are moving compressions and expansions. Sound waves move through a medium. Can sound waves move without a medium? Let's find out.

Put an electric bell into a large jar like the one shown. Start the bell ringing. Then pump the air out of the jar. As the air leaves the jar, the sound of the bell becomes softer. Soon it can hardly be heard. Air is a medium for sound waves. Without air, the sound waves have no medium in which to travel. Sound waves cannot travel without a medium. Let the air back into the jar. The sound of the bell can be heard again. The sound has a medium to travel through again.

▶ **What happens to sound waves if there is no medium?**

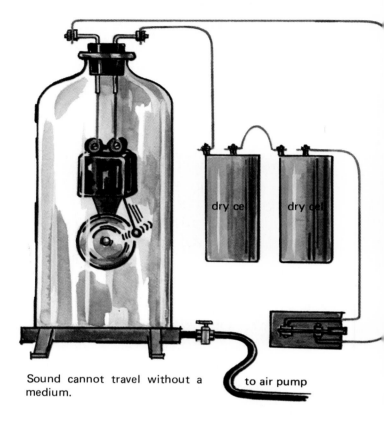

dry cell dry cell

Sound cannot travel without a medium.

to air pump

Why do sounds need a medium? When air was taken out of the jar, a <u>vacuum</u> (VAK-yoom) was formed. There is no matter in a vacuum. A vacuum is empty space. In empty space, there is nothing to compress or expand. If there are no compressions and expansions, then there can be no sound waves. Sounds cannot travel through a vacuum. If there were a big explosion on the moon, we would never hear it. There is empty space between the earth and the moon. The sound of the explosion could not travel across empty space. Sounds cannot travel without a medium.

▶ **Why can't sounds travel through empty space?**

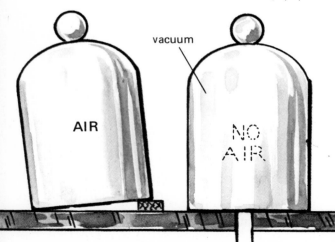

A vacuum is empty space.

vacuum

AIR

NO AIR

to air pump

wall

Can sounds move through solids, liquids, and gases? Air is made up of gases. We already know that sounds can travel through air. Can sounds travel through a liquid? Water is a liquid. Many animals that live in the sea make sounds. Other animals in the sea can hear the sounds. Sounds can travel through liquids. Liquids can be a medium for sound waves.

Place your ear against a wall. You may hear sounds from another room. Sounds can move through solid walls. Sounds can travel through any kind of matter. It makes no difference if the matter is a solid, liquid, or gas. Any kind of matter can be a medium for sound waves.

▶ **What can sounds travel through?**

WHAT YOU LEARNED

1. Sound waves need a medium to travel through.
2. Solids, liquids, and gases can all carry sound waves.

SCIENCE WORD

vacuum (VAK-yoom)
a space where there is no matter; empty space

ANSWER THESE

1. Sounds can travel through
   a. air only
   b. solids, liquids, and gases
   c. a vacuum
2. A vacuum is
   a. empty space
   b. another name for air
   c. a mixture of solids and liquids

3. A sound could not travel from the moon to the earth because
   a. there is a vacuum between them
   b. the earth is too noisy
   c. the moon is too heavy
4. Animals can send sounds underwater because
   a. there is air underwater
   b. sounds can move through water
   c. animals know how to send sounds without a medium

NOW TRY THIS

Match the words in column A with the ones in column B that fit them.

A	B
Pitch	Measure of loudness
Vacuum	Frequency
Medium	A longitudinal wave
Sound wave	Empty space
Vibrations	Carries sound waves
Decibel	Back-and-forth movements

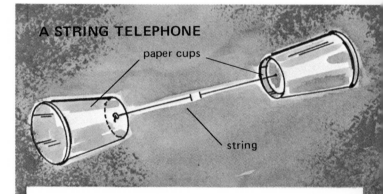

A STRING TELEPHONE

paper cups

string

DO THIS AT HOME

Sounds can travel through solids. A string is a solid. You can use some string to make a kind of telephone. You will need about 10 meters of string and two paper cups. Make a small hole in the bottom of each cup. Thread the ends of the string through the holes and knot them as shown in the picture.

Have a friend hold one paper cup while you hold the other. Keep the string stretched tightly between you. Speak softly into your cup while your friend holds the other cup to his ear. He should be able to hear you clearly. The sound of your voice travels to him through the string. The string is a medium for the sound.

UNIT 7
Sound
6

How fast does sound travel?

First you see it, then you hear it. During a thunderstorm, the lightning and the thunder happen at the same time. But after you see a flash of lightning, it takes a few seconds until you hear the thunder. Those few seconds is the time it takes for the sound of the thunder to reach you. The light from the lightning reaches your eye much sooner than the sound of the thunder reaches your ear. Comparing thunder and lightning helps show that sound travels more slowly than light.

▶ **Why does it take a few seconds before you hear the thunder from a lightning flash?**

Sound travels more slowly than light.

The speed of sound in air. Sound travels at about 335 meters per second in air. It takes sound 3 seconds to travel 1 kilometer. You can use the speed of sound to figure out how far away a lightning flash is. When you see the flash of lightning, count the seconds until you hear the thunder. If it takes three seconds for you to hear the thunder, then the flash was about 1 kilometer away. If it takes six seconds, the flash was about 2 kilometers away. For each second it takes the sound to reach you, it has traveled about one-third of a kilometer.

▶ **How fast does sound travel in air?**

Speeding up sound. Sounds travel at different speeds in different materials. Sounds travel at about 335 meters per second in air. In water, sounds travel at about 1,500 meters per second. In steel, sounds travel at about 5,000 meters per second.

▶ **How fast do sounds travel in water?**

DISTANCE SOUND TRAVELS IN 1 SECOND

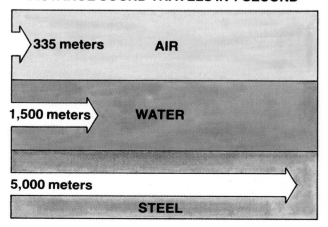

335 meters — AIR

1,500 meters — WATER

5,000 meters — STEEL

Soaking up sounds. Some materials do not carry sound well. The heavy materials often used for curtains do not carry sound well. The soft, heavy material soaks up the sound waves. Rooms with heavy curtains are usually very quiet rooms.

Hard floors, walls, and ceilings carry sounds very well. Sounds bounce off these hard materials. Rooms that have these materials often seem very noisy. Some rooms have soft, cork-like ceilings. Often school rooms have them. A ceiling like this helps to make a room less noisy. The ceiling soaks up sounds. Using special materials to make a room quiet is called sound-proofing.

▶ **What is soundproofing?**

Soundproofing the ceiling of a room.

WHAT YOU LEARNED
1. Sound takes time to travel.
2. Sounds travel more slowly than light.
3. Sounds travel at different speeds in different materials.
4. Some materials carry sounds very poorly.

ANSWER THESE
1. The speed of sound in air is
   a. 3 kilometers per second
   b. 1 kilometer per second
   c. ⅓ kilometer per second
2. A flash of lightning is seen. Fifteen seconds later, the thunder is heard. How far away was the lightning?
   a. 5 kilometers
   b. 15 kilometers
   c. 45 kilometers
3. Heavy curtains in a room
   a. make a lot of noise
   b. make sounds seem louder
   c. soak up sounds
4. Which material will carry sounds fastest?
   a. air
   b. water
   c. steel

NOW TRY THIS
Marty and Stanley were out camping. They saw a flash of lightning, and heard the thunder 15 seconds later. After a while, they saw another flash of lightning. This time they heard the thunder 3 seconds later. Stanley told Marty that they had better head for the tent. The thunderstorm was coming toward them quickly. He said it was now only about one kilometer away. How was Stanley able to figure this out?

WHAT'S HAPPENING
Speeds faster than sound are called supersonic (SOO-per-SAHN-ic) speeds. Many jet planes can fly faster than sound. When jets fly faster than sound, they make a very loud noise. This noise is called a sonic boom.

Sonic boom has become a problem for our neighborhoods. The loud noise disturbs many people. It can also break windows. Most jets are not allowed to fly at supersonic speeds over land. They are allowed to fly at these speeds only over water.

What is a sound's quality?

VIOLIN

TRUMPET

The same old pitch. A trumpet player and a clarinet player play the same note. The sounds they make have exactly the same frequency. They play with the same loudness. But the sounds are very different. The same note is played on a violin. The sound is different again. The sounds made by a trumpet, a clarinet, and a violin have different qualities (KWAL-ih-teez). The quality of a sound is caused by extra sounds. These extra sounds are called overtones (OH-ver-tones). The sounds of a trumpet, a clarinet, and a violin have different qualities because they have different overtones.

▶ Why do a trumpet and a clarinet sound different even when they play the same note?

CLARINET

Where do overtones come from? A tuning fork makes a pure sound. Its sound has only one frequency. It has no overtones. A trumpet sound has many frequencies, or overtones, in it. The overtones are caused by the vibrations of different parts of the trumpet. Some parts vibrate with the frequency of the note being played. Other parts vibrate with twice that frequency. Still other parts vibrate three times as fast. Each of these higher frequencies is an overtone. The overtones mix together and give the trumpet its special quality. A clarinet or a violin has a different mixture of overtones. Each has its own special quality.

▶ What causes the overtones that a trumpet sound has?

I know that voice. You don't have to see a friend to recognize him. You just have to hear his voice. People's voices are different because they have different overtones. When you talk or sing, your throat vibrates. Your chest vibrates. Your whole body vibrates. Touch your chest while singing. You can feel the vibrations. All these vibrating parts of your body make overtones. No two people are exactly alike. So the overtones in their voices are not exactly alike, either. Their voice qualities are different.

▶ Why are people's voices different?

WHAT YOU LEARNED

1. Sounds may have different qualities.
2. Differences in quality are caused by overtones.
3. Overtones are caused by vibrations of different parts of the object making the sound.

SCIENCE WORDS

quality (KWAL-ih-tee)
the difference in sounds due to different overtones
overtones (OH-ver-tones)
the extra frequencies that give a sound its quality

ANSWER THESE

1. Two sounds have the same pitch and loudness, yet they sound different. This is because they have
   a. the same frequency
   b. different frequencies
   c. different overtones
2. Trumpets and clarinets make sounds of different quality because
   a. they can't be played at the same pitch
   b. they are played by different people
   c. they vibrate in different ways
3. When you sing, the quality of your voice comes from
   a. the pitch you are singing at
   b. the loudness of your voice
   c. the vibrations of your body

NOW TRY THIS

You can hear the difference between a piano and a trombone even when they are playing the same note. Why do these musical instruments sound different?

DO THIS AT HOME

You can make a whistle from a soda straw. Get two different straws of the same length. Follow the instructions in the diagram to make the straws into whistles. Be sure both straws are the same length.

Do both straw whistles make the same sound when you blow on them? Can you explain why not? What is the difference between the two whistles?

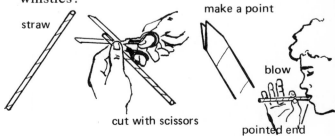

straw · make a point · cut with scissors · blow · pointed end

What are echoes?

Bats in the belfry. Many people think of horror movies when they hear about bats. They think of bats flying around in the dark. Bats are very unusual animals. They have a special way of finding their way around in the dark. Bats make very high pitched sounds while they fly. These sounds bounce off objects. Sounds that bounce off objects are called <u>echoes</u> (EK-ohz). The bats can hear these echoes. They can tell where objects are by listening to the echoes from them. Bats are so good at this that they can fly in the dark without bumping into anything.

▶ **What are echoes?**

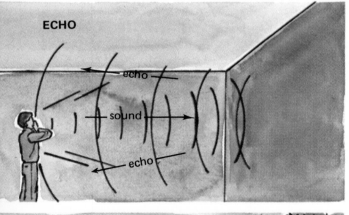

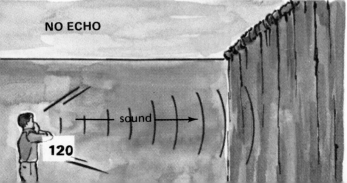

Why don't we always hear echoes? We hear echoes when sounds bounce back to our ears. Large rooms may often have echoes. But in many places we don't hear echoes. You learned that soft materials soak up sounds. The sounds are not bounced back. Then there is no echo. A room with heavy drapes all around will not have echoes. The drapes will soak up sounds.

There is another reason why echoes may not be heard in a room. In a small room, sounds have only a short distance to travel. If there are echoes, they bounce back to our ears very quickly. They come back so fast that our ears can't hear the difference between the sound and the echo. We hear only one sound. Usually only large rooms can have echoes.

▶ **Why don't we hear echoes in a room that has drapes all around?**

120

Echoes in water. <u>Sonar</u> (SOH-nahr) is a way of using echoes to find out the depth of water. A sound is sent from a boat to the bottom of the ocean. The time it takes for the sound to reach the bottom and bounce back to the boat is measured. Then the time is divided in half. This tells how long it took the sound to go one way.

When we know how much time the sound takes, we can find the distance it traveled. Sound travels through water at 1,500 meters per second. Suppose it took 4 seconds for the sound to go from the boat to the bottom and back to the boat again. Then it took 2 seconds for the sound to go one way. In 2 seconds, the sound would travel about 3,000 meters. So we know that the water is about 3,000 meters deep.

Objects under water cause echoes. Fishermen can use sonar to find schools of fish. Long before the discovery of sonar, porpoises (POR-pus-ez) were using it to find their way. As bats use echoes in air, porpoises use echoes under water to help them find their way. Underwater echoes also help porpoises find the food they eat.

▶ **Why can sonar be used to find schools of fish?**

HOW SONAR IS USED

WHAT YOU LEARNED

1. Echoes are sounds that bounce off objects.
2. Soft materials prevent echoes by soaking up sounds.
3. Sonar is a way of using echoes to measure distances under water.

SCIENCE WORDS

echo (EK-oh)
  a sound that is bounced back by an object
sonar (SOH-nahr)
  a way of using underwater echoes to find distances

ANSWER THESE

1. Sounds that bounce off objects are called _____.
2. Bats can fly in the dark without bumping into anything because
   a. they have very good eyesight
   b. they can hear the echoes of objects around them
   c. they fly only in open spaces
3. We cannot hear echoes in a small room because
   a. there are no echoes in a small room
   b. there are too many echoes in a small room
   c. the echoes come back to our ears too fast for us to hear them
4. _____ is a way to use echoes to find the depth of water.

NOW TRY THIS

A ship sent a sound signal to the bottom of the ocean. The echo came back 6 seconds later. How deep was the ocean in that place?

DO THIS AT HOME

See if you can find out what is causing an echo. Make a loud noise on the street where you live, or in a park. Listen for an echo. Look around you. Can you figure out what the sound is bouncing back from? If there is no echo, can you explain why?

How can pitch be changed?

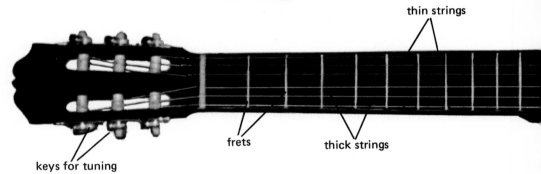

thin strings

keys for tuning

frets

thick strings

What is a stringed instrument? An instrument that uses vibrating strings to make music is called a stringed instrument. The guitar, banjo, bass fiddle, and violin are all stringed instruments. Some stringed instruments, such as the violin, are played with bows. Others are plucked, like the guitar. Stringed instruments can make sounds of many different pitches. In music, sounds of different pitch are called <u>notes</u>.

▶ **What are some stringed instruments?**

Change your pitch. A guitar can make sounds of many different pitches. How can it do this? Look at the strings on a guitar. Some are thick. Some are thin. The thick strings make sounds of lower pitch than the thin ones. A stringed instrument can have different pitches by using strings of different thicknesses. Thick strings sound lower notes than thin ones.

▶ **How does the thickness of a string affect its pitch?**

Play it again, Sam. There are keys at the top of a guitar. They are used to tighten and loosen the strings. They change the <u>tension</u> (TEN-shun) of the strings. Pluck a guitar string. Listen to its pitch. Now increase the tension by tightening the string. Play it again. The string makes a sound of higher pitch when it is tightened. When we increase the tension of a string, we make its pitch higher. When we decrease the tension of a string, we make its pitch lower.

▶ **How does the tension of a string affect its pitch?**

Don't fret. Notice the thin bars that go across the neck of the guitar, under the strings. They are called frets. When you press down on a string, it touches the fret near your finger. Only the part of the string below the fret can vibrate. This is like shortening the string.

Pluck one of the strings. Listen to the pitch. Then press down on the string to shorten it. Pluck it again. The pitch is higher when the string is shorter. Shortening a string makes its pitch higher. Lengthening a string makes its pitch lower.

▶ **How does the length of a string affect its pitch?**

GUITAR

WHAT YOU LEARNED

1. Stringed instruments can make sounds of many different pitches.
2. Three ways to change pitch in a stringed instrument are:
   a. Change the thickness of the string (thin string—high pitch; thick string—low pitch).
   b. Change the tension of the string (tight string—high pitch; loose string—low pitch).
   c. Change the length of the string (short string—high pitch; long string—low pitch).

SCIENCE WORDS

notes
  musical sounds of different pitches
tension (TEN-shun)
  the tightness of a string

ANSWER THESE

Choose the correct word and copy the sentence.
1. To make a string have a higher pitch, (increase, decrease) its length.
2. To lower the pitch of a string, (increase, decrease) its tension.
3. Thin strings have (higher, lower) pitch than thick ones.
4. Long strings have (higher, lower) pitch than short ones.
5. Tight strings have (higher, lower) pitch than loose ones.

NOW TRY THESE

Copy these sentences and fill in the missing words.
1. One guitar string plays a higher note than a second string of the same length and tension. The first string must be _____ than the other.
2. One guitar string plays a lower note than a second string of the same thickness and tension. The first string must be _____ than the other.
3. One guitar string plays a higher note than a second string of the same length and thickness. The first string must be _____ than the other.

What is music?

Beat it. The beat in music is called rhythm (RITH-um). Some music is made up only of rhythm. Drum music is an example of this. Some African, American Indian, and Latin-American music use only the rhythm of drums. Very complex music can be played using only rhythm.

▶ **What is rhythm?**

The musical scale. The musical scale is made up of eight notes arranged in order. Each note has a letter. The symbols for the notes are written on a musical staff. Musicians can read the symbols the same way that you read letters and words.

▶ **What is the musical scale?**

NOTES OF THE SCALE

NAME	LETTER
do	C
re	D
mi	E
fa	F
sol	G
la	A
ti	B
do	C

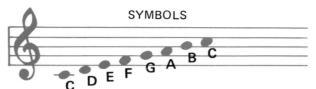

SYMBOLS

The tune. In addition to rhythm, most music has a tune, or melody (MEL-uh-dee). When you sing a song, you sing different notes from the scale. The notes make up the melody of the song. If you clap your hands as you sing, you have added rhythm.

▶ **What does music usually have besides rhythm?**

Getting it together. Often, groups of people sing together. They play different instruments together. Many different notes are heard at the same time. The notes combine to make sounds called <u>chords</u> (CORDS). A chord is usually three or more notes played at the same time. Combining notes is called <u>harmony</u> (HAR-muh-nee). Good harmony makes music sound better.

▶ **What is a chord?**

The art of music is a science. Each musical note has its own pitch. Each set of eight notes in the scale is called an <u>octave</u> (OK-tiv). The last note in the octave has twice the frequency of the first note. The octaves repeat. The frequency doubles with each new octave. The human ear can hear a total of about 10 octaves.

▶ **What is an octave?**

WHAT YOU LEARNED

1. Music is composed of rhythm, melody, and harmony.
2. Each note in the musical scale has its own frequency.
3. Notes combine to form chords.

SCIENCE WORDS

rhythm (RITH-um)
 the beat of music
melody (MEL-uh-dee)
 the tune of music
chord (CORD)
 three or more notes played together
harmony (HAR-muh-nee)
 combining musical notes
octave (OK-tiv)
 a set of eight notes of the musical scale

ANSWER THESE

1. Which part of music do we hear when drums play alone?
  a. rhythm
  b. melody
  c. harmony
2. The melody of a song is made up of
  a. different notes
  b. the same note
  c. rhythm
3. A singer sings a note. Then he sings the same note an octave higher. The frequency of the second note is
  a. half the frequency of the first note
  b. the same as the frequency of the first note
  c. twice the frequency of the first note
4. You have harmony when
  a. several people sing the same note at the same time
  b. several people sing different notes at the same time
  c. one person sings one note after another

NOW TRY THIS

The letters of these notes spell out a word that means "to get fainter." Can you figure it out?

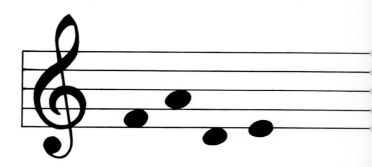

What are the different kinds of musical instruments?

CYMBALS

PERCUSSION INSTRUMENTS

XYLOPHONE

KETTLE DRUM

SNARE DRUM

Groups of instruments. Musical instruments can be divided into three groups. Each group makes its sounds in a different way. But they all follow the same rules about sound that you have learned.

▶ How are the three groups of musical instruments different from each other?

Percussion. Musical instruments that are played by hitting belong to the <u>percussion</u> (per-CUSH-un) group. Among the percussion instruments are the drums and the cymbals. The drums are hit with sticks, or with the hands. The cymbals are struck together to make sounds. Both are percussion instruments.

▶ What kinds of instruments are in the percussion group?

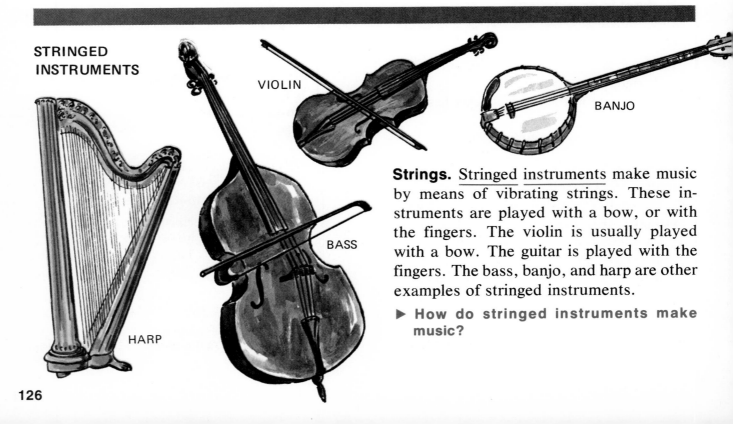

STRINGED INSTRUMENTS

VIOLIN

BANJO

HARP

BASS

Strings. <u>Stringed</u> <u>instruments</u> make music by means of vibrating strings. These instruments are played with a bow, or with the fingers. The violin is usually played with a bow. The guitar is played with the fingers. The bass, banjo, and harp are other examples of stringed instruments.

▶ How do stringed instruments make music?

Winds. <u>Wind</u> <u>instruments</u> are played by blowing. There are two kinds of wind instruments: woodwinds and brass. Some woodwinds are the clarinet, the oboe, and the saxophone. A woodwind has a thin piece of wood in the mouthpiece. It is called a reed. The reed vibrates to produce sounds when air is blown over it by the musician. There are holes along the sides of a woodwind. As these holes are opened and closed, different notes are made.

Brass instruments do not have a reed in the mouthpiece. The sounds are made partly by vibrations of the player's lips on the mouthpiece. Some brass instruments are the trumpet, the trombone, and the tuba. Most brass instruments have parts called valves. The valves are used to change the pitch of the instrument. The player can also change pitch by changing the vibrations of the lips. The trombone is a little different from other brass instruments. It has a sliding tube instead of valves. As the tube is moved back and forth, the pitch changes.

▶ **What does the reed in a woodwind do?**

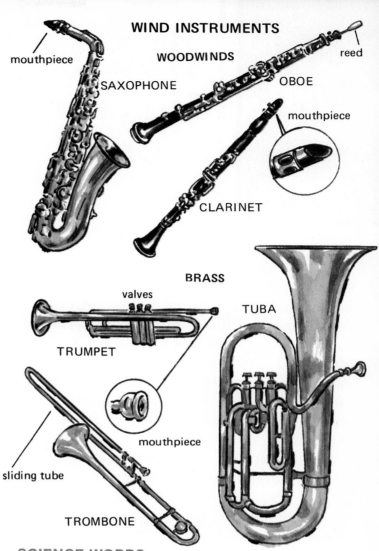

WIND INSTRUMENTS

WOODWINDS

mouthpiece — SAXOPHONE — OBOE — reed

mouthpiece

CLARINET

BRASS

valves — TUBA

TRUMPET

sliding tube — mouthpiece

TROMBONE

KINDS OF INSTRUMENTS			
Strings	**Brass**	**Woodwinds**	**Percussion**
Violin	Bugle	Piccolo	Bass drum
Viola	Cornet	Flute	Bells
Cello	Trumpet	Oboe	Castanets
Bass	Trombone	English horn	Cymbals
Banjo	Tuba	Clarinet	Kettle drum
Guitar	French horn	Saxophone	Snare drum
Harp		Bassoon	Tambourine
Piano			Triangle
			Xylophone

WHAT YOU LEARNED

The three groups of musical instruments are percussion, strings, and winds.

SCIENCE WORDS

percussion (per-CUSH-un) **instruments**
musical instruments played by hitting
stringed instruments
musical instruments that make their sound by means of vibrating strings
wind instruments
musical instruments played by blowing

ANSWER THESE

1. A percussion instrument is played by _____ it, and a wind instrument is played by _____ it.
2. The _____ in brass instruments are used to change the pitch. The player can also change the pitch by changing the vibrations of the _____.
3. Sounds are produced in woodwinds when air passes over the _____.
4. Vibrating _____ make music in the stringed instruments.

How do musical instruments work?

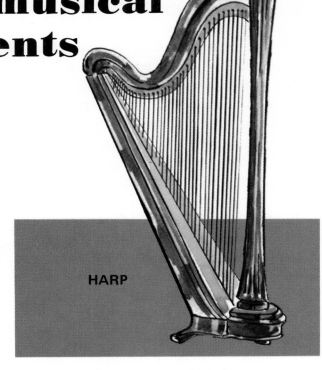

HARP

Going by the rules. All musical instruments follow the same rules. You learned rules about how strings make sounds. The same rules apply to wind and percussion instruments. In the stringed instruments, strings vibrate. In the wind instruments, air vibrates. In the percussion instruments, materials such as wood, metal, or a drum skin vibrate.

If the material that vibrates is made longer or larger, lower notes are produced. If it is made shorter or smaller, higher notes are produced. When the material that vibrates is tightened, higher notes are made. When it is loosened, lower notes are made. These rules do not change from one instrument to another.

▶ **What happens to the notes played when a vibrating material is tightened?**

How do stringed instruments work?

You learned how a guitar changes its pitch. Other stringed instruments, such as the harp or violin, work in the same way.

High Notes:	Low Notes:
Short string	Long string
Tight string	Loose string
Thin string	Thick string

▶ **What kind of note does a loose, thick string make?**

How do wind instruments work? A wind instrument is like a tube of air. The air inside a wind instrument vibrates to make sound. Look at the holes on the side of a clarinet. When these holes are opened and closed, it is like changing the length of the tube of air inside. When the vibrating tube of air is long, low notes are played. When it is short, higher notes are played. The trumpet has valves instead of holes. Opening and closing the valves is like changing the length of the tube of air inside. Different notes are played by adjusting the valves differently. Almost all wind instruments change their pitch by making a tube of vibrating air longer or shorter.

▶ **How do wind instruments change their pitch?**

CLARINET

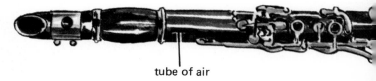

tube of air

How do percussion instruments work?

Percussion instruments are hit. They vibrate to make sounds. Drums, bells, and cymbals are some percussion instruments. The rules of sound apply to these instruments also. Large drums make low-pitched sounds. Small drums make higher-pitched sounds. Large bells play lower notes than smaller bells. If you tighten the top of a drum, it makes a higher sound. If you loosen it, the sound is lower. These rules never change.

▶ **What kinds of notes do large bells make?**

high pitch

low pitch

WHAT YOU LEARNED

All musical instruments follow the same rules for producing different sounds.

ANSWER THESE

1. _____ vibrates to produce sound in a wind instrument.
2. Opening and closing the holes in a clarinet changes its _____.
3. The sound of a large bell is (lower/higher) than the sound of a small bell.

NOW TRY THESE

1. Why does a harp have strings of different lengths?
2. Which end of the harp plays the low notes?
3. Look at the pairs of musical instruments. How do you think the sounds would differ in each pair? Try to explain why.

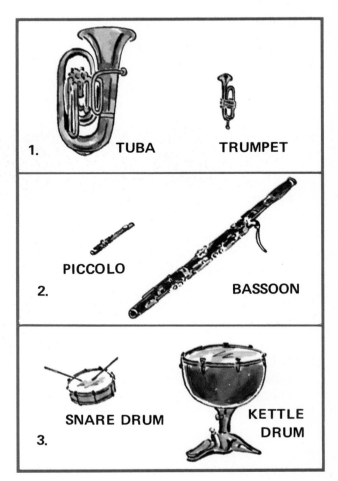

1. TUBA   TRUMPET

2. PICCOLO   BASSOON

3. SNARE DRUM   KETTLE DRUM

Do the following questions on a separate sheet of paper.

Matching   *Write down each of the statements in Column I, leaving one line of space after each statement. On the blank line following each statement, write the word from Column II that is described by that statement.*

Column I

1. A material that carries a wave.
2. A quickly repeated back-and-forth movement.
3. A unit for measuring loudness of a sound.
4. How high or low a sound is.
5. The number of vibrations per second.
6. A unit for measuring frequency.
7. A region where material is squeezed together.
8. Extra frequencies that give a sound its quality.
9. A sound that has been bounced back.
10. Three or more notes sounded together.

Column II

vibration
compression
echo
hertz
overtones
pitch
decibel
chord
medium
frequency

Multiple Choice   *Write the letter of the choice that best completes the statement or answers the question.*

1. A tuning fork produces a sound
   a. when its handle is twirled quickly
   b. when its arms are compressed
   c. when its arms move rapidly back and forth
2. A loud sound has
   a. more energy than a soft sound
   b. more vibrations than a soft sound
   c. more overtones than a soft sound
3. The pitch of a sound can be made higher by increasing its
   a. amplitude
   b. frequency
   c. decibels
4. One hertz is the same as
   a. one vibration
   b. 1000 vibrations per second
   c. one vibration per second

5. A sound wave in air
   a. is made up of compressions and expansions
   b. is like an up-and-down wave in a rope
   c. can be seen in bright light
6. Sound waves can travel
   a. only through empty space
   b. only in air
   c. through any kind of matter
7. Thunder was heard 3 seconds after a lightning flash. How far was the lightning?
   a. 1 kilometer
   b. 3 kilometers
   c. 300 kilometers
8. A violinist makes the pitch of a string higher by making it
   a. thicker
   b. longer
   c. tighter

UNIT 8

Light

Unit Lessons

1. What is light?
2. How does light travel?
3. Where does light come from?
4. What kinds of shadows are there?
5. How is light reflected?
6. How do mirrors work?
7. How can light be bent?
8. How can refraction be explained?
9. How does a lens work?
10. How do we see?
11. What is white light made of?
12. What is invisible light?
13. Why do objects have different colors?
14. How can light energy be changed?
15. What is laser light?

Goals and Objectives

After completing this unit, you should be able to:

*   recognize that light is a form of energy.
*   describe wave motion in terms of wavelength, frequency, and amplitude.
*   describe some sources of light and how light travels from a source.
*   describe what happens when light strikes different surfaces.
*   understand the difference between reflection and refraction.
*   explain the formation of images by different kinds of mirrors and lenses.
*   give examples of some practical uses for different kinds of mirrors and lenses.
*   describe how the human eye works.
*   explain the visible and invisible portions of the electromagnetic spectrum in terms of wavelength.
*   identify the colors of the visible spectrum and explain why objects have different colors.
*   describe how light energy can be changed to other forms of energy.

What is light?

Let the sunshine in. Objects warm up in sunlight. A radiometer spins in sunlight. Photoelectric cells can make electricity from sunlight. Light can do work. Light is a form of energy. Light energy can be changed into heat, electricity, and other forms of energy.

▶ What is light?

Empty space. The space between the earth and the sun is a vacuum. Light comes to us from the sun. But no sounds reach us from the sun. Sounds cannot reach us from the sun because sound waves need a medium to travel through. Light does not need a medium. It can travel through a vacuum. This is an important difference between sound and light.

▶ What is an important difference between sound and light?

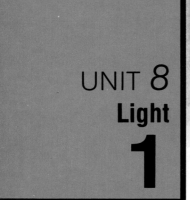

rubber hose

light

See you around the corner. Can light travel around corners? Find out. Get a piece of rubber hose. Bend it in the middle. Point one end toward a light bulb. Look into the other end. You can't see the light bulb. Light cannot travel around corners. Straighten out the hose and try again. Now you can see the bulb. Light travels in straight lines.

▶ Why can't you see a light bulb through a curved hose?

Faster than a speeding bullet. A bullet moves so fast that we cannot see it moving. But compared to light, a bullet moves very slowly. Light travels at 300,000 kilometers per second. This is the fastest possible speed that anything can have. Nothing can go faster than the speed of light.

▶ What is the fastest possible speed a thing can have?

Light-years. Light travels 300,000 kilometers in one second. It takes less than two seconds for light to reach us from the moon. It takes light about eight minutes to travel the 150 million kilometers from the sun to the earth. The distance that light travels in one year is called one light-year. This distance is about 10 trillion kilometers. One light-year equals about ten trillion kilometers. It takes light 4.2 years to reach us from the nearest star. We say that the nearest star is 4.2 light-years away.

▶ **What is meant by one light-year?**

WHAT YOU LEARNED

1. Light is a form of energy.
2. Light does not need a medium to travel through.
3. Light travels in straight lines.
4. The speed of light is the fastest possible speed.
5. A light-year is the distance light travels in one year.

SCIENCE WORD

light-year
the distance that light travels in one year

ANSWER THESE

1. Light is a form of
   a. motion
   b. energy
   c. speed
2. Light can reach us from the sun because it
   a. does not require a medium
   b. travels very fast
   c. has only a short distance to travel
3. Light travels in
   a. circles
   b. straight lines
   c. zigzags

DO THIS AT HOME

Check to see if light travels in straight lines. Get three index cards. Make a small hole in the center of each one. Line up the cards as shown in the picture. Can you see the flashlight through the holes when they are lined up? Move the center card about two centimeters to the side. Can you still see the flashlight? Explain why or why not.

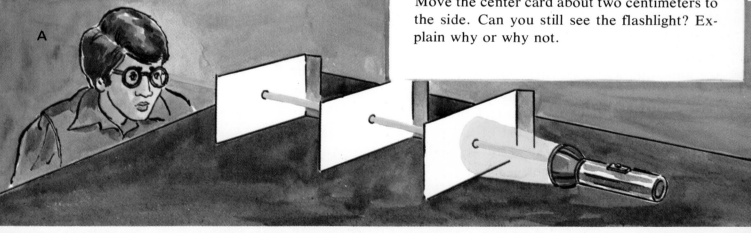

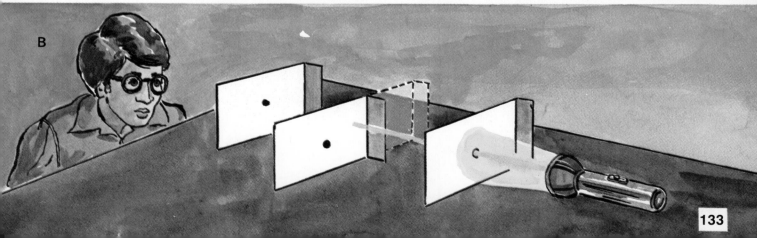

How does light travel?

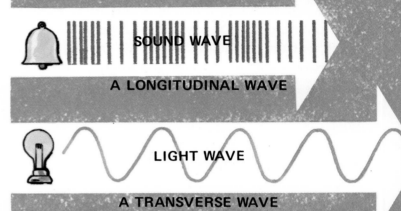

SOUND WAVE

A LONGITUDINAL WAVE

LIGHT WAVE

A TRANSVERSE WAVE

Energy can travel in waves. You learned that sound energy travels in waves. Light energy also travels in waves. Light waves are different from sound waves. Sound waves are like waves in a Slinky toy. They are longitudinal waves. Light waves are like water waves. They are called transverse (TRANZ-VERSE) waves.

▶ What kind of waves are light waves?

How can we describe a light wave? We can measure four properties of light waves. They are speed, wavelength, frequency, and amplitude.

Speed. You already know the speed of light. It is about 300,000 kilometers per second—the fastest possible speed.

Wavelength. The top of each wave is called the crest. The distance from the crest of one wave to the crest of the next wave is called the wavelength. It is the length of one wave of light.

Frequency. The number of waves that pass by each second is the frequency of the wave. Light waves move by very quickly. Many millions of light waves go by each second.

Amplitude. The height of a light wave is its amplitude. When a sound is loud, its wave has a large amplitude. When a light is bright, its wave has a large amplitude.

▶ What four properties of light waves can we measure?

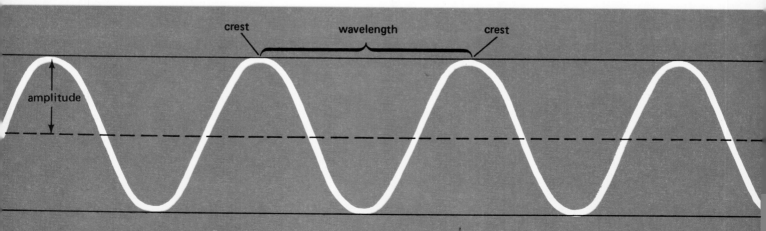

crest   wavelength   crest

amplitude

Rays of light. Light waves travel through millions of kilometers of space from the sun to the earth. Waves of light travel out from a lamp to all parts of a room. Wherever the waves are moving, they are moving in straight lines. A straight line that shows the direction of a light wave is called a ray. Rays are very helpful in understanding light. We will use rays of light to explain how mirrors and lenses work.

▶ **What is a ray of light?**

ray of light

WHAT YOU LEARNED

1. Light travels in transverse waves.
2. The four properties of light waves are speed, wavelength, frequency, and amplitude.
3. Light rays are lines that show the direction of a light wave.

SCIENCE WORDS

transverse (TRANZ-VERSE) **wave**
  a wave shaped like a water wave
ray
  a line that shows the direction of a light wave

ANSWER THESE

1. Light is a form of
   a. energy
   b. sound
   c. speed
2. Light travels as a
   a. longitudinal wave
   b. transverse wave
   c. water wave
3. Wavelength is measured from
   a. top to bottom
   b. front to back
   c. crest to crest
4. When light is bright, its wave has a large
   a. amplitude
   b. wavelength
   c. frequency

NOW TRY THESE

1. Compare light and sound. In what ways are they the same?
2. Suppose that light needed a medium to travel through, as sound does. How would the world be different?

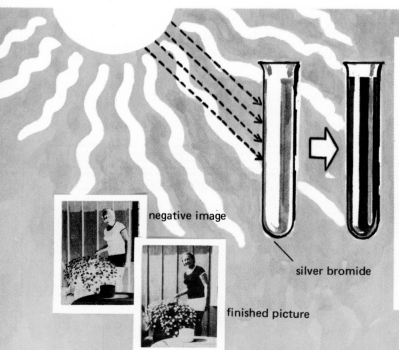
negative image
finished picture
silver bromide

WHAT'S HAPPENING

Light energy can cause a chemical change. Silver bromide is a white chemical. When light shines on silver bromide, it turns dark. Silver bromide is used in camera film. Light going through the camera lens causes a chemical change on parts of the film. Where light hits the film, the film becomes dark. Other parts of the film are not changed. An image is made on the film. This image is called a negative image. The light parts of the picture are dark on the negative. A picture can then be made from the negative image.

3 Where does light come from?

SUN — luminous

illuminated

luminous   illuminated

Let your light shine. Objects that give off their own light are called luminous (LOOM-in-us) objects. The sun is luminous. A lighted lamp is luminous. Objects that light shines on are called illuminated (ih-LOOM-ih-nate-ed) objects. Light from the sun or from a lamp shines on this book. This book is illuminated. For an object to be seen, it must be either luminous or illuminated.

▶ Why is the sun called a luminous object?

Points of light. Some luminous objects are small. They are like a point of light. A small luminous object is called a point source (SORSS) of light. Stars are very large, luminous objects, but they are very far away. Stars seem to be small because of their great distance. They act like point sources of light.

▶ What kind of light sources are stars?

Other light sources. Some luminous objects are large and close. They are called extended (eck-STEN-ded) sources of light. The lights in your classroom are extended light sources. Light comes from all the different points in an extended source. An extended source is like a group of many point sources.

▶ Where does light come from in an extended light source?

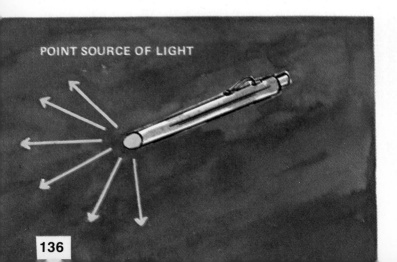

POINT SOURCE OF LIGHT

EXTENDED SOURCE OF LIGHT

In the shadows. Shadows are made when light is blocked. Materials that block all the light hitting them are called <u>opaque</u> (oh-PAKE) <u>materials</u>. Some materials let light pass right through. These are called <u>transparent</u> (trans-PAIR-ent) <u>materials</u>. You can see right through transparent materials. Clear glass, air, and water are transparent materials. Some materials are not transparent or opaque. They let just some of the light pass through them. These are called <u>translucent</u> (trans-LOOSE-ent) <u>materials</u>. Frosted glass is translucent. It lets some light through, but you can't see clearly through it.

▶ **What are opaque materials?**

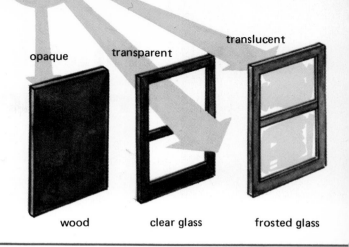

opaque   transparent   translucent

wood   clear glass   frosted glass

WHAT YOU LEARNED

1. Luminous objects give off their own light.
2. Objects that light shines on are illuminated.
3. Tiny or distant lights act like point sources of light.
4. Extended light sources are like many point sources of light combined.
5. Opaque materials block all light. Transparent materials let light pass through. Translucent materials block some light, and let some pass through.

SCIENCE WORDS

luminous (LOOM-in-us) **objects**
   objects that give off their own light
illuminated (ih-LOOM-ih-nate-ed) **objects**
   objects that light shines on
point source (SORSS)
   a tiny point of light
extended (eck-STEN-ded) **source**
   a light source made up of many point sources
opaque (oh-PAKE) **materials**
   materials that block all light
transparent (trans-PAIR-ent) **materials**
   materials that let light pass through them
translucent (trans-LOOSE-ent) **materials**
   materials that let just some light pass through

ANSWER THESE

1. Which of the following are luminous?
   a. a burning match
   b. a mirror
   c. a sheet of paper
   d. the sun
   e. the stars
   f. a light bulb that is not lit
2. Which of the following are extended light sources?
   a. a star at a very great distance
   b. a table lamp
   c. a group of point sources
   d. classroom lights
3. What is the difference between opaque and transparent materials?

NOW TRY THIS

Tell which of the materials are transparent, which are translucent, and which are opaque.

Eyeglass lens	Penny
Cotton handkerchief	Water
Paper	Air
Wood	Window pane

FINDING OUT MORE

Lights come in many kinds and sizes. Among the brightest are those used in lighthouses. The beams from these can be seen for many kilometers. Some of the smallest lights are used by doctors. A doctor uses a tiny light to look inside your ear. What kind of light does a dentist use to see inside your mouth?

What kinds of shadows are there?

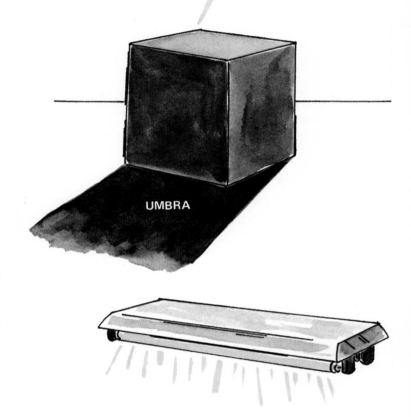

Cast a long shadow. On a sunny afternoon you may cast a long shadow. Your body is opaque. It blocks the sun's light. Look at your shadow. You can see exactly where the shadow ends. The shadow is black. A sharp, black shadow is called an <u>umbra</u> (UM-bruh).

▶ **What is an umbra?**

How is an umbra formed? The sun acts almost like a point source of light. It is very large, but very far away. When you are outdoors, some of the sun's light is completely blocked by your body. Where light is completely blocked, dark shadows form. A point source of light makes a black shadow, or umbra. No light reaches the umbra.

▶ **What kind of shadow is made by a point source of light?**

UMBRA

Gray shadows. Inside your school you also cast a shadow. This shadow comes from the school lights. How is this shadow different from your shadow in the sun? Look at your shadow indoors. It has two parts. There is a gray, outer part around a black umbra. This gray, outer part of a shadow is called a <u>penumbra</u> (pih-NUM-bruh).

▶ **What is a penumbra?**

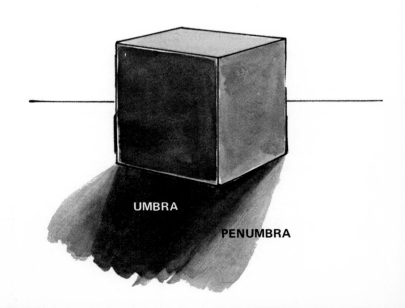

UMBRA

PENUMBRA

138

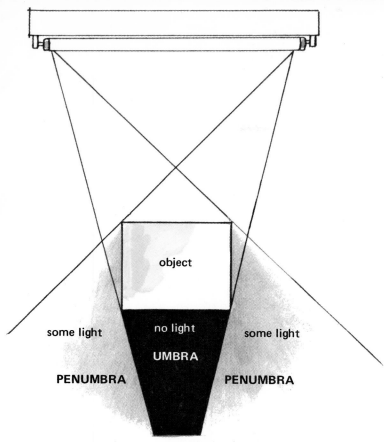

object

some light

no light

UMBRA

some light

PENUMBRA   PENUMBRA

How is a penumbra formed? Classroom lights are extended light sources. Light comes from all parts of an extended source. Some of the light is blocked by your body. But some gets by and lightens up part of your shadow. Extended light sources make shadows with two parts: a black umbra, and a gray penumbra. No light reaches the umbra. Some light does reach the penumbra. Test a light to see if it is a point source. Make a shadow. If the shadow has only an umbra, it is a point source. If the shadow has an umbra and a penumbra, then the light is an extended source.

▶ What kinds of shadows are made by extended light sources?

ANSWER THESE

1. No light reaches the part of a shadow called the
   a. umbra
   b. edge
   c. penumbra
2. Some light reaches the part of a shadow called the
   a. center
   b. umbra
   c. penumbra
3. A point source of light makes a shadow with
   a. only an umbra
   b. only a penumbra
   c. an umbra and a penumbra
4. An extended light source makes a shadow with
   a. only an umbra
   b. only a penumbra
   c. an umbra and a penumbra

FINDING OUT MORE

Shadows can be used to tell time. A sundial uses a shadow made by the sun to tell the time. A marker on the sundial casts a shadow in sunlight. As the sun moves from east to west, the shadow moves around the sundial. The position of the shadow on the dial shows the time. Some days the sundial can't be used. Can you guess why?

SUN DIAL

How is light reflected?

Follow the bouncing ball. A ball hits the wall and bounces off. Light also bounces when it hits an object. The light that bounces back is called <u>reflected</u> (ruh-FLEK-tid) <u>light</u>. Reflected light is light that has bounced off something.

▶ What is reflected light?

Reflected light. A ray of light hits a mirror and is reflected. The ray of light that hits the mirror is called the <u>incident</u> (IN-suh-dint) <u>ray</u>. The ray of light that bounces off the mirror is called the <u>reflected ray</u>.

A line can be drawn that makes a 90° angle, or right angle, with the mirror. This line is called a <u>normal line</u>. The angle between the incident ray and the normal line is called the <u>angle of incidence</u> (IN-suh-dinse). The angle between the reflected ray and the normal line is called the <u>angle of reflection</u> (ruh-FLEK-shun).

▶ What is the angle of reflection?

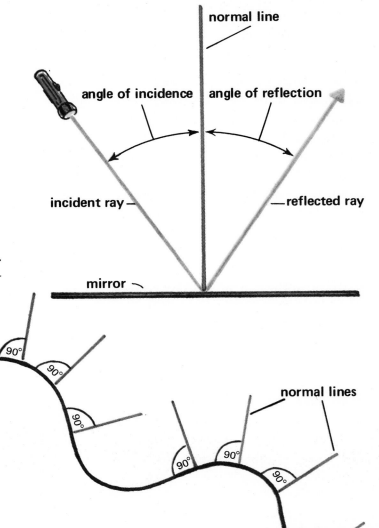

What's normal? A normal line can be drawn at any place on a surface. The normal line always forms a right angle with the surface. If a surface is curvy, then normal lines will point in different directions at different places along the surface.

▶ Where can a normal line be drawn?

Reflected light follows a rule. Shine a flashlight on a flat mirror. Notice the angle of incidence. Notice the angle of reflection. The angle of incidence is the same as the angle of reflection. Change the angle of incidence. The new angle of reflection is equal to the new angle of incidence. Shine the light beam along the normal line. The reflected ray travels back along the normal line. The angle of incidence is zero. The angle of reflection is also zero. The angle of incidence is always equal to the angle of reflection.

▶ **How does the angle of incidence compare with the angle of reflection?**

WHAT YOU LEARNED

1. When light shines on an object, it is reflected.
2. The angle of incidence of a light ray equals the angle of reflection.

SCIENCE WORDS

reflected (ruh-FLEK-tid) **light**
    light that has bounced off something
incident (IN-suh-dint) **ray**
    the ray of light that hits something
reflected ray
    the ray of light that bounces off something
normal line
    a line drawn at right angles to a surface
angle of incidence (IN-suh-dinse)
    the angle between the incident ray and the normal line
angle of reflection (ruh-FLEK-shun)
    the angle between the reflected ray and the normal line

ANSWER THESE

1. Reflected light is light that has
    a. changed color
    b. bounced off something
    c. been made brighter
2. The angle that a normal line forms with a surface is
    a. 0 degrees
    b. 45 degrees
    c. 90 degrees

3. The ray of light that hits something is called the
    a. reflected ray
    b. normal line
    c. incident ray
4. The angle of reflection is between the normal line and the
    a. reflected ray
    b. incident ray
    c. surface
5. If the angle of incidence is 30 degrees, then the angle of reflection is
    a. 60 degrees
    b. 30 degrees
    c. 90 degrees

NOW TRY THESE

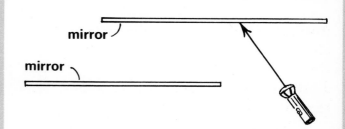

1. A light ray can be reflected more than once. Each time it is reflected, it obeys the law of reflection. Copy the diagram onto a separate sheet of paper. Then use a ruler and protractor to show how the ray will be reflected by the mirrors.

2. A normal line can be drawn at any place on a surface. Copy the diagram onto a separate sheet of paper. Then use a ruler and a protractor to draw normal lines at the places shown.

How do mirrors work?

A smooth surface gives regular reflections.

A rough surface gives diffuse reflections.

Take a look at yourself. You can see your reflection in a mirror. The reflection you see is called an image (IM-ij). Mirrors have a very smooth surface. When rays of light coming from the same direction hit a smooth surface, they are all reflected in the same direction. The reflected rays come to your eyes just as direct rays from the object would. You see the image just as you would see the object. Reflection that gives clear images is called regular reflection.

▶ What is regular reflection?

Images in water. On a calm day, the smooth surface of a pond makes a good mirror. The smooth surface gives regular reflection. You can see images clearly in the water. On a windy day, the surface of a pond is rough. Rays that come to the surface from the same direction are reflected in many different directions. These scattered rays cannot form an image. You cannot see an image in the pond when the surface is rough. The kind of reflection from rough surfaces is called diffuse (dih-FYOOS) reflection. No images can be seen with diffuse reflection.

▶ What is diffuse reflection?

An image in a mirror is backwards. It appears to be as far behind the mirror as the object is in front of the mirror.

Mirror images. Place a ruler in front of a mirror. Touch the one-centimeter mark. Your image also touches the one-centimeter mark. Move your finger to the six-centimeter mark. Your image does the same. The image of your finger seems to be just as far behind the mirror as your finger is in front of it. Hold a book up to a mirror. Try to read the words. All the letters are backwards. The image in a flat mirror is backwards, or reversed.

▶ **Why is it hard to read words reflected in a mirror?**

WHAT YOU LEARNED

1. Smooth surfaces give regular reflection.
2. Rough surfaces give diffuse reflection.
3. A flat mirror image seems to be as far behind the mirror as the object is in front of it.
4. Flat mirror images are reversed.

SCIENCE WORDS

image (IM-ij)
reflection in a mirror
regular reflection
reflection from a smooth surface; reflection that gives clear images
diffuse (dih-FYOOS) **reflection**
reflection from a rough surface; reflection that does not give images

ANSWER THESE

Fill in the blanks on a separate sheet of paper.
1. You cannot see reflections in a pond on a windy day because the water is _____. When the wind stops, the water becomes _____. Calm water is like a _____. It gives _____ reflection.
2. The image in a flat mirror seems to be just as far behind the mirror as the _____ is in front of the mirror.
3. It is hard to read writing that is reflected in a mirror because all the letters are _____.

NOW TRY THIS

Hold this page in front of a mirror. You will be able to read the name and the author of a book about a mirror. Writing like this is called mirror writing. Try to write your name in mirror writing.

"Through The Looking Glass"
by LEWIS CARROLL

FINDING OUT MORE

Flat mirrors are used for seeing yourself while dressing. They are also used in periscopes and binoculars. Mirrors can also be curved. Curved mirrors have special uses. They are used in some telescopes to gather light. They are used in auto headlights and flashlights to make strong beams. Curved mirrors can also make things look larger. Shaving and makeup mirrors are often curved. They make your face look bigger.

How can light be bent?

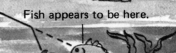

Fish appears to be here.

Rays of light. Light waves travel in straight lines called rays. Light rays can be bent. Light rays are bent when light is reflected. They can also be bent when light passes from one medium into another at an angle. Light rays bend when they pass at an angle from air into water. They also bend when they pass from air into glass. Air, water, and glass are <u>media</u> (MEE-dee-uh) that light can travel through. The bending of light as it travels from one medium to another medium is called <u>refraction</u> (ruh-FRAK-shun). Refraction takes place when light travels from one medium to another at an angle.

▶ **When does refraction take place?**

To catch the fish, the bird must not be fooled by the bending of light.

The laws of refraction. Different materials have different densities. Water is more dense than air. Glass is also more dense than air. A material's density affects the way it refracts light. The laws of refraction tell how light is refracted as it passes between media of different densities.

The Laws of Refraction

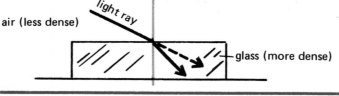

1. When light moves at an angle from a less dense medium to a more dense medium, it is bent toward the normal line.

2. When light moves at an angle from a more dense medium to a less dense medium, it is bent away from the normal line.

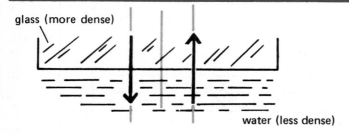

3. When light moves from medium to medium along the normal line, it is not bent.

▶ **Which way is light bent when it moves from a more dense medium to a less dense medium at an angle?**

144

Now you see it, now you don't. Put a penny into a small bowl. Then move back from the bowl until the penny is just out of sight. The light rays reflected from the penny move in straight lines. The side of the bowl blocks them from reaching your eye. Have a friend fill the bowl with water while you stay in the same place. Now you can see the penny again. As light from the penny passes from the water into the air, it is refracted. It is bent away from the normal line, and toward your eye. You can see the penny again.

▶ How did filling the bowl with water help you see the penny again?

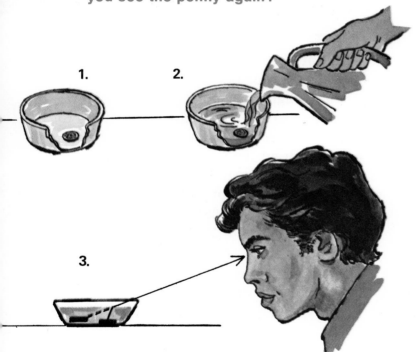

1.

2.

3.

WHAT YOU LEARNED

1. Light bends as it moves from one medium to another medium at an angle.
2. Light does not bend when it moves along the normal line.

SCIENCE WORDS

media (MEE-dee-uh)
   more than one medium
refraction (ruh-FRAK-shun)
   the bending of light as it passes from one medium to another medium at an angle

ANSWER THESE

1. Light rays can be bent
   a. only by reflection
   b. only by refraction
   c. by reflection and refraction
2. When light passes from a more dense medium to a less dense medium at an angle, it is
   a. bent toward the normal line
   b. bent away from the normal line
   c. not bent
3. When light passes from a less dense medium to a more dense medium at an angle, it is
   a. bent toward the normal line
   b. bent away from the normal line
   c. not bent
4. When light moves from a more dense medium to a less dense medium along the normal line, it is
   a. bent toward the normal line
   b. bent away from the normal line
   c. not bent

NOW TRY THIS

Copy the diagrams onto a separate sheet of paper. Show how the light rays will be bent.

DO THIS AT HOME

Stand a pencil in a glass of water. Notice how the pencil seems to be bent. Can you explain why?

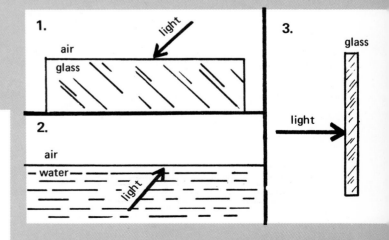

1.
air
glass

2.
air
water
light

3.
glass
light

How can refraction be explained?

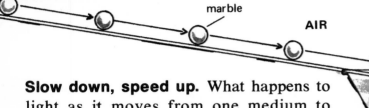

marble

AIR

WATER

Slow down, speed up. What happens to light as it moves from one medium to another? Compare the movement of light to the movement of other things. Roll a marble into water. The marble slows down when it hits the water. Light also slows down when it goes from air into water. Water is more dense than air. Light slows down when it enters a more dense medium. When light moves from air to glass, it slows down. When it leaves the glass, it speeds up. Light moves faster when it moves through less dense media.

▶ **What happens to light when it moves through more dense media?**

Straight through. Light can move from medium to medium along a normal line. Then the light does not bend. How can we explain this? Let's compare a light wave to a row of marbles rolling into water. The marbles all hit the water at the same time. They all slow down together. The "wave" of marbles is not bent. A light wave moving from medium to medium along the normal line is also slowed down all at once. It is not bent. It goes straight through.

▶ **What happens to a light wave moving from medium to medium along the normal line?**

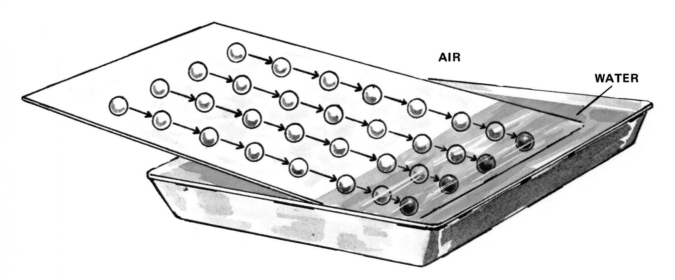

AIR

WATER

From air to glass. Light often moves from medium to medium at an angle. Can we explain why it is refracted? Let's compare a light wave to a row of marbles moving into water at an angle. As the first marble enters the water, it slows down. The rest of the marbles keep moving along at the same speed. The next marble soon reaches the water. Then it, too, slows down. The wave of marbles begins to turn. Soon all the marbles have entered the water. They have all been slowed down. The wave of marbles has been turned toward the normal line. Light waves act the same way. When light waves move from air to glass, they slow down and turn toward the normal. The rays of light are bent toward the normal.

▶ **What happens to light waves when they move from air to glass?**

From glass to air. When light leaves a more dense medium, it speeds up. Glass is more dense than air. When light moves from glass to air, it speeds up. The light wave is bent away from the normal this time. Whenever light moves from medium to medium at an angle, it is bent. The light bends because its speed changes from one medium to another.

▶ **Why does light bend when it moves from one medium to another?**

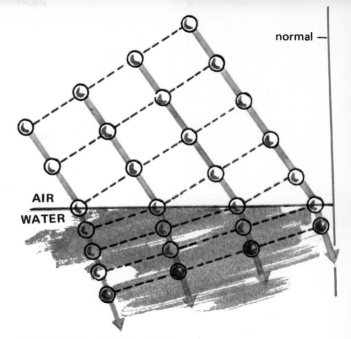

WHAT YOU LEARNED

1. When light moves into a more dense medium, it slows down.
2. When light moves into a less dense medium, it speeds up.

ANSWER THESE

1. What happens to the speed of light as it moves from air into glass?
2. On a separate sheet of paper, complete the diagram of a light wave going from air into glass. Show which way the wave bends.

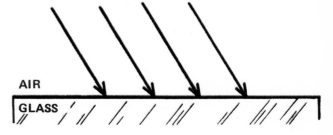

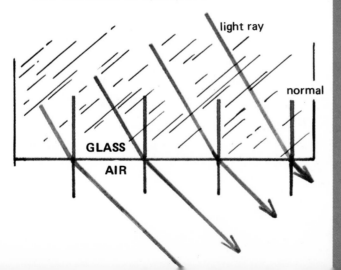

DO THIS AT HOME

You can see the refraction of light. Fill a fish tank with water. Add some iodine to color the water. Tape some cardboard over the front of a flashlight. Then cut a slit in the cardboard so that the flashlight makes a narrow beam. Shine the beam into the water at an angle. Explain why the light bends. Shine the light straight down into the water. Does the light bend? Explain why or why not.

How does a lens work?

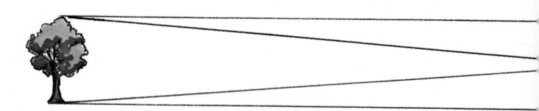

Bending light rays. When light rays pass from air into glass, they may be bent. Curved glass is used to bend light in special ways. A <u>lens</u> (LENZ) is a curved piece of glass. Lenses are used in eyeglasses, magnifying glasses, cameras, microscopes, and telescopes. All lenses bend light in a special way.

▶ **What is a lens?**

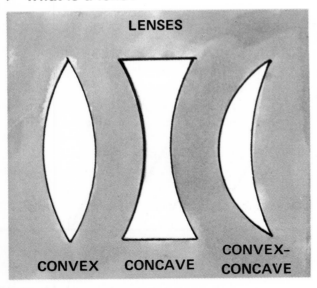

The shape of a lens. Some lenses are curved outward. These are <u>convex</u> (CON-VEX) <u>lenses</u>. Some lenses are curved inward. These are <u>concave</u> (CON-CAVE) <u>lenses</u>. Eyeglass lenses are usually curved outward on one side, and inward on the other. Lenses like these are called convex-concave.

▶ **What is a convex lens?**

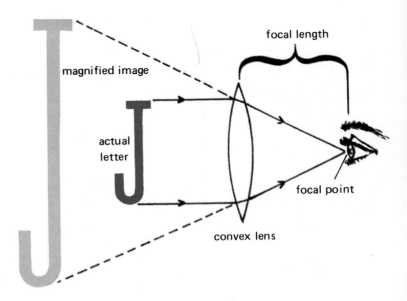

How does a convex lens work? A convex lens can be used as a magnifying glass. It makes nearby objects look larger. Light coming from the letter in the diagram is bent as it passes through the lens. The light rays meet at a point called the <u>focal</u> (FOH-kul) <u>point</u>. The distance from the focal point to the lens is called the <u>focal length</u> of the lens. Your eye is at the focal point of the lens. The light rays seem to spread away from the focal point. When you look through the lens, the letter looks larger. It is magnified.

▶ **What kind of lens is used for a magnifying glass?**

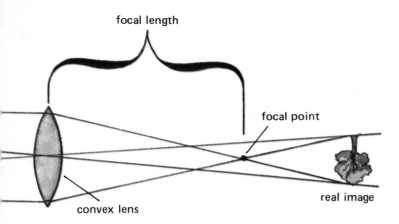

focal length

focal point

real image

convex lens

SCIENCE WORDS

lens (LENZ)
　　a curved piece of glass
convex (CON-VEX) **lens**
　　a lens that is curved outward
concave (CON-CAVE) **lens**
　　a lens that is curved inward
focal (FOH-kul) **point**
　　the place where light rays from a lens meet
focal length
　　the distance from the focal point to the lens
real image
　　an image that can be projected

Creating an image.

Creating an image. A convex lens can be used to make an image of a distant object. The image can be projected onto a screen. An image that can be projected on a screen is called a real image. The image of the tree in the diagram is upside down. The image is past the focal point of the lens. The image is smaller than the object. You can use a convex lens to magnify nearby objects. But the image you see is in your mind. It cannot be projected on a screen. It is not a real image.

▶ What is a real image?

WHAT YOU LEARNED

1. A lens is a curved piece of glass used to bend light.
2. A convex lens can magnify nearby objects.
3. A convex lens can project real images of distant objects.

ANSWER THESE

1. Lenses are used to
   a. reflect light
   b. bend light
   c. block light
2. Concave lenses are
   a. curved inward
   b. curved outward
   c. flat

3. Light rays bent by a convex lens meet at the
   a. main point
   b. center point
   c. focal point

4. The image of a distant object made by a convex lens is
   a. the same size as the object
   b. smaller than the object
   c. larger than the object

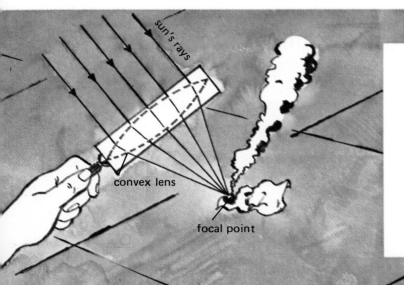

sun's rays

convex lens

focal point

DO THIS AT HOME

A convex lens can project an image of the sun. The sun appears as a tiny point of bright light. The light from the sun is concentrated in one small spot. Place a small piece of paper on the sidewalk. Have an adult help you use a magnifying glass to project the image of the sun onto the paper. The paper will soon begin to smoke. Then it will catch fire. A convex lens used like this is called a burning glass.

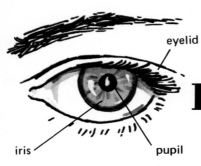

eyelid

iris   pupil

FRONT VIEW OF EYE

How do we see?

I'll be seeing you. When light from an object enters your eye, you are able to see the object. Different parts of the eye work together to help you see. The eye is protected by the eyelid. Tears help clean the eye. They also help keep it moist. The eye is set into the bones of the face to protect it.

▶ **When are you able to see an object?**

Clear through. The front of the eye is clear. It is called the cornea (COR-nee-uh). The cornea covers the pupil (PYOO-pul). The pupil is the opening into the eye. Around the pupil is the iris (EYE-ris). The iris regulates the amount of light coming into the eye. It changes the size of the pupil. When light is bright, the pupil gets smaller. Less light gets into the eye. In dim light the pupil opens wide. More light can then enter the eye.

You can see your iris work. Look at your eyes in a mirror in a dim room. Notice how wide open the pupils are. Then turn on the light. You will see your pupils get smaller. They protect your eyes from too much light. They also help gather light when it is dim.

▶ **What does the iris do?**

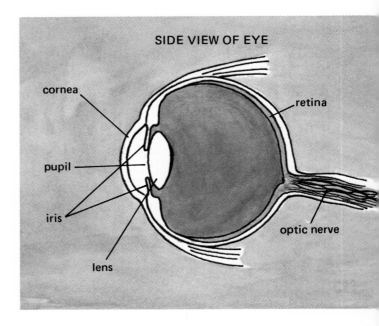

SIDE VIEW OF EYE

cornea

pupil

iris

lens

retina

optic nerve

In focus. Light rays that enter the eye pass through a convex lens. This lens focuses the light rays on the retina (RET-in-uh). The retina is at the back of the eye. The retina changes light into nerve signals. These signals are carried to the brain by the optic (OP-tik) nerve. The brain interprets the signals. It helps us to see and recognize objects.

▶ **What kind of lens is in the eye?**

DIM LIGHT

BRIGHT LIGHT

Right-side up. The image formed on the retina is upside down. This happens because the eye has a convex lens. Why don't we see everything upside down? Our brain takes care of that. The brain is able to interpret the upside-down image and turn it right-side up. An experiment was once done to show that this is so. A man was given special eyeglasses that made everything appear upside down. After he had worn the glasses for a while, everything seemed right-side up again. His brain had adjusted to the special glasses. When he took the glasses off, everything seemed upside down without them. But after a while, his brain again adjusted. Everything seemed right-side up once more.

▶ **Why don't we see objects upside down?**

WHAT YOU LEARNED

1. You are able to see an object when light from the object enters your eye.
2. The lens of the eye forms an upside-down image on the retina.
3. The brain interprets nerve signals from the eye.

SCIENCE WORDS

cornea (COR-nee-uh)
 the clear front of the eye
pupil (PYOO-pul)
 the opening into the eye
iris (EYE-ris)
 the part that controls the amount of light entering the eye
retina (RET-in-uh)
 the back part of the eye on which images form
optic (OP-tik) **nerve**
 the nerve that carries signals from the eye to the brain

ANSWER THESE

1. The eye is protected by the
   a. retina
   b. lens
   c. eyelid
2. The cornea is
   a. at the front of the eye
   b. in the middle of the eye
   c. at the back of the eye
3. The amount of light coming into the eye is controlled by the
   a. retina
   b. iris
   c. optic nerve
4. The image made by the lens of the eye is
   a. upside down
   b. right-side up
   c. larger than the object

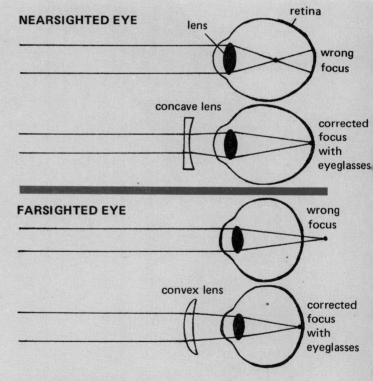

WHAT'S HAPPENING

Our eyes change as we grow older. Often the lens is no longer able to focus a clear image on the retina. We get blurred vision. Eyeglasses are used to help correct some vision problems. The lens in the eyeglass works with the lens in your eye. The two lenses together form a clear image.

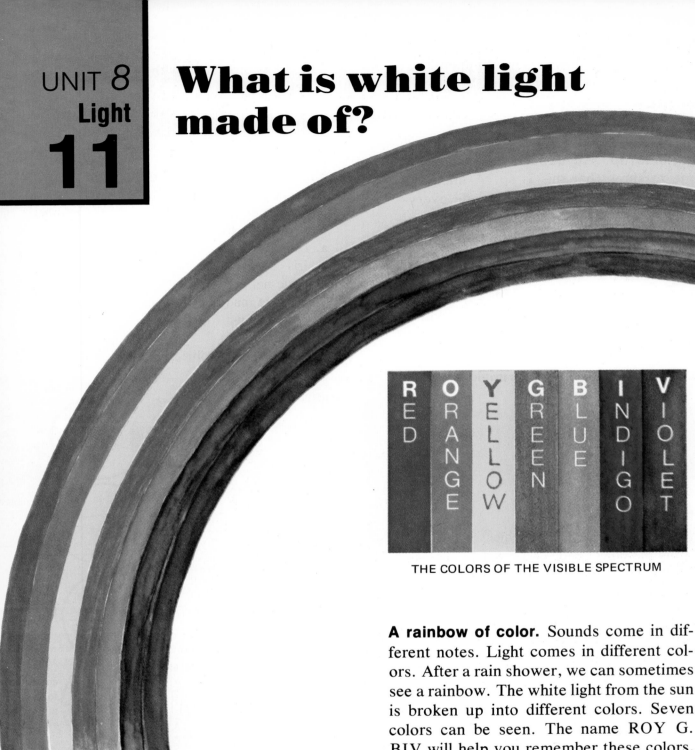

What is white light made of?

RED **O**RANGE **Y**ELLOW **G**REEN **B**LUE **I**NDIGO **V**IOLET

THE COLORS OF THE VISIBLE SPECTRUM

A rainbow of color. Sounds come in different notes. Light comes in different colors. After a rain shower, we can sometimes see a rainbow. The white light from the sun is broken up into different colors. Seven colors can be seen. The name ROY G. BIV will help you remember these colors. That is the name spelled when the first letters of the colors are put together. The seven colors in the rainbow are called the colors of the <u>visible</u> <u>spectrum</u> (VIZ-uh-bul SPEK-trum).

▶ What are the colors of the visible spectrum?

Breaking up light. The colors of the visible spectrum can be seen in a diamond ring or on an oily puddle in sunlight. The colors can also be seen when light shines through a prism (PRIZ-um). A prism is a piece of glass shaped like a triangle.

The laws of refraction help explain how a prism works. White light contains all the colors of the visible spectrum. As white light passes through a prism, it is bent. Each color in the white light is bent differently. Red is bent the least. Violet is bent the most. The white light spreads out into its colors. Each color of the visible spectrum can be seen.

▶ **What happens to white light when it passes through a prism?**

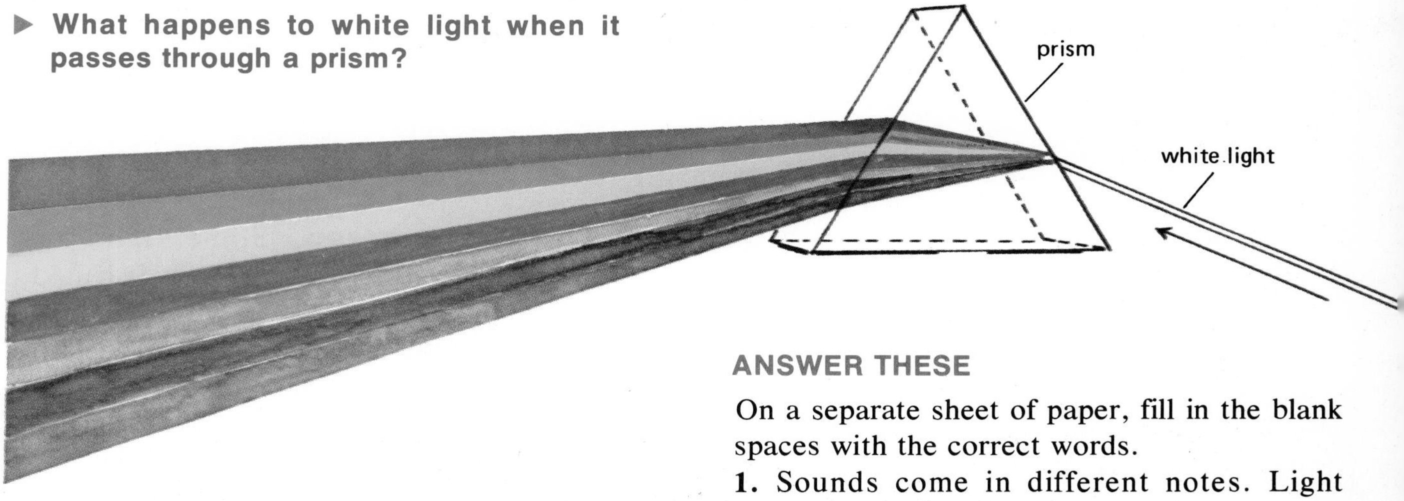

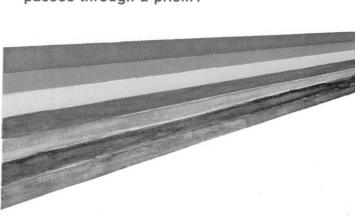

Over the rainbow. Rainbows usually form in the late afternoon, after a summer shower. Droplets of water in the air act like tiny prisms. They separate the sun's light into the colors of the visible spectrum. That is what makes the rainbow we see.

▶ **What causes a rainbow to form?**

prism

white light

ANSWER THESE

On a separate sheet of paper, fill in the blank spaces with the correct words.
1. Sounds come in different notes. Light comes in different _____.
2. The colors of the rainbow are called the colors of the _____ _____.
3. There are _____ different colors in the visible spectrum.
4. The color that is bent the least as light passes through a prism is the color _____.
5. For a rainbow to form, both sunlight and _____ _____ are needed.

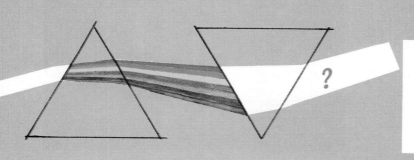

NOW TRY THIS

White light passed through a prism. The light then went into another prism. What color do you think the light coming out of the second prism was? Explain your answer.

UNIT 8
Light
12

What is invisible light?

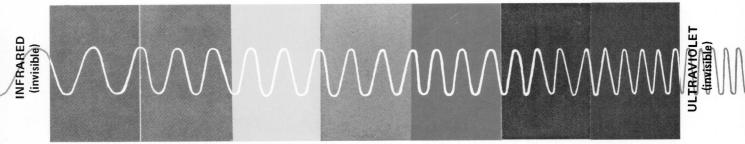

LONGER WAVES ——————————————————————————— SHORTER WAVES

INFRARED (invisible)

ULTRAVIOLET (invisible)

Color me violet. The color of light depends on its wavelength. Violet has the shortest wavelength of all the colors of the visible spectrum. Red has the longest wavelength. The colors in between have wavelengths longer than violet, but shorter than red.

▶ **What does the color of light depend on?**

Shorter than violet. Light can have wavelengths shorter than violet. It is then called <u>ultraviolet</u> (ul-truh-VYE-uh-let) <u>light</u>. Our eyes are not able to see ultraviolet light. Ultraviolet light is invisible. A lot of ultraviolet light comes to us from the sun. It is the ultraviolet light in the sun's rays that causes sunburn. Ultraviolet light cannot go through window glass. You cannot get sunburned through a closed window. Ultraviolet light can make some materials glow. "Black light" posters glow. The "black light" is really ultraviolet light.

▶ **How is ultraviolet light different from ordinary light?**

Longer than red. Some light has a wavelength longer than red. It is called <u>infrared</u> (in-fruh-RED) <u>light</u>. We cannot see this light either, but we can feel it. It feels like heat. Much of the sun's warmth comes to us as infrared light. Heat lamps also produce infrared light. Infrared light from a heat lamp can make sore muscles feel better. But a heat lamp can cause burns if it is not used carefully.

▶ **What does infrared light feel like?**

154

The larger spectrum. The visible spectrum is a small part of a large spectrum. The large spectrum is called the electromagnetic (uh-lek-tro-mag-NET-ic) spectrum. It has many parts. Light, radio waves, X rays, gamma rays, and cosmic rays are all parts of the electromagnetic spectrum. The different parts of the electromagnetic spectrum have different wavelengths. Most of the electromagnetic spectrum is invisible. Only the colors of the visible spectrum can be seen by the human eye.

▶ What are some parts and uses of electromagnetic spectrum?

THE ELECTROMAGNETIC SPECTRUM

Part	Radio waves	Infrared	Visible light	Ultra-violet	X-rays	Gamma rays	Cosmic rays
Uses	Radio broadcasting, television, radar	Heat lamps, baking	Lighting, laser beams, photography	Fluorescent lamps, suntan lamps, killing germs	Medical examinations, treating disease, inspecting metals	Treating cancer	Atomic research

WHAT YOU LEARNED

1. The color of light depends on its wavelength.
2. Ultraviolet and infrared are invisible forms of light.
3. The visible spectrum is a small part of the elecromagnetic spectrum.

SCIENCE WORDS

ultraviolet (ul-truh-VYE-uh-let) **light**
  invisible light with wavelengths shorter than violet
infrared (in-fruh-RED) **light**
  invisible light with wavelengths longer than red
electromagnetic (uh-lek-tro-mag-NET-ic) **spectrum**
  the spectrum made up of radio waves, infrared, visible light, ultraviolet, X rays, gamma rays, and cosmic rays

ANSWER THESE

1. The color of light with the longest wavelength is
   a. red   **b.** violet   **c.** green
2. When you change the wavelength of light, you change its
   a. speed   **b.** brightness   **c.** color
3. Sunburn is caused by
   a. visible light   **c.** infrared light
   b. ultraviolet light
4. The electromagnetic spectrum does NOT include
   a. X rays   **b.** visible light   **c.** sound waves

PEOPLE IN SCIENCE

Isabella Karle
Dr. Karle studies the structure of crystals by using X-rays. Since 1959 she has been head of the X-ray analysis section of the U.S. Naval Research Laboratory. In 1963 she developed a new method of determining crystal structure. The new method greatly reduced the time required for crystal structure analysis.

Dorothy Hodgkin
Dr. Hodgkin is a scientist who studies the structure of chemicals. In her research she is able to analyze the three dimensional shape of compounds by using x-rays. Penicillin, Vitamin B_{12}, and insulin are some of the compounds she has analyzed. In 1964 she was awarded the Nobel Prize in Chemistry for her work in determining the structure of penicillin and vitamin B_{12}.

Why do objects have different colors?

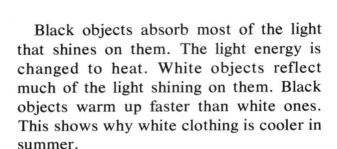

Objects of different colors. How do objects get their colors? An object's color depends on the color of light that it reflects. An object that reflects all colors is seen as white. An object that does not reflect any colors is seen as black.

▶ **What does the color of an object depend on?**

Reflecting the visible spectrum. Remember that white light is made up of seven different colors. Different objects reflect the different parts of white light. Most plant leaves reflect the green part of light. When white light shines on a leaf, mainly green is reflected to our eyes. The rest of the light is <u>absorbed</u> (ab-ZORBED), or soaked up, by the leaf. The light energy that is absorbed is used by the plant to make food.

Black objects absorb most of the light that shines on them. The light energy is changed to heat. White objects reflect much of the light shining on them. Black objects warm up faster than white ones. This shows why white clothing is cooler in summer.

▶ **What color does a green leaf reflect best?**

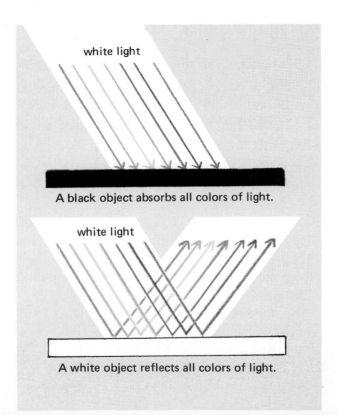

A black object absorbs all colors of light.

white light

A white object reflects all colors of light.

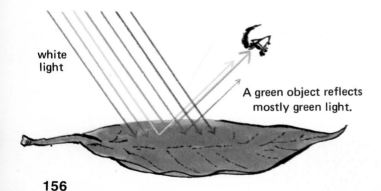

white light

A green object reflects mostly green light.

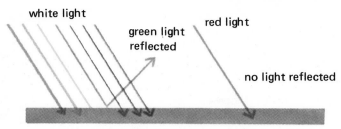

A green object appears black in red light.

Changing colors. Shine a red light on a white card. The card appears red. In green light, the card appears green. White objects reflect all colors. So white objects appear to change color in different lights. Now try shining a red light on a green card. The card appears black. Green objects reflect mainly green. Red light shining on a green object is not reflected. Objects that do not reflect much light appear black.

▶ **What color does a white card appear to be in green light?**

Shining through. Transparent and translucent objects <u>transmit</u> (trans-MIT) light. This means they allow light to pass through them. Shine a white light through a piece of green plastic. Only green is transmitted. Try it with a piece of red plastic. Now only red is transmitted. Transparent and translucent objects transmit the colors that they are. Green plastic transmits green light. Red plastic transmits red light.

Shine a white light through two pieces of plastic: one red, and the other blue. The red plastic blocks all the light but red. The blue plastic blocks all light except blue. Materials that transmit some colors of light and block others are called <u>filters</u>. A combination of red and blue filters blocks nearly all light.

▶ **What color of light is transmitted by a piece of red plastic?**

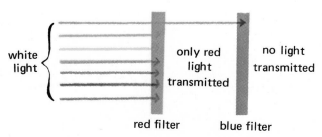

WHAT YOU LEARNED

1. White objects reflect all colors.
2. Black objects reflect no colors.
3. Opaque objects are the color they reflect.
4. Transparent and translucent objects transmit the color that they are.

SCIENCE WORDS

absorb (ab-ZORB)
  soak up
transmit (trans-MIT)
  allow to pass through
filter
  a material that transmits some colors of light and blocks others

ANSWER THESE

1. The color of an object that reflects all colors is
   a. white
   b. black
   c. red
2. The color of an object that does not reflect light is
   a. white
   b. red
   c. black
3. When red light shines on a green leaf, the leaf seems to be
   a. red
   b. black
   c. green
4. A green filter transmits
   a. red
   b. blue
   c. green

NOW TRY THESE

1. A girl buys a dress at a store that has special colored lights. When she gets home, she thinks the dress has changed color. What has happened?
2. During a show, the actors' clothing seems to change colors. Sometimes it seems green, sometimes blue, and sometimes red. When all the lights go on at the end, the clothing is seen to be white. What could have made the clothing seem to change color?

How can light energy be changed?

Forms of energy. Light is a form of energy. Energy cannot be created or destroyed. But energy can be changed into different forms. Light energy can be changed into heat energy. Fill two glasses with water. Place a thermometer in each glass. Stand one glass in sunlight, and the other in shade. The water standing in sunlight becomes warmer than the water in shade. Light energy in sunlight has been changed into heat energy in the glass. Homes can be heated in this way. Water warmed by sunlight heats the house.

▶ **What causes water standing in sunlight to become warm?**

Food from light energy. Green plants use light energy to help them make food. This is called photosynthesis (foh-toh-SIN-thuh-sis). During photosynthesis, light energy is changed into chemical energy. The chemical energy is then stored in the food the plant makes. Light energy from the sun is used by green plants to make food.

▶ **What do green plants use light energy for?**

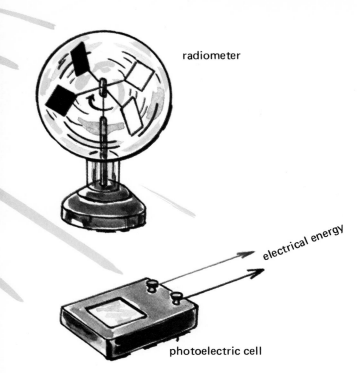

radiometer

electrical energy

photoelectric cell

Particles of light. Sometimes light energy acts like a stream of tiny particles. These particles of light are called photons (FOH-tonz). Light acts like a stream of photons when it makes electricity in a photoelectric cell. Photons of light hit the cell. They make electrons in the cell move. Moving electrons make an electric current.

▶ **What is a photon?**

WHAT YOU LEARNED

1. Light energy can be changed into other forms of energy.
2. Sometimes light acts like a stream of photons.

SCIENCE WORDS

photoelectric (foh-toh-uh-LEC-tric) **cell**
a cell that changes light into electricity
photon (FOH-ton)
a tiny particle of light

ANSWER THESE

1. Light is a form of _____.
2. Green plants use light energy to help make _____.
3. Plants store _____ energy in the food they make.
4. A radiometer changes light energy into _____ energy.
5. A _____ cell can change light into electricity.
6. Tiny particles of light are called _____.

Motion from light energy. Place a radiometer in sunlight. It begins to spin. Light energy is being changed into mechanical energy. The mechanical energy of a radiometer is too small to be of much use. A photoelectric (foh-toh-uh-LEC-tric) cell can get larger amounts of useful energy from light. When light shines on a photoelectric cell, electricity is produced. The electrical energy can be stored in batteries. It can then be used to supply power for radios and other electrical devices.

▶ **What kind of energy does a photoelectric cell change light into?**

FINDING OUT MORE

The sunlight falling on one acre of land is enough to supply all the energy needed by a small town. Two days' worth of sunlight falling on the earth has more energy than all the world's oil. This energy cannot be easily collected and stored. One way to collect and store a small part of this energy is with photoelectric cells and batteries. Some day this pollution-free source of energy may be more widely used on earth.

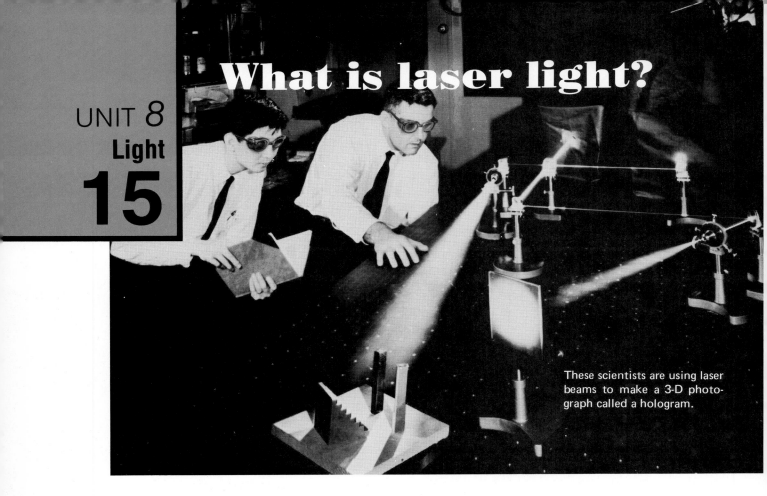

What is laser light?

These scientists are using laser beams to make a 3-D photograph called a hologram.

Zap! A powerful beam of light cuts through a steel plate. This light is different from ordinary light. This light comes from a laser (LAY-zer). A laser produces a light beam with a huge amount of energy. Light from a laser can travel to the moon and back. Laser light can cut through metals. It is more powerful than ordinary light.

▶ **What kind of light can cut through metals?**

What's special about laser light?
Ordinary light contains a mixture of many wavelengths. Light from a laser is special. All the waves in laser light have the same wavelength. This means that the light is all one color. All of the light waves move along together. This makes the light energy in a laser beam very concentrated.

▶ **How are laser light waves different from ordinary light waves?**

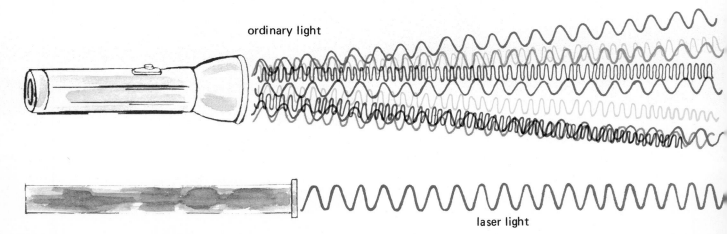

ordinary light

laser light

Lasers can be used by doctors. The retina is a part of the eye. Sometimes the retina can come loose from the back part of the eye. This is called a detached retina. It can cause blindness if it is not treated. A laser beam can be used to fix the retina back in place. The laser causes a tiny burn that does not hurt. The burn sticks the retina in place again.

▶ How can a laser be used to treat a detached retina?

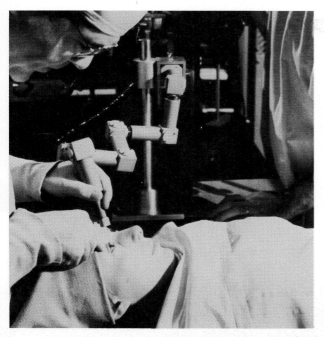
Using a laser beam to operate on the eye.

3-D photographs. Have you ever seen a 3-D movie? You need special glasses to view a 3-D movie. 3-D photographs can be made with a laser. No special glasses are needed to look at the photo. A 3-D photograph made with a laser is called a hologram (HOH-luh-gram). A hologram doesn't look like a regular photo. It is something like a fingerprint of light. You look through the hologram to see a picture in 3-D. Scientists are working to make 3-D television. They are experimenting with things that are something like holograms.

▶ What is a hologram?

WHAT YOU LEARNED

1. Light from a laser has a huge amount of energy.
2. Light from a laser is all one color.
3. Laser light waves all travel along together.

SCIENCE WORDS

laser (LAY-zer)
   a device that makes one-color, high-energy light
hologram (HOH-luh-gram)
   a 3-D photograph made with a laser

ANSWER THESE

If a sentence is true, mark it true on a separate sheet of paper. If it is false, change the word in capital letters to make it true.
1. Laser light has LESS energy than ordinary light.
2. Laser light has ONE color in it.
3. Laser light waves all travel along TOGETHER.
4. Lasers CANNOT be used to treat disease.
5. A 3-D laser photograph is called a PHOTON.

WHAT'S HAPPENING

Atoms can absorb energy. When an atom absorbs energy, the electrons in it move farther away from the nucleus. When the electrons later move back to their places, light is given off. In ordinary light, electrons are moving back and forth all the time. Light waves come from different atoms at different times. Laser light comes from electrons in millions and millions of different atoms all moving at the same time. The light waves all come out together. This is what makes a laser beam.

UNIT 8 Review

Do the following questions on a separate sheet of paper.

Matching *Write each of the statements in Column I, leaving one line of space after each statement. On the blank line following each statement, write the word or phrase from Column II that is described by that statement.*

Column I

1. Distance light travels in one year.
2. A wave shaped like a water wave.
3. A tiny point of light.
4. Sharp, black shadow.
5. Gray, outer shadow.
6. Ray of light that hits something.
7. A lens that is curved outward.
8. A lens that is curved inward.
9. The opening into the eye.
10. A tiny particle of light.

Column II

point source
concave lens
transverse wave
incident ray
light-year
pupil
photon
umbra
penumbra
convex lens

Multiple Choice *Write the letter of the choice that best completes the statement or answers the question.*

1. The speed of light is
   a. 30,000 km per second
   b. 300,000 km per second
   c. 3,000,000 km per second
2. The angle of incidence is always
   a. half the angle of reflection
   b. equal to the angle of reflection
   c. twice the angle of reflection
3. Reflection from a rough surface is called
   a. diffuse reflection
   b. regular reflection
   c. mirror image
4. When light moves from glass to air, it
   a. speeds up
   b. slows down
   c. does not change its speed

5. The retina changes light into
   a. sound impulses
   b. nerve signals
   c. shadows
6. When passing through a prism, each color in white light is
   a. bent the same amount
   b. reflected
   c. bent a different amount
7. The color of light depends upon its
   a. speed
   b. wavelength
   c. temperature
8. When light shines on a photoelectric cell,
   a. electricity is produced
   b. a photograph is made
   c. it is refracted

Unit Lessons

1. What is electricity?
2. What are insulators and conductors?
3. What is a switch?
4. What makes charges move?
5. How does an electric cell make electric current?
6. What is an electric circuit?
7. What is a parallel circuit?
8. How is electric current measured?
9. What is electromotive force?
10. How is electromotive force measured?
11. What is resistance?
12. What is Ohm's law?
13. What happens when the resistance is changed in an electric circuit?

Goals and Objectives

After completing this unit, you should be able to:

- understand that electric currents carry energy.
- describe different switches and how they work.
- describe how a wet cell or a dry cell is constructed.
- recognize that electricity travels in closed circuits.
- recognize that electrons need a force to make them move.
- recognize that electricity moves more easily through some materials than others.
- explain how a fuse is blown or a circuit is shorted.

What is electricity?

All charged up. Rub your feet on a carpet on a cool, dry day. Then bring your hand close to a metal object. A spark jumps between your hand and the metal. The spark is made by electricity (e-lec-TRISS-i-tee). Rubbing your feet across the carpet gave your body an electric (e-LEC-tric) charge. The electric charge then moved between your hand and the metal. The moving electric charge heated the air and made it glow.

▶ **How can you give your body an electric charge?**

Lightning strikes! In a thunderstorm, there are strong winds and currents of air. The moving air causes an electric charge to build up on the clouds. Suddenly the charge jumps between a cloud and the ground. There is a bright flash of lightning as the moving charge heats the air. It is like the spark from your hand. But it is much more powerful.

▶ **What causes lightning?**

Moving charges have energy. Moving charges make an electric current (CUR-rent). An electric current has energy. Lightning is a very large electric current flowing through the air. Its energy produces a bright flash of light and a loud clap of thunder. Electric currents flowing through wires also have energy. The energy of electric currents can be very useful. Toasters, lamps, motors, radios, and

TV sets are a few examples. All of them use the energy of electric currents.

▶ **Why can electric currents be useful?**

Electricity can be dangerous. Before people knew anything about electricity, they knew that lightning was dangerous. Wires that carry electric power can also be dangerous. If you touch the bare wires, enough charge my flow through your body to hurt you. You may even be electrocuted (e-LEC-tro-kew-ted), or killed by it. Electricity at home must always be used carefully. Never use anything with loose or broken electric wires.

▶ **What might happen if electricity is not used carefully?**

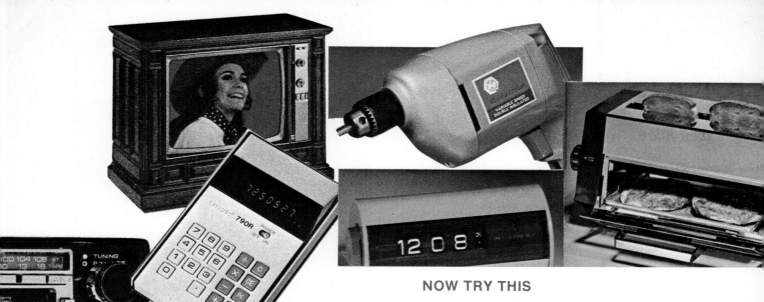

We use the energy of electric currents in many ways.

WHAT YOU LEARNED

1. An electric current is a flow of electric charge.
2. Electric currents carry energy.
3. The energy of electric currents can be used in many ways.
4. Electric currents can be dangerous.

SCIENCE WORDS

electric (e-LEC-tric) **charge**
   a condition produced by electricity

electric current (CUR-rent)
   a flow of electric charge

electrocuted (e-LEC-tro-kew-ted)
   killed by an electric current

ANSWER THESE

1. Lightning is
   a. not really dangerous
   b. caused by an electric current through the air
   c. very useful
2. Electric currents are useful because
   a. they carry energy
   b. they are hot
   c. they are moving
3. An electric current can be dangerous when it
   a. flows through your body
   b. flows through wires
   c. stops moving

NOW TRY THIS

Copy this on a sheet of paper. Use the new words you learned to fill in the blank spaces.

Moving electric charges make an electric _ _ _ _ _ _ _. This can be useful because it carries _ _ _ _ _ _. But if too much goes through your body, you could be _ _ _ _ _ _ _ _ _ _ _ _ _.

NOW TRY THIS

The presence of a small electrical charge can be shown very easily. Tear a piece of newspaper into very small pieces. Run a plastic or rubber comb quickly through your hair. Hold the comb just above the pieces of newspaper. What happens? Rubbing the comb through your hair causes an electrical charge to be built up on the comb. The charge on the comb is not large enough to cause a spark to jump. It is large enough to attract the charges on the paper. Note: This exercise works best in cool dry weather.

What are insulators and conductors?

What is insulation? Look at the electric cord that comes from a lamp. It is really two wires side by side. The wires are covered with a material called insulation (in-suh-LAY-shun). Electricity cannot go through the insulation. It stays in the wires. Anything that electricity cannot move through is called an insulator (IN-suh-lay-ter).

▶ **What does insulation do?**

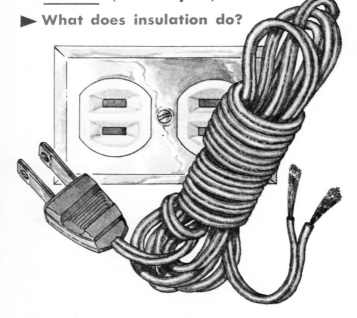

What are insulators made of? Some insulators are made of plastic. Glass and rubber are also good insulators. Electricians often wear rubber gloves when they work. Their tools may have rubber or plastic handles. But there is no perfect insulator. An electric current with a high voltage (VOLE-tij) can go through an insulator. Lightning is a high-voltage electric current. Rubber gloves cannot protect you from lightning.

▶ **What are some good insulators?**

What is a conductor? An electric current can pass through some materials. These materials are called conductors (con-DUCK-ters). An electric cord has good conductors on the inside, and a good insulator on the outside. Many electric cords are made of copper wire covered with plastic. Copper is one of the best conductors. Silver, gold, and aluminum are also very good conductors. All metals are good conductors.

▶ **When is something a good conductor?**

Using insulators and conductors. It is very important to use the right materials for power lines. The conductor must be good enough to carry the electric current a long distance. The insulator must be good enough to keep the high-voltage electricity from getting out of the wire. In many places, the power lines are underground. They are covered with thick layers of plastic and rubber. Plastic and rubber are good insulators. They keep electricity in the wires.

▶**What would happen if power lines were not well insulated?**

WHAT YOU LEARNED

1. Insulators keep electricity from getting out of a wire.
2. Rubber, glass, and plastic are good insulators.
3. Conductors are materials that carry electric current well.
4. Metals are good conductors of electricity.

SCIENCE WORDS

insulator (IN-suh-lay-ter)
  a material that electricity cannot go through
conductor (con-DUCK-ter)
  a material that electricity can go through very well

ANSWER THESE

1. The covering of an electrical wire should be made of
   a. a good conductor
   b. a good insulator
   c. metal

2. The best conductors are
   a. copper, silver, gold, and aluminum
   b. glass, plastic, and rubber
   c. copper and plastic

3. Good conductors
   a. are never used in electrical wires
   b. stop electric currents
   c. let electric currents move through them easily

NOW TRY THIS

See how many words you can make by using the letters in the word CONDUCTOR. For example, you could make the words, OR, NUT, and DOOR. How many words can you make by using the letters in INSULATOR?

DO THIS AT HOME

Someday you will probably apply for a job. Here is an ad that might interest you if you like working with electricity. Write a letter to Mr. Jones telling him why you think this job is for you.

HELP WANTED

Young man or woman to learn to repair television sets. We will pay for night school for the right person. Starting salary of $14,000. Send letter of application to Mr. Jones, ABC Television Company, 100 Main Street.

What is a switch?

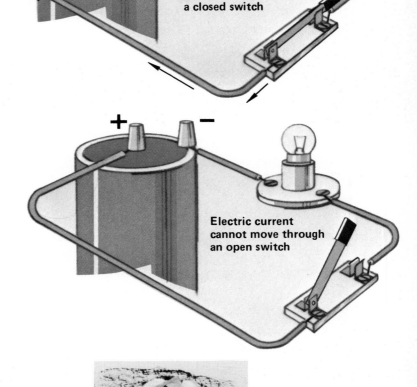

Electric current moves through a closed switch

Electric current cannot move through an open switch

What does a switch do? No one has ever been able to turn off a lightning bolt. But everyone knows how to turn off an electric light. A switch turns the light on and off. To turn the light on, you close the switch. Then electricity can flow through the switch to make the light bulb light. To turn the light off, you open the switch. Then electricity cannot flow through the switch, and the light bulb cannot light.

► **Why does an electric light need a switch?**

The knife switch. There are different kinds of switches. Each kind is good for a certain kind of job. A knife switch is good for doing experiments in electricity with low voltage. The switch is not covered with insulation. You can see if the switch is open or closed. You will use knife switches when you do experiments with dry cells. Dry cells have low voltage. If you touch the metal of the switch, you won't get a shock.

► **Why can you see if a knife switch is open or closed just by looking at it?**

The toggle switch. The switch that is put on a wall to turn a light on and off is a toggle (TOG-gull) switch. You cannot see the inside of the switch because it is covered with insulation. The insulation on the switch keeps you from getting an electric shock when you use it.

► **Why must a home light switch be insulated?**

The pushbutton switch. A <u>pushbutton switch</u> is good for doorbells. When you push the button, you close the switch. The doorbell rings. When you let go of the button, the switch opens by itself. The doorbell stops ringing. The drawing shows what a pushbutton switch looks like inside.

▶ **How do you open a pushbutton switch?**

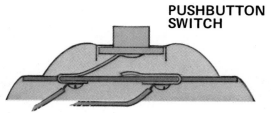

PUSHBUTTON SWITCH

WHAT YOU LEARNED

1. Switches turn electric currents on and off.
2. Electric current moves through a switch when it is closed.
3. Electric current cannot move through a switch when it is open.
4. Three kinds of switches are knife switches, toggle switches, and pushbutton switches.

SCIENCE WORDS

switch
   something used to turn electric current on and off
knife switch
   a kind of switch that is good for doing low-voltage experiments
toggle (TOG-gull) **switch**
   a kind of switch that is used for lights in a home
pushbutton switch
   a kind of switch that opens when you take your finger off the button

ANSWER THESE

Are these sentences true or false? Copy each sentence on a sheet of paper. If the sentence is false, change the colored word to make the sentence true.

1. To turn electric current on and off, you use a switch.

2. To make a light bulb light, you open the switch.

3. To open a knife switch, you just let go so it can open by itself.

NOW TRY THESE

Unscramble the mixed-up words.

1. TEGLOG WITSCHES are used in a home to turn lights on and off.

2. SHUPTOBUNT THICSWES are used to ring doorbells.

3. FENIK HICTSEWS are good for doing electrical experiments.

DO THIS AT HOME

Make a list of the different kinds of switches that you can find around your home. For each switch you find, write down what kind it is and where you found it. Use a table like the one below.

KIND OF SWITCH	WHERE I FOUND IT
toggle switch	kitchen

FINDING OUT MORE

The mercury switch is a kind of toggle switch that doesn't make a click when you use it. Mercury (MURK-yuh-ree) is a liquid metal. It is a good conductor of electricity. The mercury is in a tiny container in the switch. When the container is tipped over, the mercury touches both wires. The switch is closed. When the container is stood up on its end, the mercury flows away from one of the wires. The switch is open. The handle on the switch moves the mercury container. The mercury doesn't make any noise, so the switch is very quiet.

SWITCH CLOSED   **SWITCH OPEN**

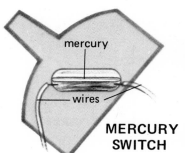
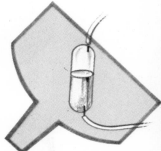

mercury

wires

MERCURY SWITCH

What makes charges move?

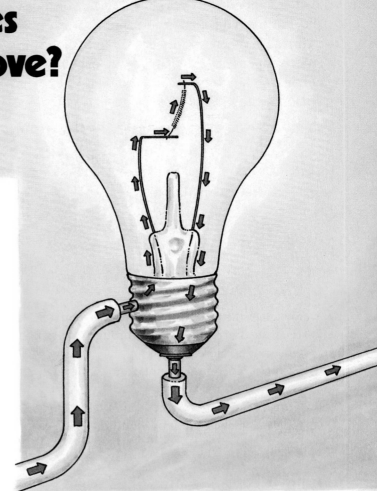

Charges on the move. Flick the switch and an electric current flows through a light bulb. An electric current is made of moving electric charge. Moving charges have <u>electrical</u> (e-LEC-tri-cul) <u>energy</u>. In the light bulb, the electrical energy is changed to heat energy and light energy.

▶ **What kind of energy do moving charges have?**

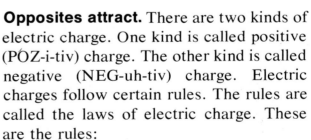

LIKE CHARGES REPEL

OPPOSITE CHARGES ATTRACT

Opposites attract. There are two kinds of electric charge. One kind is called positive (PÓZ-i-tiv) charge. The other kind is called negative (NEG-uh-tiv) charge. Electric charges follow certain rules. The rules are called the laws of electric charge. These are the rules:

1. Negative charges <u>repel</u> (ree-PEL), or push away, other negative charges.
2. Positive charges repel other positive charges.
3. Negative and positive charges attract each other.

You can remember the rules like this:
   Like charges repel.
   Opposite charges attract.

▶ **What are the laws of electric charge?**

Where do charges come from? Every atom of matter has electric charges in it. The central part of the atom has a positive charge. Tiny particles called electrons (e-LEC-trons) spin around the outside of the atom. Electrons have a negative charge. The positive charge at the center of the atom attracts the negative charge of the electrons. This attraction holds the parts of the atom together.

▶ **What parts of an atom have a negative charge?**

Pushing electrons around. In metals, some of the electrons can move from atom to atom. An electric current in a metal is made of moving electrons. All electrons have a negative charge. They repel each other. They push each other along as they go from atom to atom. The positive charges in the atoms cannot move through metals the way the negative charges can.

▶ **What is moving when an electric current goes through a metal wire?**

WHAT YOU LEARNED

1. In a light bulb, electrical energy is changed to heat energy and light energy.
2. Electric charges can be positive or negative.
3. Like electric charges repel each other.
4. Opposite electric charges attract each other.
5. Electrons have a negative charge.
6. An electric current in a metal is made of moving electrons.

SCIENCE WORDS

electrical (e-LEC-tri-cul) **energy**
the kind of energy that moving charges have
repel (ree-PEL)
push away
electron (e-LEC-tron)
a tiny particle with a negative charge

ANSWER THESE

Copy these sentences and fill in the missing words:
1. Moving _____ make an electric current.
2. Electrons _____ each other.
3. Positive charges _____ electrons.

NOW TRY THIS

Write down whether each charge in Column 1 attracts or repels the charge in Column 2.

Column 1	Column 2
negative charge	negative charge
positive charge	negative charge
negative charge	positive charge
positive charge	positive charge

FINDING OUT MORE

Electrical energy can be changed to other forms of energy, (see pages 8-11). In the chart below, list the forms of energy—light, heat, mechanical, chemical, or sound—that electrical energy is changed to when each electrical device is operated.

ELECTRICAL DEVICE	FORMS OF ENERGY
light bulb	
drill	
clock	
doorbell	
elevator	
stove	
pump	

PLEASE DO NOT WRITE IN THIS BOOK.

How does an electric cell make electric current?

WET CELL

zinc electrode

copper electrode

dilute sulfuric acid electrolyte

The wet cell. The diagram shows a <u>wet cell</u>. The copper and zinc strips are called the <u>electrodes</u> (e-LEC-trodes). The dilute sulfuric acid is the <u>electrolyte</u> (e-LEC-tro-lite). The electrolyte is a liquid that can conduct electricity.

▶ **What is the liquid in a wet cell called?**

How a wet cell works. In a wet cell, the zinc electrode and the sulfuric acid react together. The reaction causes electrons to collect on the zinc electrode. The zinc electrode gets a negative charge. The copper electrode gets a positive charge. When the zinc and the copper are connected by a wire, electrons move through the wire. Electrons from the negative zinc electrode push each other through the wire to the positive copper electrode. The moving electrons make an electric current.

▶ **Which electrode in this wet cell has more electrons on it?**

DRY CELL

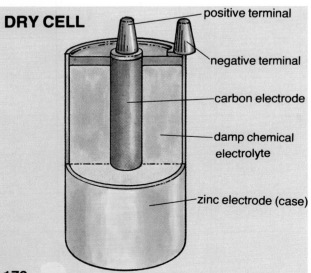

positive terminal

negative terminal

carbon electrode

damp chemical electrolyte

zinc electrode (case)

The dry cell. If you tipped over a wet cell, the electrolyte would spill out. Wet cells cannot be used in flashlights or in other things that are carried around. For these things, <u>dry cells</u> are used. Dry cells are another kind of electric cell. Dry cells can be made very small. They can be carried around easily. Flashlights, transistor radios, and many toys use dry cells.

▶ **Why are dry cells very useful?**

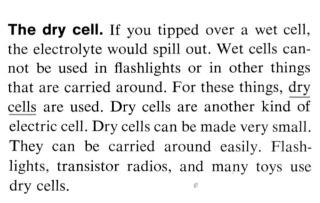 **How a dry cell works.** A dry cell is not completely dry. It has a moist electrolyte inside it. The whole outside case of a dry cell is the negative electrode. It is made of zinc. Part of the negative electrode sticks up at the top of the cell, near the edge. There is a place to connect a wire to the zinc. This is

172

called the negative terminal (TURM-i-nul). The positive electrode in a dry cell is a carbon rod. It goes down the center of the dry cell. The positive terminal is attached to the top of the carbon rod.

A chemical reaction between the electrolyte and the zinc electrode makes electrons collect on the zinc. When the positive and negative terminals of the dry cell are connected with a wire, electrons move through the wire. They move from the negative terminal to the positive terminal. Electric current always moves from a negative terminal to a positive terminal.

▶ **Which way do the electrons from a dry cell move?**

WHAT YOU LEARNED

1. An electric current can be made by a wet cell.
2. An electric current can be made by a dry cell.
3. An electric current always moves from a negative terminal to a positive terminal.

SCIENCE WORDS

electrode (e-LEC-trode)
   the negative or positive part of an electrical cell
electrolyte (e-LEC-tro-lite)
   a liquid or moist substance that can conduct electricity
wet cell
   an electrical cell that has a liquid electrolyte
dry cell
   an electrical cell that has a moist electrolyte
terminal (TURM-i-nul)
   the negative or positive end of an electrical cell

ANSWER THESE

1. What are the metal strips in a wet cell called?
2. How are wet cells and dry cells different?
3. What do you call the substance that is between the electrodes of an electrical cell?
4. Which way does the electricity of an electrical cell move?

NOW TRY THIS

Look at the letters on the diagram. Write the name of the part that each letter is pointing to.

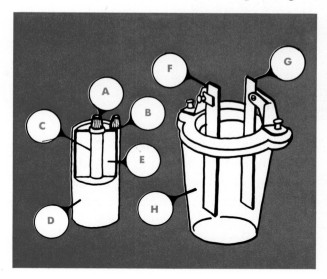

DO THIS AT HOME

Cut a raw potato in half. Attach copper wires to the terminals of a dry cell. Stick the other ends of the wires into the potato. Take the wires out of the potato after about two minutes. Look at the holes made by the wires. One of them will have a colored ring around it. What color do you see? Which terminal was this wire connected to? If you can't remember, do the experiment again.

You can use this test to find the positive terminal of any electrical cell.

What is an electric circuit?

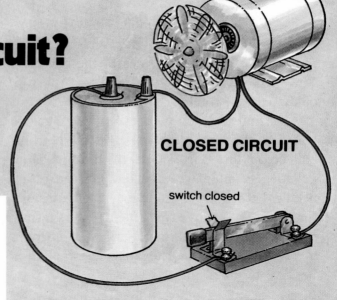

CLOSED CIRCUIT

switch closed

Electricity follows a path. Cars run on roads. A train follows the tracks. Cars and trains follow paths. Electricity follows a path, too. The path that an electric current follows is called an <u>electric circuit</u> (SURK-ut).

▶ **What is an electric circuit?**

An electric circuit can be closed or open. An electric circuit is <u>closed</u> if an electric current can move through it. If a switch is open, electric current cannot move through the circuit. The circuit is <u>open.</u> No electricity can move anywhere in the circuit. When the switch is closed, then the circuit is closed. Once again, electric current can move through the circuit. If a wire gets broken, the circuit is open. Electricity cannot move through the circuit.

A <u>closed circuit</u> is complete. An <u>open circuit</u> is incomplete. Electric current can move through a closed or complete circuit. It cannot move through an open or incomplete circuit.

▶ **What kind of circuit can an electric current move through?**

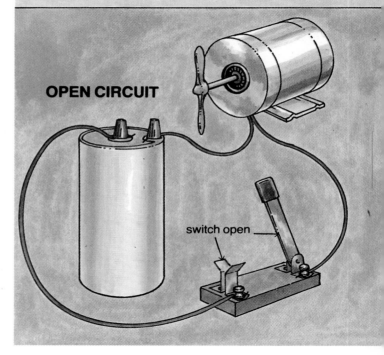

OPEN CIRCUIT

switch open

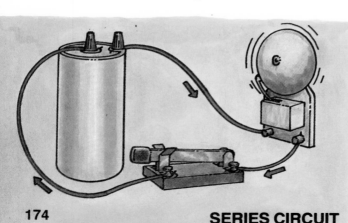

SERIES CIRCUIT

The series circuit. You can make a simple electric circuit with a dry cell, some wire, a switch, and a bell. Connect them all together as shown in the diagram. This kind of circuit is called a <u>series</u> (SEER-eez) <u>circuit</u>. Follow the electric current along as it moves through the circuit. There is only one path for the electricity to follow. In a series circuit, the electric current has only one path to follow.

▶ **How many paths can an electric current follow in a series circuit?**

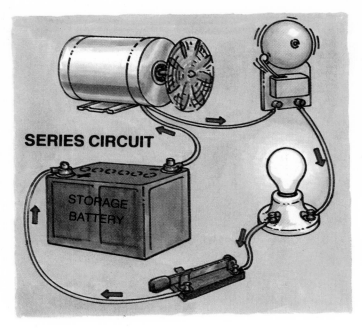

SERIES CIRCUIT

STORAGE BATTERY

Series circuits may have many things in them. The series circuit shown in the diagram has a bell, a light bulb, a motor, a switch, and a battery. When the switch is closed, electric current moves in a single path through the bell, the light bulb, and the motor. If the bulb burned out, the electric current would not be able to complete its path. The circuit would be open. The bell and the motor would stop working. Whenever one thing in a series circuit stops working, everything in the circuit stops working. The electricity cannot get past the open part of the circuit. Series circuits are used mostly for just one bell, or one light bulb, or one motor.

▶ **When one part of a series circuit is open, what happens to the current in the circuit?**

WHAT YOU LEARNED

1. Electricity follows a path called an electric circuit.
2. A closed circuit is a complete path that electricity can move along.
3. An open circuit is an incomplete path that electricity cannot move along.
4. In a series circuit, there is just one path for the electricity to follow.

SCIENCE WORDS

electric circuit (SURK-ut)
   the path that an electric current follows
closed circuit
   a complete path for electricity to move along
open circuit
   an incomplete path that electricity cannot move along
series (SEER-eez) **circuit**
   a circuit that has just one path for the electric current to follow

ANSWER THESE

1. A train goes along its tracks. An electric current goes along a _____.
2. When a switch in a circuit is open, the circuit is _____.
3. A _____ circuit has only one path for the electric current.

NOW TRY THIS

Copy the diagram into your notebook. Then try to fit all of the new words you have learned into the diagram. Some letters are in the right place to help you get started.

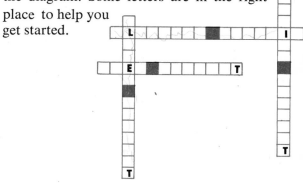

FINDING OUT MORE

Fuses

A fuse (FEWZ) helps protect your home from electrical fires. When too much electric current goes through a wire, the wire gets hot. The wire inside a fuse quickly melts when it gets hot. When the wire is melted, no more electricity can go through the fuse. We say the fuse has blown. The blown fuse makes the circuit incomplete. No more electricity can go through the circuit. Do you think a fuse is wired in a series circuit? Why?

What is a parallel circuit?

How are the lights in your home wired?

If one light in your home burns out, do all the other lights go out? No, they don't. This tells you that the lights in your home are NOT connected in series. Remember, when one bulb in a series circuit goes out, they all go out. This does not happen in your home. The lights are not connected in series.

▶ **Are the lights in your home wired in a series circuit? How do you know?**

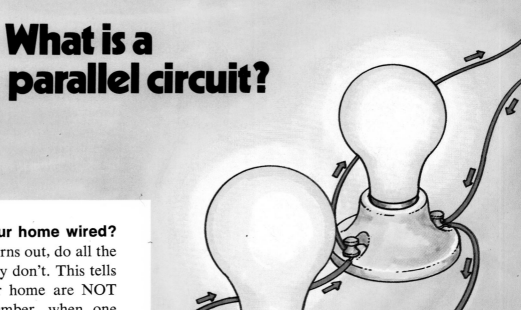

PARALLEL CIRCUIT

Parallel circuits. The lights in your home are wired like the ones in the diagram. Follow the arrows in the diagram. How many paths can the electricity follow? If one of the bulbs burns out, only its part of the circuit is broken. Electric current can still flow through the other parts of the circuit. The other bulbs can still light. A circuit that has more than one path for the electric current to follow is called a parallel (PA-ruh-lel) circuit.

▶ **What is a parallel circuit?**

Parallel circuits in your home. You may have a lamp at home that has two or three light bulbs. Do you think they are wired in a series circuit or in parallel circuits? If they are in a series circuit, they will all go out when one goes out. If they are in parallel circuits, the good bulbs will stay lit when one goes out.

▶ **What kind of circuit is used in a lamp with three light bulbs?**

Homes, schools, and offices use parallel circuits. Each room in a building may be part of a large parallel circuit. All the lights in a room are separate parts of the circuit. The electric current has many different paths to follow. If one part of the circuit becomes open, the rest stay closed. If one light bulb burns out, the rest stay lit.

▶ **Why are parallel circuits useful in buildings?**

WHAT YOU LEARNED

1. A parallel circuit has more than one path for the electricity to follow.
2. When one part of a parallel circuit burns out, the other parts will work.

SCIENCE WORD

parallel (PA-ruh-lel) **circuit**
a circuit that has more than one path for the electricity to follow

ANSWER THESE

Draw a picture of the circuits you would build to make these things work:
1. A lamp with two bulbs. One bulb must stay lit if the other burns out.
2. A motor with a light that tells when the motor is running. If the motor stops working, the light must go out.

FINDING OUT MORE

A Shorthand Way To Draw Electric Circuits
Chemists use symbols for writing the names of the elements. Physicists (FIZ-i-sists) and electricians (e-lek-TRISH-unz) use symbols to draw electric circuits. Here are some of the symbols they use:

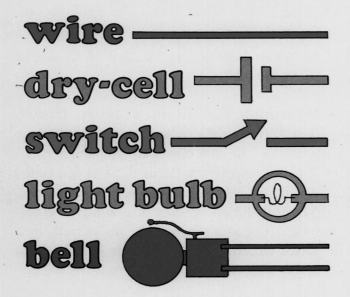

This is how the symbols would be used to show a series circuit with a dry cell, a switch, and a light bulb:

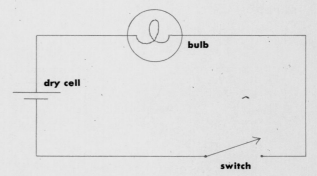

A parallel circuit with a dry cell, a light bulb, and a bell would look like this:

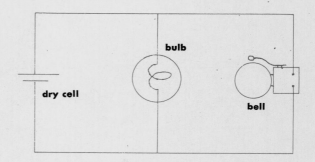

Use the symbols to draw a circuit with a dry cell, a switch, a bell, and two light bulbs.

How is electric current measured?

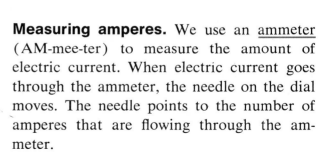

AMMETER

Moving electrons make an electric current. Water flows through a pipe. Electrons flow through a wire. The amount of water that flows through a pipe is measured in gallons per second. The amount of electric current that flows through a wire is measured in amperes (AM-peers). One ampere is just about the amount of current that flows through a 100-watt bulb when it is turned on. One ampere is a flow of about 6 *billion billion* electrons per second!

► In what unit is electric current measured?

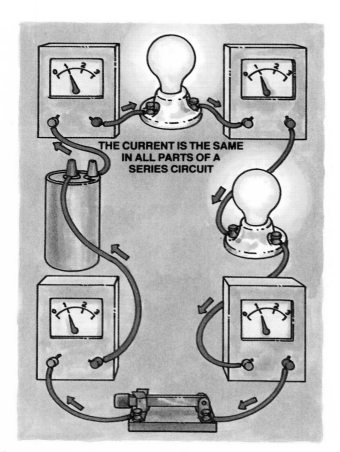

THE CURRENT IS THE SAME
IN ALL PARTS OF A
SERIES CIRCUIT

Measuring amperes. We use an ammeter (AM-mee-ter) to measure the amount of electric current. When electric current goes through the ammeter, the needle on the dial moves. The needle points to the number of amperes that are flowing through the ammeter.

► What instrument is used to measure amperes?

Measuring current in a series circuit. The drawing shows a series circuit with four ammeters in different parts of the circuit. The current is the same in all parts of a series circuit. So all the ammeters read the same. They all show 1 ampere of current. One ammeter is enough to measure the current in a series circuit. The ammeter is connected in series with the circuit at any part of the circuit.

► How should you connect an ammeter to measure the current in a series circuit?

Measuring current in parallel circuits.

Look at this drawing of a parallel circuit. In a parallel circuit, the electric current flows through more than one path. The amount of current may be different in different parts of the circuit. To measure the current in one part of the circuit, connect an ammeter in series with that part. The ammeter will show the amount of current in its part of the circuit.

▶ **How should you connect an ammeter to measure the current in one part of a parallel circuit?**

Never connect an ammeter directly to a dry cell

Using ammeters carefully. Never connect an ammeter to a battery all by itself. The current will be too large! A current that is too large will damage the ammeter.

▶ **What will happen if the current in an ammeter is too large?**

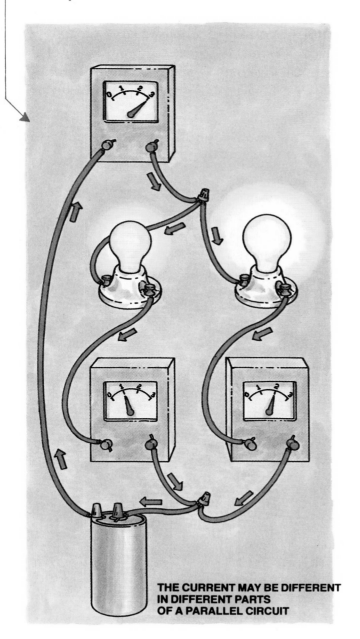
THE CURRENT MAY BE DIFFERENT IN DIFFERENT PARTS OF A PARALLEL CIRCUIT

WHAT YOU LEARNED

1. Electric current is measured in amperes.
2. An ammeter is used to measure the amount of electric current.
3. The amount of current is the same in all parts of a series circuit.
4. The amount of current can be different in different parts of a parallel circuit.

SCIENCE WORDS

ampere (AM-peer)
the unit for measuring electric current
ammeter (AM-mee-ter)
an instrument for measuring electric current

ANSWER THESE

If the sentence is true, mark it "true." If the sentence is false, change the underlined word to make it true.
1. An ammeter <u>makes</u> electric current.
2. Electric current is measured in <u>electrons</u>.
3. An ammeter is connected in <u>series</u> with a circuit. **PLEASE DO NOT WRITE**
4. Electric current is the same everywhere in a <u>parallel</u> circuit. **IN THIS BOOK.**
5. An ammeter is easily damaged by a <u>large</u> electric current.

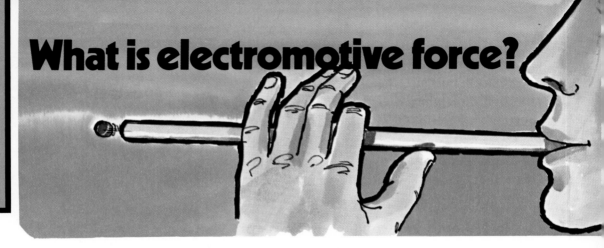

What is electromotive force?

What makes electrons move? You have learned that moving electrons make an electric current. The force that makes electrons move is called <u>electromotive</u> (e-LEC-troh-MOH-tiv) <u>force.</u> A force is a push. "Electro" is short for electricity, and "motive" means "moving." Electromotive force is the push that makes electricity move. A short way to write "electromotive force" is "EMF."

▶ **What is electromotive force?**

What is a volt? What happens when you turn on a portable radio? Electric current is pushed through the radio by the battery. The amount of push is the electromotive force (EMF). It is measured in <u>volts</u> (VOHLTS). Many portable radios use 9 volts of EMF. A dry cell used in flashlights has only 1½ volts of EMF. The electricity used in your home has about 110 volts of EMF.

▶ **How much EMF does each dry cell in a flashlight have?**

Connecting electrical cells together. Two dry cells can be connected together. If they are connected in series, their combined <u>voltage</u> (VOHL-tij) will be raised. The negative terminal of one cell must be connected to the positive terminal of the other cell. Two 1½-volt cells connected this way will give 3 volts.

Two dry cells can also be connected in parallel. The negative and positive terminals must be connected as shown in the drawing. Two 1½-volt dry cells connected in parallel will still give only 1½ volts. But the dry cells will last longer when they are connected this way.

▶ **How should you connect dry cells to get more voltage?**

SERIES CONNECTION

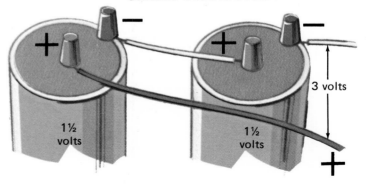

PARALLEL CONNECTION

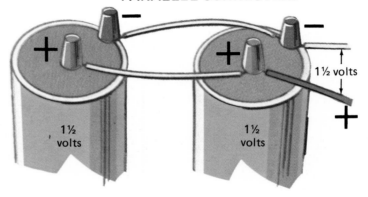

Making a battery. When electrical cells are connected together, they are called a <u>battery</u> (BAT-uh-ree). Six 1½-volt dry cells connected in series would make a 9-volt battery.

▶ **How many 1½-volt dry cells would you need to make a 9-volt battery?**

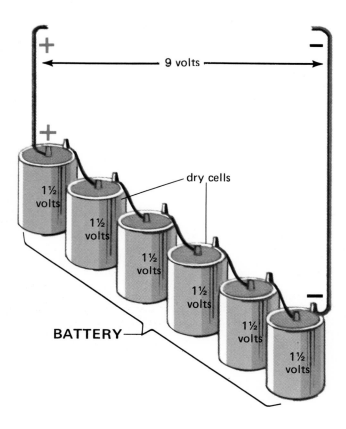

BATTERY

dry cells

9 volts

1½ volts (×6)

WHAT YOU LEARNED

1. Electromotive force makes electricity move.
2. Two or more electrical cells connected together make a battery.
3. Connecting dry cells in series raises their voltage.

SCIENCE WORDS

electromotive (e-LEC-troh-MOH-tiv) **force**
the push that makes electricity move
volt (VOHLT)
the unit for measuring electromotive force
voltage (VOHL-tij)
the number of volts
battery (BAT-uh-ree)
two or more electrical cells connected together

ANSWER THESE

1. Electrons are moved by
   a. an ammeter
   b. a current
   c. electromotive force
2. Electromotive force is measured in
   a. amperes
   b. volts
   c. electric current
3. A battery has
   a. two or more electrical cells
   b. only one electrical cell
   c. no electrical cells
4. To increase EMF, you should connect dry cells
   a. in parallel
   b. in series
   c. to an ammeter

FINDING OUT MORE

Danger—High Voltage

Have you ever rubbed your shoes on a rug and then gotten an electric shock? The shock was probably caused by thousands of volts. Yet it didn't harm you. The electricity used in your home is only about 110 volts. But it can be very dangerous if you are not careful with it. Why should 110 volts be dangerous while thousands of volts are not?

When you got a shock from rubbing your shoes on a rug, the electric current was very small. If you got a shock from the electricity in your home, the current would be very large. It is not the voltage that is dangerous. It is the amount of electric current. The voltage only tells how hard the electricity is being pushed. The amount of current tells how much electricity there is.

Think of a water pistol and a hose. The water is squirted very hard out of a water pistol. But it cannot hurt you because there is so little of it. The water coming out of a big hose may not be pushed as hard. But there is so much of it, it could knock you over.

It might be better for signs that say DANGER —HIGH VOLTAGE to say DANGER— LARGE CURRENT.

How is electromotive force measured?

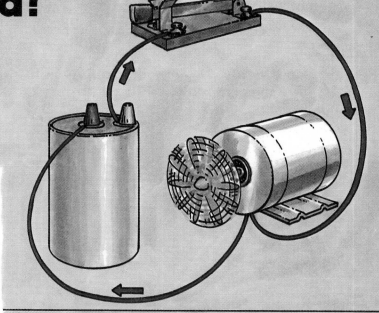

How is electricity like water? Electric circuits are something like water pipes. Water flows through pipes. Electric current flows through wires. Valves turn water on and off. Switches turn electric current on and off. Pressure (PRESH-ur) makes water move. Electromotive force makes electricity move. Water pressure can come from a pump. Electromotive force can come from a dry cell. Moving water can turn a wheel. Moving electricity can turn a motor.

► **How is an electric wire like a water pipe?**

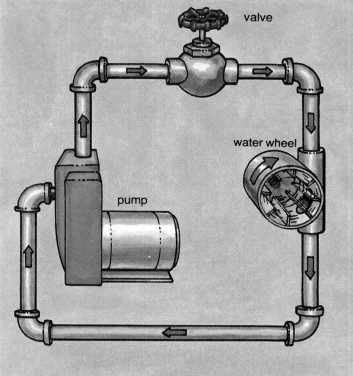

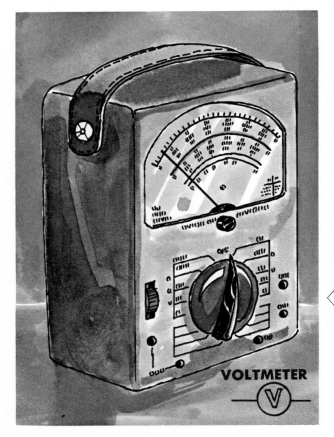

VOLTMETER

⇔ **How can you measure electromotive force?** EMF is measured in volts. A voltmeter (VOHLT-mee-ter) will tell you how many volts of EMF are pushing the electrons along in a circuit.

► **What can you use to measure the voltage in a circuit?**

Using the voltmeter. A voltmeter is always connected in parallel in a circuit. The needle on the voltmeter dial points to the number of volts.

▶ **How should a voltmeter be connected in a circuit?**

VOLTMETERS ARE CONNECTED IN PARALLEL

WHAT YOU LEARNED

1. Electromotive force is measured with a voltmeter.
2. A voltmeter is connected in parallel in a circuit.

SCIENCE WORD

voltmeter (VOHLT-mee-ter)
an instrument for measuring electromotive force

ANSWER THIS

Complete the chart showing how electricity is like water.

Electricity	Water	
electrons	are like	_____
_____	is like	moving water
wire	is like	_____
_____	is like	valve
electrical cell	is like	_____
_____	is like	water pressure
motor	is like	_____

Making Wet Cells

You can make a wet cell from a lemon and two different metal strips. The lemon juice will be the electrolyte. The metal strips will be the electrodes. The skin of the lemon will be the case that holds everything together. The juicier the lemon, the better the wet cell will work.

First attach wires to the ends of a strip of copper and a strip of zinc. Then stick the copper strip into one end of the lemon. Stick the zinc strip into the other end. Use a voltmeter to measure the EMF of your "lemon cell." How much voltage does the cell make?

Try using other metals for the electrodes. You can try an iron nail, a piece of rolled-up aluminum foil, and a brass key. Remember that the two electrodes must be different metals. Does the voltage change when you use different pairs of electrodes?

Try making electrical cells with different fruits and vegetables. You could use an orange, a grapefruit, a tomato, and a potato. Use the voltmeter to find out if changing the fruit or vegetable makes the voltage change.

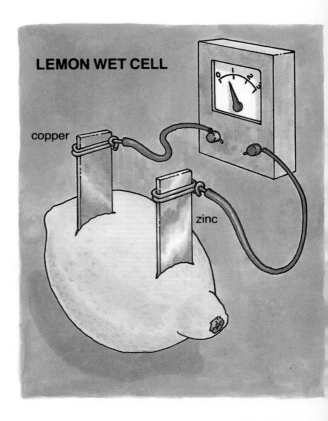

LEMON WET CELL

copper

zinc

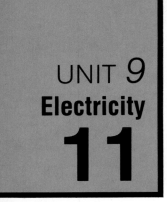

What is resistance?

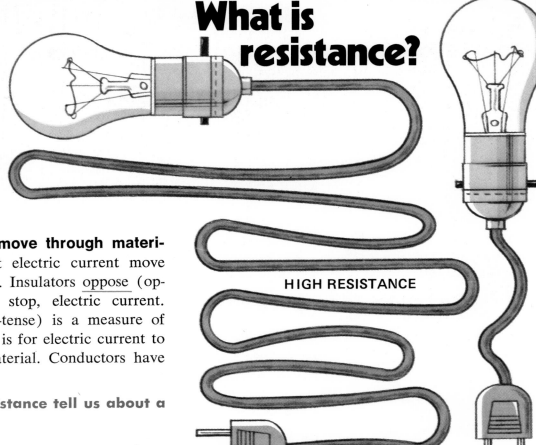

HIGH RESISTANCE

LOW RESISTANCE

Electric currents move through materials. Conductors let electric current move through them easily. Insulators oppose (op-POZE), or try to stop, electric current. Resistance (ree-ZIS-tense) is a measure of how easy or hard it is for electric current to move through a material. Conductors have low resistance.

▶ **What does resistance tell us about a material?**

Wires can have different amounts of resistance. The electric currents you are studying move mostly through wires. All wires do not have the same resistance. The resistance of a wire depends on four things:

1. the length of the wire
2. the thickness of the wire
3. the material the wire is made of
4. the temperature of the wire

▶ **What does the resistance of a wire depend on?**

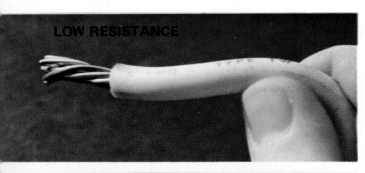

LOW RESISTANCE

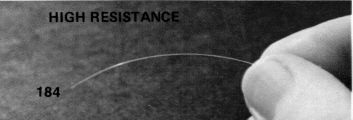

HIGH RESISTANCE

The length of the wire. The longer a wire is, the greater its resistance. Suppose you use a long extension cord to plug in a lamp. Then less electric current will go through the wire. The wire has greater resistance when you make it longer.

▶ **Which has more resistance, a long wire or a short wire?**

The thickness of the wire. The thinner a wire is, the greater its resistance. Have you ever seen power lines along a road or in the basement of a building? The power lines, or cables, are very thick. Thin wires have too much resistance to carry large amounts of current. The thick cables have low resistance. Large electric currents can move through them easily.

▶ **Which has more resistance, a thick wire or a thin wire?**

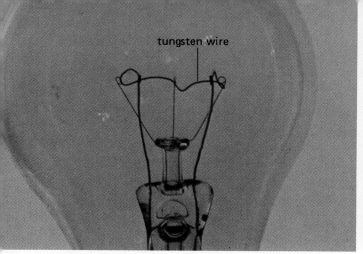

tungsten wire

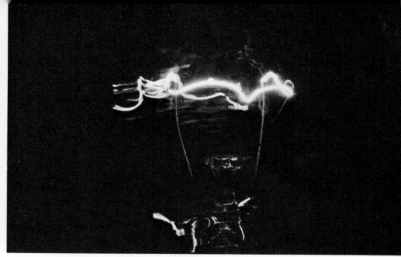

The material the wire is made of. Wires can be made of different materials. Some materials are better conductors than others. Copper is a very good conductor. Aluminum is also a good conductor. Both copper and aluminum have low resistance. Wires made of copper or aluminum are used to carry electric current across long distances.

Nichrome (NY-crome) is a metal. Nichrome is a conductor, but it has a higher resistance than copper or aluminum. When a large electric current goes through a nichrome wire, the wire gets hot. Toasters and electric heaters use wires made of nichrome. Tungsten (TUNG-sten) is another metal that has a higher resistance than copper or aluminum. Like nichrome, tungsten also gets hot when a large electric current moves through it. Wires made of tungsten are used in light bulbs. When you switch on a light bulb, the tungsten gets so hot that it glows.

▶ **What material is good for making the wires in a toaster?**

The temperature of the wire. When a wire is cooled, its resistance gets lower. Some materials lose all their resistance at very low temperatures. These materials are called superconductors (SOO-per-con-DUCK-ters). Mercury is a good conductor at ordinary temperatures. It becomes a superconductor at 270° below zero Celsius.

▶ **Which has more resistance, a hot wire or a cold wire made of the same metal?**

WHAT YOU LEARNED

1. Resistance is a measure of how easy or hard it is for electric current to move through a material.
2. Conductors have low resistance, and insulators have high resistance.
3. The resistance of a wire depends on its length, its thickness, the material it is made of, and its temperature.

SCIENCE WORDS

oppose (op-POZE)
  try to stop
resistance (ree-ZIS-tense)
  a measure of how easy or hard it is for electric current to move through a material
nichrome (NY-crome)
  a high-resistance metal used to make wires for toasters
tungsten (TUNG-sten)
  a high-resistance metal used to make wires for light bulbs
superconductor (SOO-per-con-DUCK-ter)
  a material that loses all its resistance when it is very cold

ANSWER THESE

Which wire in each pair has more resistance?
1. **a.** a long, thin copper wire
   b. a long, thick copper wire
2. **a.** a thin, 10-centimeter copper wire
   b. a thin, 10-centimeter nichrome wire
3. **a.** a 10-centimeter aluminum wire at 75°C
   b. the same 10-centimeter aluminum wire at 0°C

What is Ohm's law?

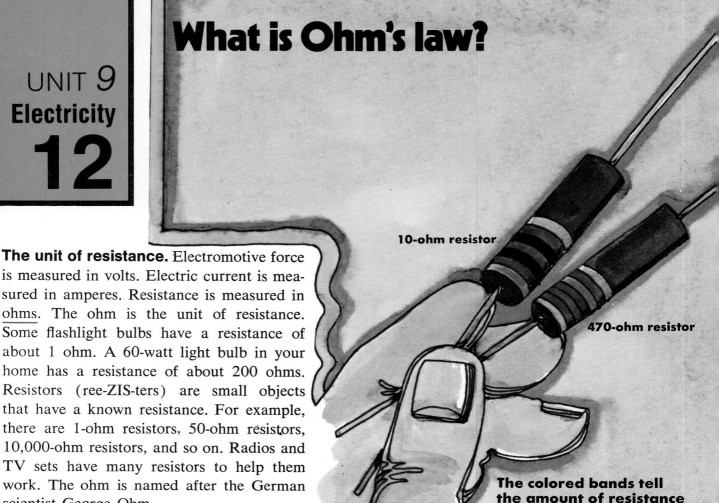

10-ohm resistor

470-ohm resistor

The colored bands tell the amount of resistance according to a special code

The unit of resistance. Electromotive force is measured in volts. Electric current is measured in amperes. Resistance is measured in ohms. The ohm is the unit of resistance. Some flashlight bulbs have a resistance of about 1 ohm. A 60-watt light bulb in your home has a resistance of about 200 ohms. Resistors (ree-ZIS-ters) are small objects that have a known resistance. For example, there are 1-ohm resistors, 50-ohm resistors, 10,000-ohm resistors, and so on. Radios and TV sets have many resistors to help them work. The ohm is named after the German scientist George Ohm.

▶ **What is an ohm?**

Electrical shorthand. Like chemists, physicists use a kind of shorthand to write things down. Here are the electrical symbols that physicists use:

	SYMBOL	UNIT
electromotive force	V	volt
electric current	I	ampere
resistance	R	ohm

▶ **What are the symbols for EMF, electric current, and resistance?**

Ohm's law. George Ohm found that the electric current in a circuit is affected by the EMF and the resistance. He described the effect by a scientific rule, or law. Ohm's law says that the electric current in a circuit is equal to the EMF divided by the resistance. This is how Ohm's law can be written down:

OHM'S LAW

$$\text{electric current (amperes)} = \frac{\text{electromotive force (volts)}}{\text{resistance (ohms)}}$$

$$I = \frac{V}{R}$$

▶ **What is Ohm's law?**

Testing Ohm's law. Connect two dry cells together to make a 3-volt battery. Connect the battery to a 1-ohm resistor. Ohm's law predicts (pree-DICTS) that there will be a current of 3 amperes.

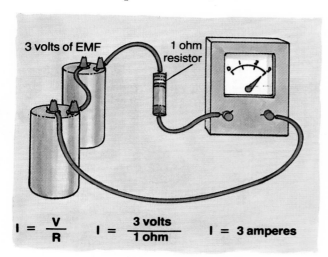

$$I = \frac{V}{R} \qquad I = \frac{3 \text{ volts}}{1 \text{ ohm}} \qquad I = 3 \text{ amperes}$$

Add an ammeter to the circuit. What is the reading on the ammeter? Did Ohm's law predict the amount of current correctly?

▶ **How can you test Ohm's law?**

Changing EMF. Disconnect one of the dry cells from the circuit you made. With one dry cell, the circuit now has an EMF of 1½ volts. How will this affect the amount of current? Look at the ammeter. Does it read 1½ amperes? Ohm's law will give you the same answer. When the EMF in a circuit is decreased, the electric current is also decreased.

▶ **What happens when you decrease the EMF in a circuit?**

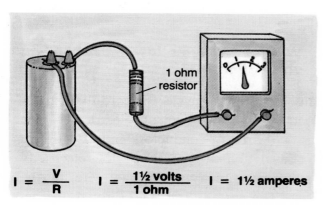

$$I = \frac{V}{R} \qquad I = \frac{1½ \text{ volts}}{1 \text{ ohm}} \qquad I = 1½ \text{ amperes}$$

WHAT YOU LEARNED

1. Resistance is measured in ohms.
2. Ohm's law says that the electric current in a circuit is equal to the EMF divided by the resistance.

SCIENCE WORDS

ohm
the unit of resistance
predict (pree-DICT)
tell what will happen

ANSWER THESE 1. Complete the chart.

	Symbol	Unit
EMF		
	I	
		ohm

PLEASE DO NOT WRITE IN THIS BOOK.

2. How much current will flow in a flashlight that has a 6-volt battery and a bulb with 3 ohms of resistance?
3. How much current will flow if a 3-volt battery is used with a bulb that has 3 ohms of resistance?
4. Most homes use 110-volt electricity. Suppose a toaster has 10 ohms of resistance. How much current will flow through the toaster when it is plugged in?

NOW TRY THIS

There are 15 words about electricity hidden in the square of letters below. See if you can find them all. You can read across or down to find the words.

```
O A B C F U S E I Q
H D E M F E W F N R
M B E L L G I H S S
C U R R E N T K U C
W I R E I J C L L I
C O P P E R H M A R
N A M M E T E R T C
E L E C T R O N O U
O W E T C E L L R I
S H O C K P V O L T
```

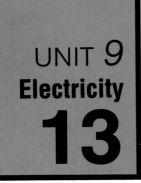

What happens when the resistance is changed in an electric circuit?

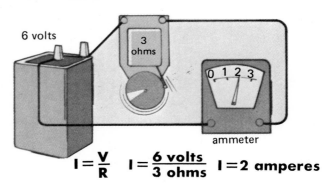

6 volts

3 ohms

0 1 2 3

ammeter

$$I = \frac{V}{R} \quad I = \frac{6 \text{ volts}}{3 \text{ ohms}} \quad I = 2 \text{ amperes}$$

Increasing resistance. What happens in an electric circuit when the resistance is made larger? An experiment like the one in this drawing can tell the answer.

When another bell is added to the circuit, the resistance is increased. The electric current gets smaller. Ohm's law predicts what will happen to the electric current. Ohm's law gives the same answer as the ammeter.

▶ **What happens to the electric current in a circuit when you double the resistance?**

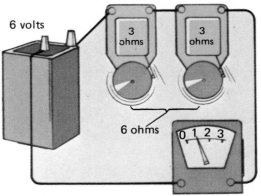

6 volts

3 ohms

3 ohms

6 ohms

0 1 2 3

$$I = \frac{V}{R} \quad I = \frac{6 \text{ volts}}{6 \text{ ohms}} \quad I = 1 \text{ ampere}$$

Using Ohm's law. Ohm's law can predict the current in any simple electric circuit. Here is an example: An electric toaster has a resistance of 10 ohms. An electric light bulb has a resistance of 100 ohms. Both use 110-volt electricity. Which uses more electric current? Ohm's law can tell you the answer.

▶ **What can Ohm's law tell about an electric current?**

Short circuits. The electric cord that carries electricity to and from an electrical device has two wires, or conductors, in it. Each wire has insulation around it, so the electricity cannot go directly from one wire to the other. The current has to go through the device.

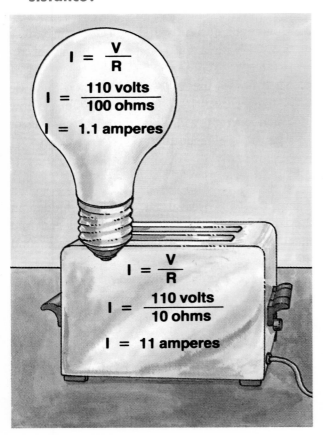

$$I = \frac{V}{R}$$

$$I = \frac{110 \text{ volts}}{100 \text{ ohms}}$$

$$I = 1.1 \text{ amperes}$$

$$I = \frac{V}{R}$$

$$I = \frac{110 \text{ volts}}{10 \text{ ohms}}$$

$$I = 11 \text{ amperes}$$

Sometimes the insulation of an electric cord gets torn or broken. Then the two wires may touch. If that happens, the current can go directly from one wire to the other. It doesn't have to go through the electrical device. This is called a short circuit.

A short circuit has a very low resistance. Ohm's law tells us that a very large current will flow through a short circuit. You remember that a large current can make wires very hot. The hot wires in a short circuit could start a fire.

▶ **Why is a short circuit dangerous?**

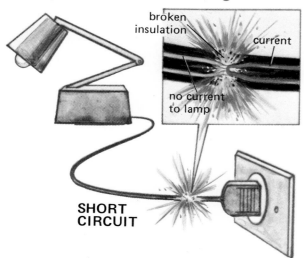

broken insulation

current

no current to lamp

SHORT CIRCUIT

Fuses. The fuses in your home protect against short circuits. Fuses are connected in series with the electrical circuits in your home. When a short circuit occurs, the large current flows through a fuse. The large current heats the fuse and makes it melt, or "blow." This opens the circuit, and stops the flow of current. A fuse blows so quickly that the wires in the circuit don't have a chance to get hot.

▶ **What happens to a fuse when a short circuit occurs?**

WHAT YOU LEARNED

1. When the resistance is increased in a circuit, the current becomes smaller.
2. A "short circuit" has very low resistance.
3. A fuse opens a circuit when there is too much current.

SCIENCE WORDS

short circuit
a short electrical path that has very low resistance

ANSWER THESE

1. What law tells what will happen in an electric circuit?
2. What can happen when there is a short circuit?
3. What device protects us from the dangers of short circuits?

NOW TRY THIS

Ohm's law can help you find the EMF, the current, or the resistance in an electric circuit. To find any one of them, you must know the other two. The circle shows how to use Ohm's law. Cover what you want to find. Then follow the signs to divide or multiply the other two. That will give you the correct answer.

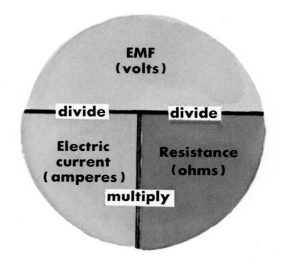

EMF (volts)

divide   divide

Electric current (amperes)   Resistance (ohms)

multiply

Use the circle to help you answer these questions:
1. An electric drill uses 110 volts and 1 ampere of electricity. How much resistance does it have?
2. An electric fan uses 110 volts and has 110 ohms of resistance. How much electric current does it use?
3. A TV set has 55 ohms of resistance, and uses 2 amperes of current. What is the voltage?

Do the following questions on a separate sheet of paper.

Fill in the Blank   *Write down the statements in Column I. Where there is a blank line in each statement, write the word or phrase from Column II that best completes the meaning of the statement.*

Column I	Column II
1. Torn insulation can cause a _____.	electrode
2. A short circuit can cause a _____.	tungsten
3. A metal with a high resistance is_____.	short circuit
4. A metal with a low resistance is_____.	volts
5. EMF is measured in _____.	electrolyte
6. Electric current is measured in _____.	blown fuse
7. A closed circuit is _____.	complete
8. An open circuit is_____.	amperes
9. Zinc is used as a(n) _____.	copper
10. Dilute sulfuric acid is used as a(n) _____.	incomplete

Multiple Choice   *Write the letter of the choice that best completes the statement or answers the question.*

1. A conductor is a material that
   a. electricity cannot pass through
   b. provides insulation
   c. electricity can pass through

2. When you turn on a light, you are
   a. closing a circuit
   b. opening a circuit
   c. causing a short-circuit

3. An electric current is made of
   a. solar energy
   b. a stream of neutral particles
   c. moving electric charges

4. A dry cell has a
   a. liquid electrolyte
   b. moist electrolyte
   c. dry electrolyte

5. A parallel circuit has more than one
   a. switch
   b. path for electricity to follow
   c. electrical device hooked up to it

6. Two 2-volt cells connected in parallel will give
   a. 2 volts
   b. 3 volts
   c. 4 volts

7. Superconductors lose all their resistance at very
   a. high temperatures
   b. low temperatures
   c. small thicknesses

8. Resistance is measured in
   a. amperes
   b. ohms
   c. volts

10 Magnetism

Unit Lessons

1. What is a magnet?
2. How can magnetism be explained?
3. What is a magnetic field?
4. How is the earth like a magnet?
5. How can magnetism be destroyed?
6. How can magnetism be made with electricity?
7. How can you make an electromagnet stronger?
8. How can you make electricity with a magnet?
9. How can an electromagnet induce electricity?
10. What is a transformer?

Goals and Objectives

After completing this unit, you should be able to:

- tell which materials are magnetic and which are not.
- describe how an iron nail can be made into a magnet.
- explain why some materials are magnetic.
- demonstrate the existence of a magnetic field.
- explain what is meant by the North and South magnetic poles.
- describe how electricity and magnetism are related.
- differentiate between direct and alternating current.

What is a magnet?

What does a magnet attract? Find out what things are attracted to a magnet. Hold a magnet over paper, wood, glass, copper, lead, and tin. None of these things is attracted to the magnet. Hold the magnet over an iron nail. The nail is attracted to the magnet. Only three metals are attracted to a magnet. They are iron, nickel, and cobalt (COH-bawlt). Some materials made from these metals will also be attracted to a magnet.

▶ **What three metals are attracted to a magnet?**

The poles of a magnet. The picture shows a bar magnet. The ends of a magnet are called its poles. Test a bar magnet to see which part of it is strongest. Spread some paper clips on a table. The paper clips are made of steel, which is mostly iron. The clips will be attracted to the magnet. Lower the magnet over the paper clips. Where do most of the paper clips stick to the magnet? Most of the clips stick to the magnet at its poles. The poles of a magnet have the strongest magnetism.

▶ **Where is a magnet strongest?**

iron

cobalt

nickel

POLES

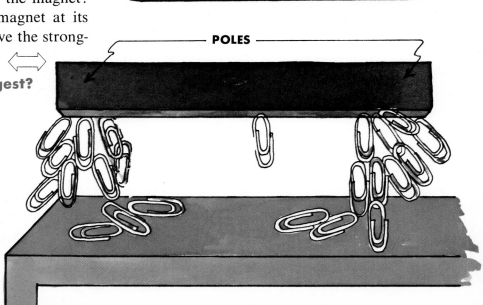

North and south poles. Make a mark at one end of a bar magnet, and hang the magnet from a string. Tie the string around the middle of the magnet. See which way the marked end of the magnet is pointing when the magnet stops swinging. Then give the magnet a little push and let it come to rest again. The marked end of the magnet will point in the same direction again.

One pole of the magnet always points toward the north. This is the north-seeking pole, or simply the north pole, of the magnet. The other end of the magnet points south. This is the south-seeking, or south, pole. Every magnet has a north pole and a south pole.

▶ **Which pole of a magnet points toward the north?**

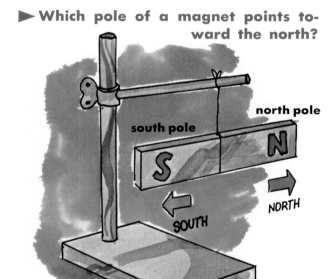

The law of magnetic poles. Place two bar magnets on a smooth table. Push the north pole of one magnet toward the south pole of the other. The two magnets stick together. North and south are unlike poles. Unlike magnetic poles attract each other. Try to put the two north poles together. They repel each other. Try the two south poles. They also repel each other. Like magnetic poles always repel each other. The law of magnetic poles says that unlike magnetic poles attract, and like magnetic poles repel.

▶ **What is the law of magnetic poles?**

WHAT YOU LEARNED

1. A magnet attracts only iron, nickel, and cobalt.
2. A magnet is strongest at its poles.
3. Unlike magnetic poles attract; like magnetic poles repel.

SCIENCE WORD

poles
the ends of a magnet

ANSWER THESE

1. A magnet attracts
   a. all metals
   b. iron, zinc, and tin
   c. iron, cobalt, and nickel
2. The strength of a magnet is
   a. greatest in the middle
   b. greatest at the poles
   c. the same all over
3. Like magnetic poles
   a. attract each other
   b. repel each other
   c. have no effect on each other
4. Unlike magnetic poles
   a. attract each other
   b. repel each other
   c. have no effect on each other

LOOKING BACK IN SCIENCE

Hundreds of years ago, sailors found an important use for magnets. They discovered that a magnet could help them find directions at sea. No matter where they were, the magnet would always show them which way was north. The sailors put the magnet inside a device called a compass. Today, magnetic compasses help people find directions on land, at sea, and in the air.

WHAT'S HAPPENING

Did you ever see a pair of small plastic dogs that do tricks? When you move one dog near the other one, sometimes they jump together. Other times, one dog may spin around or jump away. It all depends on which way the dogs are pointing. Can you guess what makes the dogs do their tricks? Each dog has a metal base. What metal do you think might be used to make the base?

How can magnetism be explained?

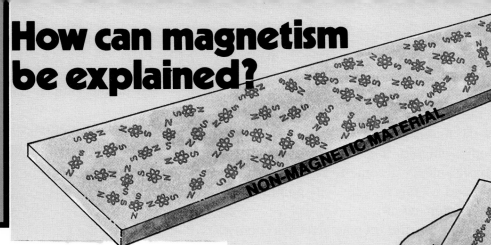

NON-MAGNETIC MATERIAL

Magnetic materials. Atoms may have north and south magnetic poles. Some atoms act like tiny magnets. In most materials, the atoms are not lined up in any special way. They point in all different directions. They cancel out each other's magnetism. The material is not magnetic.

Iron, cobalt, and nickel are magnetic materials. Their atoms can be lined up so that many of them face the same way. When many of the atoms face the same way, the material becomes a good magnet.

▶ **How are the atoms arranged in a magnet?**

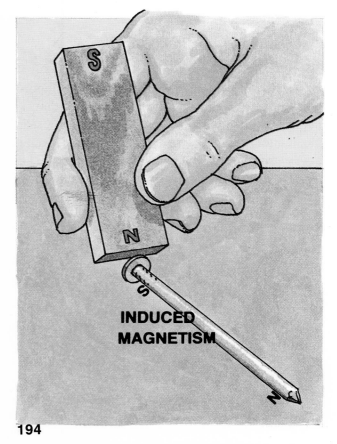

INDUCED MAGNETISM

MAGNETIC MATERIAL

Making a magnet. Hold one end of a bar magnet near one end of an iron nail. The magnet attracts the nail. Some of the atoms in the iron nail turn. Their north and south poles line up. The nail becomes a magnet. If the north pole of the magnet is used, the end of the nail that is near it will be a south pole. Magnetism that is made this way is called induced (in-DOOSED) magnetism.

▶ **How can you turn an iron nail into a magnet?**

194

Making a stronger magnet. Rub one end of a bar magnet along an iron nail. Do it 10 times. Rub in the same direction each time, not back and forth. The rubbing will magnetize (MAG-nuh-tize) the nail, or make it into a magnet. Each time you rub the magnet along the nail, some of the atoms in the nail line up. The more atoms that line up, the more magnetism the nail will get. Suppose you are using the north pole of the magnet. Then the end of the nail that the magnet touches last will be a south pole.

▶ **What is a good way to magnetize an iron nail?**

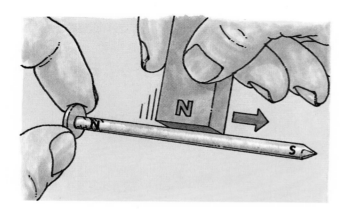

Using the earth to make a magnet. The earth acts like a large magnet. Point an iron rod north. The rod is lined up with the earth's magnetism. A few of the atoms in the rod may be lined up in the same direction. Hit the end of the iron rod with a hammer. Now some more of the atoms in the rod may line up. If you point an iron rod north and hit it with a hammer, you can make it into a magnet.

▶ **How can you use the earth to make a magnet?**

WHAT YOU LEARNED

1. Atoms may act like tiny magnets.
2. In a magnetic material, the atoms can line up so their poles face the same way.
3. Many atoms facing the same way make a magnet.
4. Magnets can be made by using other magnets.

SCIENCE WORDS

induced (in-DOOSED) magnetism
    magnetism caused by touching or being near a magnet
magnetize (MAG-nuh-tize)
    make into a magnet

ANSWER THESE

1. In most materials, the north and south poles of atoms
    a. all point in the same direction
    b. point in many different directions
    c. are made of iron
2. A magnet can be made by
    a. heating an iron nail
    b. rubbing an iron nail with a magnet
    c. placing an iron nail in the earth
3. The earth acts as if it were
    a. a huge atom
    b. a huge compass
    c. a huge magnet

NOW TRY THIS

The Floating Paper Clip

One day a magician showed some people a trick. He made a paper clip float in the air. The paper clip had a thread attached to the bottom, but not the top. The picture shows what the trick looked like.

Someone wanted to look inside the box that was over the clip. But the magician wouldn't let him. He said a mysterious substance was in the box. See if you can guess the magician's trick.

1. What do you think was in the box?
2. Why did the paper clip have a thread at the bottom?
3. What was holding up the paper clip?

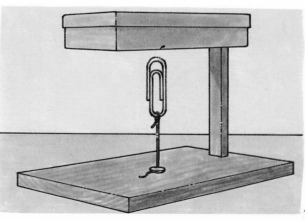

What is a magnetic field?

Seeing magnetic fields. There is an invisible pattern of magnetism around every magnet. This pattern is called a <u>magnetic field</u> (mag-NET-ic FEELD). There is a way you can see this magnetic field. Place a sheet of paper over a bar magnet. Sprinkle some iron filings on the paper. Then tap the paper gently.

You will see the iron filings make a pattern on the paper. This is a picture of the magnetic field of the magnet. The lines you see are called <u>lines of force</u>. They are closest together at the poles of the magnet. A magnet is strongest at the poles. You can tell where the magnet's poles are by looking at the lines of force.

► **What is a magnetic field?**

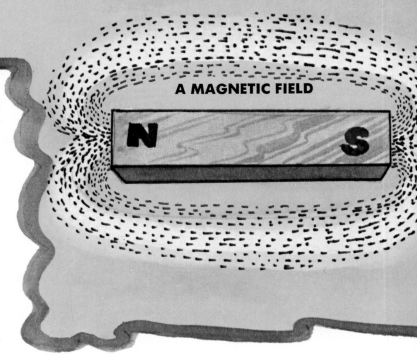

A MAGNETIC FIELD

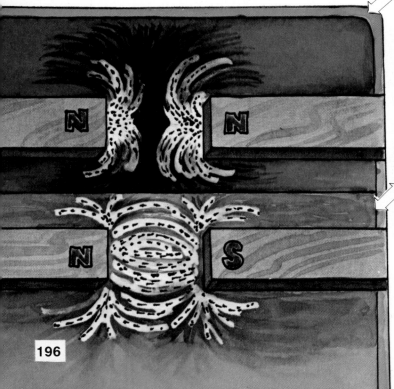

Magnetic fields affect each other. Put the north poles of two bar magnets near each other, without letting them touch. Then make a picture of their magnetic fields with paper and iron filings. The picture shows that the magnetic fields bend away from each other. You learned in another lesson that like magnetic poles repel each other. The lines of force show this.

Now arrange the magnets so that unlike poles are facing each other. Make a picture of the magnetic fields now. The lines of force snow that the two unlike poles attract each other.

Every magnet has a magnetic field around it. The magnetic field of one magnet affects the magnetic field of another magnet.

► **What do the lines of force show when two magnetic poles are near each other?**

196

WHAT YOU LEARNED

1. Every magnet has a magnetic field around it.
2. Magnetic fields affect each other.

SCIENCE WORDS

magnetic field (mag-NET-ic FEELD)
   the pattern of magnetism around a magnet
lines of force
   the lines that show a magnetic field

ANSWER THESE

1. Magnetic fields are
   a. weakest at the poles of a magnet
   b. strongest at the poles of a magnet
   c. visible when they go through paper
2. Pictures of magnetic fields
   a. can help you find magnetic poles
   b. show the difference between north and south poles
   c. are all the same

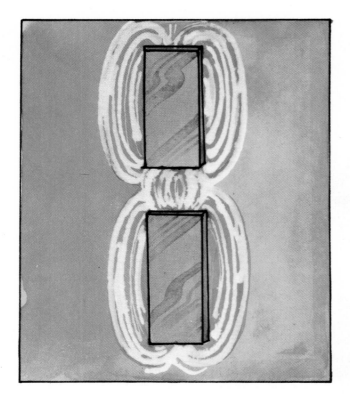

3. This picture of a magnetic field shows
   a. two north poles facing each other
   b. two south poles facing each other
   c. a north pole and a south pole facing each other

NOW TRY THIS

Here are some pictures of magnetic fields. In each picture, one of the magnetic poles is labeled. Copy each picture and then label the other pole.

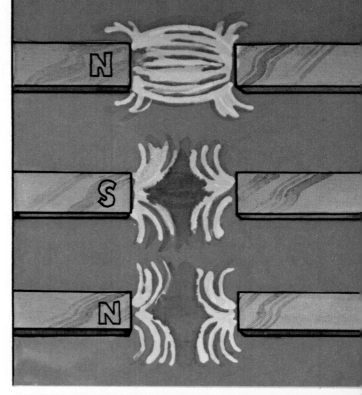

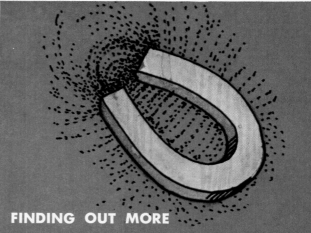

FINDING OUT MORE

Horseshoe Magnets

The picture shows the magnetic field around a horseshoe magnet. See if you can answer the following question by studying the picture: Why can a horseshoe magnet pick up more iron than a bar magnet of the same strength?

How is the earth like a magnet?

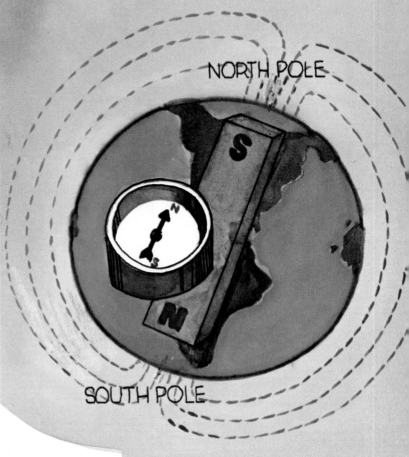

The earth is like a magnet. The earth acts as if it had a very big bar magnet inside it. The earth has two magnetic poles, just like any magnet. One of the earth's magnetic poles is in Canada. It is about 2000 kilometers from the earth's North Pole. This magnetic pole is called the North Magnetic Pole, because it is in the north. The other magnetic pole of the earth is near the South Pole. This is called the South Magnetic Pole.

▶ What are the two magnetic poles of the earth called?

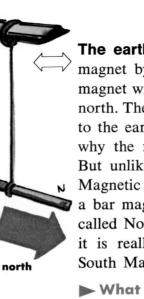

The earth's magnetic poles. Hang a bar magnet by a string around its middle. The magnet will turn so its north pole is pointing north. The north pole of a magnet is attracted to the earth's North Magnetic Pole. That is why the magnet's north pole points north. But unlike poles attract. The earth's North Magnetic Pole must be like the south pole of a bar magnet! The North Magnetic Pole is called North because it is in the north. But it is really a south pole. And the earth's South Magnetic Pole is really a north pole.

▶ What kind of magnetic pole is the North Magnetic Pole?

The magnetic compass. A magnetic compass is used to find directions. It could not work if the earth did not act like a magnet.

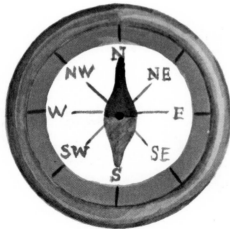

The north pole of the magnet in the compass is attracted to the earth's North Magnetic Pole. It points to the north. At almost every place on earth, the compass can tell you which way north is. The compass does not point exactly north. It points to the North Magnetic Pole.

▶ **Where does a magnetic compass point?**

WHAT YOU LEARNED

1. The earth acts like a magnet.
2. The North Magnetic Pole of the earth is really a south magnetic pole.
3. A magnetic compass points to the North Magnetic Pole.

ANSWER THESE

1. The earth acts as if it had
   a. a large compass inside it
   b. a large dry cell inside it
   c. a large magnet inside it
2. The north pole of a magnetic compass points to the earth's
   a. South Magnetic Pole
   b. North Pole
   c. North Magnetic Pole
3. The North Pole and the North Magnetic Pole of the earth are
   a. in exactly the same place
   b. about 2000 kilometers apart
   c. at opposite ends of the earth

WHAT'S HAPPENING

The Gyroscope

You may have seen or used a toy gyroscope (JY-ruh-scope). A gyroscope is a kind of top. When a gyroscope is spinning fast, it stays pointed in one direction. The faster it spins, the harder it is to change the way it is pointing.

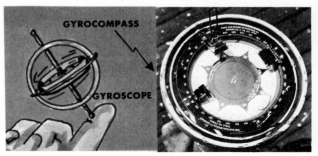

But a gyroscope is not just a toy. It can be used to make a kind of compass. A motor makes the gyroscope spin very fast. The gyroscope is pointed north. As long as it is spinning fast, the gyroscope will keep pointing north. This kind of compass is called a gyrocompass (JY-roh-com-pus). It can be used instead of a magnetic compass on ships, planes, and submarines.

Make a Magnetic Compass

Rub a sewing needle several times against a magnet. Rub the needle in the same direction each time. This will magnetize the needle. Then put a thumbtack in the bottom of a cork. Put the cork into a bowl of water, with the tack down. Now lay the needle down on top of the cork. When the needle stops turning, it will be pointed north and south. Give the needle a little push to start it turning again. It will point north and south again when it stops.

How can magnetism be destroyed?

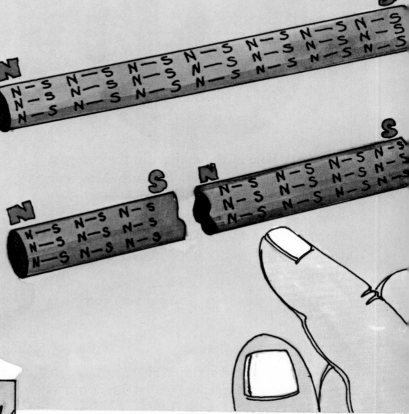

What happens when you break a magnet? Magnetize an iron wire by rubbing it with a magnet. Test it by seeing if it will pick up a paper clip. See if one end of the magnet you made will attract one end of a compass needle. It should also repel the other end of the compass needle.

Now break the magnet you made into two pieces. Test each piece with a compass needle. The test shows that each piece of the broken magnet is a complete magnet by itself. It has a north pole and a south pole. Breaking a magnet does not destroy its magnetism.

▶ **Will a magnet still be a magnet if it is broken in half?**

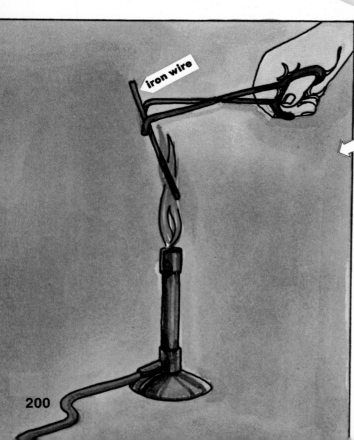

iron wire

What happens when you heat a magnet? Make another magnet out of an iron wire. Use tongs to hold the magnet over a flame. Heat it until it is red hot. Now test it for magnetism with a compass needle. You will see that any part of the wire will attract both ends of the compass needle. The wire is not a magnet any more. It does not have two different poles. When you made the wire into a magnet, you lined up its atoms in a certain way. The heat made the atoms get out of order. They are no longer lined up to make north and south poles. Heating made the wire lose its magnetism.

▶ **Will a magnet still be a magnet if it is heated?**

What happens if you hit a magnet? Hit a magnetized iron wire several times with a hammer. Then test it with a compass needle. Each end of the wire attracts both ends of the compass needle. The wire is not a magnet any more. Hitting the wire made the atoms in it move out of line. The wire lost its magnetism when you hit it. The same thing could happen if you dropped a magnet many times.

▶ **Will a magnet still be a magnet if it is hit with a hammer many times?**

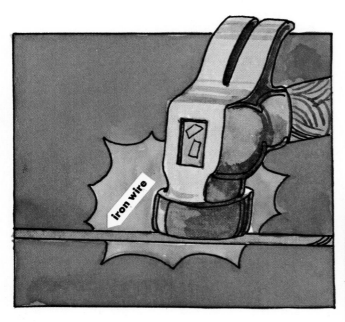

Destroying magnetism. Things made of iron, cobalt, or nickel can become magnets when their atoms are lined up. If the atoms are moved out of line again, the magnetism is destroyed. Dropping, hitting, or heating a magnet can make the atoms move out of line. Any of these things can destroy a magnet's magnetism.

▶ **How can magnetism be destroyed?**

WHAT YOU LEARNED

1. Breaking a magnet does not destroy its magnetism.
2. Hitting or heating a magnet can destroy its magnetism.
3. When the atoms in a magnet get out of line, magnetism is destroyed.

ANSWER THESE

1. When a bar magnet is broken in half,
   a. it loses its magnetism
   b. both halves are magnets
   c. one half has two south poles and the other half has two north poles
2. If one end of an iron wire attracts both ends of a compass needle, then the iron wire
   a. is a magnet
   b. is not a magnet
   c. cannot be used to make a magnet
3. Magnets lose their magnetism when they are
   a. heated
   b. cooled
   c. put in water
4. Dropping a magnet
   a. does not affect it
   b. makes it stronger
   c. makes it weaker

FINDING OUT MORE

Temporary and Permanent Magnets

An iron nail can be magnetized. But it does not keep its magnetism very long. The iron used in nails is called soft iron. A soft iron magnet loses its magnetism quickly. It is called a temporary (TEM-puh-reh-ree) magnet.

Steel is made of iron with some other elements added. When steel is magnetized, it keeps its magnetism a long time. A magnet that keeps its magnetism well is called a permanent (PERM-uh-nent) magnet. Some of the strongest permanent magnets are made of a material called alnico (AL-nih-co). Alnico is a mixture of five metals. It is made of aluminum, nickel, cobalt, copper, and iron. Two of these metals are not magnetic materials. But even so, alnico magnets are many times stronger than iron magnets the same size. And they keep their magnetism well for many years.

How can magnetism be made with electricity?

UNIT 10
Magnetism
6

Oersted's discovery. Many scientific discoveries are made by accident. Hans Christian Oersted (UR-sted) was a Danish scientist and teacher who was born about 200 years ago. One day he was teaching his class about electricity. He showed them a battery with a wire connected to one terminal. Then he connected the other end of the wire to the other terminal. There was a compass on the desk near the wire. When Oersted completed the electric circuit, he saw the compass needle move! When he disconnected the wire, the compass needle moved back to its first position. Nobody had ever noticed this happen before. Oersted wondered why a wire connected to a battery could make a compass needle move.

▶ **What happened to the compass needle when Oersted connected the wire to the battery?**

Oersted's theory. Oersted knew that a compass needle is affected by magnetism. He saw that the compass needle moved when electric current was moving through a wire nearby. So Oersted decided that an electric current must cause magnetism. When he stopped the electric current, the magnetism disappeared. The compass needle moved back to where it was pointing before. Oersted said that whenever there is an electric current, there is magnetism around it.

▶ **What did Oersted discover about electric currents and magnetism?**

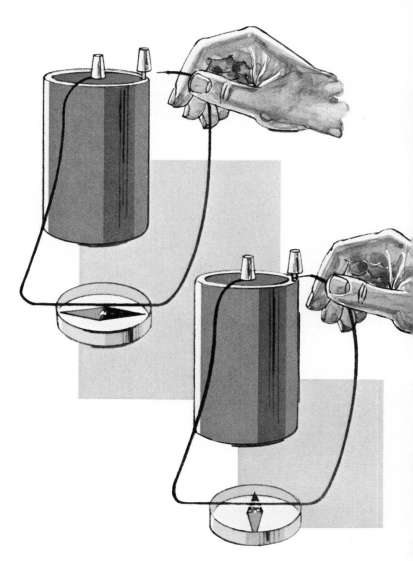

Atoms are tiny magnets. Atoms have electrons moving around their centers. Moving electrons make an electric current. So there are tiny electric currents in every atom. These electric currents produce magnetism. The electrons in an atom move in many different directions. In most atoms, the different magnetic fields of the electrons cancel out. But in magnetic elements, the tiny magnetic fields add together.

▶ **What makes tiny electric currents in atoms?**

202

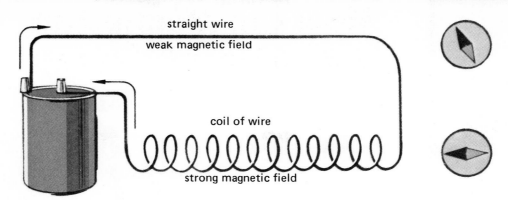

straight wire
weak magnetic field
coil of wire
strong magnetic field

Making a magnet out of wire.

A wire carrying an electric current always has a magnetic field around it. The magnetic field around a straight wire is not very strong. If the wire is wound up into a coil, the magnetic field becomes much stronger. The magnetic fields of all the loops or turns add together. A coil of wire that uses an electric current to make a strong magnetic field is called an <u>electromagnet</u> (e-LEC-tro-MAG-net).

▶ **When is there a magnetic field around a wire?**

Magnets with a difference.

An ordinary magnet can not be turned off. An electromagnet can be turned off. Just stop the current, and the electromagnet stops working. Electromagnets are used to pick up old cars in junkyards. To put the car down, you turn off the current. An electromagnet is like an ordinary magnet in many ways. One way that they are alike is that they both have two poles. One end of an electromagnet is a south pole. The other end is a north pole.

▶ **How many poles does an electromagnet have?**

WHAT YOU LEARNED

1. Every electric current has a magnetic field around it.
2. Moving electrons inside atoms make tiny magnetic fields.
3. An electromagnet is a coil of wire that uses an electric current to make a strong magnetic field.
4. An electromagnet can be turned on and off.

SCIENCE WORD

electromagnet (e-LEC-tro-MAG-net)
a coil of wire that uses an electric current to make a strong magnetic field

ANSWER THESE

1. Who discovered that electric currents have magnetism?
2. What was he doing when he made the discovery?
3. What produces magnetism inside an atom?
4. Why does a coil of wire carrying an electric current have a stronger magnetic field than a straight wire?
5. How is an electromagnet like an ordinary magnet?
6. How is an electromagnet different from an ordinary magnet?

WHAT'S HAPPENING

Swinging Signs

Did you ever see a swinging sign in a store window? Part of the sign keeps swinging back and forth all day. Can you guess what makes it do that?

Behind the sign there is an electromagnet. The part of the sign that swings has an iron rod attached to it. The electromagnet attracts the iron rod, making the moving part of the sign swing toward it. But when the iron rod gets near the electromagnet, a switch opens. The current is turned off, and the electromagnet loses its magnetism. The iron rod swings back. When it gets to the other side, the switch closes again. Now the electromagnet attracts the iron rod again. This keeps happening over and over, and the sign keeps swinging back and forth.

How can you make an electromagnet stronger?

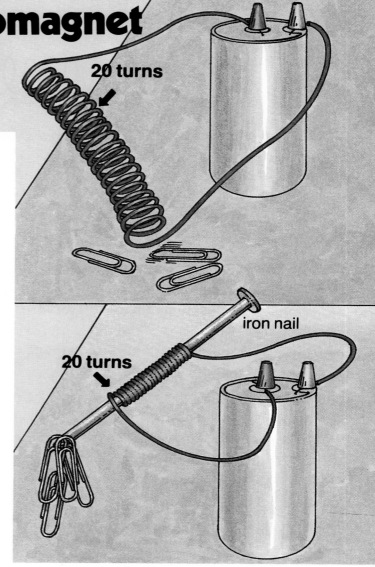

20 turns

iron nail

20 turns

Putting iron inside an electromagnet. Make an electromagnet with 20 turns of wire. Connect it to a 1½-volt dry cell. This electromagnet will probably be too weak to pick up even one paper clip. Now put an iron nail in the center of the coil. Tighten the coil of wire around the nail. With the nail inside it, the electromagnet should be able to pick up a few paper clips.

The iron in the center of the electromagnet is called a core. A core made from a magnetic material makes an electromagnet stronger. Iron, nickel, and cobalt can be used to make cores for electromagnets.

▶ **What materials can be used to make a core for an electromagnet?**

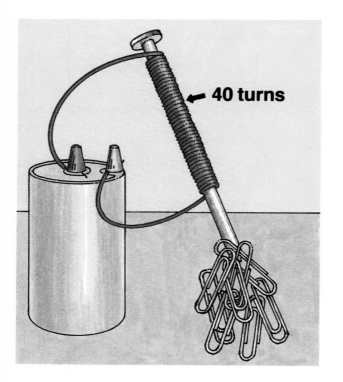

◀ **40 turns**

Increasing the number of turns. Count how many paper clips you can pick up with the electromagnet you made. Then make another electromagnet that has 40 turns of wire instead of 20. Both electromagnets should have an iron core. You will see that the electromagnet with 40 turns is stronger. It can pick up more paper clips than the electromagnet with 20 turns. Adding more turns makes an electromagnet stronger.

▶ **What happens to an electromagnet if you increase the number of turns?**

Increasing the electric current. You have been using one 1½-volt dry cell to test your electromagnets. Now wire two 1½-volt dry cells together in series. This will increase the current to the electromagnet. Connect the electromagnet with 40 turns to the two dry cells. It will pick up more paper clips than before. Increasing the electric current makes an electromagnet stronger.

▶ **What happens when you increase the current in an electromagnet?**

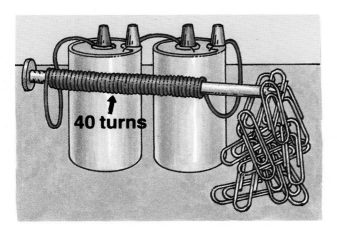

40 turns

WHAT YOU LEARNED

1. A core of magnetic material increases the strength of an electromagnet.
2. Increasing the number of turns increases the strength of an electromagnet.
3. Increasing the electric current increases the strength of an electromagnet.

SCIENCE WORD

core
the material in the center of an electromagnet

ANSWER THESE

Tell which is the stronger electromagnet in each of the following pairs.
1. **a.** an electromagnet with 20 turns
   b. an electromagnet with 40 turns
2. **a.** an electromagnet with an iron core
   b. an electromagnet with no core
3. **a.** an electromagnet with 20 turns that uses 1 ampere of current
   b. an electromagnet with 20 turns that uses 3 amperes of current

FINDING OUT MORE

The Telegraph

One important use for electromagnets is in the telegraph. A telegraph sends messages by means of buzzing sounds. The first telegraph message was sent in 1844 by Samuel Morse. Morse invented the telegraph. He also made up a code for the telegraph, called the Morse code. The most famous Morse code signal is the SOS. This is a call for help. The code for SOS is:

DOT DOT DOT　　DASH DASH DASH　　DOT DOT DOT

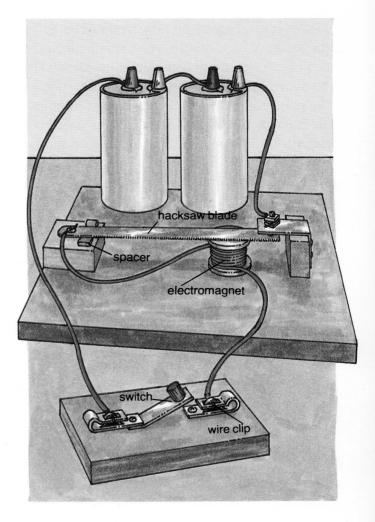

hacksaw blade

spacer

electromagnet

switch

wire clip

DO THIS AT HOME

Use the diagram to help you make a model telegraph buzzer. Practice sending messages with it. You can find the Morse code in a dictionary. Or you can make up your own code.

How can you make electricity with a magnet?

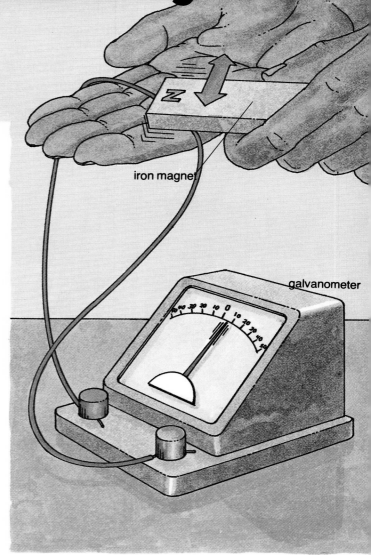

iron magnet

galvanometer

Electricity and magnetism. You know that an electric current has a magnetic field around it. Moving electricity makes magnetism. Can moving magnetism make electricity? Connect both ends of a wire to a galvanometer (gal-va-NOM-uh-ter). The galvanometer will measure very small electric currents. Watch the galvanometer needle while you move an iron bar magnet past the wire. The galvanometer needle moves as you move the magnet. This shows that there is an electric current in the wire. When you stop moving the magnet, the current stops. A moving magnet can make current flow in a wire. An electric current made this way is called an <u>induced</u> (in-DOOSED) <u>current</u>.

▶ **How can a magnet make current flow in a wire?**

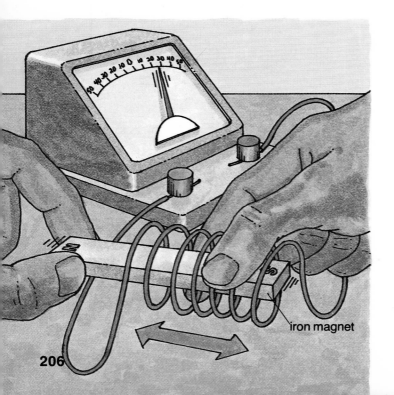

iron magnet

Moving a magnet through a coil. Make a coil out of the wire you have been using. Push the iron bar magnet through the coil. Now the galvanometer shows a larger electric current than before. Coiling the wire increases the amount of electric current. The more turns there are in the coil, the larger the induced current.

▶ **What can you do to a wire to induce a larger current in it?**

206

Using a stronger magnet. Magnets made of alnico are stronger than magnets made of iron. Move an alnico bar magnet through the coil of wire you made. The galvanometer shows a larger current than you got with the iron magnet. Using a stronger magnet induces a larger current in a wire.

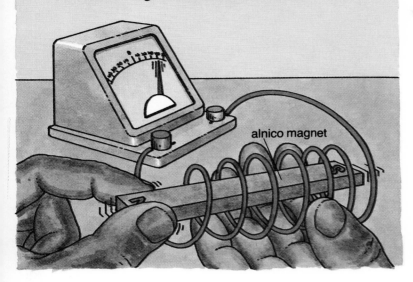

alnico magnet

▶ **How does the kind of magnet you use affect the current induced in a wire?**

Moving the magnet faster. Move a bar magnet slowly back and forth inside the wire coil. Watch the galvanometer needle. Now move the same magnet back and forth quickly in the coil. The galvanometer needle moves farther when you move the magnet quickly. A larger current is induced by the fast-moving magnet. Moving a magnet faster increases the current induced in a wire.

▶ **How does the speed of a moving magnet affect the current it induces?**

WHAT YOU LEARNED

1. A moving magnetic field can induce an electric current in a wire.
2. Induced electric currents can be made stronger by coiling the wire, using a stronger magnet, or moving the magnet faster.

SCIENCE WORDS

galvanometer (gal-va-NOM-uh-ter)
 a tool for measuring very small electric currents
induced (in-DOOSED) **current**
 an electric current made by a moving magnetic field

ANSWER THESE

1. A moving magnetic field
    a. changes its poles
    b. induces an electric current
    c. loses its power
2. Moving a magnet faster in a coil
    a. increases its magnetism
    b. increases the induced electric current
    c. decreases the induced electric current
3. A stronger magnet induces
    a. a weaker electric current
    b. a weaker magnetic field
    c. a stronger electric current
4. To induce a larger electric current,
    a. use a straight wire
    b. use a coil of wire
    c. do not use any wire

PEOPLE IN SCIENCE

Thomas Dawson

Thomas Dawson, an American Indian, is an electrical engineer and inventor. He has worked as an aircraft flight test engineer. In 1963 he joined M.I.T.'s Laboratory for Nuclear Science. At M.I.T. he has been involved in the Mariner, Pioneer, and Explorer space programs. Mr. Dawson has invented several devices that are currently used in space program projects.

How can an electromagnet induce electricity?

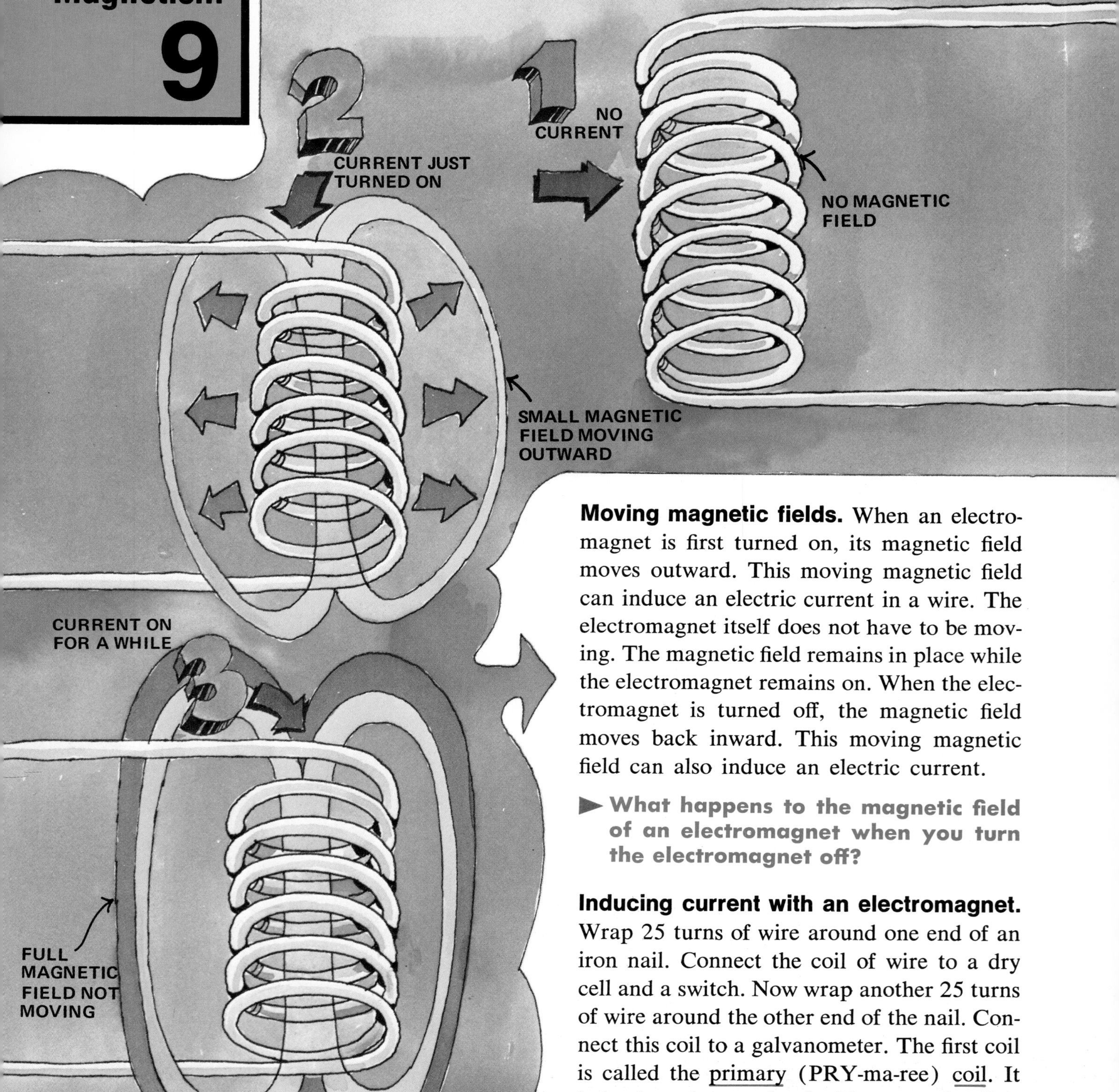

2

CURRENT JUST
TURNED ON

1

NO
CURRENT

NO MAGNETIC
FIELD

SMALL MAGNETIC
FIELD MOVING
OUTWARD

CURRENT ON
FOR A WHILE

3

FULL
MAGNETIC
FIELD NOT
MOVING

Moving magnetic fields. When an electromagnet is first turned on, its magnetic field moves outward. This moving magnetic field can induce an electric current in a wire. The electromagnet itself does not have to be moving. The magnetic field remains in place while the electromagnet remains on. When the electromagnet is turned off, the magnetic field moves back inward. This moving magnetic field can also induce an electric current.

▶ **What happens to the magnetic field of an electromagnet when you turn the electromagnet off?**

Inducing current with an electromagnet. Wrap 25 turns of wire around one end of an iron nail. Connect the coil of wire to a dry cell and a switch. Now wrap another 25 turns of wire around the other end of the nail. Connect this coil to a galvanometer. The first coil is called the <u>primary</u> (PRY-ma-ree) <u>coil</u>. It is in the primary circuit. The second coil is the <u>secondary</u> (SEC-un-DER-ree) <u>coil</u>. It is in the secondary circuit.

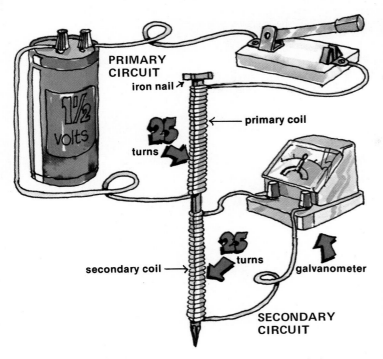

PRIMARY
CIRCUIT

iron nail

primary coil

25 turns

secondary coil

25 turns

galvanometer

SECONDARY
CIRCUIT

Close the switch in the primary circuit. The galvanometer shows a current in the secondary circuit. But the current lasts only a moment. Now open the switch in the primary circuit again. Again there is a current in the secondary circuit for a short time. Whenever the current in the primary circuit is turned on or off, there is a current in the secondary circuit. This current lasts only a short time. The magnetic field moving out from or back to the primary coil induces an electric current in the secondary coil. When the magnetic field is steady, there is no current in the secondary coil.

▶ **When can the current in a primary coil induce a current in a secondary coil?**

WHAT YOU LEARNED

1. The magnetic field around an electromagnet moves when the electromagnet is turned on and off.
2. A magnetic field moving out from or back to a primary coil can induce an electric current in a secondary coil.
3. A primary and secondary coil working together make an induction coil.

Primary and secondary coils work together. A primary coil and a secondary coil working together are called an induction (in-DUCK-shun) coil. Induction coils can change high voltage to low voltage. They can also change low voltage to high voltage. The more turns there are in the secondary coil, the higher the voltage that will be induced in it. The spark plugs in a car need very high voltage. But the car's battery is only 12 volts. Induction coils increase the voltage for the spark plugs.

▶ **What is an induction coil?**

spark plug

SCIENCE WORDS

primary (PRY-ma-ree) **coil**
a coil that induces a current in another coil
secondary (SEC-un-DER-ree) **coil**
a coil in which current is induced
induction (in-DUCK-shun) **coil**
a primary and secondary coil working together

ANSWER THESE

1. At the moment the switch in the primary circuit is closed, there is
   a. no current in the primary coil
   b. no current in the secondary coil
   c. a current in the secondary coil
2. After the switch in the primary circuit has been closed for a while, there is
   a. no current in the primary coil
   b. a current in both the primary coil and the secondary coil
   c. a current in the primary coil but not in the secondary coil
3. As soon as the switch in the primary coil is opened, there is
   a. a current in the primary coil
   b. a current in the secondary coil
   c. no current in either coil

What is a transformer?

DIRECT CURRENT

GOES IN ONE DIRECTION

ALTERNATING CURRENT

CHANGES DIRECTION

Different kinds of electric current. There are two kinds of electric current. Direct current moves through a circuit in one direction only. Dry cells produce direct current. Alternating (ALL-ter-NAY-ting) current keeps changing direction in a circuit. It keeps moving back and forth. Alternating current is used in your home.

▶ **What are the two kinds of electric current?**

Inducing currents in a coil. Electricity is induced in an induction coil only when the switch is being opened or closed. A direct current moving steadily through the primary coil will not induce a current in the secondary coil. A transformer (trans-FOR-mer) is a kind of induction coil that uses alternating current. The transformer has a primary coil, a secondary coil, and an iron core. Each time

the current changes direction in the primary coil, a current is induced in the secondary coil. The switch does not have to be turned on and off. The current flowing back and forth in the primary coil keeps inducing currents in the secondary coil.

▶ **What is a transformer?**

Transformers can increase voltage. A transformer can be used to make voltages larger. This is called stepping up the voltage. A step-up transformer has more turns in the secondary coil than in the primary coil. The more turns in the secondary coil, the higher the voltage.

▶ **Which coil in a step-up transformer has more turns?**

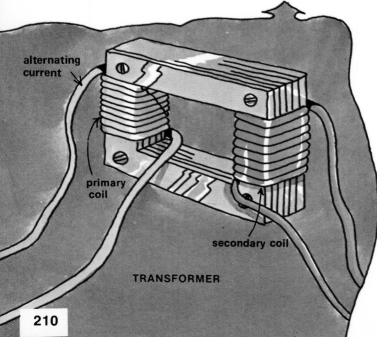

alternating current

primary coil

secondary coil

TRANSFORMER

Transformers can decrease voltage. A transformer can also make voltages smaller. This is called stepping down the voltage. A step-down transformer has fewer turns in the secondary coil than in the primary coil. The fewer the turns in the secondary coil, the lower the voltage.

▶ **Which coil in a step-down transformer has fewer turns?**

Using step-up transformers. Radios and television sets need higher voltages than those that come to our homes. Step-up transformers produce the voltages needed to run them. The transformer is inside the radio or TV set. Very high voltages are needed to carry electricity long distances through power lines. Huge transformers produce these high voltages also.

▶ **Why is a step-up transformer needed in a TV set?**

Using step-down transformers. The electricity used in most homes is about 110 volts. But a doorbell usually works on only 6 volts. A step-down transformer changes the house voltage to the lower voltage needed for the doorbell. Power lines carry electricity at thousands of volts. Transformers step down the electricity to about 110 volts before it enters our homes.

▶ **What kind of transformer is used in a doorbell?**

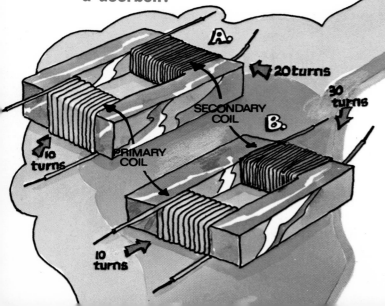

WHAT YOU LEARNED

1. Current can be either direct or alternating.
2. Transformers use alternating current.
3. Transformers can either increase or decrease voltage.

SCIENCE WORDS

direct current
electric current that moves in one direction only
alternating (ALL-ter-NAY-ting) **current**
electric current that keeps moving back and forth
transformer (trans-FOR-mer)
an induction coil that uses alternating current

ANSWER THESE

1. What are the three parts of a transformer?
2. Which coil of a step-up transformer has more turns?
3. What kind of transformer changes 110 volts to 6 volts?
4. What kind of electricity does a transformer use?

FINDING OUT MORE

The number of turns in each coil of a transformer can tell you something. It tells you just how much the transformer will change voltage.

Look at the transformer marked A in the diagram. It has twice as many turns in the secondary coil as in the primary coil. It can double the voltage that goes into it. It can change 10 volts to 20 volts, or 4 volts to 8 volts. Transformer B has three times as many turns in the secondary coil as in the primary coil. It can triple the voltage that goes into it. It can change 3 volts to 9 volts, or 15 volts to 45 volts.

Suppose the coils in transformer A were changed around. Then the secondary coil would have only half as many turns as the primary coil. Can you figure out just how this would change the voltage? What would 10 volts be changed to in this transformer?

UNIT 10 Review

Do the following review questions on a separate sheet of paper.

Modified True/False   *Write down each of the following statements, leaving a blank line between each line you write. Before the number for each statement, write T if the statement is true and F if the statement is false. For the false statements, cross out the word written in capital letters and write above it a word that will make the statement true.*

1. The POLES are the ends of a magnet.
2. Rubbing a nail on a magnet will MAGNETIZE the nail.
3. Lines of force are lines that show a magnetic ATTRACTION.
4. The North Magnetic Pole is really a NORTH pole.
5. The South Magnetic Pole is really a NORTH pole.
6. Hitting a magnet could INCREASE its magnetism.
7. A coil of wire can be used to make an ELECTROMAGNET.
8. The more turns in the coil, the WEAKER the magnet.
9. Small electric currents are measured with a GALVANOMETER.
10. Electric current that moves in one direction only is called a DIRECT CURRENT.

Multiple Choice   *Write the letter of the choice that best completes the statement or answers the question.*

1. If you hold the south poles of two magnets together, they will
   a. attract each other
   b. repel each other
   c. lose their magnetism
2. Lines of force come closer together near
   a. the poles of a magnet
   b. the middle of a magnet
   c. the north pole of a magnet
3. Heating a magnet could cause it to
   a. become more magnetic
   b. become an induced magnet
   c. become less magnetic
4. The magnetic field around a coiled wire is
   a. greater than that around a straight wire
   b. less than that around a straight wire
   c. the same as that around a straight wire

5. An iron core will make an electromagnet
   a. stronger
   b. weaker
   c. non-magnetic
6. In order to induce current, a magnet has to
   a. be bent
   b. be coiled
   c. move
7. In a transformer, high voltage can be changed to low voltage in
   a. the primary coil
   b. the secondary coil
   c. the induction
8. A step-down transformer is used to
   a. lower voltage
   b. induce a current
   c. increase voltage

11 Elements

Unit Lessons

1. What is matter?
2. In what forms is matter found?
3. Can matter change its form?
4. What are the simplest kinds of substances?
5. What are metals and non-metals?
6. What are chemical symbols?
   Periodic Table of the Elements
7. What does the periodic table tell about the elements?

Goals and Objectives

After completing this unit, you should be able to:
- define matter.
- recognize the three forms of matter.
- explain how matter may change its form.
- describe the properties that distinguish metals from non-metals.
- recognize the symbols that chemists use to describe elements.

What is matter?

Things around you. Look all around you. What do you see? Nearly everything you see around you is <u>matter</u>. Anything that has mass and takes up space is called matter.

▶ **What do we call something that has weight and takes up space?**

Matter has mass. Take two glasses. Fill one with water. Lift both glasses. Which one feels heavier? Water has mass because water is matter. The mass of the water makes the glass feel heavier.

▶ **Why does a glass of water feel heavier than a glass without water?**

Air is matter. Press a basketball as flat as you can, and find its mass. Fill the basketball with air and find its mass again. This time, the ball is heavier. Air has mass because air is matter. The mass of the air in the ball makes the ball heavier.

▶ **Why does the basketball weigh more when it is filled with air?**

Matter takes up space. Fill a glass with water. Put a rock in the glass. The rock is matter. It takes up space in the glass. The rock pushes some of the water out. The amount of space the rock takes up is called its <u>volume</u> (VOL-yoom).

Air is matter. It takes up space. When you blow air into a balloon, the air makes the balloon take up more space. The volume of the balloon gets bigger.

▶ **Why does a balloon take up more space when you blow air into it?**

You are matter. Step on a scale. How much do you weigh? Does the water level get higher in a bathtub when you step into it? Why does that happen? You have mass. You take up space. You are matter.

▶ **How can you show that you are matter?**

What is chemistry? Matter makes up almost everything you see in the world. Scientists who study matter are called chemists (KEM-ists). Chemistry (KEM-iss-tree) is the study of matter.

▶ **What does a chemist do?**

WHAT YOU LEARNED

1. Matter is anything that has mass and takes up space.
2. Nearly everything you see in the world is made of matter.
3. Chemistry is the study of matter.

SCIENCE WORDS

matter
   anything that has mass and takes up space
volume (VOL-yoom)
   the amount of space matter takes up
chemistry (KEM-iss-tree)
   the study of matter

ANSWER THESE

1. Why does a bicycle tire get heavier when you pump air into it?
2. What properties of air make you think that air is matter?
3. Matter
   a. can push water out of a glass
   b. cannot push water out of a glass
   c. cannot push air out of a glass
4. The amount of space matter takes up is called
   a. weight
   b. volume
   c. chemistry
5. What do we call a person who studies matter?

NOW TRY THESE

What is "it"?

"It" has mass and takes up space.
The amount of space "it" takes up is called _____.

Scientists who study "it" are called _____. "It" is _____.

DO THIS AT HOME

Stuff a tissue or a napkin into the bottom of a glass. Turn the glass upside down and push it straight down into a sink or pail full of water. Then pull the glass straight out of the water. Feel the tissue. Did it get wet? What kept the water out of the glass? How does this experiment show that air is matter?

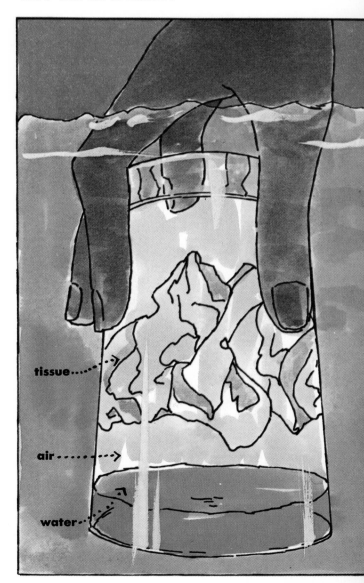

tissue

air

water

In what forms is matter found?

All matter is not the same. There are different forms of matter in the picture. The fence is made of steel. The steel is different from the water in the drinking fountain. Both are different from the air the boys and girls are breathing. There are three main forms of matter. The form that matter comes in is called its phase.

▶ **How many different phases can matter be in?**

Matter can be solid. The bricks in the wall have a definite shape. They have a definite volume. The volume is the amount of space they take up. The bricks are solid (SOL-id). Solids always have a definite shape and take up a definite amount of space. Some solids are hard, like the bricks. Other solids may be soft, like the children's clothing.

▶ **Why do we say that bricks are solid?**

Matter can be liquid. Pour some water into a plastic bag and close the bag tightly. What happens when you squeeze the bag gently? The water changes its shape inside the bag. Water is not a solid. It does not have a definite shape, as bricks do. Pour 100 cubic centimeters of water into several different containers. It always takes up 100 cubic centimeters of space. The shape of the water changes, but it has a definite volume. Water is a liquid (LIK-wid). Liquids have a definite volume.

▶ **How are liquids different from solids?**

Gases are another form of matter. Fill a balloon with air. Squeeze the balloon. You can change the shape of the air in the balloon by squeezing it. What is the shape of the air in a basketball, a football, or a bicycle tire? Air is a gas (GASS). Gases always have the shape of whatever they are in. Gases always fill a container completely. Squeeze the balloon you have blown up. Can you find any place where there is no air? A container of liquid can be half full. A container of gas is always completely full.

▶ **Why can't a balloon be only half full of air?**

Matter comes in tiny bits. <u>Molecules</u> (MOL-uh-kewls) are tiny bits of matter. In a solid, the molecules are tightly packed together. They cannot change position easily. They can only <u>vibrate</u> (VY-brate) in place. In a liquid, the molecules are able to slide past each other. They can easily change position in the liquid. In a gas, the molecules are much farther apart than in solids or liquids. They have plenty of space to move around in. They can easily spread out through all the space in the container.

▶ In which state of matter are the molecules farthest apart?

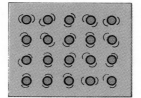

Molecules in a solid vibrate in place.

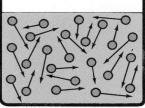

Molecules in a liquid can slide past each other.

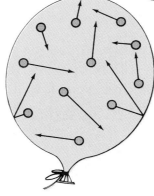

Molecules in a gas are far apart and move freely to all parts of a container.

WHAT YOU LEARNED

1. There are three phases of matter: solids, liquids, and gases.
2. Solids have a definite shape and a definite volume.
3. Liquids have a definite volume, but their shape can change.
4. Gases do not have a definite shape or a definite volume.
5. The molecules in a solid cannot change position. They can only vibrate in place.
6. The molecules in a liquid can slide past each other and change position.
7. The molecules in a gas are far apart. They can easily spread out to all parts of a container.

SCIENCE WORDS

phase

one of the forms in which matter may be found

solid (SOL-id)

the form of matter that has a definite shape and volume

liquid (LIK-wid)

the form of matter that has a definite volume but no definite shape

gas (GASS)

the form of matter that has no definite shape or volume

molecules (MOL-uh-kewls)

the tiny bits that make up matter

vibrate (VY-brate)

move back and forth quickly in a small space

ANSWER THESE

1. The form matter comes in is called its
   a. shape
   b. phase
   c. volume
2. When you pour milk from a carton into a glass, the milk changes its
   a. volume
   b. shape
   c. mass
3. In a container of gas, the molecules are
   a. mostly at the bottom
   b. mostly at the top
   c. spread out evenly

NOW TRY THESE

1. A beaker has a volume of 500 cubic centimeters. It is half full of water. The water is poured into a tall jar that has a volume of 1,000 cubic centimeters. How much of the jar will be filled?
2. Tell which of the following are solids, which are liquids, and which are gases?

water	sugar
iron	oil
alcohol	soda
air	bubbles in soda
salt	this page

Can matter change its form?

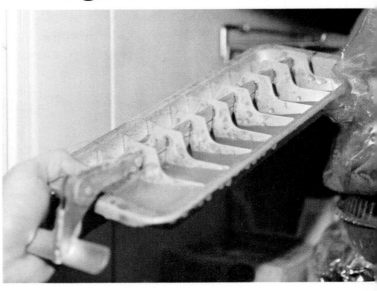

Water can change to ice. Fill an ice tray with water and place it in the freezer. The temperature inside the freezer is low. It is below the freezing point of water. Heat goes out of the water into the colder surroundings. As the liquid water loses heat, it changes to ice. The ice cubes have a definite shape. Ice is a solid. When a liquid loses heat, it can change to the solid phase. This is called freezing.

▶ **What is the phase of ice?**

Changing ice to water. Let the ice cubes stand in the warm air of the room. Heat flows into the ice from the air. The ice changes back to water. When a solid gains heat, it can change to the liquid phase. This is called melting.

▶ **What may happen when a solid gains heat?**

evaporating water

water lost by evaporation

Boiling water. Place a pan of water on the stove, and heat it until it boils. Watch the bubbles coming up from the bottom of the pan. When water is made hot enough to boil, it changes to a gas called steam. Each bubble is filled with steam. When the bubbles come to the top of the water, the steam escapes into the air. If you keep the water boiling, it will all change to steam.

▶ **What does boiling water change to?**

Disappearing water. Water can change to a gas without boiling. Put some water in a glass. Make a mark on the glass to show the water level. Check the water level after several days. You will see that the water level is lower than the mark. Some of the water has disappeared. If you let the glass stand long enough, all the water will disappear. This happens because molecules of water escape from the liquid into the air. This is called evaporation (ee-VAP-uh-RAY-shun). Liquids evaporate (ee-VAP-uh-rate) when they are left open to the air.

▶ **What happens to water when it stands open to air?**

Gases can change to liquids. Put some ice cubes in a bowl. Hold the bowl over boiling water. Be careful not to let the steam burn your hand. Soon you will see drops of water on the outside of the bowl. Heat from the stove made the water boil and change to steam. When the steam touched the cool bowl, heat was taken out of the steam. It changed back to liquid water. Changing a gas to a liquid is called condensation (CON-den-SAY-shun).

▶ What is condensation?

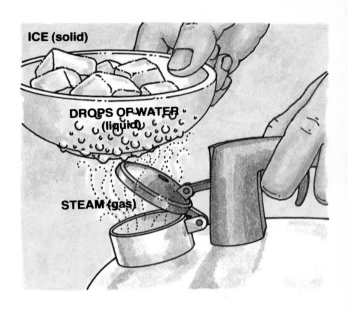

ICE (solid)

DROPS OF WATER (liquid)

STEAM (gas)

WHAT YOU LEARNED

1. Liquids may change to solids by losing heat.
2. Solids may change to liquids by gaining heat.
3. When a liquid boils, it changes to a gas.
4. A liquid can change to a gas by evaporation.
5. A gas can change to a liquid by condensation.

SCIENCE WORDS

freezing
   changing from a liquid to a solid
melting
   changing from a solid to a liquid
evaporation (ee-VAP-uh-RAY-shun)
   changing from a liquid to a gas when the liquid is left open to the air.
condensation (CON-den-SAY-shun)
   changing from a gas to a liquid

ANSWER THESE

1. To change a solid to a liquid, you
   a. add heat
   b. remove heat
   c. add cold
2. Changing a solid to a liquid is called
   a. melting
   b. freezing
   c. cooling
3. Water changes from a liquid to a gas when it
   a. melts
   b. loses heat
   c. evaporates

NOW TRY THIS

Tell whether each of the following forms of water is a solid, a liquid, or a gas.

rain	steam
snowball	icicle
iceberg	hail
pond	cloud

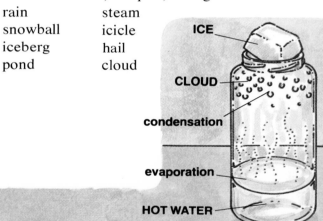

ICE

CLOUD

condensation

evaporation

HOT WATER

DO THIS AT HOME

Put a small amount of hot water in a bottle or jar. Then place an ice cube over the top of the bottle so it won't fall in. After a little while, you will see a cloud near the top of the bottle. Water vapor is in the bottle because the warm water you put in is evaporating. The water vapor is warm. But the air near the ice cube is cool. When the water vapor meets the cool air near the ice cube, it starts to condense. It changes back to tiny droplets of water. The water droplets make the cloud that you see. If the water droplets get big enough, some of them might fall to the bottom of the bottle. How would that be like rain?

What are the simplest kinds of substances?

The elements. Some substances can be broken down into other substances. Water can be broken down into hydrogen and oxygen. Sugar can be broken down into carbon, hydrogen, and oxygen. Salt can be broken down into sodium and chlorine. But hydrogen, oxygen, carbon, sodium, and chlorine cannot be broken down. These substances are called elements (EL-uh-ments). Elements are substances that cannot be broken down into anything else.

▶ **What is an element?**

All substances are made of elements. There are more than 100 elements that we know about. Every substance on earth is made of one or more of these elements. Elements are simple substances. They are the building blocks of all other substances.

▶ **What are substances made of?**

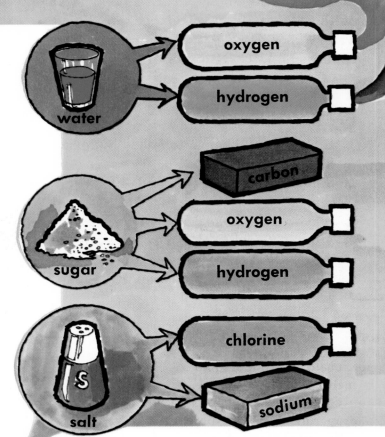

Elements can be solids, liquids, or gases. Most elements are solids at ordinary temperatures. Some elements are gases. A few elements are liquids.

▶ **In what phases of matter are elements found?**

Some substances are composed of only one element. An iron nail contains only the element iron. Aluminum foil is composed of only the element aluminum. The "lead" in the pencil you write with is not really lead at all. It is graphite (GRAF-ite). Graphite is composed of the element carbon.

▶ **What are some things that are composed of only one element?**

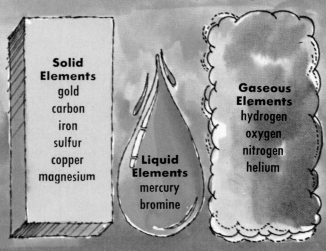

Elements can be solids, liquids, or gases

Solid Elements
gold
carbon
iron
sulfur
copper
magnesium

Liquid Elements
mercury
bromine

Gaseous Elements
hydrogen
oxygen
nitrogen
helium

Some substances contain more than one element. Water is composed of the two elements hydrogen and oxygen. Sugar contains carbon, hydrogen, and oxygen. Brass is a mixture of the elements copper and zinc. Mercuric oxide contains the elements mercury and oxygen.

It is not hard to break mercuric oxide into its two elements. Heat some mercuric oxide in a test tube. At first it turns black. If you keep heating it, drops of a silver-colored liquid form on the inside of the test tube. This liquid is the element mercury. If you then put a glowing wood splint into the test tube, the splint will burst into flame. This shows that the test tube also contains the invisible gas oxygen. Oxygen can make a glowing wood splint burst into flame.

▶ **What elements is mercuric oxide composed of?**

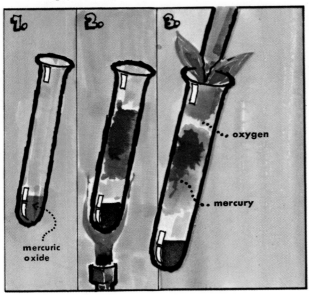

oxygen

mercury

mercuric oxide

WHAT YOU LEARNED

1. All substances are composed of elements.
2. An element is a simple substance that cannot be broken down into other substances.
3. There are more than 100 known elements.

SCIENCE WORD

element (EL-uh-ment)
   a simple substance that cannot be broken down into simpler substances

ANSWER THESE

1. Which of the following substances are elements?

water	mercury
oxygen	sugar
iron	carbon
salt	wood
hydrogen	nitrogen

2. The number of known elements is _____.
3. An element that is a silver-colored liquid is
   - **a.** hydrogen
   - **b.** mercury
   - **c.** silver
   - **d.** carbon
4. An element that is an invisible gas is
   - **a.** gold
   - **b.** copper
   - **c.** iron
   - **d.** oxygen
5. What elements are found in each of the following substances?
   - **a.** carbon dioxide
   - **b.** iron sulfide
   - **c.** silver bromide
   - **d.** carbon tetrachloride
   - **e.** magnesium hydroxide

NOW TRY THIS

Unscramble the letters to find the names of some elements.

CRANBO	DOGL
CHINEROL	PORPEC

FINDING OUT MORE

Although there are more than 100 known elements, only 88 are found naturally on the earth. These are called naturally occurring elements. The remaining elements do not occur anywhere on the earth. These elements have been made in scientific laboratories. They are called artificial elements. Some of these elements have been named after famous scientists. For example, the artificial element einsteinium is named after Albert Einstein.

What are metals and non-metals?

The properties of elements. How are you able to pick out a friend in a crowd of people? The things that help you identify (eye-DEN-ti-fy) or recognize something are called its properties (PROP-er-teez). Your friend has properties that help you to identify him. Each element also has its own special properties that help us identify it.

▶ **How do we identify elements?**

The properties of metals. All of the elements shown in the picture are metals (MET-uls). They are called metallic (muh-TAL-ic) elements. Metallic elements have similar properties. All metals, except mercury, are solids at room temperature. Mercury is a liquid. Metals have a bright and shiny luster (LUS-ter), or appearance. Metals are malleable (MAL-ee-uh-bul). That means they can be hammered into different shapes. Most metals are silver-gray in color. Copper and gold are exceptions.

▶ **What kind of luster do metals have?**

Metals are good conductors of electricity. Connect a dry cell and a light bulb as shown in Diagram A. The bulb does not light because the circuit is open. Put a penny across the bare wires. Now the bulb lights. Electric current can flow through the penny. It is a good conductor of electricity. A penny is made of several metals mixed together. All metals are good conductors of electricity. That is why the penny is a good conductor of electricity.

▶ **Why are electrical wires made of metal?**

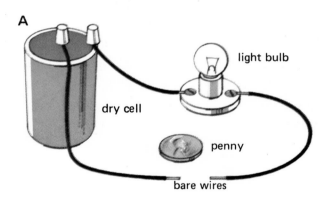

A

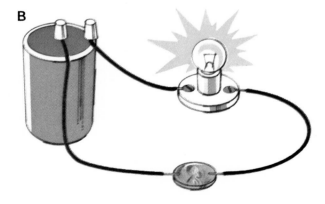

B

Metals are good conductors of heat.

Find an iron nail and a piece of wood about the same length. Hold one in each hand, with their ends over a flame. The nail soon becomes too hot to hold. But the end of the wood you are holding does not become very hot. You can still hold it even when the other end begins to burn. The heat was carried quickly from one end of the nail to the other. The nail is a good conductor of heat. It is made of the metal iron. The wood did not conduct the heat very well. Wood is not a metal.

▶ Why are cooking pots made of metal?

Some elements are not metals.

The elements that are not metals are called non-metallic elements, or just non-metals. Non-metals may be solid, liquid, or gas. They have many different colors. Most non-metals are poor conductors of heat and electricity.

▶ What do we call elements that are not metals?

Non-metals and metals have different properties.

This chart compares the properties of metals and non-metals.

METALLIC AND NON-METALLIC PROPERTIES		
PROPERTIES	METALS	NON-METALS
STATE	solids — except mercury	solids, liquids or gases
LUSTER	bright and shiny	dull
COLOR	silver-gray — except gold and copper	different colors
ELECTRICAL CONDUCTIVITY	good conductors	poor conductors
HEAT CONDUCTIVITY	good conductors	poor conductors

▶ Are the properties of metals and non-metals generally similar, or generally opposite?

WHAT YOU LEARNED

1. Metals can be identified by their properties.
2. Some properties of metals are:
   a. Metals are solids at room temperature (except mercury).
   b. Metals have a silver-gray color (except gold and copper).
   c. Metals have a shiny luster.
   d. Metals are malleable.
   e. Metals are good conductors of electricity and heat.
3. Elements that are not metals are called non-metals.
4. Metals and non-metals generally have opposite properties.

SCIENCE WORDS

identify (eye-DEN-ti-fy)
recognize or find out what something is
properties (PROP-er-teez)
things that help identify something
luster (LUS-ter)
the shininess of a material
malleable (MAL-ee-uh-bul)
able to be hammered into different shapes
metals (MET-uls)
elements that have certain properties
non-metals
elements with properties that are the opposite of metals

ANSWER THESE

1. On clean paper copy the chart below. On the copy fill in the empty spaces.

PROPERTIES	METALS	NON-METALS
LUSTER	shiny	
HEAT CONDUCTIVITY	good	
MALLEABILITY	malleable	
ELECTRICAL CONDUCTIVITY		poor

2. How are the properties of non-metals different from the properties of metals?

What are chemical symbols?

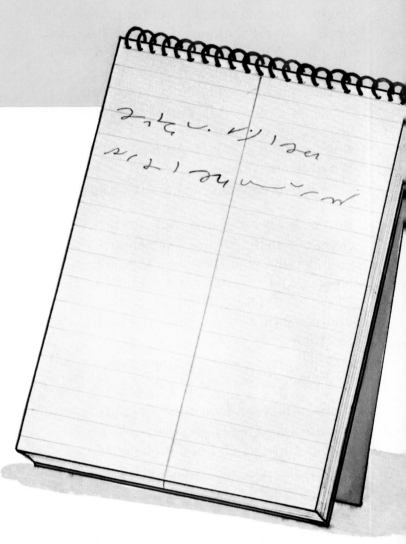

A shorthand for chemists. <u>Chemical symbols</u> (SIM-buls) are something like the shorthand writing used by stenographers (ste-NOG-ra-fers). Shorthand helps stenographers to write a lot of words quickly and in a small space. It is a way of shortening the words to take up less space and less time to write. Chemists have their own shorthand for writing the names of the elements. These shortened names for the elements are called chemical symbols.

▶ **What do we call the shortened names that chemists use for the elements?**

The language of chemistry. Chemists all over the world use the same symbols for the elements. The symbol "Fe" always means iron to a chemist. It doesn't matter whether the chemist lives in the United States, Russia, China, Africa, South America, or anywhere else. Chemical symbols are a <u>universal</u> (YEW-ni-VERS-al) language that all chemists understand.

▶ **What element does Fe stand for in Russia?**

The rules for writing chemical symbols. For everyone to understand them, the chemical symbols must always be written the same way. Here are the rules for writing them:

1. The symbol is always either one letter or two letters.
2. If the symbol is just one letter, that letter is a capital letter.
3. If the symbol has two letters, then the first letter is a capital letter and the second letter is a small letter.

▶ **How many letters are there in a chemical symbol?**

Learning the symbols for the elements.

The best way to learn the symbols is to memorize them. Copy the names of the elements and their symbols into your science notebook. Practice writing them several times until you know them by heart.

THE FIRST TWENTY ELEMENTS			
aluminum	Al	lithium	Li
argon	Ar	magnesium	Mg
beryllium	Be	neon	Ne
boron	B	nitrogen	N
calcium	Ca	oxygen	O
carbon	C	phosphorus	P
chlorine	Cl	potassium	K
fluorine	F	silicon	Si
helium	He	sodium	Na
hydrogen	H	sulfur	S

SOME OTHER IMPORTANT ELEMENTS			
bromine	Br	mercury	Hg
chromium	Cr	nickel	Ni
cobalt	Co	platinum	Pt
copper	Cu	radium	Ra
gold	Au	silver	Ag
iodine	I	tin	Sn
iron	Fe	tungsten	W
krypton	Kr	uranium	U
lead	Pb	xenon	Xe
manganese	Mn	zinc	Zn

WHAT YOU LEARNED

1. Chemists use symbols for the names of the elements.
2. The symbols for the elements are the same all over the world.
3. Chemical symbols always contain one or two letters. The first letter is always a capital, and the second letter is always a small letter.

SCIENCE WORDS

chemical symbols (SIM-buls)
a short way of writing the names of the elements

universal (YEW-ni-VERS-al)
worldwide; the same all over the world

ANSWER THIS

Match the elements in one column with their symbols in the other column.

copper	C
magnesium	B
carbon	He
silver	Al
boron	Mg
helium	Cl
chlorine	Cu
aluminum	Ag

NOW TRY THIS

Use the symbols below to find the names of the elements needed to complete the crossword puzzle.

Across	Down
1. N	**2.** W
4. Xe	**3.** Ne
6. Fe	**5.** Ni
9. Kr	**7.** O
10. Sn	**8.** I

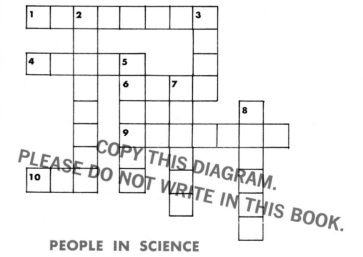

PEOPLE IN SCIENCE

Jons Jakob Berzelius was a Swedish chemist who lived from 1779 to 1848. Berzelius discovered the elements selenium, cerium, and thorium. But he is remembered most for working out the method we now use for writing chemical symbols. Besides working in his laboratory, Berzelius taught chemistry and medicine at the University of Stockholm in Sweden. The Swedish government made Berzelius a baron for his important work in science.

METALS

*Elements marked with a star (*) are not found naturally on the earth. They have all been made artificially.

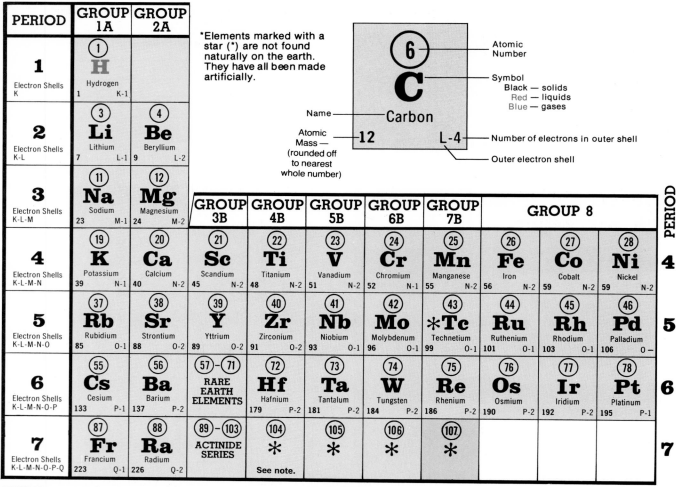

Atomic Number — 6
Symbol
  Black — solids
  Red — liquids
  Blue — gases
Name — Carbon
Atomic Mass — 12 (rounded off to nearest whole number)
L-4 — Number of electrons in outer shell
Outer electron shell

PERIOD	GROUP 1A	GROUP 2A	GROUP 3B	GROUP 4B	GROUP 5B	GROUP 6B	GROUP 7B	GROUP 8		
1 Electron Shells K	(1) **H** Hydrogen 1 K-1									
2 Electron Shells K-L	(3) **Li** Lithium 7 L-1	(4) **Be** Beryllium 9 L-2								
3 Electron Shells K-L-M	(11) **Na** Sodium 23 M-1	(12) **Mg** Magnesium 24 M-2								
4 Electron Shells K-L-M-N	(19) **K** Potassium 39 N-1	(20) **Ca** Calcium 40 N-2	(21) **Sc** Scandium 45 N-2	(22) **Ti** Titanium 48 N-2	(23) **V** Vanadium 51 N-2	(24) **Cr** Chromium 52 N-1	(25) **Mn** Manganese 55 N-2	(26) **Fe** Iron 56 N-2	(27) **Co** Cobalt 59 N-2	(28) **Ni** Nickel 59 N-2
5 Electron Shells K-L-M-N-O	(37) **Rb** Rubidium 85 O-1	(38) **Sr** Strontium 88 O-2	(39) **Y** Yttrium 89 O-2	(40) **Zr** Zirconium 91 O-2	(41) **Nb** Niobium 93 O-1	(42) **Mo** Molybdenum 96 O-1	(43) *****Tc** Technetium 99 O-1	(44) **Ru** Ruthenium 101 O-1	(45) **Rh** Rhodium 103 O-1	(46) **Pd** Palladium 106 O –
6 Electron Shells K-L-M-N-O-P	(55) **Cs** Cesium 133 P-1	(56) **Ba** Barium 137 P-2	(57)–(71) **RARE EARTH ELEMENTS**	(72) **Hf** Hafnium 179 P-2	(73) **Ta** Tantalum 181 P-2	(74) **W** Tungsten 184 P-2	(75) **Re** Rhenium 186 P-2	(76) **Os** Osmium 190 P-2	(77) **Ir** Iridium 192 P-2	(78) **Pt** Platinum 195 P-1
7 Electron Shells K-L-M-N-O-P-Q	(87) **Fr** Francium 223 Q-1	(88) **Ra** Radium 226 Q-2	(89)–(103) **ACTINIDE SERIES** See note.	(104) *****	(105) *****	(106) *****	(107) *****			

NOTE: The names and symbols of elements 104, 105, 106, and 107 have not been agreed upon

RARE EARTH ELEMENTS (57)–(71)							
(57) **La** Lanthanum 139 P-2	(58) **Ce** Cerium 140 P-2	(59) **Pr** Praseodymium 141 P-2	(60) **Nd** Neodymium 144 P-2	(61) **Pm** Promethium 147 P-2	(62) **Sm** Samarium 150 P-2	(63) **Eu** Europium 152 P-2	(64) **Gd** Gadolinium 157 P-2

ACTINIDE SERIES (89)–(103)							
(89) **Ac** Actinium 227 Q-2	(90) **Th** Thorium 232 Q-2	(91) **Pa** Protactinium 231 Q-2	(92) **U** Uranium 238 Q-2	(93) *****Np** Neptunium 237 Q-2	(94) *****Pu** Plutonium 242 Q-2	(95) *****Am** Americium 243 Q-2	(96) *****Cm** Curium 247 Q-2

THE ELEMENTS

NON-METALS

	GROUP 3A	GROUP 4A	GROUP 5A	GROUP 6A	GROUP 7A	GROUP O	PERIOD
1						② **He** Helium 4 K-2	**1**
2	⑤ **B** Boron 11 L-3	⑥ **C** Carbon 12 L-4	⑦ **N** Nitrogen 14 L-5	⑧ **O** Oxygen 16 L-6	⑨ **F** Fluorine 19 L-7	⑩ **Ne** Neon 20 L-8	**2**
3	⑬ **Al** Aluminum 27 M-3	⑭ **Si** Silicon 28 M-4	⑮ **P** Phosphorus 31 M-5	⑯ **S** Sulfur 32 M-6	⑰ **Cl** Chlorine 35 M-7	⑱ **Ar** Argon 40 M-8	**3**

	GROUP 1B	GROUP 2B							
4	㉙ **Cu** Copper 64 N-1	㉚ **Zn** Zinc 65 N2	㉛ **Ga** Gallium 70 N-3	㉜ **Ge** Germanium 73 N-4	㉝ **As** Arsenic /5 N-5	㉞ **Se** Selenium 79 N-6	㉟ **Br** Bromine 80 N-7	㊱ **Kr** Krypton 84 N-8	**4**
5	㊼ **Ag** Silver 108 O-1	㊽ **Cd** Cadmium 112 O-2	㊾ **In** Indium 115 O-3	㊿ **Sn** Tin 119 O-4	51 **Sb** Antimony 122 O-5	52 **Te** Tellurium 128 O-6	53 **I** Iodine 127 O-7	54 **Xe** Xenon 131 O-8	**5**
6	79 **Au** Gold 197 P-1	80 **Hg** Mercury 201 P-2	81 **Tl** Thallium 204 P-3	82 **Pb** Lead 207 P-4	83 **Bi** Bismuth 209 P-5	84 **Po** Polonium 210 P-6	85 **At** Astatine 210 P-7	86 **Rn** Radon 222 P-8	**6**
7									**7**

65 **Tb** Terbium 159 P-2	66 **Dy** Dysprosium 163 P-2	67 **Ho** Holmium 165 P-2	68 **Er** Erbium 167 P-2	69 **Tm** Thulium 169 P-2	70 **Yb** Ytterbium 173 P-2	71 **Lu** Lutetium 175 P-2

97 ***Bk** Berkelium 249 Q-2	98 ***Cf** Californium 251 Q-2	99 ***Es** Einsteinium 254 Q-2	100 ***Fm** Fermium 253 Q-2	101 ***Md** Mendelevium 256 Q-2	102 ***No** Nobelium 254 Q-2	103 ***Lw** Lawrencium 257 Q-2

What does the periodic table tell about the elements?

UNIT 11
Elements
7

Arranging elements by weight. In the 1800's, scientists were trying to find new elements. At first, only a few elements were known. Then, more and more were found. Scientists tried to put these elements in order. A scientist named Mendeleev (MEN-de-LAY-ef) made a list of the known elements by weight. He put the lighter elements first, and the heavier elements last. Then he arranged them in rows in a chart. Mendeleev found that elements with similar properties were in the same column of his chart, one under the other. His chart was the first periodic (peer-ee-ODD-ic) table of the elements.

▶ **How did Mendeleev arrange the elements?**

Arranging elements by atomic number. Mendeleev's table of the elements was very useful, but it was not perfect. Some of the elements were out of place. For many years, scientists tried to improve the periodic table. Each element was given a number, called the atomic (uh-TOM-ic) number. When the elements were arranged by atomic number, all the elements fell into place in the table. Atomic numbers are used to arrange the elements in the modern periodic table. The elements are numbered from 1 to 107.

▶ **How are the elements arranged today in a periodic table?**

Elements are arranged in groups. Look at the periodic table. Each column of elements, from top to bottom, is called a group. A group of elements is like a family. All of the elements in a group have similar properties. Each group has a number and a letter.

▶ **What are the first two elements in group 6A?**

Elements are arranged in periods. Another kind of family of elements is called a period (PEER-ee-ud). A period is a line of elements that goes across the periodic table.

Look at the periodic table. You can see that period 1 contains only two elements, hydrogen (H) and helium (He). Period 5 contains 18 elements. Count how many elements are in period 2.

▶ **Which element in period 2 is also in group 2A?**

228

Metals and non-metals. Look for a heavy black line on the periodic table. It starts next to boron (B), and goes down the chart like a flight of steps. This line divides the periodic table into metals and non-metals. The metals are on the left side of the line. The non-metals are on the right side of the line. The metals are in blue boxes, and the non-metals are in red boxes. Count whether there are more metals or non-metals in the periodic table.

▶ **Which element in group 3A is a non-metal?**

Solids, liquids, and gases. The elements whose symbols are shown in black, like $\boxed{C}$, are solids at room temperature. Red symbols, like $\boxed{Hg}$, are for liquids. Blue symbols, like $\boxed{O}$, are for gases. Artificial elements are shown with a star in front of the symbol, like $\boxed{*Pu}$.

▶ **Which element in group 7A is a liquid?**

WHAT YOU LEARNED

1. The periodic table is a chart showing the elements in order of atomic number.
2. Metals are on the left side of the chart, and non-metals are on the right side.
3. Elements are arranged in groups and periods in the table.

SCIENCE WORDS

atomic (uh-TOM-ic) **number**
a number used to identify an element and show its place in the periodic table

group
a family of elements going down the periodic table

period (PEER-ee-ud)
a family of elements going across the periodic table

ANSWER THESE

1. An element in group 1A that is also in period 4 is
   a. K **b.** Ca **c.** Na **d.** Li

2. A metallic element found in group 3A is
   a. B **b.** Al **c.** Ni **d.** Cu

3. A non-metallic element found in group 5A is
   a. Sb **b.** Bi **c.** P **d.** O

4. A gas found in group 6A is
   a. N **b.** H **c.** S **d.** O

5. The atomic number of neon is
   a. 7 **b.** 10 **c.** 20 **d.** 30

6. An element in the same period as argon is
   a. Ne **b.** O **c.** N **d.** S

NOW TRY THESE

1. Name two elements that are liquids at room temperature.
2. Name three elements that are gases at room temperature.
3. How many artificial elements can you find on the periodic table?
4. Elements are arranged in the modern periodic table based on their **a.** atomic number **b.** atomic weight **c.** atomic mass

PEOPLE IN SCIENCE

Dmitri Mendeleev (1834-1907)
Dmitri Mendeleev was a Russian chemist. He put together the first useful table of the elements. He listed the elements in order of their atomic weight. Hydrogen came first in the table, followed by the heavier elements in order. There were empty spaces in Mendeleev's periodic table. Later, scientists found new elements that fit in the spaces in the table.

Marguerite Perey (1909-1975)
Marguerite Perey began her career as a laboratory assistant to Marie Curie. At the age of 30 she discovered a new radioactive element, called francium. She was appointed professor of nuclear chemistry at Strasbourg University and Director of the Strasbourg Center for Nuclear Research. In 1962 she became the first woman member of the French Academy of Sciences.

UNIT 11 Review

Do the following questions on a separate sheet of paper.

Matching   *Write down each of the statements in Column I, leaving one line of space after each statement. On the blank line following each statement, write the word or phrase from Column II that is described by that statement.*

Column I

1. Symbol for sodium.
2. Symbol for sulfur.
3. The shininess of a material.
4. Changing from a liquid to a solid.
5. Changing from a solid to a liquid.
6. The tiny bits that make up matter.
7. Definite volume, definite shape.
8. No definite shape or volume.
9. Definite volume, no definite shape.
10. The amount of space matter takes up.

Column II

S
molecules
Na
volume
solid
luster
melting
freezing
liquid
gas

Multiple Choice   *Write the letter of the choice that best completes the statement or answers the question.*

1. Anything that has mass and takes up space is
   a. a vacuum
   b. matter
   c. an element
2. Liquids are different from solids because they
   a. have a definite volume
   b. can change shape
   c. are made of matter
3. Molecules are most widely spread apart in
   a. gases
   b. liquids
   c. solids
4. Molecules in a solid
   a. are completely still
   b. vibrate in place
   c. can slide past each other

5. Changing a gas to a liquid is called
   a. condensation
   b. evaporation
   c. vaporization
6. At ordinary temperatures, most elements are
   a. solids
   b. liquids
   c. gases
7. Mercury is the only metal that is
   a. silver in apperance
   b. liquid at room temperature
   c. malleable
8. Dmitri Mendeleev is best known for
   a. the first periodic table
   b. discovering oxygen
   c. creating the language of chemistry

UNIT 12

Atoms

Unit Lessons

1. What are atoms?
2. What are atoms composed of?
3. What is an element's atomic number?
4. What is atomic mass?
5. How are electrons arranged in an atom?

Goals and Objectives

After completing this unit, you should be able to:

- understand how atoms of different elements differ.
- name the components of an atom and their properties.
- understand how numbers are used to describe different aspects of an atom.
- describe the structure of an atom.

What are atoms?

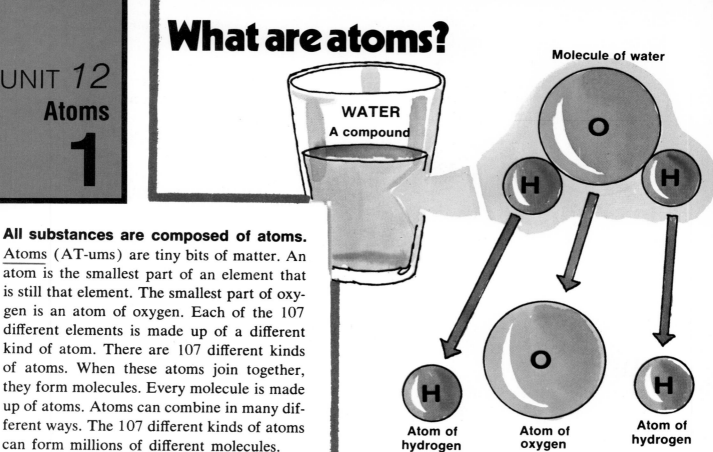

Molecule of water

WATER
A compound

Atom of hydrogen

Atom of oxygen

Atom of hydrogen

ALL MATTER IS COMPOSED OF ATOMS

All substances are composed of atoms. Atoms (AT-ums) are tiny bits of matter. An atom is the smallest part of an element that is still that element. The smallest part of oxygen is an atom of oxygen. Each of the 107 different elements is made up of a different kind of atom. There are 107 different kinds of atoms. When these atoms join together, they form molecules. Every molecule is made up of atoms. Atoms can combine in many different ways. The 107 different kinds of atoms can form millions of different molecules.

▶ **What is an atom?**

Atoms are very small. A million million atoms could fit in the period at the end of this sentence. How can scientists study atoms if they are so small? Atoms are too small to be seen, even with the most powerful microscope. But scientists have other tools that help them to study atoms. Before these tools were invented, scientists made some good guesses about atoms.

About 2000 years ago, a Greek teacher named Democritus (duh-MOC-ri-tus) studied matter. He guessed that it was made up of tiny particles. He was the first to call these particles atoms. Democritus thought atoms were solid particles that could not be broken apart. Scientists no longer believe this is true. But the ideas of Democritus were a help to later scientists who studied atoms.

▶ **What did Democritus think atoms were like?**

Ideas about atoms. About 150 years ago, an English chemist named John Dalton stated a theory about atoms. Here is what Dalton's theory said:

1. All elements are made of tiny particles called atoms.
2. All atoms of the same element have the same weight. Atoms of different elements have different weights.
3. Atoms are solid particles that cannot be split apart.
4. Atoms of one element can combine with atoms of other elements to form compounds.

Like Democritus, Dalton had some ideas about atoms that scientists no longer agree with. But Dalton's theory was the beginning of our present ideas about the atom.

▶ **What did Dalton say about the weights of atoms?**

Chemical changes do not affect atoms.

During some chemical reactions, atoms combine to form molecules. During other chemical reactions, molecules are broken down into atoms. But the atoms themselves never change in a chemical reaction.

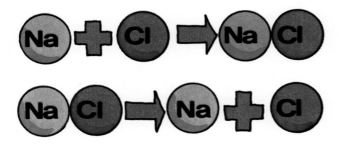

One atom of sodium combines with one atom of chlorine to form one molecule of sodium chloride. The atoms of sodium and chlorine do not change. The molecule of sodium chloride can be broken down into the same atoms of sodium and chlorine. Chemical reactions produce new substances, but they do not produce new atoms. The new substances always contain the same kind and number of atoms as the old substances did.

▶ **What do chemical reactions produce?**

SCIENCE WORD

atom (AT-um)
  the smallest part of an element that is still that element

WHAT YOU LEARNED

1. An atom is the smallest part of an element that is still that element.
2. Atoms are very small.
3. Atoms do not change in a chemical reaction.

ANSWER THESE

1. The first person to call tiny particles of matter atoms was _____.
2. The smallest bit of gold that is still gold is _____.
3. When atoms join together, they form _____.
4. Dalton's theory says that all atoms of the same element have the same _____, and that atoms of different elements have different _____.

5. Atoms (do/do not) change in a chemical reaction.

NOW TRY THESE

1. What idea did Democritus and Dalton have about the atom that scientists today no longer agree with?
2. What atoms are needed to make a molecule of water?

FINDING OUT MORE

Taking atoms apart. An atom is the smallest bit of an element that is still that element. But an atom is not the very smallest bit of matter. Atoms are made of still smaller particles called protons, electrons, and neutrons. Scientists use protons and electrons as a kind of "bullet" to study the structure of matter. They shoot these bullets at samples of matter. When the particles hit the atoms in the sample, the atoms may break apart or give off new particles or radiation. By studying these results, scientists can find out about the forces that hold the parts of atoms together.

These experiments are carried out in machines called "atom smashers," or particle accelerators. There are several types of accelerators. All of them accelerate, or speed up, particles to very high speeds. One type of accelerator, called a cyclotron, accelerates particles outward in a huge spiral. Some accelerators, called linear accelerators, speed up particles in a straight line. Sometimes the line is stretched over many kilometers. The longer the path, the faster the particles can be accelerated. A high speed means that there will be great energy in the collisions and that many particles will be set free to study.

This "atom smasher" is called a Bevatron. It can shoot 800 billion protons in a single burst.

What are atoms composed of?

PROTON
POSITIVE

ELECTRON
NEGATIVE

NEUTRON
NEUTRAL

Atoms are made up of particles. All matter is made up of atoms. Atoms are made up of smaller particles. Atoms contain protons (PROH-tons), electrons (e-LEC-trons), and neutrons (NEW-trons). These atomic particles have electrical (e-LEC-tri-cul) properties. A proton has a positive (POS-i-tiv) charge. An electron has a negative (NEG-uh-tiv) charge. A neutron has neither a positive nor a negative charge. It is neutral (NEW-trul). In an atom, the number of protons is the same as the number of electrons. Their electrical charges balance, so the atom as a whole is neutral.

▶ **What three particles are found in atoms?**

The law of electrical charges. Substances that have the same electrical charge repel, or move away from, each other. Substances that have different electrical charges attract, or move toward, each other. Here is the law of electrical charges:

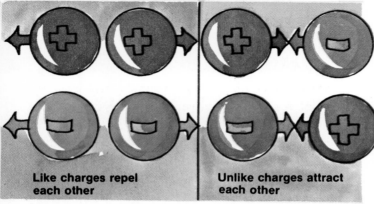

Like charges repel each other

Unlike charges attract each other

▶ **How do different electrical charges affect each other?**

Making objects move apart. Rub a rubber rod with fur, and hang the rod from a stand. Rub another rubber rod with fur, and hold it near the first rod. The hanging rod moves away.

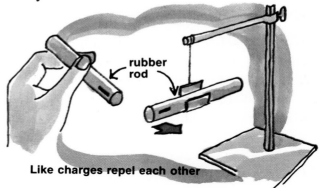

rubber rod

Like charges repel each other

Ordinarily, a piece of matter is electrically neutral. Its atoms have just as many protons as electrons. When you rub a rubber rod with fur, electrons move from the fur to the rubber. The rubber now has more electrons than protons. The extra electrons give the rubber a negative charge. In this experiment, both rods were rubbed with fur. Both got negative charges. Since like charges repel each other, the two rods with negative charges repelled each other.

▶ **What kind of charge did the extra electrons give the rubber rods?**

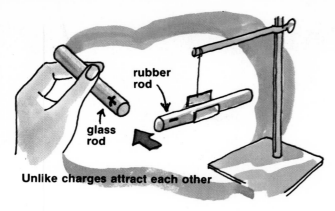

Unlike charges attract each other

Making objects move together.

Rub a glass rod with silk. Hold it near the rubber rod hanging from the stand. The rubber rod swings toward the glass rod. It is attracted to the glass rod. When you rub a glass rod with silk, electrons move from the glass to the silk. The glass rod now has more protons than electrons. It has a positive charge. The rubber rod has a negative charge. The unlike charges attract each other, and the rubber rod swings toward the glass rod.

▶ **What happens when you rub a glass rod with silk?**

WHAT YOU LEARNED

1. Atoms contain protons, electrons, and neutrons.
2. Protons have a positive charge; electrons have a negative charge; neutrons are neutral.
3. Like electrical charges repel each other; unlike charges attract each other.

SCIENCE WORDS

proton (PROH-ton)
 a positively charged atomic particle
electron (e-LEC-tron)
 a negatively charged atomic particle
neutron (NEW-tron)
 a neutral atomic particle
positive (POS-i-tiv) **charge**
 opposite of negative charge; the kind of charge on a proton
negative (NEG-uh-tiv) **charge**
 opposite of positive charge; the kind of charge on an electron
neutral (NEW-trul)
 neither positively nor negatively charged

ANSWER THESE

1. Particle having a positive electrical charge: _____
2. Particle having a negative electrical charge: _____
3. Neutral particle: _____
4. Adding electrons gives a substance a _____ charge.
5. Removing electrons gives a substance a _____ charge.

DO THIS AT HOME
Making an Electroscope

An electroscope (uh-LEC-tro-scope) is a device that can store electrical charges. Use the diagram to make your own working electroscope at home.

 First attach two strips of aluminum foil to one end of a metal rod. Push the other end of the rod through a one-hole rubber stopper. Make it stick out a little. Fit the stopper into a flask, bottle, or jar. Then put a metal ball on top of the rod. You can use some rolled-up aluminum foil. Now run

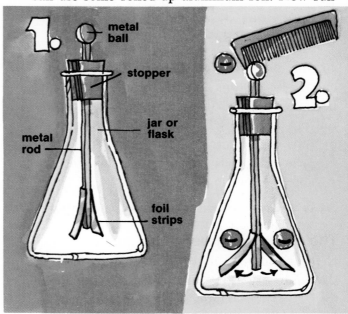

a rubber comb through your hair to give the comb a negative charge. Touch the comb to the metal ball. Watch the foil strips (called leaves) at the bottom of the metal rod. You will see them move apart.

 When you touched the comb to the metal ball, electrons moved from the comb to the ball. They traveled down the rod to the metal foil. Both leaves of the electroscope got a negative charge, so they moved apart.

What is an element's atomic number?

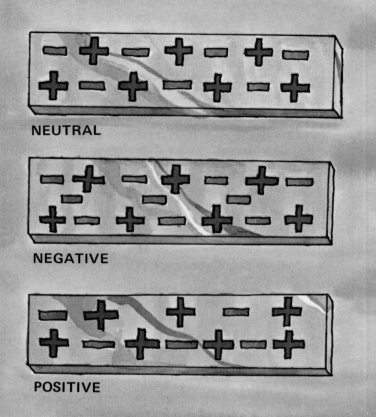

NEUTRAL

NEGATIVE

POSITIVE

Positive and negative charges. Most substances are electrically neutral. They have the same number of positive and negative charges. Positive charges are carried by protons. Negative charges are carried by electrons. A substance becomes negatively charged if it gets extra electrons. A substance becomes positively charged if it loses some electrons.

▶ **How does a substance become positively charged?**

Atoms are neutral. Electrical charges are carried by protons and electrons. A substance becomes charged if it has more of one than the other. Atoms have the same number of protons and electrons. They have the same number of positive and negative charges. Atoms are electrically neutral.

▶ **Why are atoms electrically neutral?**

The atomic number of an element. Look at the periodic table of the elements on pages 226 and 227. The elements are numbered 1 to 107. These numbers are the atomic numbers of the elements. An element's atomic number is the number of protons in each atom of the element. Each hydrogen atom has one proton, so hydrogen's atomic number is 1. A helium atom has two protons, so helium's atomic number is 2. Uranium atoms have 92 protons each, so uranium's atomic number is 92. The atomic number of any element tells

you the number of protons that are in each atom of the element.

▶ **What does an element's atomic number tell you about its atoms?**

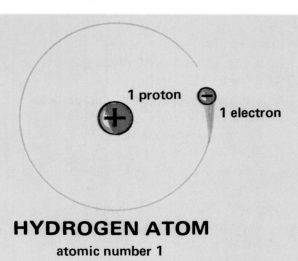

1 proton

1 electron

HYDROGEN ATOM

atomic number 1

Finding the number of electrons in an atom. Atoms are electrically neutral. They have the same number of protons and electrons. If the atomic number of an element is 8, then an atom of that element has 8 protons. If the atom has 8 protons, then it also has 8 electrons. The atomic number of an element can tell you the number of electrons in each atom of the element.

▶ **How can you find the number of electrons in an element's atoms?**

Element	Symbol	Atomic Number	Number of Protons	Number of Electrons
carbon	C	6	6	6
sodium	Na	11	11	11
iron	Fe	26	26	26
gold	Au	79	79	79

Arranging elements by atomic number. Mendeleev arranged the elements by weight in his periodic table. Today we know that the number of protons in each atom of an element is more important than the weight of the atom. An element's chemical properties depend on the number of protons in each of its atoms. The number of protons in each atom is the same as the element's atomic number. In the modern periodic table, we arrange the elements by atomic number, instead of by atomic weight. Hydrogen, with 1 proton in each of its atoms, is number 1 in the table. Radium, with 88 protons, is number 88.

▶ **How are elements arranged in the modern periodic table?**

WHAT YOU LEARNED

1. The atomic number of an element is the number of protons in each atom of the element.
2. An atom has the same number of protons and electrons.

ANSWER THESE

Write down the number of protons found in each atom of each of the following elements. (Use the periodic table on pages 226 and 227.)

1. neon (Ne)
2. aluminum (Al)
3. potassium (K)
4. mercury (Hg)
5. helium (He)

FINDING OUT MORE

Radiation

Certain elements give off tiny particles, or rays. This is called radiation (RAY-dee-AY-shun). These elements are said to be radioactive (RAY-dee-oh-AC-tiv). Three different kinds of radiation are given off by radioactive elements. They are called alpha, beta, and gamma. Alpha rays are positive. Beta rays are negative. Gamma rays are neutral. Alpha and beta rays are bent in different directions by a magnet. Gamma rays are not affected by a magnet.

PEOPLE IN SCIENCE

Marie Curie (1867-1934)

In 1892 Marie Curie and her husband, Pierre, discovered the radioactive element polonium. Later that year they discovered radium, another radioactive element. For these discoveries the Curies received the Nobel Prize in Chemistry in 1903. After her husband's death, Marie Curie continued research on radium. In 1911 she again was awarded the Nobel Prize for her work on that element. Thus she became the first person to be awarded two Nobel Prizes.

Irene Joliot-Curie (1897-1956)

Irene Joliot-Curie was the daughter of Marie and Pierre Curie. She carried on the research work of her parents. She and her husband discovered a method for making certain elements artificially radioactive. For this important discovery, they were awarded the Nobel Prize in Chemistry in 1935.

What is atomic mass?

electron

nucleus

orbit or shell

proton   neutron

HELIUM ATOM

Atoms are made up of particles. Atoms contain protons, neutrons, and electrons. The protons and neutrons are together in the center of the atom. The center of the atom is called the nucleus (NEW-clee-us). The protons and neutrons are in the nucleus of the atom. The electrons move around the nucleus. They move in paths called orbits (OR-bits). These orbits are also called shells.

▶ **What is the center of an atom called?**

Atomic mass. The mass of an atom is very small. scientists do not measure the mass of atoms in grams. They use a special unit called an atomic mass unit. A proton has a mass of one atomic mass unit. A neutron also has a mass of one atomic mass unit. The atomic mass of an atom is the total mass of its protons and neutrons. Atomic mass is sometimes called "atomic weight."

The atomic mass of an atom is always the same as the total number of protons and neutrons in the nucleus of the atom. Electrons have much less mass than protons or neutrons. In fact, they are practically "weightless." Electrons add almost nothing to the mass of an atom. They don't have to be counted to find atomic mass.

A hydrogen atom has 1 proton and no neutrons in its nucleus. Its atomic mass is 1. A helium atom has 2 protons and 2 neutrons. Its atomic mass is 4. A sodium atom has 11 protons and 12 neutrons. Its atomic mass is 23. The atomic mass of an atom is the same as its number of protons and neutrons.

▶ **What is atomic mass?**

Finding the number of neutrons in an atom. Atomic mass tells you the number of protons and neutrons in an atom. The atomic number tells you the number of protons in the atom. Suppose you know the atomic mass and the atomic number of an atom. Then you can figure out how many neutrons it has. Just subtract the atomic number from the atomic mass. Atomic mass (number of protons + neutrons) minus atomic number (number of protons) equals the number of neutrons.

▶ **How can you figure out the number of neutrons in an atom?**

LITHIUM
atomic mass 7   atomic number 3

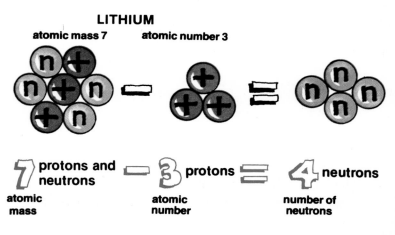

7 protons and neutrons   —   3 protons   =   4 neutrons

atomic mass   atomic number   number of neutrons

WHAT YOU LEARNED

1. Protons and neutrons are in the nucleus of an atom. Electrons move in orbits or shells around the nucleus.
2. Atomic mass is the number of protons and neutrons in an atom.

ANSWER THIS

The center of an atom is called the _____. It contains _____ and _____. Electrons move around the _____ in paths called _____ or _____. Most of an atom's mass is in its _____. The atom's atomic mass tells the number of _____ and _____ it has in its _____.

SCIENCE WORDS

nucleus (NEW-clee-us)
the center of an atom
orbit (OR-bit)
a path that electrons follow around the nucleus
atomic mass
the total number of protons and neutrons in an atom's nucleus; also called "atomic weight"

NOW TRY THIS
Fill in the blank spaces in the chart.

Element	Symbol	Atomic Number	Atomic Mass	Protons	Neutrons	Electrons
nitrogen	N	7	14			
oxygen	O	8	16			
sulfur	S	16	32			
nickel	Ni	28	59			
tin	Sn	50	119			
plutonium	Pu	94	242			

PLEASE DO NOT WRITE IN THIS BOOK.

FINDING OUT MORE

Atoms of an element do not always have the same number of neutrons. Sometimes the number of neutrons can be different for different atoms of the same element. The atomic masses of these atoms will be different from each other. Atoms of the same element that have different atomic masses are called isotopes (EYE-so-topes). Isotopes of an element have the same number of protons, but different numbers of neutrons.

Hydrogen is an example of an element with several isotopes. The periodic table shows that hydrogen has an atomic mass of 1. But there are isotopes of hydrogen that have atomic weights of 2 and 3. Atoms of these isotopes have extra neutrons in their nucleus. Atoms with a mass of 2 have 1 proton and 1 neutron. Atoms with a mass of 3 have 1 proton and 2 neutrons. The mass shown in the periodic table for an element is the average mass of its atoms.

PEOPLE IN SCIENCE

Chien-Shiung Wu
Dr. Wu is a professor of physics at Columbia University. She was educated in China and in the United States. Her research has involved understanding the forces that exist within atoms. She is best known for proving that a basic law of physics was not correct under certain conditions. She was the first woman to receive the Comstock Prize from the National Academy of Sciences.

Shirley Ann Jackson
Dr. Jackson received her doctoral degree in physics from M.I.T. She was the first American black woman to receive such a degree from that institution. Her work involves research in the basic properties of matter. During her career she has taught at Fisk University and at M.I.T. She has also worked at the Fermi Accelerator Laboratory in Illinois. She currently works as a research scientist at Bell Laboratories.

How are electrons arranged in an atom?

Electron paths. An atom has the same number of electrons as protons. The electrons travel around the nucleus in paths called orbits. An orbit is a single path. But electrons can take many paths around the nucleus. All of the electron paths put together make an <u>electron shell</u>.

▶ **What is an electron shell?**

Numbers of electron shells. Hydrogen and helium are the elements in the first period of the periodic table. Atoms of elements in the first period have 1 electron shell. Atoms of elements in the second period have 2 electron shells. Atoms of elements in the third period have 3 electron shells, and so on. Letters are used to name the shells. The first shell is called the K shell. The others follow in alphabetical order, from L to Q.

▶ **How many electron shells do atoms in the second period have?**

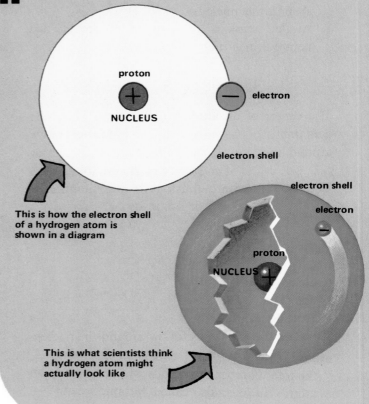

proton

electron

NUCLEUS

electron shell

This is how the electron shell of a hydrogen atom is shown in a diagram

electron shell

electron

proton

NUCLEUS

This is what scientists think a hydrogen atom might actually look like

Filling the shells. Each electron shell can hold only a certain number of electrons. The diagram and chart show how many electrons each of the first four shells can hold.

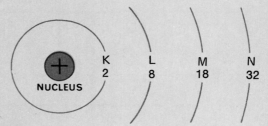

NUCLEUS K 2 L 8 M 18 N 32

SHELL	NUMBER OF ELECTRONS SHELL CAN HOLD
K	2
L	8
M	18
N	32

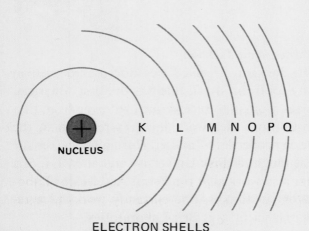

NUCLEUS K L M N O P Q

ELECTRON SHELLS

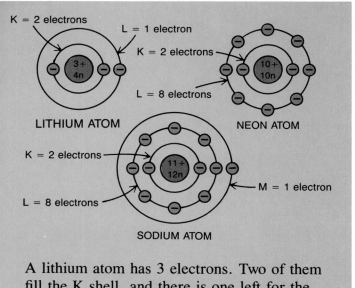

K = 2 electrons
L = 1 electron
K = 2 electrons
3+
4n
LITHIUM ATOM

K = 2 electrons
L = 8 electrons
10+
10n
NEON ATOM

K = 2 electrons
L = 8 electrons
11+
12n
M = 1 electron
SODIUM ATOM

A lithium atom has 3 electrons. Two of them fill the K shell, and there is one left for the L shell. Neon has 10 electrons. It needs only 2 electron shells. Sodium has 11 electrons, so it needs a third shell.

▶ **How many electron shells does an atom with 10 electrons need?**

Inner and outer shells. A K shell is complete when it has two electrons. An L shell is complete when it has 8 electrons. M and N shells can hold 18 and 32 electrons when they are inner shells. Inner shells are inside other shells. When an M or N shell is the outer shell, it can hold only 8 electrons. An outer shell can never hold more than 8 electrons. Eight electrons make an outer shell complete.

▶ **How many electrons can an N shell hold when it is the outer shell?**

WHAT YOU LEARNED

1. Electrons are found in shells around the nucleus of an atom.
2. An electron shell can hold only a certain number of electrons.
3. A complete outer shell has 8 electrons (except for the K shell, which has 2).

SCIENCE WORD

electron shell

   all of an electron's orbits, or paths.

ANSWER THESE

Use the periodic table on pages 226 and 227 to help you answer the following.

1. A silicon atom has _____ electron shells.
2. A silver atom has _____ electron shells.
3. An argon atom has _____ electrons in its outer shell.
4. For each of the elements in the chart, fill in the letter of its outer shell and the number of electrons in that shell.

ELEMENT	SYMBOL	LETTER OF OUTER SHELL	NUMBER OF ELECTRONS IN OUTER SHELL
sulfur	S		
helium	He		
chlorine	Cl		

PEOPLE IN SCIENCE

Luis Walter Alvarez

Dr. Alvarez has been a professor of physics at the University of California, Berkeley since 1938. He has invented instruments and developed computer programs to analyze basic particles of matter. In 1960 he discovered two types of atomic particles. In 1968 he was awarded a Nobel Prize for his contributions to the study of matter.

Maria Goeppert Mayer (1906-1972)

Dr. Mayer was educated in Europe. She came to the United States in 1930. In 1946 she became professor at the University of Chicago. She also was senior scientist at the Argonne National Laboratory. There she developed a theory to explain the arrangement of protons and neutrons within the nuclei of different elements. In 1963 Dr. Mayer was awarded the Nobel Prize in Physics for her theory of nuclear structure.

Do the following questions on a separate sheet of paper.

Fill in the Blank   *Write down the statements in Column I. Where there is a blank line in each statement, write the word or phrase from Column II that best completes the meaning of the statement.*

Column I	Column II
1. An atom can have only 2 electrons in the _____.	atoms
2. An M shell is complete when it holds _____electrons.	l
3. The atomic mass of a hydrogen atom is _____.	K shell
4. Atomic mass is sometimes called _____.	proton
5. Electrical charges are carried by_____ .	elements
6. If an atom has 8 protons, its atomic number is _____.	atomic weight
7. A positively charged atomic particle is the_____.	neutral
8. An atom that is neither positively nor negatively charged is _____.	8
9. Molecules are made up of_____ .	protons and electrons
10. There are 107 different_____.	

Multiple Choice   *Write the letter of the choice that best completes the statement or answers the question.*

1. In a chemical reaction, the atoms
   a. break into smaller particles
   b. do not change
   c. become new atoms
2. Scientists no longer believe atoms
   a. cannot be broken down
   b. are the smallest units of an element
   c. are made of matter
3. A glass rod with more protons than electrons has
   a. a negative charge
   b. no charge
   c. a positive charge
4. A negatively charged atomic particle is the
   a. proton
   b. neutron
   c. electron

5. The atomic number of an element tells you
   a. the charge on its atoms
   b. the number of protons in each atom
   c. the number of neutrons in each atom
6. A proton's mass is equal to
   a. an electron's mass
   b. zero atomic mass units
   c. one atomic mass unit
7. A helium atom has 2 protons and 2 neutrons. Its atomic mass is
   a. 2
   b. 4
   c. 0
8. An outer shell can never hold more than
   a. 8 electrons
   b. 2 electrons
   c. 6 electrons

UNIT 13 Compounds

Unit Lessons

1. What is a compound?
2. What is water composed of?
3. What does the formula for a compound tell us?
4. What are molecules?
5. What happens when elements combine with oxygen?
6. What are the properties of carbon dioxide?
7. What are physical and chemical changes?
8. What are chemical equations?
9. How are compounds and mixtures different?

Goals and Objectives

After completing this unit, you should be able to:
- explain how compounds differ from mixtures.
- demonstrate that water is a compound.
- read and understand chemical formulas and equations.
- understand the difference between fast and slow oxidation.
- give examples of chemical and physical changes.

What is a compound?

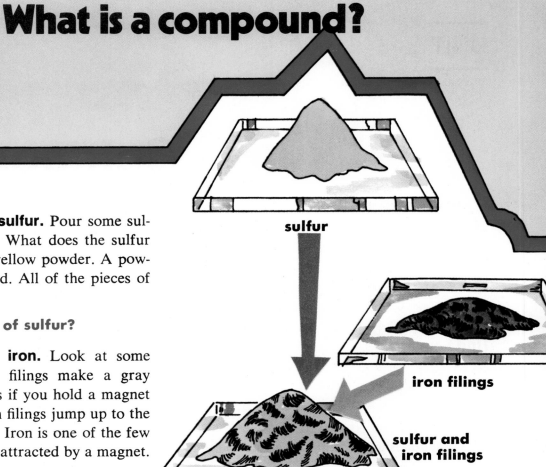

sulfur

iron filings

sulfur and
iron filings

Some properties of sulfur. Pour some sulfur onto a glass plate. What does the sulfur look like? Sulfur is a yellow powder. A powder is a ground-up solid. All of the pieces of sulfur look alike.

▶ **What is the color of sulfur?**

Some properties of iron. Look at some iron filings. The iron filings make a gray powder. What happens if you hold a magnet over the iron? The iron filings jump up to the magnet and stick to it. Iron is one of the few substances that can be attracted by a magnet.

▶ **What happens when you hold a magnet over iron filings?**

Mixing iron with sulfur. Mix the iron filings and the sulfur together on a glass plate. Look at the mixture carefully. Can you still see the iron filings and the sulfur? Have the properties of the iron filings or the sulfur changed?

Hold a magnet over the mixture. The iron filings jump up to the magnet. The sulfur stays on the plate. You can easily separate the iron from the sulfur with a magnet.

Now look at the iron and sulfur again. Do they look the same as they did before you mixed them together? The properties of the iron and sulfur did not change when you mixed them. When elements are put together in a mixture, their properties do not change.

▶ **How can a mixture of iron and sulfur be separated?**

Combining iron with sulfur. Mix the iron filings and sulfur together again. Put them in a test tube. Heat the test tube until the mixture begins to glow. Then take it away from the flame and let it cool.

Remove the cool material from the test tube. Can you see the iron and the yellow sulfur now? Can you remove the iron with a magnet? The new material does not have the properties of either iron or sulfur. It does not look like either one, and you cannot separate it with a magnet.

In the test tube, the iron and sulfur combined to make a new material. The iron and sulfur together became iron sulfide (SUL-fide). Iron sulfide is not like iron or sulfur.

244

It has different properties. Iron sulfide is a compound (COM-pound) of iron and sulfur. When elements are combined to make a new material, that material is called a compound. A compound has different properties from the elements that make it up.

► **How is a compound formed?**

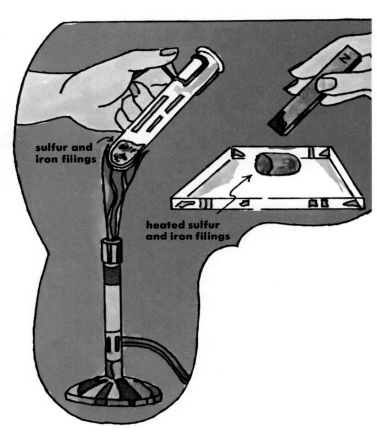

sulfur and
iron filings

heated sulfur
and iron filings

Other compounds. Most of the matter making up the earth is composed of compounds. The salt you use on your table is a compound. It is made of the elements sodium and chlorine. Sodium is a metal that burns very easily. It would be dangerous to eat. Chlorine is a poisonous gas. When sodium and chlorine combine, they form sodium chloride. When it is on our table, we call it salt. But salt is not green. It is not a gas. It does not burn. And it is certainly not poisonous. The sodium and chlorine combine to make a white powder

that we can use on our food. Salt is not at all like the elements that make it up. Sand is made up of many different compounds. One type of sand is formed when silicon combines with oxygen. The chemical name for this sand is silicon dioxide. Glass and quartz are other forms of silicon dioxide.

► **How is salt different from the elements that form it?**

WHAT YOU LEARNED

1. A compound is a combination of elements.
2. A compound has different properties from the elements that make it up.

SCIENCE WORD

compound (COM-pound)
a combination of elements that has different properties from the elements that make it up

ANSWER THESE

1. When iron and sulfur are mixed together,
   a. the sulfur can be removed with a magnet
   b. the iron can be removed with a magnet
   c. they cannot be separated with a magnet
2. When iron and sulfur are heated together until they glow,
   a. they can be separated with a magnet while they're hot
   b. they can be separated with a magnet after they cool
   c. they cannot be separated with a magnet
3. A compound is
   a. a combination of elements that can be easily separated
   b. a combination of elements that cannot be easily separated
   c. any mixture of elements that is not attracted by a magnet

NOW TRY THESE

1. How does sand differ from the elements that form it?
2. Is carbon dioxide an element or a compound? Why?

What is water composed of?

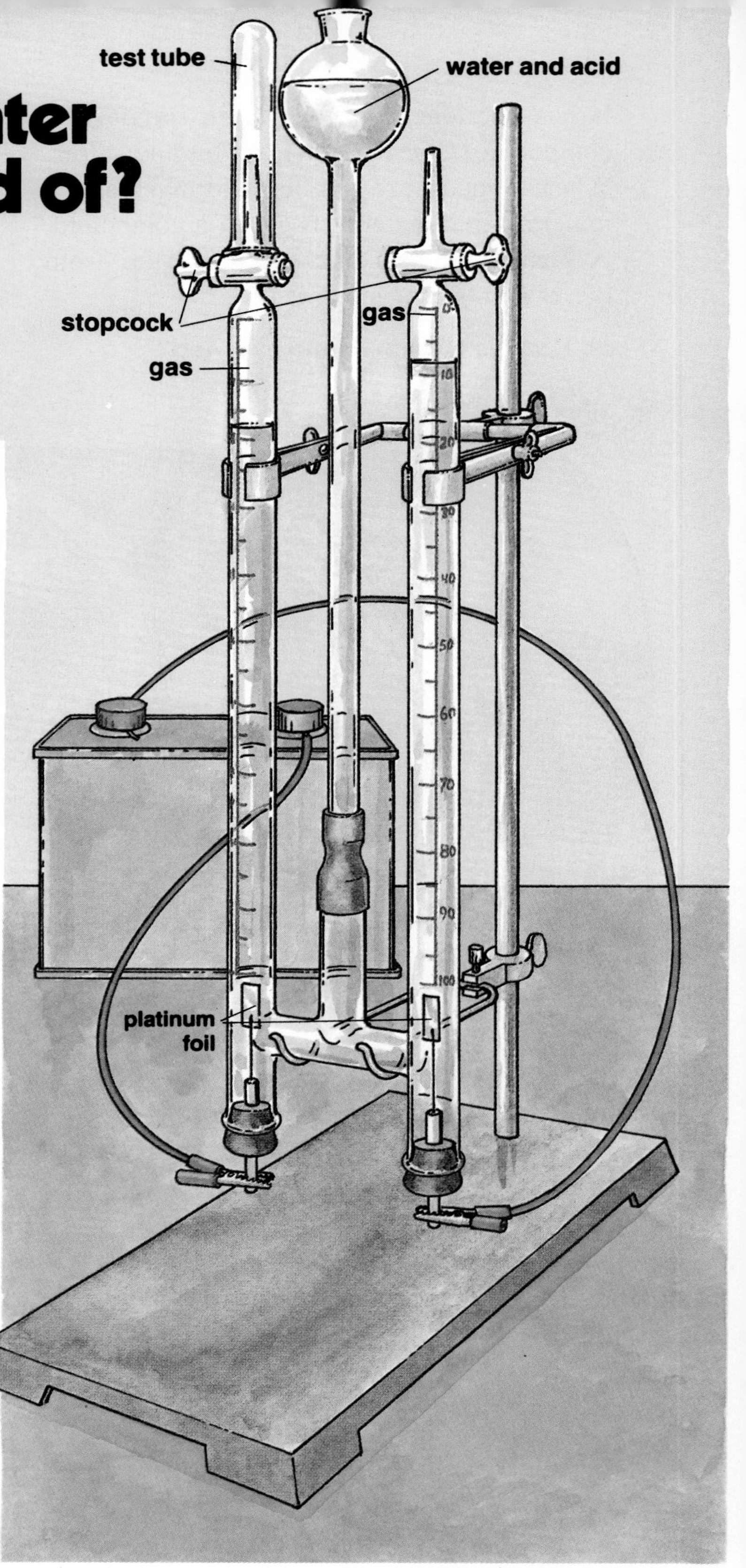

test tube

water and acid

stopcock

gas

gas

platinum foil

Taking water apart. The diagram shows a device called the Hoffman apparatus (HOFF-mun AP-uh-RAT-us). It can be used to take water apart. Water is a compound. The Hoffman apparatus can separate water into the elements that make it up. An electric current goes through the water. The electric current breaks the water into its elements.

▶ What can the Hoffman apparatus do?

Water is made up of two gases. When the Hoffman apparatus is turned on, electricity flows through the water. At the end of each electrical wire, there is some platinum foil. Gas is produced at the platinum foil. Bubbles of gas rise through the water from the foil. The gas collects at the top of each tube. The stopcock keeps the gas from getting out of the tube.

Measure how much gas is collected in each tube. There is twice as much gas in one tube as in the other. This happens whenever water is broken down. The gases being collected in the two tubes are not the same. There is a different gas in each tube.

▶ How many gases are produced when water is taken apart?

Identifying the gases that make up water. Hold a test tube over the top of the Hoffman tube that has more gas in it. Turn the stopcock to let some of the gas into the test tube. Then hold a burning wooden splint near the mouth of the test tube. You will hear a pop, and see flames come out of the test tube.

Hydrogen is a gas that burns very easily. A burning splint is used to test for hydrogen. The test shows that the gas from the Hoffman tube was hydrogen.

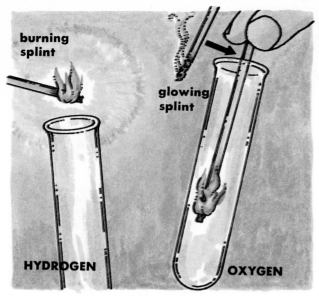

burning splint

glowing splint

HYDROGEN

OXYGEN

Now collect some gas from the other tube in the Hoffman apparatus. To test this gas, use a splint that is not burning, but just glowing. When you put the glowing splint into the test tube, the splint bursts into flame. Oxygen is a gas that helps things burn. A glowing splint is used to test for oxygen. The test shows that the second gas was oxygen.

► **What two gases are produced when water is taken apart?**

Water is composed of hydrogen and oxygen. Water is a compound. When water is broken down, two gases are produced. The gases are hydrogen and oxygen. Twice as much hydrogen is produced as oxygen. Water is made up of the elements hydrogen and oxygen. There is twice as much hydrogen in water as oxygen. Water is two parts hydrogen and one part oxygen.

► **What is water composed of?**

WHAT YOU LEARNED

1. The Hoffman apparatus can be used to break water down into its elements.
2. Water is a compound made up of hydrogen and oxygen.
3. There is twice as much hydrogen in water as oxygen.

SCIENCE WORD

Hoffman apparatus (HOFF-mun AP-uh-RAT-us) a device that can break water down into its elements

ANSWER THESE

1. Water is
   a. an element
   b. a compound
   c. a metal

2. Water is composed of
   a. carbon and oxygen
   b. hydrogen and oxygen
   c. sodium and chlorine

3. A gas that burns when a burning splint is held near it is
   a. oxygen
   b. nitrogen
   c. hydrogen

4. A gas that makes a glowing splint burst into flame is
   a. oxygen
   b. nitrogen
   c. hydrogen

```
C H L O R I N E A T
W A T E R N I E N A
W I R O N T C L A M
T N E B R I K A R E
S E N O A Z E E G R
O O A R T N L Y O C
D N E O X Y G E N U
I T I N C O P P E R
U S A G O L D D R Y
M S I L V E R A M G
```

NOW TRY THIS

The word puzzle has the names of some of the elements hidden in it. To find them, you can read the letters down or across. How many hidden elements can you find?

FINDING OUT MORE

Water can be broken down into hydrogen and oxygen. Hydrogen and oxygen can also be combined to make water. Collect some hydrogen in a dry test tube. Hold a burning splint near the mouth of the test tube. The hydrogen burns quickly, and then goes out. Now look carefully at the inside of the test tube. Do you see moisture on the inside of the test tube? The moisture is water. Oxygen from the air helped the hydrogen burn. The oxygen combined with the hydrogen to make water.

What does the formula for a compound tell us?

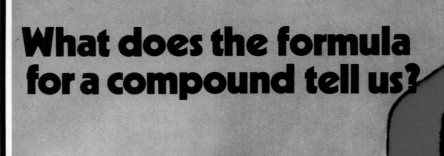

What is H_2O? Scientists use symbols as a shorthand way of writing the names of elements. A <u>chemical formula</u> (KEM-i-kul FOR-mew-luh) is a shorthand way to write the name of a compound. The formula for the compound water is H_2O.

H_2O is a shorthand way to write water.

▶ **What is a chemical formula?**

Chemical formulas contain symbols. A formula tells the elements that make up a compound. The letters in the formula are the symbols for the elements that make up the compound. The formula H_2O tells you that water is made up of hydrogen (H) and oxygen (O). You will find out what the "2" means in the next section. The chart shows some more compounds and their formulas.

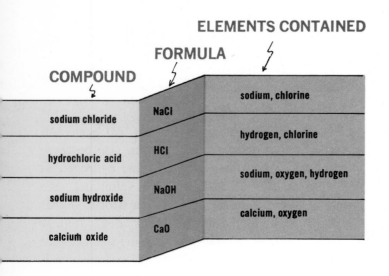

COMPOUND	FORMULA	ELEMENTS CONTAINED
sodium chloride	NaCl	sodium, chlorine
hydrochloric acid	HCl	hydrogen, chlorine
sodium hydroxide	NaOH	sodium, oxygen, hydrogen
calcium oxide	CaO	calcium, oxygen

▶ **What do the symbols in a chemical formula tell you about a compound?**

Some chemical formulas contain numbers. The formula for water has the number 2 in it after the symbol H. A number that follows a symbol in a chemical formula is called a <u>subscript</u> (SUB-script). The subscript is placed after the symbol for an element, and a little bit below it. The subscript tells how much of an element is in a compound. The subscript 2 in H_2O shows that water is two parts hydrogen. Water is also one part oxygen. But there is no subscript after O in H_2O. The subscript 1 doesn't have to be written down. When there is no subscript after a symbol in a formula, it means 1. The chart on the next page shows more compounds and their formulas. It also shows how much of each element is in them.

COMPOUND	FORMULA	AMOUNT OF EACH ELEMENT
carbon dioxide	CO_2	1 part carbon 2 parts oxygen
aluminum chloride	$AlCl_3$	1 part aluminum 3 parts chlorine
aluminum oxide	Al_2O_3	2 parts aluminum 3 parts oxygen
potassium chloride	KCl	1 part potassium 1 part chlorine
sugar	$C_{12}H_{22}O_{11}$	12 parts carbon 22 parts hydrogen 11 parts oxygen

▶ **What do the subscripts in a formula tell you about a compound?**

Writing the formulas of compounds. In many compounds, a metallic element is combined with a non-metallic element. Sodium chloride is made up of the metal sodium and the non-metal chlorine. In a chemical formula, the symbol for the metallic element is always written first. The scientific names of many compounds are like their formulas. The name tells the elements that make up the compound. The chart below shows some compounds and the metallic and non-metallic elements that make them up.

COMPOUND	FORMULA	METALLIC ELEMENT	NON-METALLIC ELEMENT
sodium chloride	$NaCl$	Na (sodium)	Cl (chlorine)
mercuric oxide	HgO	Hg (mercury)	O (oxygen)
barium chloride	$BaCl_2$	Ba (barium)	Cl (chlorine)
silver sulfide	Ag_2S	Ag (silver)	S (sulfur)
lead iodide	PbI	Pb (lead)	I (iodine)

▶ **In a formula for a compound of a metal and a non-metal, which symbol is written first?**

WHAT YOU LEARNED

1. A chemical formula is a shorthand way of writing the name of a compound.
2. A chemical formula tells you the name and amount of each element in a compound.

SCIENCE WORDS

chemical formula (KEM-i-kul FOR-mew-luh) a shorthand way to write the name of a compound

subscript (SUB-script) a number in a formula that tells you how much of an element is in the compound

ANSWER THESE

On a sheet of paper, list the elements that make up each compound.

COMPOUND	ELEMENTS CONTAINED			
1. carbon dioxide (CO_2)	a. ?	b. ?		
2. ammonia (NH_3)	a. ?	b. ?		
3. calcite ($CaCO_3$)	a. ?	b. ?	c. ?	
4. potassium hydroxide (KOH)	a. ?	b. ?	c. ?	
5. baking soda ($NaHCO_3$)	a. ?	b. ?	c. ?	d. ?

NOW TRY THIS

Write the chemical formula for each of the following compounds. The elements are listed in the correct order.

1. potassium chloride (1 part potassium, 1 part chlorine)
2. nitric acid (1 part hydrogen, 1 part nitrogen, 3 parts oxygen)
3. lead nitrate (1 part lead, 1 part nitrogen, 3 parts oxygen)
4. copper sulfate (1 part copper, 1 part sulfur, 4 parts oxygen)
5. hydrogen sulfide (2 parts hydrogen, 1 part sulfur)

What are molecules?

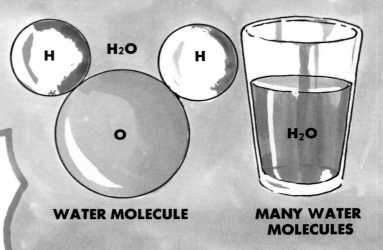

WATER MOLECULE

MANY WATER MOLECULES

Molecules are the smallest bits of a substance. Did you ever spill sugar on the floor and then walk on it? You could hear the bits of sugar being crunched into smaller pieces. Even these very small pieces can be broken into smaller pieces. The smallest piece of sugar there could be is called a molecule of sugar. A molecule is the smallest piece of an element or a compound. A molecule of water is the smallest bit of water that would still be water.

▶ **What is a molecule?**

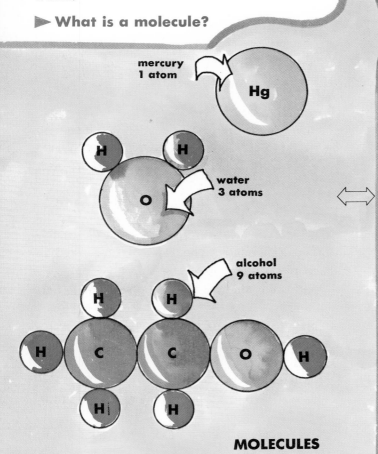

mercury
1 atom

water
3 atoms

alcohol
9 atoms

MOLECULES

Molecules are composed of atoms. The formula for water is H_2O. This tells you what elements are in the compound water. The H tells you there is hydrogen in it. The O tells you there is oxygen. The formula also tells you what atoms are in one molecule of water. One molecule of water contains 2 atoms of hydrogen and 1 atom of oxygen.

▶ **What is one molecule of water made of?**

A molecule may have one atom or many atoms. Mercury is an element. An element is made up of only one kind of atom. A molecule of mercury is just 1 atom of mercury. Water is a compound. A molecule of water (H_2O) is made of 3 atoms joined together. A molecule of alcohol (C_2H_5OH) is made of 9 atoms joined together. A molecule of table sugar ($C_{12}H_{22}O_{11}$) is made of 45 atoms joined together. (Count them up in the formula.) Some molecules in your body have thousands of atoms in them.

▶ **How many atoms are there in a molecule of water?**

All substances are composed of molecules. Molecules are packed tightly together in solids. Molecules are loosely packed in liquids. Molecules can move far apart in gases. Molecules are always moving, even in solids. Look closely at some sugar. Each grain of sugar looks like a tiny jewel. This is called a crystal (CRISS-tul). A crystal of sugar contains millions of sugar molecules packed tightly together.

► **What are sugar crystals made of?**

molecules

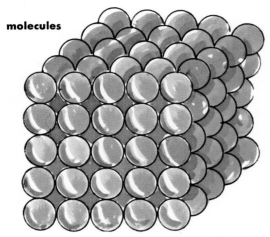

SUGAR CRYSTAL — $C_{12}H_{22}O_{11}$

WHAT YOU LEARNED

1. A molecule is the smallest piece of an element or compound that is still that element or compound.
2. Molecules are composed of atoms.

SCIENCE WORD

crystal (CRISS-tul)
   a piece of a solid that is shaped like a jewel

ANSWER THESE

1. How many atoms are there in each of these molecules?
   - **a.** C
   - **b.** CO
   - **c.** Cu
   - **d.** SO_2
   - **e.** H_2SO_4
   - **f.** KCl
   - **g.** Ag
   - **h.** $C_6H_{12}O_6$
   - **i.** O_3
   - **j.** NaOH
2. Name the atoms found in these molecules.
   - **a.** $MgCl_2$
   - **b.** NaOH
   - **c.** Pb

NOW TRY THIS

Copy these pictures of molecules onto a piece of paper. Under each picture, write the chemical formula of that molecule. Pick the formula from these: H_2S Fe_2O_3 NH_3 CH_4

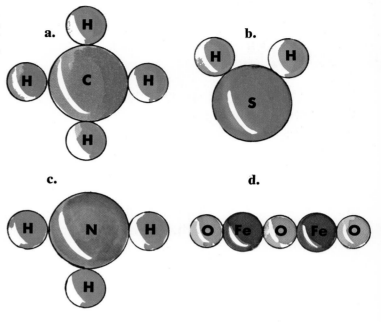

FINDING OUT MORE

Diatomic Molecules

The atoms of some elements always travel in pairs. We never find a single atom of oxygen by itself. Two single oxygen atoms would quickly combine with each other to form a molecule of oxygen. A molecule of oxygen contains two oxygen atoms joined together. That is why the chemical formula for oxygen is O_2. Oxygen is a diatomic (DIE-uh-TOM-ic) molecule. A diatomic molecule contains two atoms of the same element joined together. Some other diatomic molecules are hydrogen (H_2), nitrogen (N_2), chlorine (Cl_2), and iodine (I_2).

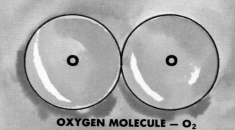

OXYGEN MOLECULE — O_2

What happens when elements combine with oxygen?

Another method of preparing oxygen. Mix some hydrogen peroxide with some manganese dioxide in a flask. You will see bubbles form in the flask. A gas is being produced. Collect some of the gas in the way shown in the diagram. Test it with a glowing splint. The splint bursts into flame when you put it into the gas. The gas is oxygen.

▶ **What two chemicals can you use to prepare oxygen?**

Burning steel wool. Steel wool contains the element iron (Fe). Heat a piece of steel wool until it glows. Then quickly put the steel wool into a bottle of oxygen. The steel wool bursts into flame. Now take the steel wool out of the bottle. The steel wool looks different. A new substance was formed when it burned. The new substance is iron oxide (Fe_2O_3). The iron in the steel wool combined with the oxygen in the bottle. It formed iron oxide.

▶ **What substance is formed when iron combines with oxygen?**

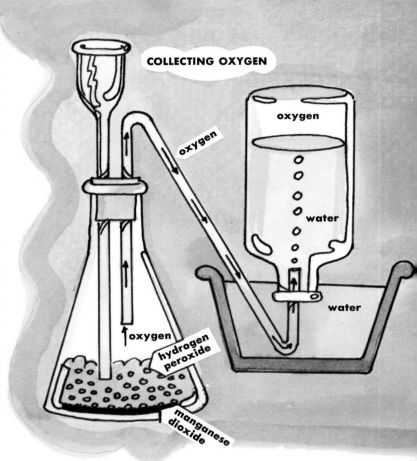

COLLECTING OXYGEN

oxygen

oxygen

water

oxygen

hydrogen peroxide

manganese dioxide

water

Combining with oxygen. Elements can combine with oxygen to form new substances. This is called oxidation (OX-i-DAY-shun). Iron oxide is a new substance that is produced by oxidation. Iron oxide is produced when some glowing steel wool is placed in oxygen. Iron oxide also forms when iron stands in moist air. Iron oxide made this way is called rust. Rusting is a form of slow oxidation. The iron combines slowly with oxygen in the air to form iron oxide.

▶ **What is oxidation?**

Rusting of iron

Burning substances in air. Look at a piece of magnesium ribbon that has been burned. The white powder that has formed is magnesium oxide (MgO). When magnesium burns, it combines with oxygen in the air. Burning is a form of oxidation. Burning occurs faster than rusting. Rusting is slow oxidation. Burning is fast oxidation.

▶ **What happens when things burn?**

Forming new substances with oxygen. When hydrogen is burned, water forms. Hydrogen combines with oxygen to produce water (H_2O). We breathe in air that contains oxygen. We eat foods that contain carbon and hydrogen. The foods are slowly oxidized in our bodies. We breathe out carbon dioxide and water vapor. The oxidation of the foods we eat also produces energy for work and play.

▶ **How do our bodies get energy?**

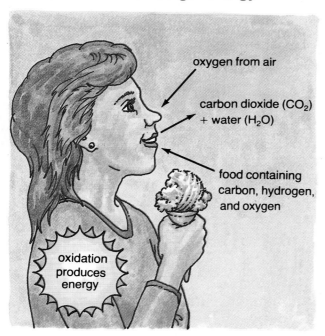

oxygen from air

carbon dioxide (CO_2) + water (H_2O)

food containing carbon, hydrogen, and oxygen

oxidation produces energy

Substances gain weight when they burn. Weigh a piece of steel wool. Then heat the steel wool until it glows. Weigh the new substance that is produced. Iron in the steel wool combined with oxygen in the air to form iron oxide. The iron oxide weighs more than the iron alone.

A piece of paper seems to be lighter after it has burned. Can you figure out why that happens? The compounds in the paper have a lot of carbon in them. When paper burns, carbon dioxide is formed. The carbon dioxide weighs more than the carbon alone. But carbon dioxide is a gas. It escapes into the air. You can't weigh it on the scale after you burn the paper.

▶ **Why does steel wool gain weight when it burns?**

WHAT YOU LEARNED

1. Elements combine with oxygen to form new substances. This is called oxidation.
2. Burning and rusting are forms of oxidation.
3. Oxidation of food in our bodies produces energy.

SCIENCE WORDS

oxidation (OX-i-DAY-shun)
   combining with oxygen
rusting
   the slow oxidation of iron
burning
   fast oxidation

ANSWER THESE

1. To produce oxygen, add _____ _____ to manganese dioxide.
2. The chemical formula for iron oxide is
   a. MnO_2 **b.** H_2O_2 **c.** Fe_2O_3
3. An example of slow oxidation is
   a. burning **b.** rusting **c.** heating
4. An example of fast oxidation is
   a. burning **b.** rusting **c.** heating
5. Why will a piece of iron gain weight when it rusts?

NOW TRY THESE

Tell what new compound is produced.
a. Burning magnesium produces _____ _____.
b. Burning carbon produces _____ _____.
c. Burning hydrogen produces _____.
d. Rusting iron produces _____ _____.
e. Burning iron produces _____ _____.

What are the properties of carbon dioxide?

Preparing carbon dioxide. Put some marble chips into a flask. The marble is calcium carbonate ($CaCO_3$). Now pour some hydrochloric acid (HCl) into the flask. Use a bottle to collect the gas that is produced. You will see that the gas has no color. Also, it has no odor. The gas is colorless and odorless.

Pour some clear limewater (LIME-water) into the bottle containing the gas. Shake the bottle gently. What happens to the limewater? You will see the limewater turn milky-white. This is what happens when limewater mixes with carbon dioxide. Limewater is used to test for carbon dioxide. The gas that was produced in the flask was carbon dioxide.

▶ **What can you use to test for carbon dioxide?**

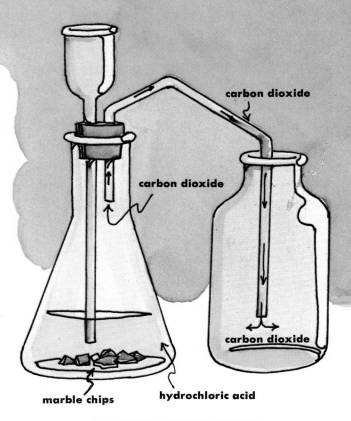

COLLECTING CARBON DIOXIDE

Burning fuels. Use a pair of tongs to hold a piece of paper. Light the paper and hold it over a bottle containing clear limewater. Shake the bottle gently. The limewater turns milky-white. Carbon dioxide has become mixed with it. There was carbon in the paper. The carbon was oxidized when the paper burned. When the carbon was oxidized, carbon dioxide was produced. Fuels like oil, gasoline, coal, and natural gas all contain carbon. When any of these fuels is burned, carbon dioxide is formed.

▶ **Why does burning paper produce carbon dioxide?**

Living things produce carbon dioxide. Blow through a straw into a bottle of limewater. Your breath makes the limewater turn milky-white. When food is oxidized in your body, carbon dioxide is produced. The carbon dioxide leaves your body when you breathe out. Your breath contains carbon dioxide. You and other living things oxidize food and produce carbon dioxide.

▶ **How can you show there is carbon dioxide in your breath?**

Putting out fires with carbon dioxide.
Collect some carbon dioxide in a bottle.
Then light a candle and place it in the bottom of an empty jar. Hold the bottle of carbon dioxide above the candle. Tip the bottle as if you were pouring something out of it. You will see the candle go out. Carbon dioxide filled the jar and put out the candle.

When you tipped the bottle over, you did pour something. You poured the carbon dioxide out of the bottle. Carbon dioxide is heavier than air. It can be poured like water. When the carbon dioxide filled the jar, no oxygen could get in. Without oxygen to help it burn, the candle went out. Carbon dioxide can put out fires. Some fire extinguishers (ex-TING-wish-ers) use carbon dioxide.

▶ **How does carbon dioxide put out a fire?**

WHAT YOU LEARNED

1. Carbon dioxide is a colorless, odorless gas. It is heavier than air and turns limewater milky-white.
2. Carbon dioxide is produced when fuels are burned. It is also produced by living things.
3. Carbon dioxide can put out fires and is used in fire extinguishers.

SCIENCE WORD

limewater (LIME-water)
a chemical that turns milky-white when it mixes with carbon dioxide

ANSWER THESE

1. Carbon dioxide is formed when carbon is
   a. oxidized
   b. breathed upon
   c. dissolved in water
2. Carbon dioxide gets into the air
   a. when fuels burn
   b. when animals breathe
   c. when both of these things happen
3. Carbon dioxide is
   a. lighter than air
   b. heavier than air
   c. the same weight as air
4. A chemical used to test for carbon dioxide is
   a. oxygen
   b. limewater
   c. hydrochloric acid

NOW TRY THESE

1. Name three properties of carbon dioxide.
2. Name three fuels that release carbon dioxide into the air when burned.

FINDING OUT MORE

Have you ever wondered what makes the fizz in soda? The tiny bubbles are carbon dioxide. Carbon dioxide is put into the soda when it is bottled. The cap is put on tightly to keep the carbon dioxide from escaping. When you open the bottle, the gas forms bubbles and goes into the air. The carbon dioxide gives soda its sparkly taste. When soda tastes flat, it's because most of the carbon dioxide has escaped from it.

DO THIS AT HOME

You can make carbon dioxide by mixing acetic (a-SEE-tic) acid and sodium bicarbonate. You probably have these chemicals at home, but don't know it. Vinegar has acetic acid in it. Baking soda is sodium bicarbonate. Put some baking soda in a cup. Add some vinegar. You will see bubbles of carbon dioxide form when these two substances mix.

What are physical and chemical changes?

Changes in size and shape. Break a wooden stick. Cut or tear a piece of paper. Stretch a rubber band. What happens? In each case, the size or shape of the material changes. The wood is still wood, the paper is still paper, and the rubber is still rubber. What happens when a drinking glass gets broken? Each piece of broken glass is still glass. The pieces just have different sizes and shapes. Changes like these are called <u>physical</u> (FIZZ-i-cul) <u>changes</u>. When a physical change happens to a substance, it stays the same substance.

▶ **What are some examples of a physical change?**

PHYSICAL CHANGES

A CHEMICAL CHANGE

paper

ashes

Producing new substances. Burn a small piece of paper. What does it look like now? Is it still paper? When substances burn, they combine with oxygen. New substances are produced. When paper burns, carbon dioxide, water vapor, and ashes are produced. None of these is paper. Changes like this are called <u>chemical</u> (KEM-i-cul) <u>changes</u>. When a chemical change happens to a substance, it is no longer the same substance. Different substances are formed from it.

▶ **What happens in a chemical change?**

Changing the state of matter. Let an ice cube melt in a dish. The solid ice becomes water. But ice and water are both H_2O. The ice did not change to a new substance when it melted. It only changed its state. Melting, freezing, evaporation, and condensation are changes in state. Changes in state are physical changes.

▶ **What kind of change is a change in state?**

A CHANGE OF STATE

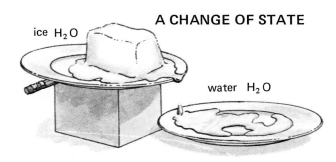

ice H_2O

water H_2O

Chemical changes form new substances.

When carbon burns, carbon dioxide is formed. When iron rusts, iron oxide is formed. Burning and other forms of oxidation are chemical changes. Mixing vinegar with baking soda produces carbon dioxide. This is also a chemical change. Heating mercuric oxide produces mercury and oxygen. The Hoffman apparatus breaks water down into hydrogen and oxygen. All of these are chemical changes. Whenever new substances are produced, the change is a chemical change.

▶ **Why is rusting a chemical change?**

WHAT YOU LEARNED

1. Physical changes are changes that do not produce new substances.
2. Chemical changes are changes that produce new substances.
3. Changes in state are physical changes.

SCIENCE WORDS

physical (FIZZ-i-cul) **change**
a change that does not produce a new substance

chemical (KEM-i-cul) **change**
a change that produces new substances

ANSWER THESE

1. A change that produces a new substance is a _____ change.
2. A change only in the size and shape of a substance is a _____ change.
3. A change of state is a _____ change.
4. Oxidation is an example of a _____ change.
5. Two ways in which water can change its state are _____ and _____.

NOW TRY THIS

Tell whether each of the following is a chemical change (C) or only a physical change (P).
1. boiling water
2. rusting nail
3. tearing clothes
4. burning gas in a stove
5. tarnishing silver
6. melting ice cream
7. lighting a match
8. sawing wood
9. chewing food
10. oxidizing food for energy

WHAT'S HAPPENING

Chemical Changes in Cooking

A cake looks much different from the batter used to make it. In the oven, the liquid batter changes to a solid cake. But the cake does not change back to a liquid when it cools. Baking a cake is more than just a physical change. In the oven, chemical changes take place. New substances are formed while the cake is baking. Chemical changes usually take place whenever foods are cooked.

A hard-boiled egg does not become liquid again when you let it cool. The egg has been changed chemically by boiling. Cooked meat is chemically different from uncooked meat. When vegetables are cooked too long, some of their vitamins are lost. The vitamins are changed chemically to new substances. Foods change chemically when they are cooked.

What are chemical equations?

CHEMICAL REACTIONS

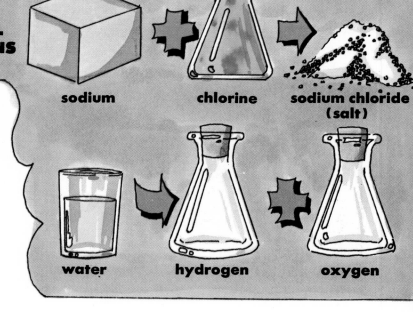

sodium   chlorine   sodium chloride (salt)

water   hydrogen   oxygen

Substances change. In a chemical change, one or more new substances are formed. A chemical change is also called a chemical reaction (ree-AC-shun). There are different kinds of chemical reactions. Sometimes, two substances combine with each other to form a new substance. Sodium combines with chlorine to form sodium chloride, or salt. Sometimes a substance breaks down to form other substances. Water can be broken down to form hydrogen and oxygen. Each of these changes is a chemical reaction.

► **Give an example of a chemical reaction.**

Chemical sentences. "Sodium combines with chlorine to produce sodium chloride." This sentence tells about a chemical reaction. Scientists have a shorter way to write this sentence. They use chemical symbols and formulas instead of words. Here is how they would write the sentence:

$$Na + Cl \rightarrow NaCl$$

This is called a chemical equation (uh-KWAY-zhun). The plus sign (+) means that sodium (Na) and chlorine (Cl) are reacting. The arrow means "produces," but the chemist uses the word yields (YEELDS), instead. To yield means to produce. The formula on the right side of the arrow tells the substance that is produced. To read the equation aloud, you would say, "Sodium plus chlorine yields sodium chloride."

► **What does the arrow in a chemical equation stand for?**

Numbers in chemical equations. Look at this equation. It tells about the chemical reaction when water is broken down.

$$2H_2O \rightarrow 2H_2 + O_2$$

There is one substance on the left side of the arrow. It is water (H_2O). Water yields the two substances on the right side. They are hydrogen (H_2) and oxygen (O_2). There is a 2 in front of the H_2O. This means that 2 molecules of water are needed for the reaction. There is a 2 in front of the H_2. This means that 2 molecules of hydrogen are produced by the reaction. The number 2 is called a coefficient (COH-uh-FISH-unt). A coefficient tells how many molecules are needed or produced in a reaction. When only one molecule is needed or produced, there is no coefficient. No coefficient means 1. There is no coefficient in front of O_2. This means that 1 molecule of oxygen (O_2) is produced.

► **What does a coefficient in a chemical equation tell you?**

Chemical equations must balance. Look at this equation. It is the chemical reaction when hydrogen and oxygen combine to produce water.

$$2H_2 + O_2 \rightarrow 2H_2O$$

It says, "2 molecules of hydrogen plus 1 molecule of oxygen yields 2 molecules of water." A chemical reaction cannot make atoms, and it cannot lose atoms. There must be the same number of hydrogen atoms after the reaction as there were before. The chemical equation must show this. The table proves that it does.

A BALANCED EQUATION			
Equation	$2H_2$	$+ O_2 \rightarrow$	$2H_2O$
Number of Molecules	2 molecules of hydrogen	1 molecule of oxygen	2 molecules of water
Molecules			
Number of Atoms	4 atoms of hydrogen	2 atoms of oxygen	4 atoms of hydrogen 2 atoms of oxygen
NUMBERS OF ATOMS BALANCE			

There are 4 atoms of hydrogen on the left and 4 on the right. There are 2 atoms of oxygen on the left and 2 on the right. We say that the equation is <u>balanced</u> (BAL-unst). The coefficients are needed to balance the equation. If you take the coefficients away, the equation won't be balanced. Try it and see.

▶ **When is an equation balanced?**

WHAT YOU LEARNED

1. A chemical reaction is a change that produces one or more new substances.
2. A chemical equation is a way of using symbols and formulas to tell about a chemical reaction.
3. A chemical equation must be balanced so that the number of atoms of each element is the same on both sides.

SCIENCE WORDS

chemical reaction (ree-AC-shun)
a change that produces one or more new substances
chemical equation (uh-KWAY-zhun)
a way of telling about a chemical reaction with symbols and formulas.
yield (YEELD)
produce
coefficient (COH-uh-FISH-unt)
a number that tells how many molecules of a substance are needed or produced in a reaction
balance (BAL-unss)
make the number of atoms of each element the same on both sides of an equation

ANSWER THESE

Copy these equations. Count the number of atoms of each element on both sides of the equations. If an equation is balanced, write B. If it is not balanced, change the coefficients or add new ones to balance it.

1. $2\,Mg + O_2 \longrightarrow 2\,MgO$
2. $C + 2\,Br_2 \longrightarrow 2\,CBr_4$
3. $Fe + O_2 \longrightarrow FeO$
4. $2B + 3\,Cl_2 \longrightarrow 2\,BCl_3$
5. $Si + O_2 \longrightarrow SiO_2$

FINDING OUT MORE
The Law of Conservation of Matter

A scientific law is not like the laws men make. It is a statement of fact. It tells something that always happens. You can sometimes disobey a man-made law, but you can never disobey a scientific law.

One important scientific law is the law of conservation of matter. This law says that matter can never be created or destroyed in a chemical change. In a chemical reaction, matter is never lost or gained. You always end up with the same amount of matter you started with. All chemical reactions obey the law of conservation of matter. This is why chemical equations must always balance.

How are compounds and mixtures different?

MIXTURE OF IRON AND SULFUR

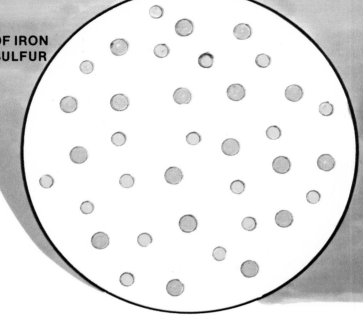

Making a mixture. Mix some iron filings and sulfur powder in a test tube. This is a mixture (MIX-chur) of iron and sulfur. The iron and sulfur particles still have their own properties. The substances in a mixture keep the properties they had before they were mixed. They can be separated from each other by physical means. The particles in this mixture can be separated with a magnet. Look at the mixture under a microscope. You will see tiny yellow sulfur particles and tiny gray iron particles.

▶ **What happens to the properties of substances in a mixture?**

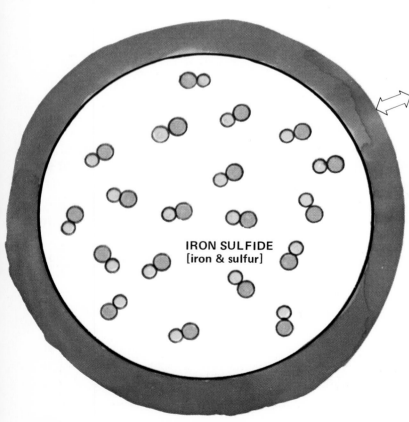

IRON SULFIDE
[iron & sulfur]

Making a compound. Heat the mixture of iron and sulfur over a burner. Now the iron and sulfur combine. They produce the compound iron sulfide. The chemical formula for iron sulfide is FeS. Each molecule of iron sulfide contains one atom of iron and one atom of sulfur. Look at the iron sulfide under a microscope. You cannot see separate particles of iron and sulfur. The iron and sulfur cannot be separated with a magnet. They have lost the properties they had. When elements combine to form compounds, they lose their own properties. They cannot be separated by physical means. The compound has new properties.

▶ **What happens when iron and sulfur combine?**

Mixtures do not have chemical formulas. A compound always has the same chemical formula. It is always made up exactly the same way. The compound iron sulfide is always one part iron and one part sulfur. Water is always two parts hydrogen and one part oxygen. A mixture can be made up in many different ways. A mixture of iron and sulfur can have the same amounts of each element. Or it could have twice as much iron as sulfur. Or three times as much sulfur as iron. There could be any amounts of iron and sulfur in the mixture. A mixture does not have a definite chemical composition. It cannot have a chemical formula.

▶ **Why can't you write a formula for a mixture?**

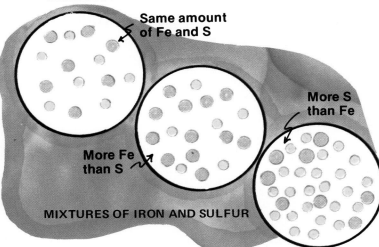

Same amount of Fe and S

More S than Fe

More Fe than S

MIXTURES OF IRON AND SULFUR

Differences between mixtures and compounds. Here is a chart that can help you remember the differences between mixtures and compounds.

MIXTURES	COMPOUNDS
Made of two or more substances mixed together	Made of two or more substances chemically combined
Substances keep their own properties	Substances lose their own properties
Can be separated by physical means	Can be separated only by chemical means
Have no definite chemical composition	Have a definite chemical composition
Have no chemical formula	Have a chemical formula

WHAT YOU LEARNED

1. Mixtures can be separated by physical means, but compounds can be separated only by chemical means.
2. Compounds have a definite chemical composition, while mixtures do not.

SCIENCE WORD

mixture (MIX-chur)
two or more substances put together that can be separated by physical means

ANSWER THESE

Tell whether each sentence describes a compound or a mixture.
1. Can be separated only by chemical means.
2. Has no definite chemical composition.
3. Made of two or more substances chemically combined.
4. Its formula is C_2H_5OH.
5. Can be separated with a magnet.
6. Substances that make it up lose their own properties.

FINDING OUT MORE

There are many different kinds of mixtures. Substances can be mixed with other substances in the same state or in different states. Iron and sulfur is a mixture of two solids. Salt and water is a mixture of a solid and a liquid. You cannot see the particles of salt mixed with the water. But you can taste the salt. The salt did not lose its own properties.

Here are some other mixtures and the substances they contain.

MIXTURE	SUBSTANCES CONTAINED	STATES OF SUBSTANCES
club soda	carbon dioxide and water	gas and liquid
brass	copper and zinc	solid and solid
steel	iron and carbon	solid and solid
tincture of iodine	iodine and alcohol	solid and liquid
air	nitrogen, oxygen, argon, and other gases	all gases
sea water	salts and water	solids and liquid

Do the following review questions on a separate sheet of paper.

Modified True/False   *Write down each of the following statements, leaving a blank line between each line you write. Before the number for each statement, write T if the statement is true and F if the statement is false. For the false statements, cross out the word written in capital letters and write above it a word that will make the statement true.*

1. Mixtures can be separated by PHYSICAL means.
2. Compounds can be separated by PHYSICAL means.
3. COEFFICIENTS are needed to balance an equation.
4. A PHYSICAL change produces a new substance.
5. Carbon dioxide is a product of OXIDATION.
6. Carbon dioxide is LIGHTER THAN oxygen.
7. When hydrogen is burned, WATER forms.
8. A CRYSTAL is a piece of solid shaped like a jewel.
9. Sodium is a METAL.
10. Iron sulfide DOES have the same properties as iron and sulfur.

Multiple Choice   *Write the letter of the choice that best completes the statement or answers the question.*

1. Quartz (silicon dioxide) is a(n)
   a. element
   b. mixture
   c. compound
2. No subscript after an element really means
   a. zero
   b. one
   c. two
3. Symbols for metallic elements are usually
   a. written last in a formula
   b. written first in a formula
   c. left out of formulas
4. Rusting is a form of
   a. fast oxidation
   b. slow oxidation
   c. carbonization

5. Living things oxidize food and produce
   a. oxygen
   b. carbon monoxide
   c. carbon dioxide
6. Changing water into ice is a
   a. physical change
   b. chemical change
   c. chemical reaction
7. Atoms in a chemical reaction cannot be
   a. made or destroyed
   b. rearranged
   c. combined with unlike elements
8. A mixture does not have
   a. any elements in it
   b. different substances in it
   c. a definite chemical composition

Unit Lessons

1. What is valence?
2. How can valence be used to find the formula of a compound?
3. How do atoms share electrons?
4. What is a polyatomic ion?
5. How can we find the formulas of some other compounds?
6. Can an element have more than one valence?
7. What is formula mass?

Goals and Objectives

After completing this unit, you should be able to:
- understand what a valence number tells about an atom or group of atoms.
- describe how atoms form ions.
- understand the difference between ionic and covalent compounds.
- recognize the formula of a polyatomic ion.
- find the formula mass of a molecule.

What is valence?

Completing the outer shell. When the outer shell of an atom has 8 electrons, the shell is complete. Most atoms do not have complete outer shells. The atoms of metals have only 1, 2, or 3 electrons in the outer shell. By getting rid of these electrons, they get rid of the outer shell also. The next inner shell then becomes a complete outer shell. Non-metals have 5, 6, or 7 electrons in the outer shell. They can complete the outer shell by adding more electrons.

▶ **How many electrons are in a complete outer shell?**

Lending and borrowing electrons. A sodium atom has 1 electron in its outer shell, the M shell. If it lends this electron,

then the L shell becomes its outer shell. Now it has a complete outer shell of 8 electrons. A chlorine atom has 7 electrons in its outer shell. If it borrows an electron, then it will have a complete outer shell of 8 electrons.

A sodium atom combines with a chlorine atom in a chemical reaction. The chlorine atom borrows an electron from the sodium atom. Both atoms now have complete outer shells. The two atoms together form sodium chloride. Sodium chloride is a compound formed when sodium lends chlorine an electron.

▶ **In sodium chloride, which atom completes its outer shell by borrowing an electron?**

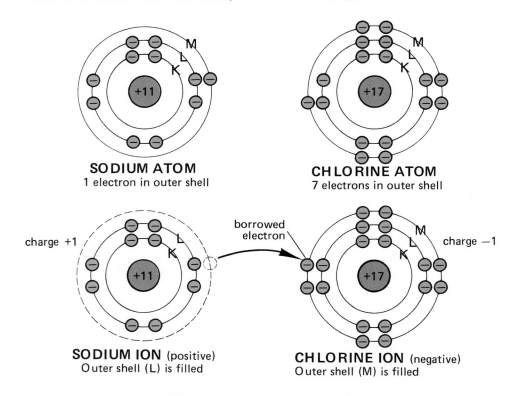

SODIUM ATOM
1 electron in outer shell

CHLORINE ATOM
7 electrons in outer shell

charge +1

borrowed electron

charge −1

SODIUM ION (positive)
Outer shell (L) is filled

CHLORINE ION (negative)
Outer shell (M) is filled

Forming ions. Atoms of metals usually lend electrons during chemical reactions. When an atom lends electrons, it becomes a positive <u>ion</u> (EYE-on). An atom that has lost one or more electrons is a positive ion. The atoms of non-metals usually borrow or gain electrons during chemical reactions. Atoms that gain electrons become negative ions. Metals usually form positive ions. Non-metals usually form negative ions.

▶ **How does an atom become a positive ion?**

Valence. The number of electrons an atom can lend or borrow is called its <u>valence</u> (VAIL-ens). Elements in group 1A have a valence of +1. They have 1 electron to lend. They form positive ions. Elements in group 2A have a valence of +2.

Elements in group 7A have a valence of −1. They would like to borrow 1 electron. They form negative ions. Elements in group 6A have a valence of −2.

Atoms that lend electrons have a positive valence. Atoms that borrow electrons have a negative valence.

▶ **What is valence?**

GROUP	VALENCE
1A	+1
2A	+2
3A	+3
4A	+4 −4
5A	−3
6A	−2
7A	−1
0	0

WHAT YOU LEARNED

1. Atoms can have their outer shells filled by losing or gaining electrons.
2. Atoms can combine to form compounds by lending and borrowing electrons.
3. An atom that loses or lends an electron becomes a positive ion.
4. An atom that gains or borrows an electron becomes a negative ion.
5. The number of electrons an atom can lend or borrow is called its valence.

SCIENCE WORDS

ion (EYE-on)
  an atom that is electrically charged because it has lost or gained electrons
valence (VAIL-ens)
  the number of electrons an atom borrows or lends

ANSWER THESE

1. An atom of sulfur has 6 electrons in its outer shell. It can fill its outer shell by
   a. borrowing 2 electrons
   b. borrowing 6 electrons
   c. lending 2 electrons
2. Sulfur forms
   a. positive ions
   b. no ions
   c. negative ions
3. An atom with 2 electrons in its outer shell has a valence of
   a. −2
   b. −6
   c. +2

NOW TRY THIS

Find the valence of the following elements. (Hint: Use the periodic table to find the group they are in.)

potassium	sodium
calcium	magnesium
iodine	chlorine
oxygen	sulfur

How can valence be used to find the formula of a compound?

NaCl

NaOH   NH₃ CO_2 $AlCl_3$ H_2O

Forming compounds. Elements may form compounds by borrowing and lending electrons. An atom of the metal sodium has 1 electron to lend. An atom of the non-metal chlorine has 7 electrons. It can borrow 1 electron. Sodium can lend 1 electron to chlorine. This is how the compound sodium chloride forms. The compound sodium chloride is composed of 1 atom of sodium and 1 atom of chlorine. The chemical formula for sodium chloride is NaCl. Remember that in a chemical formula, the symbol for the metal is always written first.

▶ **In sodium chloride, how many electrons does each sodium atom lend?**

Some compounds are made of ions. Sodium chloride is a compound formed when sodium atoms lend electrons to chlorine atoms. When a sodium atom lends an electron, it becomes a sodium ion. When a chlorine atom borrows an electron, it becomes a chlorine ion. Sodium chloride is a compound made of sodium ions and chlorine ions. A compound like that is called an <u>ionic</u> (eye-ON-ic) compound. Ionic compounds form when atoms lend and borrow electrons. Ionic compounds are made of ions.

▶ **What is an ionic compound?**

Finding the formula of a compound. An atom of calcium has 2 electrons to lend. An atom of chlorine can borrow 1 electron. An atom of calcium can lend 1 electron to an atom of chlorine. The calcium atom still has 1 electron left to lend. It can lend that electron to a second atom of chlorine. The calcium atom and both chlorine atoms now have complete outer shells. They have formed the compound calcium chloride. The formula of the compound is $CaCl_2$. 2 atoms of chlorine combine with 1 atom of calcium to form calcium chloride. Calcium chloride is an ionic compound.

▶ **How many electrons does an atom of calcium have to lend?**

FORMING CALCIUM CHLORIDE ($CaCl_2$)

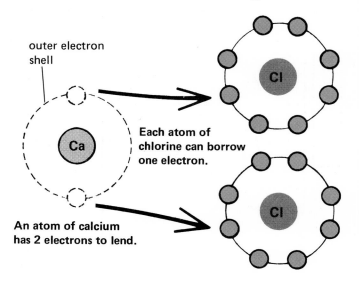

outer electron shell

Ca

Each atom of chlorine can borrow one electron.

An atom of calcium has 2 electrons to lend.

Cl

Cl

Using valence to find formulas. The valence of an element tells if it lends (+) or borrows (−) electrons. Valence also tells how many electrons are lent or borrowed. A valence of +2 means an atom has two electrons to lend. Knowing the valence of elements can help you find the formulas of compounds. Calcium has a valence of +2. Chlorine has a valence of −1. Let us use these valences to find the formula of calcium chloride.

1. Write down the symbols for each element.	Ca Cl
2. Place the valence of each element above the symbol.	$\overset{+2}{Ca}\ \overset{-1}{Cl}$
3. Cross out the + and − signs.	$\overset{2}{Ca}\ \overset{1}{Cl}$
4. Criss-cross the valence numbers and use them as subscripts. The number 1 is never written. The formula for calcium chloride is ⟶	$\overset{2}{Ca}\underset{1}{\diagdown}\overset{1}{Cl}\underset{2}{}$ $CaCl_2$

▶ **What does a valence of +2 mean?**

WHAT YOU LEARNED

1. Elements may form compounds by lending and borrowing electrons.
2. Ionic compounds are formed when atoms lend and borrow electrons.
3. Valence can be used to find the formulas of compounds.

SCIENCE WORD

ionic (eye-ON-ic) **compound**
   the kind of compound formed when atoms combine by lending and borrowing electrons

ANSWER THESE

1. The formula for water is H_2O. A molecule of water has
   a. 1 atom of hydrogen and 1 atom of oxygen
   b. 1 atom of hydrogen and 2 atoms of oxygen
   c. 2 atoms of hydrogen and 1 atom of oxygen
2. A molecule of calcium chloride has
   a. 1 atom of calcium and 1 atom of chlorine
   b. 1 atom of calcium and 2 atoms of chlorine
   c. 2 atoms of calcium and 1 atom of chlorine
3. The formula for aluminum chloride is $AlCl_3$. A molecule of aluminum chloride has _____ atom(s) of aluminum and _____ atom(s) of chlorine.

METALS	NON-METALS				
	Cl^{-1}	Br^{-1}	I^{-1}	O^{-2}	S^{-2}
H^{+1}	HCl			H_2O	
Na^{+1}	NaCl				
Au^{+1}					
Mg^{+2}					
Ca^{+2}	$CaCl_2$				
Al^{+3}					
COMPOUNDS					

COPY THIS DIAGRAM. PLEASE DO NOT WRITE IN THIS BOOK.

NOW TRY THIS

Complete the chart on a separate sheet of paper. Use the valences given to find the formulas of the compounds that will be formed when each metal combines with each non-metal.

How do atoms share electrons?

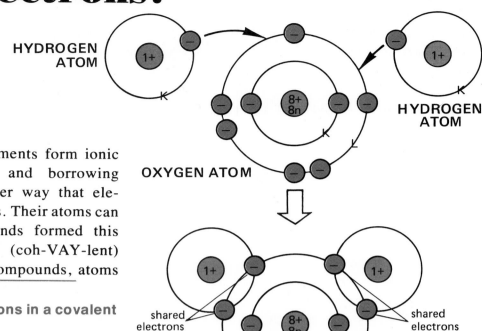

HYDROGEN ATOM

HYDROGEN ATOM

OXYGEN ATOM

shared electrons

shared electrons

WATER MOLECULE

Sharing electrons. Elements form ionic compounds by lending and borrowing electrons. There is another way that elements can form compounds. Their atoms can share electrons. Compounds formed this way are called covalent (coh-VAY-lent) compounds. In covalent compounds, atoms share their electrons.

▶ **What happens to electrons in a covalent compound?**

Water is a covalent compound. An oxygen atom has 6 electrons in its outer shell. It needs 2 more to complete the shell. A hydrogen atom has only one electron shell. It has only 1 electron in its shell. Remember that this shell is complete when it has 2 electrons. So a hydrogen atom needs only 1 more electron to complete its shell.

Two hydrogen atoms combine with one oxygen atom to form a molecule of water. Each hydrogen atom shares its electron with the oxygen atom. The oxygen atom shares one of its electrons with each hydrogen atom. None of the atoms gives up

any of its electrons. The electrons are shared by the atoms. The oxygen atom has a complete outer shell of 8 electrons. Each hydrogen atom has a complete outer shell of 2 electrons. Water is a covalent compound in which atoms share electrons.

▶ **What kind of compound is water?**

Another example. A carbon atom has 4 electrons in its outer shell. A chlorine atom has 7 electrons in its outer shell. One carbon atom can combine with 4 chlorine atoms by sharing electrons. The drawing shows how this is done. The carbon atom now has 8 electrons in its outer shell. Each chlorine atom also has 8 electrons in its outer shell. This covalent compound is called carbon tetrachloride. Its formula is CCl_4.

▶ **How many chlorine atoms can one carbon atom share electrons with?**

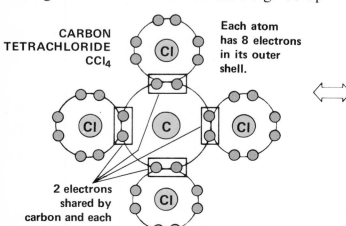

CARBON TETRACHLORIDE CCl_4

Each atom has 8 electrons in its outer shell.

2 electrons shared by carbon and each chlorine atom.

Covalent compounds do not contain ions.
Atoms sharing electrons do not lose or gain any electrons. Each atom keeps the same number of electrons it started with. Each atom keeps the same number of electrons as protons. The atoms remain electrically neutral. They do not become positively or negatively charged ions. There are no ions in a molecule of a covalent compound.

▶ **Why don't the atoms in covalent molecules become ions?**

Comparing ionic and covalent compounds.
Here are the main points to remember about ionic and covalent compounds.

IONIC COMPOUNDS	COVALENT COMPOUNDS
Atoms complete outer shell	Atoms complete outer shell
Electrons borrowed and lent	Electrons shared
Atoms lose and gain electrons	No electrons lost or gained
Atoms form ions	No ions formed

▶ **In what way are ionic and covalent compounds alike?**

WHAT YOU LEARNED

1. Atoms share electrons in covalent compounds.
2. Ions are not formed in covalent compounds.

SCIENCE WORD

covalent (coh-VAY-lent) **compound**
   a compound in which atoms share electrons

ANSWER THESE

Choose the word from Column B that fits each compound described in column A. You can use the same word from column B more than once.

A	B
1. Compound formed when atoms borrow and lend electrons	covalent
2. Compound formed when atoms share electrons	ionic
3. Compound that contains ions	electronic

NOW TRY THIS

Draw a diagram of a methane molecule. Methane is a covalent molecule with the formula CH_4. The carbon atom has 4 electrons in its outer shell. Each hydrogen atom has 1 electron. How many electrons are shared in the methane molecule?

FINDING OUT MORE

Every carbon atom has 4 electrons it can share with other atoms. Carbon atoms can share electrons with one another as well as with other elements. They can form large, complex molecules with hundreds of atoms in chains and rings. These compounds are called organic (or-GAN-ic) compounds, because they are found in living organisms. The formulas of organic compounds are written in a special way. These formulas show how the atoms are joined together. They are called structural (STRUCK-chur-ul) formulas. In a structural formula, each line stands for a pair of shared electrons. Here is the structural formula of glucose, a kind of sugar.

Glucose

What is a polyatomic ion?

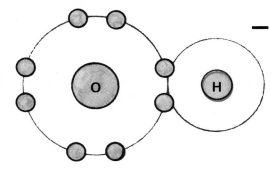

HYDROXIDE ION

8 outer electrons: 6 electrons from oxygen atom
1 electron from hydrogen atom
1 extra electron

Ions with more than one atom. There are groups of atoms that act like ions of single atoms. These groups of atoms have a charge. They stay together as a group in chemical reactions. A charged group of atoms that stays together in chemical reactions is called a polyatomic (pol-ee-uh-TOM-ic) ion. An example of a polyatomic ion is the hydroxide (hy-DROK-side) ion, OH^-. This ion is made up of 1 oxygen atom and 1 hydrogen atom, with an extra electron.

▶ **What is a polyatomic ion?**

A positive ion. The ammonium (uh-MOH-nee-um) ion, NH_4^+, is made up of 1 nitrogen atom and 4 hydrogen atoms. This ion has a charge of +1. It is the only common positive polyatomic ion.

▶ **What atoms is an ammonium ion made up of?**

Other ions. Listed in the table are some other ions with their names.

SO_4^{-2}	sulfate ion
CO_3^{-2}	carbonate ion
PO_3^{-3}	phosphate ion
NO_3^{-1}	nitrate ion
ClO_3^{-1}	chlorate ion

▶ **What is the formula of the sulfate ion?**

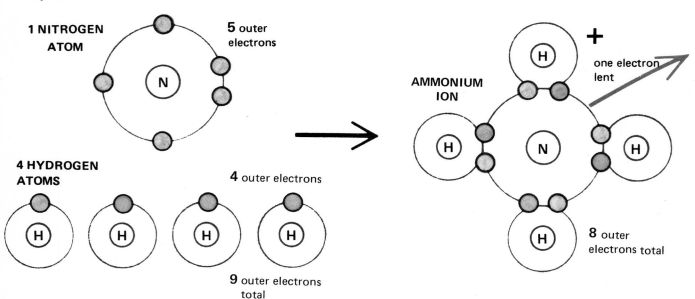

1 NITROGEN ATOM

5 outer electrons

4 HYDROGEN ATOMS

4 outer electrons

9 outer electrons total

AMMONIUM ION

one electron lent

8 outer electrons total

WHAT YOU LEARNED

1. A polyatomic ion is a charged group of atoms that acts like an ion of a single atom.
2. Polyatomic ions may be positive or negative ions.

SCIENCE WORDS

polyatomic (pol-ee-uh-TOM-ic) **ion**
a charged group of atoms that acts like the ion of a single atom

hydroxide (hy-DROK-side) **ion**
an ion containing one oxygen atom and one hydrogen atom

ANSWER THESE

1. A polyatomic ion is an electrically charged group of
   a. atoms
   b. molecules
   c. electrons
2. The formula of the hydroxide ion is
   a. OH^-
   b. OH^+
   c. HO^+
3. An ion that is a positive ion is
   a. sulfate
   b. ammonium
   c. nitrate

NOW TRY THIS

Match the formulas of the ions in column A with their names in column B.

A	B
SO_4^{-2}	ammonium
NO_3^{-1}	sulfate
NH_4^{+1}	carbonate
CO_3^{-2}	nitrate
PO_4^{-3}	phosphate

FINDING OUT MORE

All compounds that contain a hydroxide ion combined with a metallic ion are called bases. Bases are chemical compounds with special properties. Bases feel slippery. Soap is slippery because it is made from a base. Bases taste bitter, like milk of magnesia. Bases make red litmus paper turn blue.

BASES

FORMULA	CHEMICAL NAME	COMMON NAME
NaOH	sodium hydroxide	lye
$Mg(OH)_2$	magnesium hydroxide	milk of magnesia
$Ca(OH)_2$	calcium hydroxide	limewater
NH_4OH	ammonium hydroxide	ammonia water

How can we find the formulas of some other compounds?

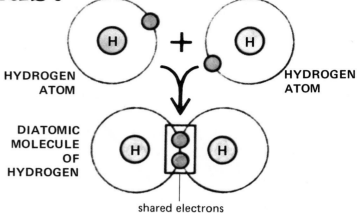

HYDROGEN ATOM + HYDROGEN ATOM

DIATOMIC MOLECULE OF HYDROGEN

shared electrons

Polyatomic ions act like ions of single atoms. Some polyatomic ions have a positive valence. They act like metals. Some polyatomic ions have a negative valence. They act like non-metals. The ammonium ion (NH_4^+) acts like a metallic ion. The hydroxide ion (OH^-) acts like a non-metallic ion. We can use their valences to find the compound they form when they combine.

$$NH_4^{+1} + OH^{-1} \longrightarrow NH_4OH$$

The ammonium ion and the hydroxide ion combine to form the compound ammonium hydroxide (NH_4OH).

▶ **What ions combine to form NH_4OH?**

Diatomic molecules. An atom of hydrogen has one electron in its outer shell. It needs one more electron to complete the shell. It can get that electron from another hydrogen atom. But the other atom cannot be left without any electrons. The two atoms can share the two electrons. Then each has a complete outer shell containing two electrons. The two atoms form a

Atoms that share electrons. The atoms of elements in covalent compounds do not borrow or lend electrons. These atoms share electrons. Carbon is an atom that always shares electrons when it forms compounds. The valence of carbon is 4. Valence tells the number of electrons an atom can share. Carbon will share electrons with chlorine to form a compound. What is the formula of the compound that one atom of carbon will form with chlorine?

$$C^{+4} + Cl^{-1} \longrightarrow CCl_4$$
(carbon tetrachloride)

After combining, the carbon atom has eight electrons in its outer shell. Each chlorine atom has eight electrons also.

▶ **What is the valence of carbon?**

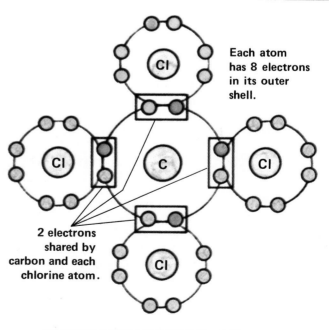

Each atom has 8 electrons in its outer shell.

2 electrons shared by carbon and each chlorine atom.

CARBON TETRACHLORIDE CCl_4

diatomic (DY-uh-TOM-ic) molecule of hydrogen. A diatomic molecule contains two atoms of the same element. We never find single atoms of hydrogen. Hydrogen is always found in diatomic molecules. Most gaseous elements form diatomic molecules.

▶ **What is a diatomic molecule made up of?**

SOME DIATOMIC MOLECULES

iodine	I_2
oxygen	O_2
nitrogen	N_2
chlorine	Cl_2
fluorine	F_2
bromine	Br_2

WHAT YOU LEARNED

1. Polyatomic ions act like ions of single atoms when they form compounds.
2. The atoms of some elements share electrons to form compounds.
3. Diatomic molecules contain two atoms of the same element.

SCIENCE WORD

diatomic (DY-uh-TOM-ic) **molecule**
a molecule containing two atoms of the same element

ANSWER THESE

1. A polyatomic ion that acts like a non-metallic ion is
   a. NH_4^+ **b.** H_3O^+ **c.** SO_4^{-2}

2. Which of the following are diatomic molecules?
   CO Cl_2 I_2
   N_2 SO_2 O_2
3. The formula for carbon tetrachloride is
   a. C_4Cl **b.** CCl_4 **c.** $4CCl$
4. The atoms of elements in covalent compounds (do/do not) share electrons.

NOW TRY THIS

Find the formulas of the compounds formed when the metallic ions combine with the non-metallic ions in the chart at the bottom of the page. Complete the chart on a sheet of paper.

FINDING OUT MORE

Oxygen is a gas found in the atmosphere. Oxygen forms diatomic molecules. Most of the oxygen in the air is in the form of O_2. High in the atmosphere, oxygen gets bombarded by high-energy radiations from the sun. These radiations change the oxygen molecule. The oxygen forms O_3. This is triatomic (TRY-uh-TOM-ic) oxygen. Each molecule contains three atoms of oxygen. Triatomic oxygen is known as ozone. Ozone is very important to life on earth. It filters out some of the dangerous radiations that enter our atmosphere. Some scientists think that supersonic jets and aerosol spray cans containing fluorocarbons will decrease the amount of ozone in the atmosphere. This could become a problem in the future. In many states the government has banned the use of fluorocarbons in spray cans, in order to protect the environment.

		NON-METALLIC IONS				
		SO_4^{-2}	NO_3^{-1}	OH^{-1}	CO_3^{-2}	PO_4^{-3}
METALLIC IONS	NH_4^{+1}			NH_4OH		
	H^{+1}	H_2SO_4				
	Na^{+1}					
	Ca^{+2}					
	Mg^{+2}					
		COMPOUNDS				

Can an element have more than one valence?

The valence of iron. Look at iron (element no. 26) in the periodic table. Its atom has 2 electrons in the outer shell. It is a metal that can lend 2 electrons. Its valence is +2. Chlorine has a valence of −1. What is the formula of the compound that iron and chlorine form? Iron and chlorine can combine to form the compound $FeCl_2$.

▶ **What is the valence of iron in $FeCl_2$?**

Another valence of iron. Chemists have found that iron and chlorine can also form the compound $FeCl_3$. In this compound, iron lends 3 electrons. The third electron comes from an inner shell. The valence of iron in this compound is +3. Iron forms two different compounds with chlorine. In one compound its valence is +2. In the other it is +3. Iron forms two different compounds with other elements and radicals, too.

▶ **What are the two valences that iron may have?**

$$Fe^{+2} + Cl^{-1} \longrightarrow FeCl_2$$

FORMING FERROUS CHLORIDE

$$Fe^{+3} + Cl^{-1} \longrightarrow FeCl_3$$

FORMING FERRIC CHLORIDE

$$Hg^{+1} + Cl^{-1} \longrightarrow HgCl$$

FORMING MERCUROUS CHLORIDE

$$Hg^{+2} + Cl^{-1} \longrightarrow HgCl_2$$

FORMING MERCURIC CHLORIDE

Many elements have two valences. According to the periodic table, mercury should have a valence of +2. It has 2 electrons in its outer shell. But in some compounds mercury has a valence of +1. Mercury forms two different compounds with chlorine.

▶ **What are the valences of mercury?**

Naming compounds. Sodium has only one valence. When it combines with chlorine, only one compound can form. The name of the compound is sodium chloride (NaCl). The name of the metal is written first. The name of the non-metal is changed to end in *ide*. It is written last.

▶ **Which element is written first in the name of a compound?**

Showing valence in the name. Many metals have two valences. The names of their compounds tell which valence the metal has in the compound. In $FeCl_2$, the iron has a valence of +2. In $FeCl_3$, the iron has a valence of +3. In naming these compounds, we change the name of the metal. In the compound that contains the metal at

VALENCES OF METALS		
METAL	HIGHER VALENCE	LOWER VALENCE
iron	+3 ferric	+2 ferrous
mercury	+2 mercuric	+1 mercurous
copper	+2 cupric	+1 cuprous
tin	+4 stannic	+2 stannous
nickel	+3 nickelic	+2 nickelous
gold	+3 auric	+1 aurous

its lower valence, the name of the metal is changed to end in *ous*. Compounds of iron use the Latin name for iron, *ferrum*. $FeCl_2$ becomes fer*rous* chloride. The name of the compound with the higher valence is changed to end in *ic*. $FeCl_3$ becomes fer*ric* chloride. HgCl is mercurous chloride. $HgCl_2$ is mercuric chloride.

▶ **What ending shows the lower valence of a metal in the name of a compound?**

Other elements with more than one valence. Most elements have more than one valence. You can find one of these valences by locating the group the element is in. The chart shows the other valence for some metals. It also shows how the name of the metal changes in compounds. For many metals, a Latin name is used in compounds.

▶ **What name is often used for metals in compounds?**

FINDING OUT MORE
There is another way of naming compounds of elements that have more than one valence. The ordinary name of the metal is used. The valence number is written after the name of the metal, in Roman numbers. Ferrous chloride becomes iron (II) chloride. Ferric chloride becomes iron (III) chloride.

WHAT YOU LEARNED
1. Elements can have more than one valence.
2. The name of a compound shows the valence of the metal in a compound.

ANSWER THESE
1. Iron has valences of
   a. +1 and +2
   b. +2 and +3
   c. +2 and −2
2. In naming compounds, the name of the non-metal is
   a. written first
   b. written last
   c. not written at all
3. The valence of iron in ferrous chloride is
   a. +1 b. +2 c. +3
4. The valence of mercury in mercuric chloride is
   a. +1 b. +2 c. +3
5. The valence of copper in cuprous chloride is
   a. +1 b. +2 c. +3

NOW TRY THESE
What are the formulas of the following compounds?
   cupric chloride
   stannous chloride   ferric bromide
   mercuric bromide   cuprous iodide

$FeCl_2$
iron (II) chloride

$FeCl_3$
iron (III) chloride

What is formula mass?

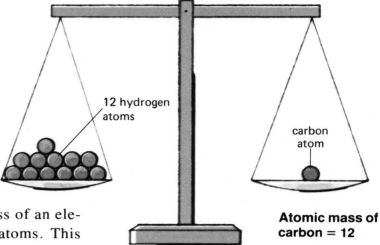

Atomic mass of hydrogen = 1

12 hydrogen atoms

carbon atom

Atomic mass of carbon = 12

Atomic mass. The atomic mass of an element is the mass of one of its atoms. This mass is not measured in ordinary units, such as grams. Instead, the mass is compared with the mass of an atom carbon. Scientists have agreed to give the carbon atom a mass of 12 units. The atomic mass of carbon is 12. The mass of a hydrogen atom is only one-twelfth (1/12) that of a carbon atom. The atomic mass of hydrogen is 1, because 1 is 1/12 of 12. An atom of magnesium has twice as much mass as an atom of carbon. The atomic mass of magnesium is 24, because 2 x 12 = 24.

▶ **What is the atomic mass of carbon?**

Finding molecular mass. Molecules contain one or more atoms. The mass of one molecule of any element or compound is called its molecular (muh-LEK-yuh-ler) mass. This is also called its formula mass. The formula mass of a molecule containing only one atom is the same as its atomic mass. How can we find the formula mass of a molecule that contains more than one atom? Adding the masses of all the atoms in the molecule gives us the formula weight.

▶ **How do we find the molecular mass of an element or compound?**

Finding formula mass. Formula mass is the sum of all the atomic masses in a molecule. A molecule of mercury contains one atom of mercury. The formula mass of mercury is the same as the atomic mass. The atomic mass of mercury is 201. The formula mass of mercury is also 201.

To find the formula mass of molecules that contain more than one item, follow these steps:

1. Write down the formula of the compound.
2. Find the atomic mass of each element in the compound. Use the periodic table.
3. Multiply the atomic mass of each element by its subscript. The subscript shows how many atoms of the element are in a molecule. If there is no subscript, that means there is only one atom of the element.
4. Add up the total masses of all the elements in the compound. That will give you the formula mass.

▶ **How does the formula tell us how many atoms of an element are in one molecule?**

MERCURY Hg

Element	Atomic mass		Subscript		
Hg	201	×	1	=	201
			Formula mass	=	**201**

HYDROGEN H₂

Element	Atomic mass		Subscript		
H	1	×	2	=	2
			Formula mass	=	**2**

WATER H₂O

Element	Atomic mass		Subscript		
H	1	×	2	=	2
O	16	×	1	=	16
			Formula mass	=	18

ETHYL CHLORIDE C₂H₅Cl

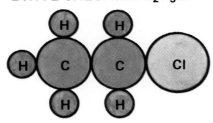

Element	Atomic mass		Subscript		
C	12	×	2	=	24
H	1	×	5	=	5
Cl	35	×	1	=	35
			Formula mass	=	64

WHAT YOU LEARNED

Formula mass is the sum of all the atomic masses in a molecule.

SCIENCE WORDS

formula mass
   The sum of all the atomic masses in a molecule
molecular (muh-LEK-yuh-ler) **mass**
   the same as formula mass
subscript
   a number that shows how many atoms of an element are in a molecule

ANSWER THESE

1. The mass of one atom of an element is the _____ mass.

2. The mass of one molecule of a compound is the _____ mass.

3. Atomic mass is a comparison between the mass of any atom and the mass of an atom of
   a. hydrogen
   b. oxygen
   c. carbon

NOW TRY THIS

Find the formula masses of the following compounds:

CO $NaCl$ $FeCl_2$
CO_2 $NaOH$ H_2SO_4

UNIT 14 Review

Do the following questions on a separate sheet of paper.

Fill in the Blank   *Write down the statements in Column I. Where there is a blank line in each statement, write the word or phrase from Column II that best completes the meaning of the statement.*

Column I

1. Atoms that have lost one or more electrons are _____ .
2. Atoms that gain electrons become _____ .
3. A negative charge is found on the _____ .
4. A positive charge is found on the _____ .
5. The number of electrons an atom borrows or lends is called its _____ .
6. Compounds formed when atoms lend or borrow electrons are called _____ .
7. Compounds formed when atoms share electrons are called _____ .
8. A molecule containing two atoms of the same element is called a _____ .
9. The valence of elements in group 1A is _____ .
10. The valence of elements in group 7A is _____ .

Column II

+1
ionic compounds
negative ions
diatomic molecule
proton
covalent compounds
electron
−1
valence
positive ions

Multiple Choice   *Write the letter of the choice that best completes the statement or answers the question.*

1. When an atom lends an electron, it becomes a
   a. positive ion
   b. negative ion
   c. metal
2. The number of electrons an atom can lend or borrow is called its
   a. atomic number
   b. valence
   c. subscript
3. If an atom has two electrons to lend, it will have
   a. a valence of +2
   b. no valence
   c. a valence of −2
4. A compound in which atoms share electrons is
   a. ionic
   b. covalent
   c. non-atomic

5. In ionic compounds, the atoms are
   a. electrically neutral
   b. covalent
   c. electrically charged
6. The only common positive polyatomic ion is
   a. ammonium
   b. sulfate
   c. carbonate
7. The iron in ferrous chloride has a valence of
   a. −2
   b. +2
   c. +3
8. The formula mass of water is
   a. 2
   b. 3
   c. 18

15 Chemical Reactions

Unit Lessons

1. Can matter be created or destroyed?
2. What is a synthesis reaction?
3. What is a decomposition reaction?
4. What is a replacement reaction?
5. What is a double replacement reaction?

Goals and Objectives

After completing this unit, you should be able to:

- understand the law of conservation of matter.
- explain how burning iron increases its weight.
- explain why rusting is a synthesis reaction.
- give an example of a decomposition reaction and a replacement reaction.
- describe a reaction between an acid and a base.

Can matter be created or destroyed?

Combining iron and oxygen. When a substance burns, it combines with oxygen. Steel wool is made mostly of iron. When iron burns, it combines with oxygen to produce ferric oxide.

$$4Fe + 3O_2 \longrightarrow 2Fe_2O_3$$

iron　　　oxygen　　　　　ferric oxide

REACTANTS　　　　　　PRODUCT

Look at the chemical equation for this reaction. Iron and oxygen are the <u>reactants</u> (ree-ACT-ents). Ferric oxide is the <u>product</u> (PROD-uct). The reactants are the substances that are changed in a chemical reaction. The new substance produced is the product.

▶ **What is the product in a chemical reaction?**

Burning is a put-on. A student weighed out 7 grams of steel wool. Steel wool contains iron. The boy held the steel wool over a flame until it turned bright red. Then he let it cool, and weighed it again. It now weighed 10 grams. The weight of the steel wool had increased by three grams. Where did the extra weight come from?

After burning, the steel wool turned black. It was not iron any more. A new substance had formed. The iron in the steel wool changed to ferric oxide. Look back at the equation in the first paragraph. Ferric oxide is iron combined with oxygen. The extra three grams the boy found was the weight of the oxygen. Oxygen from the air had combined with the iron in the steel wool. When substances are burned, they gain weight.

▶ **What is ferric oxide?**

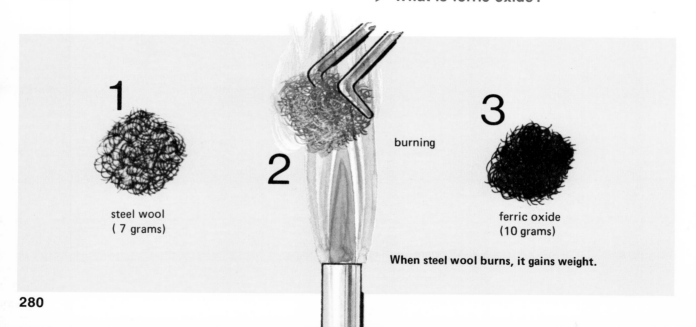

1

steel wool
(7 grams)

2

burning

3

ferric oxide
(10 grams)

When steel wool burns, it gains weight.

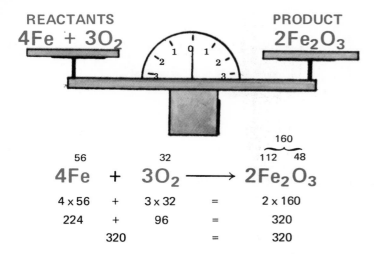

REACTANTS
$4Fe + 3O_2$

PRODUCT
$2Fe_2O_3$

$$\underset{56}{4Fe} + \underset{32}{3O_2} \longrightarrow \underset{\underset{112 \quad 48}{\overbrace{}}^{160}}{2Fe_2O_3}$$

4×56	$+$	3×32	$=$	2×160
224	$+$	96	$=$	320
		320	$=$	320

It's the law. In a chemical reaction, the weight of the products always equals the weight of the reactants. This is the law of conservation of matter. The law says that in a chemical reaction, matter can never be created or destroyed.

▶ **What is the law of conservation of matter?**

WHAT YOU LEARNED

1. When substances burn, they gain weight.
2. In a chemical reaction, the weight of the products always equals the weight of the reactants.
3. The law of conservation of matter says that in a chemical reaction, matter can never be created or destroyed.

SCIENCE WORDS

reactant (ree-ACT-ent)
   a substance that is changed in a chemical reaction
product (PROD-uct)
   a substance that is produced in a chemical reaction

ANSWER THESE

1. When substances burn, they combine with
   a. water
   b. fire
   c. oxygen
2. When substances burn, they
   a. gain weight
   b. lose weight
   c. remain the same

3. The law of conservation of matter says that in a chemical reaction,
   a. matter is destroyed
   b. matter can never be destroyed
   c. matter can sometimes be destroyed

NOW TRY THIS

Find the formula weights of the reactants and the products in the following chemical reactions. Are they the same?

1. $C + O_2 \longrightarrow CO_2$
2. $2H_2 + O_2 \longrightarrow 2H_2O$
3. $4Al + 3O_2 \longrightarrow 2Al_2O_3$

FINDING OUT MORE
The Disappearing Paper

Burn a piece of paper. The ashes seem to weigh less than the original paper. When we weigh the ashes, we see that they are lighter. Have we destroyed matter? The paper was composed of carbon, hydrogen, oxygen, and some mineral matter. When we burned the paper, it combined with oxygen from the air. What are the products of the reaction?

Carbon dioxide and water vapor are produced. They escape into the air. A mineral ash is left. The mineral ash weighs less than the paper. Some of the products have gone into the air. This is where our missing weight is. No matter was destroyed.

$$C + O_2 \longrightarrow CO_2$$

Burning carbon produces carbon dioxide.

$$2H_2 + O_2 \longrightarrow 2H_2O$$

Burning hydrogen produces water vapor.

What is a synthesis reaction?

Chemical reactions between elements.
Chemical reactions produce new substances. In some chemical reactions, the reactants are both elements. The product of the reaction is a compound. This kind of reaction is called a synthesis (SIN-thuh-sis) reaction. Look at this reaction:

$$2H_2 + O_2 \longrightarrow 2H_2O$$

ELEMENT + ELEMENT $\longrightarrow$ COMPOUND

Hydrogen and oxygen are both elements. When hydrogen is burned, it combines with oxygen. The reaction produces the compound water. This is an example of a synthesis reaction. A synthesis reaction is a reaction in which two elements combine to form a compound.

▶ **What is a synthesis reaction?**

Examples of synthesis reactions.
Metals combine with non-metals to form compounds. These reactions are synthesis reactions. When iron rusts, it combines with oxygen. The new substance formed is iron oxide, or rust. Rusting is a synthesis reaction. Carbon combines with oxygen when it burns. The compound formed is carbon dioxide. This too is a synthesis reaction. During most synthesis reactions, metals combine with non-metals.

▶ **How does iron oxide form?**

SYNTHESIS REACTIONS

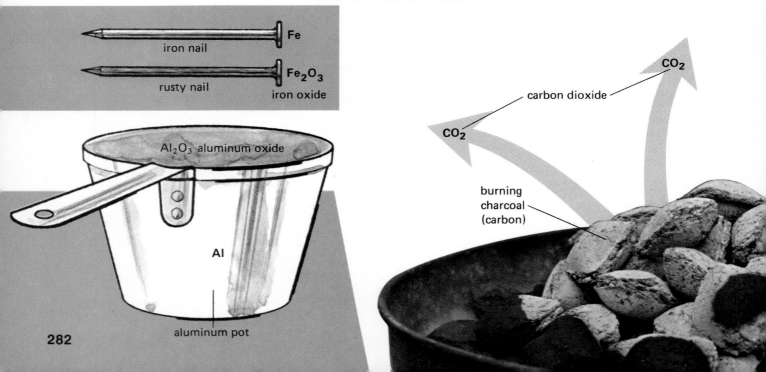

iron nail — Fe

rusty nail — Fe_2O_3 iron oxide

Al_2O_3 aluminum oxide

Al

aluminum pot

CO_2

carbon dioxide

CO_2

burning charcoal (carbon)

SOME SYNTHESIS REACTIONS

METAL		NON-METAL	COMPOUND
2Na	+	$Cl_2 \longrightarrow$	2NaCl sodium chloride
2Hg	+	$O_2 \longrightarrow$	2HgO mercuric oxide
Mg	+	$Cl_2 \longrightarrow$	$MgCl_2$ magnesium chloride
4Au	+	$3O_2 \longrightarrow$	$2Au_2O_3$ gold oxide
2K	+	$Br_2 \longrightarrow$	2KBr potassium bromide

Some other synthesis reactions. Look at the chart. In each synthesis reaction, a metal has combined with a non-metal to form a compound.

▶ **What elements combine to form mercuric oxide?**

WHAT YOU LEARNED

During synthesis reactions, two elements combine to form a compound.

SCIENCE WORD

synthesis (SIN-thuh-sis) **reaction**
   a reaction in which two elements combine to form a compound

ANSWER THESE

1. The reactants in a synthesis reaction are
   a. elements only
   b. compounds only
   c. elements and compounds
2. The product of a synthesis reaction is
   a. two elements
   b. a compound
   c. two elements and a compound
3. Reactions in which metals and non-metals combine are _____ reactions.
4. An example of a synthesis reaction is the _____ of iron.

NOW TRY THIS

Complete the synthesis reactions on a separate sheet of paper.

1. $2Na + Br_2 \longrightarrow$?

2. $2Al + 3Cl_2 \longrightarrow$?

3. $2Mg + O_2 \longrightarrow$?

4. $4Fe + 3O_2 \longrightarrow$?

FINDING OUT MORE

Exothermic and Endothermic Reactions

Some chemical reactions give off heat. When wood burns, it combines with oxygen. Burning gives off heat energy. Reactions that give off heat are called exothermic (EK-soh-THER-mik) reactions. Fuels combine with oxygen and give off heat energy. Hydrogen combines with oxygen to form water. Heat is given off. This is an exothermic reaction.

   Some reactions take in heat. To break down lead oxide, heat energy is needed. This is an endothermic (EN-doh-THER-mik) reaction. Endothermic reactions absorb, or take in, heat energy.

What is a decomposition reaction?

$$2H_2O \longrightarrow 2H_2 + O_2$$

**ELECTROLYSIS OF WATER
A DECOMPOSITION REACTION**

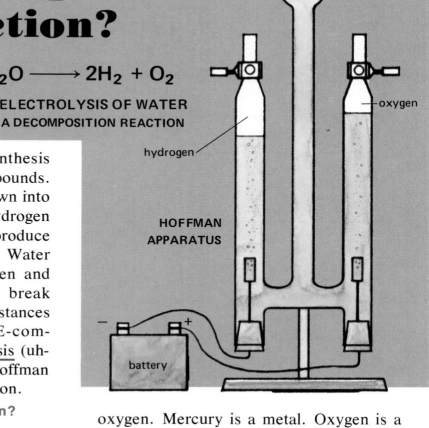

oxygen

hydrogen

**HOFFMAN
APPARATUS**

− +

battery

Breaking up is hard to do. Synthesis reactions build elements into compounds. Compounds can also be broken down into the elements they are made of. Hydrogen and oxygen can be combined to produce water. This is a synthesis reaction. Water can be broken down into hydrogen and oxygen. Chemical reactions that break down compounds into simpler substances are called <u>decomposition</u> (DEE-com-puh-ZISH-un) <u>reactions</u>. <u>Electrolysis</u> (uh-lec-TROL-uh-sis) of water in the Hoffman apparatus is a decomposition reaction.

▶ **What is a decomposition reaction?**

Decomposition reactions. Mercuric oxide is a compound composed of mercury and oxygen. When mercuric oxide is heated, it breaks down into mercury and

oxygen. Mercury is a metal. Oxygen is a non-metal. Both are elements. Some decomposition reactions produce a metal and a non-metal.

▶ **What is mercuric oxide composed of?**

Other decomposition reactions. During decomposition reactions, compounds are always broken down. Sometimes they are broken down into elements. Sometimes they are broken down into simpler compounds. The products of a decomposition

**DECOMPOSITION OF
MERCURIC OXIDE**

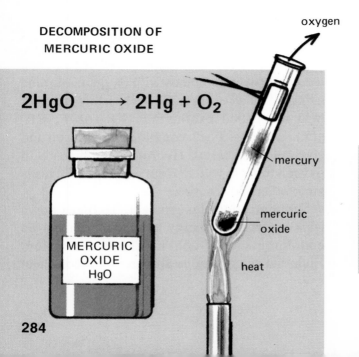

oxygen

$$2HgO \longrightarrow 2Hg + O_2$$

mercury

mercuric
oxide

heat

MERCURIC
OXIDE
HgO

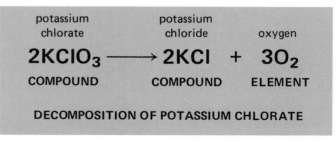

potassium chlorate		potassium chloride	oxygen
$2KClO_3$	$\longrightarrow$	$2KCl$ +	$3O_2$
COMPOUND		COMPOUND	ELEMENT

DECOMPOSITION OF POTASSIUM CHLORATE

reaction can be either elements or compounds. Potassium chlorate can be broken down into potassium chloride and oxygen. The products are a simpler compound and an element.

▶ **What substances is potassium chlorate broken down into?**

OTHER DECOMPOSITION REACTIONS

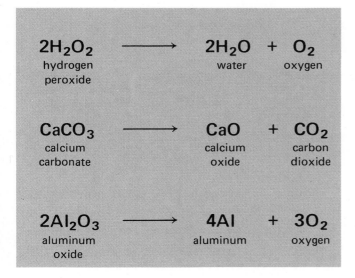

$$2H_2O_2 \longrightarrow 2H_2O + O_2$$
hydrogen peroxide   water   oxygen

$$CaCO_3 \longrightarrow CaO + CO_2$$
calcium carbonate   calcium oxide   carbon dioxide

$$2Al_2O_3 \longrightarrow 4Al + 3O_2$$
aluminum oxide   aluminum   oxygen

WHAT YOU LEARNED

Decomposition reactions are reactions that break down compounds into simpler substances.

SCIENCE WORDS

decomposition (DEE-com-puh-ZISH-un) **reaction**
a reaction that breaks down compounds into simpler substances

electrolysis (uh-lec-TROL-uh-sis)
using an electric current to break down a compound

ANSWER THESE

1. Reactions that break down compounds into simpler substances are _____ reactions.
2. The decomposition of water produces _____ and _____.
3. The decomposition of mercuric oxide produces _____ and _____.
4. The Hoffman apparatus is used in the decomposition of _____.

NOW TRY THIS

Complete the decomposition reactions on a separate sheet of paper.

1. $2H_2O_2 \longrightarrow 2H_2O + \underline{\hspace{2cm}}$

2. $2Al_2O_3 \longrightarrow 4Al + \underline{\hspace{2cm}}$

3. $2FeO \longrightarrow \underline{\hspace{1.5cm}} + \underline{\hspace{1.5cm}}$

4. $2MgCl_3 \longrightarrow 2Mg + \underline{\hspace{2cm}}$

5. $2NaCl \longrightarrow \underline{\hspace{1.5cm}} + \underline{\hspace{1.5cm}}$

FINDING OUT MORE

The formula for sugar is $C_6H_{12}O_6$. Sugar contains the elements carbon, hydrogen, and oxygen. When sugar is heated, it breaks down into carbon and water. Carbon is a black solid. It is an element. Water is a compound composed of hydrogen and oxygen. The carbon and water contain the same elements that were in the sugar.

$$C_6H_{12}O_6 \longrightarrow 6C + 6H_2O$$
sugar   carbon   water

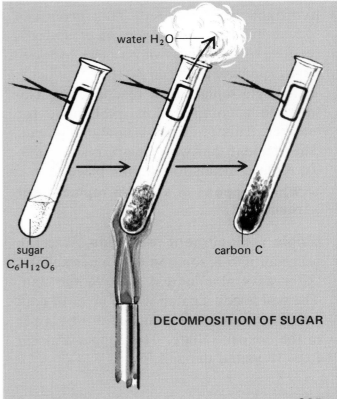

water H_2O

sugar $C_6H_{12}O_6$

carbon C

DECOMPOSITION OF SUGAR

285

What is a replacement reaction?

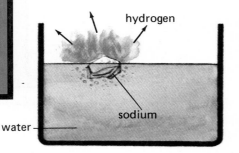

hydrogen

sodium

water

DANGER

Sodium reacts with water to produce hydrogen.

A SINGLE
REPLACEMENT
REACTION

ELEMENT		COMPOUND			COMPOUND		ELEMENT
$2Na$	$+$	$2H_2O$	$\longrightarrow$		$2NaOH$	$+$	H_2
sodium		water			sodium hydroxide		hydrogen

Exchanging elements in a compound.
When sodium is added to water, a chemical
reaction occurs. Hydrogen gas and sodium
hydroxide are produced. Heat is given off.
The heat can cause the hydrogen gas to
explode. This is a very dangerous reaction.
During the reaction, the sodium atom
changes place with one of the atoms of
hydrogen in the water. This produces
sodium hydroxide. The hydrogen atom that is
set free will combine with another hydrogen
atom to produce hydrogen gas (H_2).

In a single replacement reaction, one element in a compound is exchanged for
another. This produces a new compound.
The element that was replaced is set free.
To <u>replace</u> means to take the place of.

▶ **What happens in a single replacement
reaction?**

Single replacement reactions. Place an
iron nail into a solution of copper sulfate.
After several minutes, remove the nail.
The nail is now coated with a layer of copper. The iron was exchanged for the copper
in the copper sulfate. The copper was set
free. It coated the nail.

Place a copper strip into a solution of
silver nitrate. Remove the copper after
several minutes. It is now coated with
silver. The copper took the place of the
silver in the silver nitrate. The silver was
set free.

Cu	$+$	$AgNO_3$	$\longrightarrow$	$CuNO_3$	$+$	Ag
copper		silver nitrate		copper nitrate		silver

▶ **What happened to the copper in the
copper sulfate when it was replaced by
iron?**

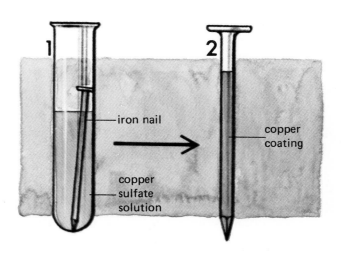

1

2

iron nail

copper coating

copper sulfate solution

$$Fe + CuSO_4 \longrightarrow FeSO_4 + Cu$$

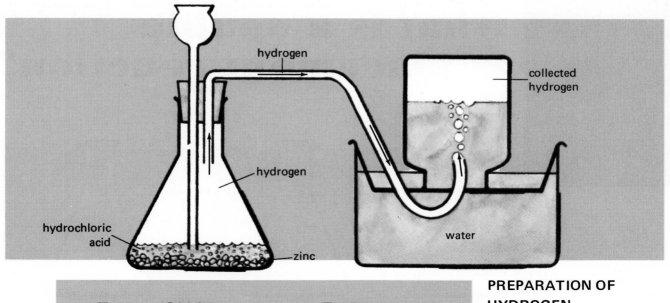

Zn + 2HCl ⟶ ZnCl₂ + H₂

zinc   hydrochloric   zinc   hydrogen
         acid   chloride

PREPARATION OF
HYDROGEN
A SINGLE REPLACEMENT
REACTION

Some other single replacement reactions.

Some metals react with acids to produce hydrogen. The metal changes place with the hydrogen in the acid. The hydrogen is set free. These reactions are single replacement reactions. Zinc is a metal that will react with hydrochloric acid. This reaction produces zinc chloride ($ZnCl_2$) and hydrogen.

▶ How can hydrogen be set free from an acid?

WHAT YOU LEARNED

1. Elements can change places with other elements in a compound. The element that is replaced is set free.

2. Some metals can replace hydrogen from acids. The hydrogen is set free.

SCIENCE WORDS

single replacement (ree-PLACE-ment) **reaction**
a chemical reaction in which one element replaces another element in a compound
replace
take the place of

ANSWER THESE

1. A reaction in which one element changes place with another element in a compound is called a _____ _____ reaction.

2. When an iron nail is placed in a copper sulfate solution, the nail becomes coated with the metal _____.

3. Metals can react with acids to produce _____.

4. When copper reacts with silver nitrate, the element _____ is set free.

NOW TRY THIS

Find the metal released in each reaction.

Fe + CuSO₄ ⟶ FeSO₄ + Cu
(example)

Cu + AgNO₃ ⟶ ?

Cu + HgCl ⟶ ?

Zn + 2AgNO₃ ⟶ ?

K + NaCl ⟶ ?

What is a double replacement reaction?

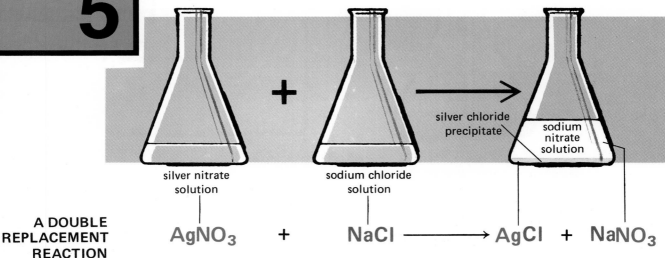

A DOUBLE REPLACEMENT REACTION

silver nitrate solution

sodium chloride solution

silver chloride precipitate

sodium nitrate solution

$$AgNO_3 \quad + \quad NaCl \longrightarrow AgCl \quad + \quad NaNO_3$$

Double replacement reactions. An atom from an element can change places with an atom from a compound. This is a single replacement reaction. An atom from one compound can change places with an atom from a second compound. This is a double replacement reaction.

▶ What is a double replacement reaction?

Changing places. Mix together solutions of silver nitrate and sodium chloride. A white solid forms in the solution and sinks to the bottom. The solid is called a precipitate (pruh-SIP-ih-tate). A precipitate is a solid that does not dissolve in water. It usually sinks to the bottom of the water.

The precipitate that forms in this reaction is silver chloride. Where did the silver chloride come from? The silver from the silver nitrate changed places with the sodium from the sodium chloride. This formed two new compounds, silver chloride and sodium nitrate.

▶ What is a precipitate?

Other double replacement reactions. Look at the chart showing some double replacement reactions. Double replacement reactions always form two new compounds. All neutralization (NOO-truh-luh-ZAY-shun) reactions are double re-

**SOME OTHER
DOUBLE REPLACEMENT REACTIONS**

$MgSO_4$	+	$2NH_4OH$	$\longrightarrow$	$(NH_4)_2SO_4$	+	$Mg(OH)_2$
$Pb(NO_3)_2$	+	K_2CrO_4	$\longrightarrow$	$PbCrO_4$	+	$2KNO_3$
$Ca(OH)_2$	+	Na_2CO_3	$\longrightarrow$	$2NaOH$	+	$CaCO_3$

NEUTRALIZATION

$$HCl + NaOH \longrightarrow NaCl + HOH$$

hydrochloric acid   sodium hydroxide   sodium chloride   water (H_2O)

acid + base ⟶ salt + water

placement reactions. In a neutralization reaction, an acid and a base form a salt plus water.

▶ **What is a neutralization reaction?**

Summary of kinds of chemical reactions.

1. Synthesis reactions—two elements combine to form a compound.

2. Decomposition reactions—compounds are broken down into elements, or into elements and simpler compounds.

3. Single replacement reactions—an element replaces another element from a compound. This produces a new compound and sets the element that is replaced free.

4. Double replacement reactions—an element from one compound changes places with an element from a second compound. This forms two new compounds.

▶ **In what kind of reaction are two new compounds always formed?**

WHAT YOU LEARNED

1. In a double replacement reaction, an element from one compound replaces an element from a second compound.
2. Two new compounds are produced in a double replacement reaction.

SCIENCE WORDS

double replacement reaction
    a reaction in which elements from two compounds change places, and two new compounds are formed

precipitate (pruh-SIP-ih-tate)
    an undissolved solid that usually sinks to the bottom of a mixture

neutralization (NOO-truh-luh-ZAY-shun) **reaction**
    a reaction in which an acid and a base form a salt plus water

ANSWER THESE

Complete the double replacement reactions on a separate sheet of paper.

1. $NaOH + HCl \longrightarrow$ _____ $+ HOH$
2. $Mg(OH)_2 + Na_2CO_3 \longrightarrow$ _____ $+$ _____
3. $KOH + HBr \longrightarrow$ _____ $+ HOH$
4. $BaCl_2 + Na_2SO_4 \longrightarrow$ _____ $+$ _____

NOW TRY THESE

What kind of reaction (synthesis, decomposition, single replacement, or double replacement) is each of the following?

1. $AgNO_3 + NaBr \longrightarrow AgBr + NaNO_3$
2. $2Na + Cl_2 \longrightarrow 2NaCl$
3. $Ca + 2H_2O \longrightarrow Ca(OH)_2 + H_2$
4. $2H_2O_2 \longrightarrow 2H_2O + O_2$
5. $2Al_2O_3 \longrightarrow 4Al + 3O_2$

UNIT 15 Review

Do the following review questions on a separate sheet of paper.

Modified True/False   *Write down each of the following statements, leaving a blank line between each line you write. Before the number for each statement, write T if the statement is true and F if the statement is false. For the false statements, cross out the word written in capital letters and write above it a word that will make the statement true.*

1. When a substance burns, it combines with NITROGEN.
2. When a substance burns, it LOSES weight.
3. Rusting is a SYNTHESIS reaction.
4. Burning hydrogen produces WATER.
5. Electrolysis of water is a DECOMPOSITION reaction.
6. The decomposition of mercuric oxide produces mercury and NITROGEN.
7. The Hoffman apparatus is used to break down SUGAR.
8. To REPLACE means "to take the place of."
9. A precipitate is a LIQUID that does not dissolve in water.
10. All neutralization reactions are DOUBLE replacement reactions.

Multiple Choice   *Write the letter of the choice that best completes the statement or answers the question.*

1. A substance that is changed in a chemical reaction is called a
   a. product
   b. catalyst
   c. reactant
2. Ferric oxide is oxygen combined with
   a. steel
   b. iron
   c. copper
3. The burning of hydrogen is a
   a. synthesis reaction
   b. diatomic reaction
   c. replacement reaction
4. When iron rusts, it combines with
   a. oxygen
   b. nitrogen
   c. carbon
5. During decomposition reaction, compounds are
   a. built up
   b. not affected
   c. broken down
6. The electrolysis of water is an example of a (n)
   a. synthesis reaction
   b. decomposition reaction
   c. oxidation reaction
7. When sodium is added to water,
   a. a single replacement reaction occurs
   b. a double replacement reaction occurs
   c. nothing happens
8. The products of the above reaction are
   a. sodium hydroxide and oxygen
   b. sodium hydroxide and hydrogen
   c. hydrogen and oxygen

UNIT 16

Reactions of Metals

Unit Lessons

1. What is an ore?
2. How do we separate a metal from its ore?
3. What is an alloy?
4. Why are some metals more active than others?
5. Why do some metals corrode?
6. How can metals be protected from corrosion?
7. How are metals plated?
8. Why do oxidation and reduction occur together?

Goals and Objectives

After completing this unit, you should be able to:

- name some common ores and the metals we get from them.
- describe the process by which metals are produced.
- describe how metals are combined with each other in different ways.
- explain the chemical process that causes the decay of metals. Understand how the oxidation and reduction of atoms are related.

What is an ore?

Metals in the earth. Metallic elements are important in our everyday lives. Iron is used in autos, buildings, home appliances, and in nails and screws. Copper is used in electrical wiring, jewelry, and pots. Aluminum is used for packaging food, for furniture, and for screen doors and windows.

These metals and many more are found in the earth. But they are not often found in a form in which they can be used. They are usually found combined with other elements. The metals are in the form of chemical compounds. These compounds are called <u>ores</u> (ORS). An ore is a mineral compound from which we can get a useful metal.

▶ **What is an ore?**

Iron ore. Iron is not found in the earth in a form that can be used. It is often found combined with oxygen, as the compound iron oxide. This is an ore of iron. Hematite (HEM-uh-tite), limonite (LY-muh-nite),

and magnetite (MAG-nuh-tite) are iron ores. In order to obtain pure iron from these ores, we must remove the oxygen from them.

▶ **What are some ores of iron?**

Other ores. Look at the chart of metallic ores. What are the metals combined with? Most ores are oxides, sulfides, or carbonates. Hematite (Fe_2O_3) and bauxite (BAWK-site) (Al_2O_3) are oxide ores. Galena (guh-LEE-nuh) (PbS) and cinnabar (SIN-nuh-bar) (HgS) are sulfide ores. Smithsonite (SMITH-suh-nite) ($ZnCO_3$) and magnesite (MAG-nuh-site) ($MgCO_3$) are carbonate ores.

▶ **What is the ore of aluminum?**

WHAT YOU LEARNED

1. Ores are mineral compounds from which we can get a useful metal.
2. Ores are usually metal oxides, sulfides, or carbonates:

SCIENCE WORD

ore (OR)
  a mineral compound from which we can get a useful metal

ANSWER THESE

1. A metal used for electrical wiring is
   a. iron
   b. copper
   c. lead

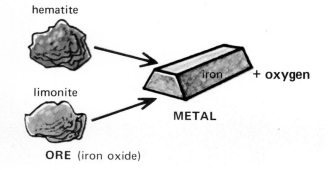

hematite

limonite

iron + oxygen

METAL

ORE (iron oxide)

METALLIC ORES

ORE	CHEMICAL FORMULA	METAL	KIND OF ORE
hematite	Fe_2O_3	iron	oxide
limonite	Fe_2O_3	iron	oxide
pyrite	FeS_2	iron	sulfide
bauxite	Al_2O_3	aluminum	oxide
galena	PbS	lead	sulfide
litharge	PbO	lead	oxide
smithsonite	$ZnCO_3$	zinc	carbonate
sphalerite	ZnS	zinc	sulfide
cuprite	Cu_2O	copper	oxide
magnesite	$MgCO_3$	magnesium	carbonate
uraninite	UO_2	uranium	oxide
cinnabar	HgS	mercury	sulfide
cassiterite	SnO_2	tin	oxide

2. Ores are usually
   a. pure metals
   b. metals combined with other elements
   c. pure non-metals
3. An ore of iron is
   a. pyrite
   b. bauxite
   c. galena
4. Al_2O_3 is the ore of
   a. iron
   b. aluminum
   c. lead

NOW TRY THIS

What useful metal can be obtained from each of these ores?

ORE	METAL
hematite	iron
bauxite	?
galena	?
uraninite	?
cinnabar	?
pyrite	?
litharge	?

FINDING OUT MORE

Ores are usually compounds. The metal may be found combined with oxygen, sulfur, or carbon and oxygen. But not all ores are compounds. Some ores are pure metals. These are called native metals. Gold, silver, and copper are examples of native metals. These elements do not combine easily with other elements. That is why they are found as native metals.

Gold is found as a pure metal.

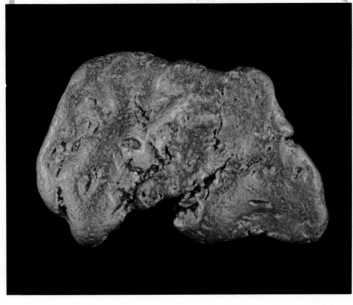

How do we separate a metal from its ore?

CO₂
carbon
dioxide

lead oxide
and charcoal

lead

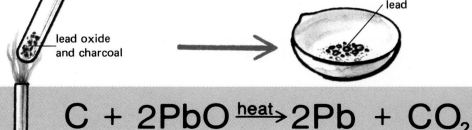

A REDUCTION
REACTION

$$C + 2PbO \xrightarrow{heat} 2Pb + CO_2$$

carbon   lead oxide   lead   carbon dioxide

REDUCTION OF OXIDE ORES

ORE						METAL OBTAINED
C	+	2CuO $\xrightarrow{heat}$	2Cu	+	CO₂	copper
C	+	2FeO $\xrightarrow{heat}$	2Fe	+	CO₂	iron
C	+	2ZnO $\xrightarrow{heat}$	2Zn	+	CO₂	zinc

Obtaining useful metals. An ore is a mineral compound that contains a useful metal. Ores may be oxides, sulfides, or carbonates. Litharge (LITH-arj) is the oxide ore of lead. In litharge (PbO), lead is chemically combined with oxygen. Lead is used in automobile batteries. But the lead in litharge must be separated from the oxygen before it can be used. Metals must be removed from their ores before they can be used.

▶ **What is litharge?**

Obtaining metals from oxide ores. Mix equal amounts of lead oxide and charcoal in a test tube. Charcoal is composed mainly of the element carbon. Heat the test tube for about five minutes. Empty it into an evaporating dish. Tiny beads of lead can be seen in the mixture. Where did the lead come from? The carbon combined with the oxygen in the lead oxide. This produced

carbon dioxide gas. The lead was set free. Removing oxygen from an ore is called reduction (ree-DUCK-shun). It is a single replacement reaction. Metals can be obtained from oxide ores by mixing the ores with carbon and heating. These are reduction reactions.

▶ **How can metals be obtained from oxide ores?**

Obtaining metals from sulfide ores. Metals cannot be set free from sulfide ores as easily as from oxide ores. Two steps are needed. The ore must first be heated in the open air. This is called roasting. Roasting causes both the metal and the sulfur to combine with oxygen. The sulfur forms sulfur dioxide, a gas that escapes into the air. The second step is reduction of the metal oxide that is left after roasting.

▶ **What is the first step in obtaining metals from sulfide ores?**

294

FREEING METALS FROM SULFIDE ORES		
Step 1. Roasting	$2CuS + 3O_2 \xrightarrow{heat} 2CuO + 2SO_2$ sulfide oxide	
Step 2. Reduction	$2CuO + C \xrightarrow{heat} 2Cu + CO_2$ oxide metal	

FREEING METALS FROM CARBONATE ORES		
Step 1. Roasting	$PbCO_3 \xrightarrow{heat} PbO + CO_2$ carbonate oxide	
Step 2. Reduction	$2PbO + C \xrightarrow{heat} 2Pb + CO_2$ oxide metal	

Obtaining metals from carbonate ores.

In carbonate ores, metals are combined with carbon and oxygen. Two steps are needed to free the metal. First the ore is roasted. This releases carbon dioxide from the carbonate ore. The metal oxide remains. The second step is reduction of the oxide.

▶ **What are metals combined with in carbonate ores?**

WHAT YOU LEARNED

1. Metals must be removed from their ores before they can be used.
2. Metals can be removed from oxide ores by reduction with carbon.
3. Metals can be removed from sulfide ores by first roasting the ores to produce an oxide. Reduction then frees the metal from the oxide.
4. Metals can be removed from carbonate ores by first roasting to produce an oxide. Reduction then frees the metal from the oxide.

SCIENCE WORDS

reduction (ree-DUCK-shun)
    removing oxygen from an ore to free the metal in the ore

roasting
    heating an ore in air to produce an oxide

ANSWER THESE

1. Metals are freed from oxide ores by
  a. roasting
  b. reduction
  c. roasting and then reduction

2. Metals are freed from sulfide ores by
  a. roasting
  b. reduction
  c. roasting and then reduction

3. Metals are freed from carbonate ores by
  a. roasting
  b. reduction
  c. roasting and then reduction

4. Roasting changes sulfide ores to
  a. carbonates
  b. oxides
  c. metals

NOW TRY THESE

1. Show the steps in freeing zinc from its carbonate ore ($ZnCO_3$).
2. Show the steps in freeing iron from its sulfide ore (FeS_2).
3. Show the steps in freeing tin from its oxide ore (SnO_2).

What is an alloy?

ALLOYS

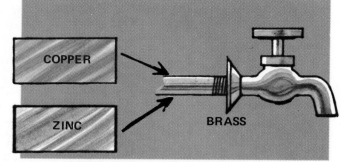

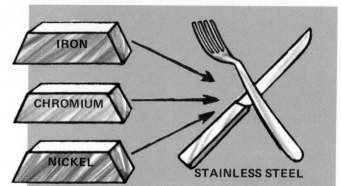

Properties of metals. Can you remember some of the properties of metallic elements?

1. Metals have a shiny luster.
2. Metals are good conductors of heat and electricity.
3. Metals are malleable. They can be hammered into different shapes.
4. Metals are ductile. They can be drawn into wires.
5. Metals are solids at room temperature, except for mercury, which is liquid.
6. Metals have a silver-gray color, except for gold and copper.

▶ **Which metal is a liquid at room temperature?**

Special properties of metals. All metals are good conductors of electricity. Silver and copper are especially good conductors. Copper is used in electrical wiring because silver is too expensive. Metals are used in construction because of their strength. Iron is strong, but very heavy. It is used in building construction, where weight is not important. Aluminum and magnesium are light metals. They are used to build airplanes, where light weight is important.

All metals have similar properties. But certain metals are better for certain jobs because of their special properties. Different metals have different uses because of their special properties.

▶ **Why are different metals used for different purposes?**

Mix and match. Metals can be mixed together. When they are mixed, their properties change. A mixture of two or more metals is an alloy (AL-loy). Brass is an alloy of copper and zinc. It is harder than either copper or zinc alone. It lasts longer when used in water pipes and faucets than most other metals do.

Stainless steel is an alloy of iron, chromium, and nickel. Iron will rust. Stainless steel will not rust. Alloys have more useful properties than the individual metals they contain. Alloys are used in place of pure metals because of the special properties that alloys have.

▶ **What is an alloy?**

Other alloys. The chart shows some other alloys and the metals they contain. An alloy may be made of two or more metals. Different alloys are used for different purposes.

▶ **How many metals can an alloy be made of?**

ALLOY	ELEMENTS CONTAINED	USES
stainless steel	iron, chromium, nickel	cooking utensils, knives, forks, spoons
brass	copper, zinc	plumbing fixtures
bronze	copper, tin	boat hardware, machine parts
pewter	tin, copper, antimony	dishes and cups
sterling silver	silver, copper	silverware, jewelry
alnico	iron, aluminum, nickel, cobalt	magnets
nichrome	nickel, iron, chromium, manganese	electrical wire
silver amalgam	mercury, silver	fillings for teeth

WHAT YOU LEARNED

1. Alloys are mixtures of two or more metals.
2. The properties of an alloy are different from the properties of the metals it contains.

SCIENCE WORD

alloy (AL-loy)
  a mixture of two or more metals

ANSWER THESE

1. Which of the following are properties of metals?
   a. brittle
   b. malleable
   c. ductile
   d. shiny luster
   e. poor conductor
2. Steel contains the element
   a. iron
   b. oxygen
   c. copper
3. Mixtures of two or more metals are
   a. compounds
   b. alloys
   c. ores
4. Copper is used in electrical wiring because
   a. it is a heavy metal
   b. it is one of the best conductors of electricity
   c. it has a red color

NOW TRY THIS

Complete the chart on a separate sheet of paper.

ALLOY	ELEMENTS CONTAINED
sterling silver	_____ , _____
_____	copper, tin
pewter	_____ , _____ , _____
_____	copper, zinc
nichrome	_____ , _____ , _____ , _____

FINDING OUT MORE

Most alloys are made by mixing metals when they are molten. Bronze is made by mixing the proper amounts of molten copper and tin. Some alloys can be made without heating the metals. A cavity in a tooth can be filled with an alloy of mercury and silver. This alloy can be mixed at room temperature. Alloys of mercury are called amalgams (uh-MAL-gums).

UNIT 16
Reactions of Metals
4

Why are some metals more active than others?

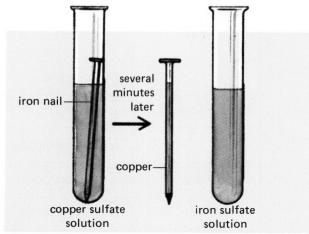

iron nail

several minutes later

copper

copper sulfate solution

iron sulfate solution

Metals replace other metals. Place a clean iron nail into a test tube containing a solution of copper sulfate. Remove the nail after several minutes, and examine it. What do you observe? The nail is coated with a layer of copper. The copper sulfate solution has turned green. The green solution is a solution of iron sulfate. Let us see what has happened chemically:

$$Fe + CuSO_4 \longrightarrow Cu + FeSO_4$$

iron + copper sulfate $\longrightarrow$ copper + iron sulfate

The iron was able to replace the copper in the copper sulfate. The copper from the copper sulfate coated the iron nail. This is a single replacement reaction. Iron always replaces copper from copper compounds.

▶ **Why did the iron nail become coated with copper?**

Some metals do not replace others. Place a copper strip into a solution of iron sulfate. Remove the copper strip after several minutes. Nothing has happened. Copper cannot replace iron from iron compounds. Iron is a <u>more</u> <u>active</u> <u>metal</u> than copper. More active metals replace less active metals from their compounds. Less active metals cannot replace more active metals.

▶ **Why didn't the copper replace the iron in the iron sulfate?**

Replacing metals. Place a zinc strip and a copper strip into each of the following solutions:

> silver nitrate—$AgNO_3$
> zinc nitrate—$Zn(NO_3)_2$
> copper nitrate—$Cu(NO_3)_2$
> lead nitrate—$Pb(NO_3)_2$

Remove the strips after several minutes. What do you observe?

Zinc replaced all the other metals from their compounds. Zinc is more active than lead, copper, or silver. Copper replaced silver. It did not replace zinc or lead. Copper is more active than silver. Copper is less active than zinc or lead. More active metals replace less active metals from their compounds.

▶ **Why did the copper strip become coated with silver?**

Metals do not all replace each other. The table shows the activity of some metals. The most active metals are at the top of the table. The least active metals are at the bottom. The table is called the electromotive series of metals.

Metals will replace metals below them from their compounds. Copper is above silver. Copper will replace silver from its

298

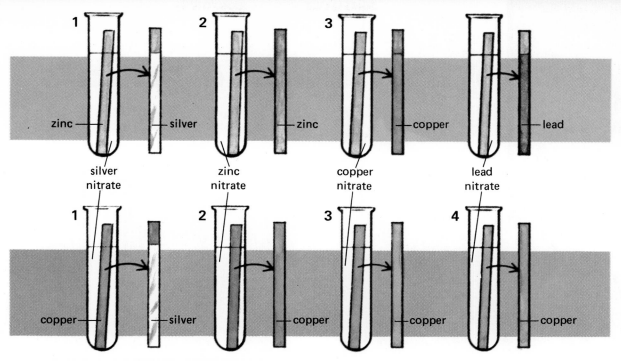

ELECTROMOTIVE SERIES OF METALS

lithium	most active	Li
potassium		K
barium		Ba
calcium		Ca
sodium		Na
magnesium		Mg
aluminum		Al
zinc		Zn
iron		Fe
tin		Sn
lead		Pb
hydrogen		H
copper		Cu
silver		Ag
platinum		Pt
gold	least active	Au

compounds. Copper is below zinc. It will not replace zinc from its compounds. Sodium will replace zinc. Lithium is the most active metal. It will replace all other metals. Gold is the least active metal. It will not replace any other metals.

▶ **Which is the least active metal?**

WHAT YOU LEARNED

1. More active metals replace less active metals from their compounds.
2. The electromotive series of metals lists metallic elements in order of their activity.
3. A metal will replace the metals listed below it in the electromotive series.

SCIENCE WORD

more active metal
   a metal that replaces another metal from its compounds

ANSWER THESE

1. If an iron nail is placed in a copper sulfate solution, it
   a. becomes coated with sulfur
   b. becomes coated with copper
   c. does not change
2. More active metals _____ less active metals from their compounds.
3. The most active metal is
   a. iron   b. copper   c. lithium
4. The electromotive series of metals lists metals in order of their
   a. color   b. weight   c. activity

NOW TRY THIS

Rearrange the following metals in order of their activity. Place the more active metals above those that are less active.

aluminum	silver
lithium	copper
barium	sodium
magnesium	gold
calcium	zinc

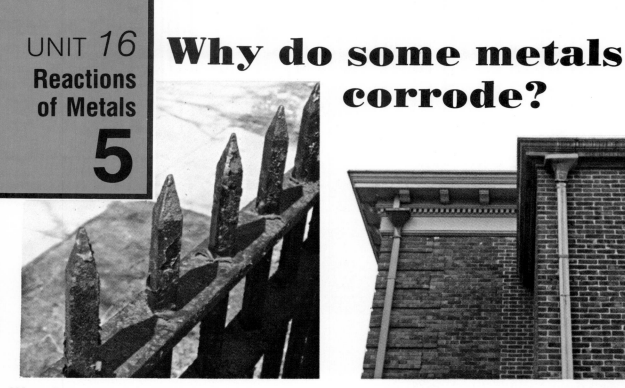

UNIT 16
Reactions of Metals
5

Why do some metals corrode?

Wearing away metals. After the paint chips off an iron railing, the iron turns a reddish-brown color. The color is caused by a coat of rust. Shiny aluminum pots become dull after a while. Copper pennies are shiny when they are new. When they get older, they become dull. Silver forks and spoons turn black when they are left in a drawer. These are examples of corrosion (cuh-ROH-zhun). Corrosion is a chemical change in metals. It is the wearing away of metals.

▶ **What is corrosion?**

Oxidation of metals. Metals may be corroded when they are exposed to air or water. Chemicals in air and water combine with some metals to make new compounds. Oxygen is a gas found in the air. It combines with iron to form iron oxide, or rust. Rusting is a form of oxidation. Oxidation of metals is a cause of corrosion.

Aluminum also combines with oxygen from the air. It changes to aluminum oxide. The dull gray coating on aluminum pots and screens is aluminum oxide. Copper combines with carbon dioxide and water to

form verdigris (VERD-uh-griss). Verdigris is the green coating you may sometimes see on pennies and copper pipes.

▶ **What is rusting?**

Losing electrons. When metals are oxidized, they combine with oxygen. Oxygen is a non-metal. When metals combine with non-metals, they lose electrons. The non-metals gain electrons. Oxidation is a loss of electrons.

Look at the equation showing how rust is formed. The 4 atoms of iron lose 12 electrons and become iron ions. The 6 atoms of

FORMATION OF RUST

iron	+	oxygen	$\longrightarrow$	rust
$4\ Fe$	+	$3O_2$	$\longrightarrow$	$2Fe_2O_3$
4 atoms of iron		6 atoms of oxygen		

$$Fe^{\circ} - 3\ electrons \longrightarrow Fe^{+3}$$
$$O^{\circ} + 2\ electrons \longrightarrow O^{-2}$$

ATOMS   **IONS**

$4 \times 3 = 12$ electrons lost

$6 \times 2 = 12$ electrons gained

300

oxygen gain 12 electrons and become oxygen ions. In a chemical reaction, the number of electrons lost always equals the number of electrons gained. When metals are oxidized, they lose electrons to non-metals.

▶ **What happens to metals when they are oxidized?**

ATOMS		IONS
Al^0 — 3 electrons $\longrightarrow$		Al^{+3}
Cu^0 — 2 electrons $\longrightarrow$		Cu^{+2}
Ag^0 — 1 electron $\longrightarrow$		Ag^{+1}

When metals are oxidized, they lose electrons and become ions.

WHAT YOU LEARNED

1. Corrosion is the wearing away of metals.
2. Oxidation of metals is a cause of corrosion.
3. When metals are oxidized, they lose electrons to non-metals.

SCIENCE WORDS

corrosion (cuh-ROH-zhun)
 the wearing away of metals
verdigris (VERD-uh-griss)
 the green coating on corroded copper

ANSWER THESE

1. Rust forms when iron combines with
    a. oxygen
    b. copper
    c. water
2. Rusting is a form of
    a. physical change
    b. cooling
    c. oxidation
3. The wearing away of metals is called
    a. oxidation
    b. corrosion
    c. burning
4. The gray coating on aluminum pots is
    a. copper oxide
    b. iron oxide
    c. aluminum oxide
5. Oxidation is a loss of _____.

NOW TRY THIS

How many electrons are lost when each of the metal atoms becomes an ion?

ATOMS			IONS
Fe^0 —	_____ electrons	$\longrightarrow$	Fe^{+3}
Cu^0 —	_____ electrons	$\longrightarrow$	Cu^{+2}
Ag^0 —	_____ electrons	$\longrightarrow$	Ag^{+1}
Al^0 —	_____ electrons	$\longrightarrow$	Al^{+3}
Ni^0 —	_____ electrons	$\longrightarrow$	Ni^{+3}
Cr^0 —	_____ electrons	$\longrightarrow$	Cr^{+3}
Ca^0 —	_____ electrons	$\longrightarrow$	Ca^{+2}
Mg^0 —	_____ electrons	$\longrightarrow$	Mg^{+2}

DO THIS AT HOME
Tarnishing of Silver

Silver will not combine with oxygen as easily as other metals do. But silver combines with sulfur compounds from the air. Sulfur gets into the air when fuels are burned. Volcanoes also release sulfur compounds into the air. The sulfur forms a black coating on silver. The black coating is silver sulfide. It is called tarnish.

Place a silver spoon or coin into hard-boiled egg yolk. Egg yolk contains sulfur. After several minutes, remove the spoon. The black coating on the spoon is silver sulfide. It can be removed with silver polish.

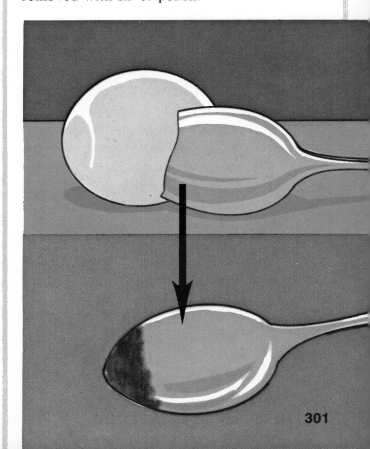

How can metals be protected from corrosion?

Corrosion weakens metals. When metals corrode, they form compounds. The compounds are not as strong as the original metal. This can cause the metal to weaken and break. Replacing metals damaged by corrosion costs many millions of dollars each year.

Iron combines with oxygen from the air to form iron oxide, or rust. Rust forms on iron surfaces. It is brittle and comes off in flakes. The remaining iron is thinner and weaker. The iron can be protected from rusting, if oxygen can be kept from getting at it.

▶ How does rusting weaken iron?

Protecting bridges from corrosion. Have you ever seen men painting a bridge? First they chip and scrape the rust from all the iron surfaces. Then they cover the bridge with a fresh coat of paint. The paint keeps air and water from getting to the metal surfaces. Then oxidation cannot occur. If the bridge were not painted, rusting would continue.

▶ How does paint protect bridges from corrosion?

Other ways of protecting metals from corrosion. Metals corrode when they are exposed to air or water. Only the outer surface of a metal is exposed to air or water. Only the outer surface will corrode. Covering the outer surface protects the metal from corrosion.

Painting protects metals from corrosion. Coating a metal with oil also protects it from corrosion. Have you ever seen brand new tools? They are often coated with a layer of oil. The oil protects the tools from corrosion. Air or water cannot get to the metal to corrode it.

The use of alloys also prevents corrosion. Stainless steel is an alloy of iron. Iron will rust. Stainless steel resists rusting. Some metals, such as zinc and tin, resist corrosion. Other metals can be coated with these corrosion-resistant metals. This protects the metal underneath from corrosion.

▶ How can new tools be protected from corrosion?

Flake off. When iron is exposed to air, rust forms. The rust flakes off the iron. This weakens the iron, and exposes new iron surfaces to the air. The rusting and flaking continue.

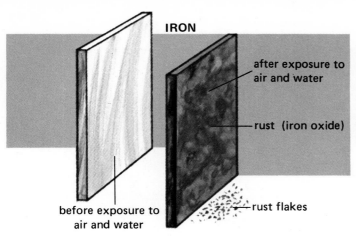

IRON

before exposure to air and water

after exposure to air and water

rust (iron oxide)

rust flakes

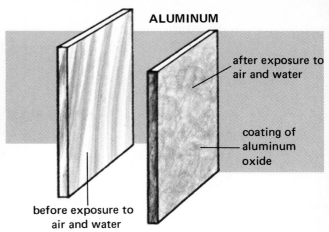

ALUMINUM

before exposure to air and water

after exposure to air and water

coating of aluminum oxide

When aluminum is exposed to air, aluminum oxide forms. The aluminum oxide does not flake off. It sticks to the surface of the aluminum. The aluminum oxide becomes a protective layer over the rest of the aluminum. Corrosion stops. Old aluminum is dull because it is covered with aluminum oxide.

▶ How does aluminum oxide stop the corrosion of aluminum?

WHAT YOU LEARNED

1. Metals corrode when they are exposed to air or water.
2. Metals can be protected from corrosion by painting, coating with oil, using corrosion-resistant alloys, or coating with corrosion-resistant metals.

ANSWER THESE

1. When iron corrodes, it changes to
   a. aluminum oxide
   b. iron oxide
   c. zinc oxide
2. Corrosion usually occurs to metal surfaces when they are
   a. exposed to air or water
   b. coated with paint
   c. coated with oil
3. Corrosion usually affects
   a. exposed surfaces
   b. oily surfaces
   c. painted surfaces
4. Oil is used to
   a. dissolve iron
   b. coat tools
   c. speed up corrosion

NOW TRY THESE

1. How are automobile bodies protected from corrosion?
2. Why are knives and forks made from stainless steel?
3. Give three examples of corrosion of metals.

DO THIS AT HOME

Get three iron nails. Coat one with oil or petroleum jelly. Paint another one with clear nail polish. Do not put anything on the third nail. Pour some water into a glass. Add a little vinegar to the water. Vinegar speeds up rusting. Place the three nails into the glass of water and leave them there overnight. What happens? How do the oil and nail polish affect the corrosion of the iron? Can you find any other substances that will protect iron nails from corrosion?

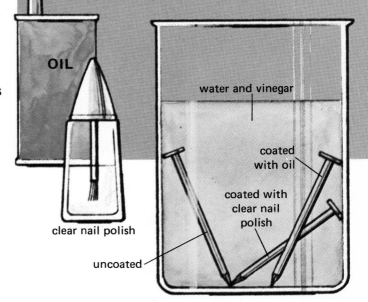

OIL

clear nail polish

water and vinegar

coated with oil

coated with clear nail polish

uncoated

How are metals plated?

GALVANIZED IRON

TIN—PLATED STEEL

Plating metals. When iron is exposed to air, it corrodes. We can protect iron against corrosion by coating it with another metal. Coating one metal with another metal is called plating (PLATE-ing).

Iron can be dipped into molten zinc. When the iron is removed, a thin layer of zinc sticks to it. Iron coated with zinc is called galvanized (GAL-vuh-nized) iron. The zinc protects the iron against corrosion. When the zinc corrodes, it forms zinc oxide. The zinc oxide sticks to the zinc. No further corrosion occurs. Garbage cans, snow shovels, and rust-proof nails are made of galvanized iron. Tin is used to plate steel. "Tin" cans are made by plating steel with tin.

▶ What is galvanized iron?

Electroplating metals. Electricity is often used to plate metals onto other metals. This is called electroplating (eh-LEC-tro-plate-ing). Nickel, silver, and copper are plated onto other metals in this way. The diagram shows how copper can be electroplated onto carbon.

Two carbon rods are placed in a solution of copper sulfate. The copper sulfate is an electrolyte (eh-LEC-tro-lite). Electrolytes are compounds that form ions when they dissolve. Solutions of electrolytes are good conductors of electricity.

The carbon rods are attached to the terminals of a battery. The carbon rod attached to the positive terminal is the positive electrode (eh-LEC-trode). An electrode is a rod that allows an electric current

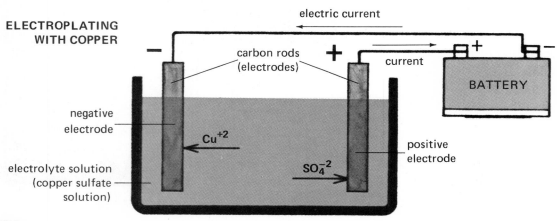

ELECTROPLATING WITH COPPER

electric current

carbon rods (electrodes)

current

BATTERY

negative electrode

Cu^{+2}

positive electrode

electrolyte solution (copper sulfate solution)

SO_4^{-2}

to enter or leave an electrolyte solution. The carbon rod attached to the negative terminal of the battery is the negative electrode. An electric current will flow through the electrodes and the electrolyte solution.

▶ **What is an electrolyte?**

Ions in motion. Copper ions (Cu^{+2}) move to the negative electrode. At the negative electrode there are extra electrons. Each copper ion gains two electrons and becomes an atom of copper.

$$Cu^{+2} \ + \ 2 \text{ electrons} \longrightarrow Cu^0$$

The copper plates itself onto the carbon rod. Metals can be plated with copper by using them as electrodes. To unplate a metal, we change the direction of the electric current.

▶ **At which electrode are there extra electrons?**

WHAT YOU LEARNED

1. Metals can be plated by dipping them into molten metals.
2. Metals can be electroplated in electrolyte solutions.
3. In an electrolyte solution, metallic ions gain electrons at the negative electrode. They then become metallic atoms.

SCIENCE WORDS

plating (PLATE-ing)
   coating one metal with another metal
galvanized (GAL-vuh-nized) **iron**
   iron that is plated with zinc
electroplating (eh-LEC-tro-plate-ing)
   using an electric current to plate one metal onto another metal
electrolyte (eh-LEC-tro-lite)
   a compound that forms ions when it dissolves
electrode (eh-LEC-trode)
   a rod that allows an electric current to enter or leave an electrolyte solution

ANSWER THESE

1. Galvanized iron is iron that is plated with
   a. zinc
   b. tin
   c. copper
2. Metals can be plated by
   a. dipping them in molten metals
   b. rubbing them against each other
   c. putting them in water
3. An electrolyte is
   a. a compound that can form ions
   b. an electrode
   c. a machine
4. Metals plate on the
   a. positive electrode
   b. negative electrode
   c. electrolyte

NOW TRY THIS

Choose the correct words.

A boy wanted to plate a penny with silver. He wired the penny to the (negative, positive) terminal of a dry cell. A piece of copper wire was attached to the other terminal. The boy used an electrolyte that contained (copper, silver) ions. (Chemical, Electrical) energy was needed to plate the penny. When the current flowed through the electrolyte, silver was plated on the (negative, positive) electrode.

Silver is very expensive. Many silver objects that you see are not made of solid silver. They are made of a cheaper metal plated with silver.

Why do oxidation and reduction occur together?

OXIDATION $2Fe + O_2 \longrightarrow 2FeO$
REDUCTION $2FeO \longrightarrow 2Fe + O_2$

Oxidation and reduction. You learned that oxidation takes place when elements combine with oxygen. Hydrogen combines with oxygen to form water. Iron combines with oxygen to form iron oxide. These are examples of oxidation. Reduction means to separate an element from oxygen. Pure metals are produced when oxide ores are reduced. Iron oxide can be reduced to produce iron. The iron is separated from the oxygen.

▶ **What is produced when ores are reduced?**

Losing electrons. Oxidation means to combine with oxygen. But it can also have another meaning. When iron combines with oxygen, the iron lends electrons to the oxygen. When water forms, hydrogen lends electrons to oxygen. The substance that is oxidized always loses some electrons. Oxidation can mean to lose electrons during a chemical reaction. Oxidation can occur even when no oxygen is involved. When sodium chloride is formed, sodium lends electrons to chlorine. The sodium loses electrons. It is oxidized.

▶ **What two things can oxidation mean?**

OXIDATION

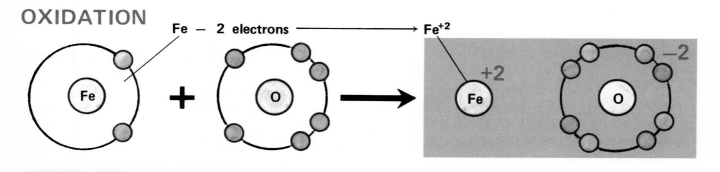

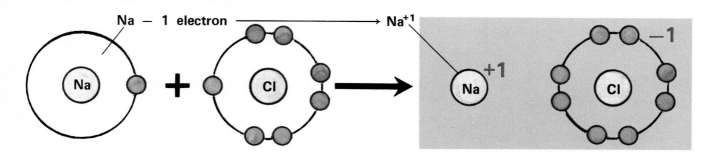

REDUCTION

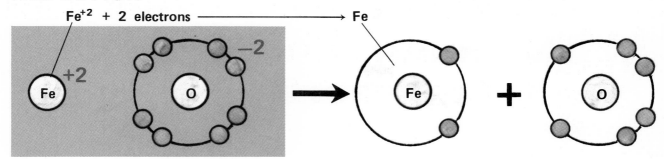

Fe^{+2} + 2 electrons ⟶ Fe

Gaining electrons. Reduction means to separate from oxygen. Reduction can also have another meaning. When ores are reduced, metal ions gain electrons and become metal atoms. When iron oxide is reduced, the iron gains electrons. <u>Reduction can mean to gain electrons during a chemical reaction.</u> Reduction can occur even when no oxygen is involved.

▶ **What two things can reduction mean?**

Oxidation and reduction occur together. When hydrogen combines with oxygen, the hydrogen loses electrons. It is oxidized. The oxygen gains electrons. It is reduced. Oxidation and reduction occur together during chemical reactions. Atoms that are oxidized lose electrons to other atoms that are reduced.

▶ **How do oxidation and reduction occur together during chemical reactions?**

WHAT YOU LEARNED

1. Oxidation is a loss of electrons.
2. Reduction is a gain of electrons.
3. Oxidation and reduction occur together during chemical reactions.

SCIENCE WORDS

oxidation
    losing electrons in a chemical reaction
reduction
    gaining electrons in a chemical reaction

ANSWER THESE

1. When elements are oxidized, they
   a. gain electrons
   b. lose electrons
   c. separate from oxygen

2. When elements are reduced, they
   a. gain electrons
   b. lose electrons
   c. combine with oxygen

3. During chemical reactions, oxidation and reduction always
   a. occur together
   b. form water
   c. change metals to non-metals

4. When metallic atoms lose electrons, they become
   a. positive ions
   b. negative ions

5. When non-metallic atoms gain electrons, they become
   a. positive ions
   b. negative ions

NOW TRY THESE

Tell whether each equation is an example of oxidation or of reduction.

1. Hg^{+2} + 2 electrons ⟶ Hg
2. O^{-2} − 2 electrons ⟶ O
3. Mg − 2 electrons ⟶ Mg^{+2}
4. Cl + 1 electron ⟶ Cl^{-1}

16 Review

Do the following questions on a separate sheet of paper.

Fill in the Blank   Write down the statements in Column I. Where there is a blank line in each statement, write the word or phrase from Column II that best completes the meaning of the statement.

Column I	Column II
1. An ore is a mineral compound from which we can get a useful_____.	zinc
2. Removing oxygen from an ore is called_____.	active metal
3. Heating an ore in open air is called _____.	metal
4. A mixture of two metals is a (n) _____.	together
5. Lithium is the most _____.	oxidation
6. Rusting is a form of_____.	reduction
7. Bauxite is an ore of_____.	air or water
8. Metals corrode when they are exposed to _____.	roasting
9. Galvanized iron is iron plated with _____.	aluminum
10. Oxidation and reduction occur_____.	alloy

Multiple Choice   Write the letter of the choice that best completes the statement or answers the question.

1. Hematite, magnetite, and limonite are ores of
   a. iron
   b. zinc
   c. copper
2. Removing oxygen from an ore is called
   a. replacement
   b. roasting
   c. reduction
3. Heating an ore in open air to produce an oxide is called
   a. replacement
   b. roasting
   c. reduction
4. Brass is an alloy of
   a. zinc and silver
   b. zinc and copper
   c. silver and copper

5. If you wanted to build something light, you would use
   a. iron
   b. aluminum
   c. steel
6. A metal that best resists corrosion is
   a. iron
   b. silver
   c. gold
7. Coating one metal with another is called
   a. plating
   b. corrosion
   c. rusting
8. When an atom is oxidized, it
   a. decomposes
   b. loses electrons
   c. gains electrons

UNIT 17 Solutions

Unit Lessons

1. What are mixtures?
2. What is a solution?
3. Do all substances dissolve in water?
4. How can liquid solutions be recognized?
5. Can solutions be made without water?
6. How can we make solutes dissolve faster?
7. How much solute can be dissolved in a solution?
8. How can we find the temperature at which liquids freeze?
9. How do solutes affect the freezing point of water?
10. What happens when liquids are heated?
11. How do solutes affect the boiling point of water?
12. How can a solute be separated from a solvent?
13. What is chromatography?
14. How are crystals formed?

Goals and Objectives

After completing this unit, you should be able to:

- give examples of liquid, gas and solid solutions.
- distinguish solutions from non-solutions.
- demonstrate how to quickly prepare solutions.
- explain the difference between saturated and unsaturated solutions.
- determine the freezing, melting, and boiling points of a solution.
- explain how solutes may be recovered from solutions and some mixtures may be separated.
- describe how super-saturated solutions can form crystals.

What are mixtures?

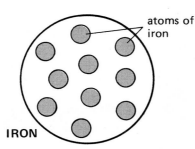

atoms of iron

IRON

molecules of hydrogen

molecules of carbon dioxide

HYDROGEN

CARBON DIOXIDE

Pure substances. An element is a pure substance. It is made up of only one kind of atom or molecule. A piece of iron contains only atoms of iron. A tank of hydrogen contains only molecules of hydrogen. A compound is a pure substance, too. Carbon dioxide is made up only of molecules of carbon dioxide. It is a pure substance.

▶ **Why are elements and compounds called pure substances?**

Mixtures. In a <u>mixture</u> (MIX-chur), different substances are mixed together. A mixture is not a pure substance. The molecules in a mixture are not all alike. Some are molecules of one substance. Some are molecules of another. There may be many different substances in a mixture. The substances in a mixture are not changed by being mixed together. They all keep their own properties.

▶ **Why is a mixture not a pure substance?**

Mixtures do not have chemical formulas. A compound always has the same chemical formula. It is always made up of the same elements combined in the same way. The compound sodium chloride always has one atom of sodium for each atom of chlorine. A mixture can be made in many different ways. A mixture of hydrogen and oxygen can have the same amount of each element. Or it can have twice as much hydrogen as oxygen. Or it can have three times as much oxygen as hydrogen. There could be any amounts of hydrogen and oxygen in the mixture. A mixture does not have a definite chemical composition. It cannot have a chemical formula.

▶ **Why can't you write a formula for a mixture?**

MIXTURES OF OXYGEN AND HYDROGEN

oxygen molecule   hydrogen molecule

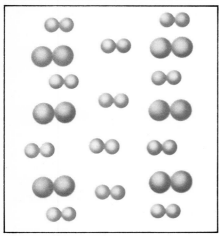

More hydrogen than oxygen

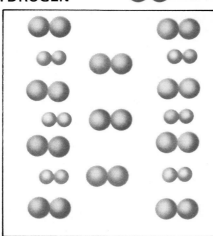

More oxygen than hydrogen

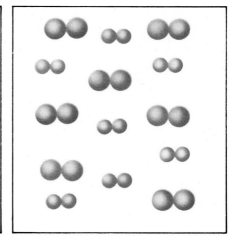

Same amounts of hydrogen and oxygen

310

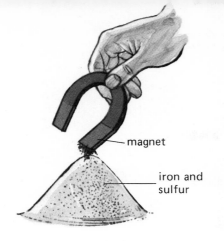

magnet

iron and sulfur

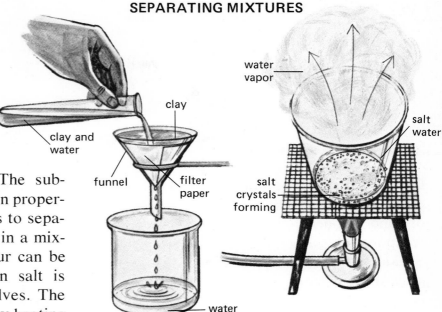

SEPARATING MIXTURES

clay and water

clay

funnel

filter paper

water

water vapor

salt water

salt crystals forming

Mixtures can be separated. The substances in a mixture keep their own properties. You can use their properties to separate one substance from another in a mixture. A mixture of iron and sulfur can be separated with a magnet. When salt is mixed with water, the salt dissolves. The salt and water can be separated by heating the solution. The water evaporates, and the salt is left behind. A mixture of clay and water can be separated by filtering the mixture. The water goes through the filter paper. The clay stays behind. You can always separate a mixture by physical means.

▶ **How can a mixture of iron and sulfur be separated?**

Differences between mixtures and compounds. This chart can help you remember the differences between mixtures and compounds.

MIXTURES	COMPOUNDS
Made of two or more substances mixed together	Made of two or more substances chemically combined
Substances keep their own properties	Have new properties, not like the substances that made the compound
Can be separated by physical means	Can be separated only by chemical means
Have no definite chemical composition	Have a definite chemical composition
Have no chemical formula	Have a chemical formula

▶ **How can a compound be separated into its elements?**

WHAT YOU LEARNED

1. A pure substance is made up of only one kind of atom or molecule.
2. A mixture is made up of different molecules mixed together.
3. A mixture does not have a chemical formula.
4. The substances in a mixture keep their own properties.
5. Mixtures can be separated by physical means.

SCIENCE WORD

mixture (MIX-chur)

two or more substances that have been put together, but have not been changed chemically

ANSWER THESE

Tell whether each sentence describes a compound or a mixture.

1. Can be separated only by chemical means.
2. Has no definite chemical composition.
3. Made of two different kinds of molecules.
4. Has a chemical formula C_2H_5OH.
5. Can be separated with a magnet.

UNIT 17
Solutions
2

What is a solution?

Disappearing chemicals. Fill two test tubes half full with water. Add ¼ teaspoon of sand to one of the test tubes. Add ¼ teaspoon of salt to the other test tube. Shake both test tubes. The sand can be seen at the bottom of its tube, but the salt has disappeared. Taste the water in the test tube to which salt was added. It tastes salty. The salt is still in the test tube, but we cannot see it. The salt is <u>dissolved</u> (dih-ZOLVED) in the water. The sand did not dissolve in the water.

▶ **What happens when salt is placed in water?**

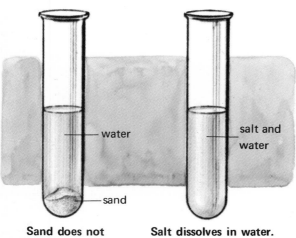

Sand does not dissolve in water.

Salt dissolves in water.

Solutions. Salt dissolves in water. Sand does not dissolve in water. A mixture of salt and water is called a <u>solution</u> (suh-LEW-shun). A solution is a special kind of mixture. Solutions are formed when substances dissolve in other substances.

▶ **How are solutions formed?**

Liquid solutions. Liquid solutions form when solids dissolve in liquids. Salt water is an example of this kind of solution. The salt, which is a solid, dissolves in the water, which is a liquid. Liquid solutions may also be formed when a gas dissolves in a liquid. Club soda is a solution of the gas carbon dioxide in the liquid water. The bubbles you see in club soda are carbon dioxide gas. Liquid solutions may also be solutions of liquids in liquids. Water and alcohol form this type of solution.

▶ **Give an example of a solution of a gas in a liquid.**

LIQUID SOLUTIONS

water (liquid)

alcohol (liquid)

solution of alcohol and water

carbon dioxide (gas) dissolved in water (liquid)

KINDS OF SOLUTIONS

SUBSTANCE	DISSOLVED IN	EXAMPLES
liquid	liquid	alcohol in water
	gas	water vapor in air
	solid	ether in rubber
gas	liquid	carbon dioxide in water (club soda)
	gas	nitrogen and oxygen mixed together (air)
	solid	hydrogen in palladium
solid	liquid	salt in water
	gas	iodine vapor in air
	solid	copper and zinc mixed together (brass)

Other types of solutions. Solutions are mixtures in which one or more substances are dissolved in another substance. These substances can be solids, liquids, or gases. You have already learned that solids, liquids, and gases can dissolve in a liquid. Solutions can also be formed by dissolving substances in solids and gases. The chart shows some examples of different kinds of solutions.

▶ **Why is air a solution?**

WHAT YOU LEARNED

1. Some substances dissolve in another substance. Some substances do not dissolve in the other substance.
2. When substances dissolve in other substances, solutions are formed.
3. A solution is a mixture of dissolved substances.

SCIENCE WORDS

dissolve (dih-ZOLV)
  become part of a solution
solution (suh-LEW-shun)
  a mixture of two or more substances that mix evenly with each other

ANSWER THESE

1. A solution is a _____ of two or more substances.
2. Club soda is an example of a solution of a liquid and a _____ .

3. Which of the following are solutions?
  air   soda water
  alcohol   brass
  salt water   sugar

NOW TRY THESE

Unscramble the following groups of letters to form some chemical terms.
  XMTIERU   SODSIVLE
  IQLDIU   LTIOUOSN

FINDING OUT MORE

Pure metals are not usually used in industry. Alloys are used instead of pure metals. Some alloys are solutions of one metal in another. Steel, brass, and bronze are examples of common alloys. Alloys are used to make coins, tools, machinery, and many other things. In fact, almost all metal objects that you buy are made of alloys.

NAME OF ALLOY	METALS IN SOLUTION	USES
steel	iron, chromium, nickel	cars, bikes, appliances, construction
brass	copper, zinc	jewelry, doorknobs, plumbing
bronze	copper, tin	medals, statues

Do all substances dissolve in water?

Luckily, many substances do not dissolve in water. How many insoluble substances can you find in this picture?

Dissolving solids in water. Fill four test tubes half full of water. Into each test tube place ¼ teaspoon of one of the following substances: sugar, iron filings, potassium dichromate, and sulfur. Place a rubber stopper in each tube, and shake the tubes. The sugar and potassium dichromate dissolve. The iron filings and sulfur do not dissolve. When a substance can dissolve in another substance, it is said to be <u>soluble</u> (SOL-yuh-bul) in that substance. Sugar and potassium dichromate are soluble in water. A substance that does not dissolve is <u>insoluble</u> (in-SOL-yuh-bul). Iron and sulfur are insoluble in water.

▶ Name two substances that are soluble in water.

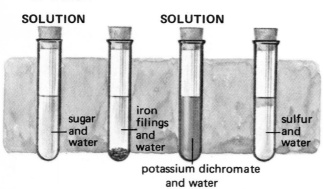

SOLUTION   SOLUTION

sugar and water | iron filings and water | potassium dichromate and water | sulfur and water

Mixing liquids with liquids. Mix ¼ of a test tube of each of the following liquids with ¼ of a test tube of water: alcohol, oil, vinegar, and benzene. Some of these liquids mix with the water to form solutions. These liquids are <u>miscible</u> (MIS-uh-bul) with water. Miscible liquids are liquids that mix together to form a solution. Alcohol and water are miscible. Vinegar and water

are miscible. Liquids that do not mix are <u>immiscible</u> (im-MIS-uh-bul). Oil and water do not mix. They are immiscible. Benzene and water are also immiscible.

Vinegar is miscible with water, but it is not miscible with oil. Vinegar forms a solution with water. It will not form a solution with oil. Liquids that are miscible with water may not be miscible with some other liquids.

▶ Name two liquids that are miscible with water.

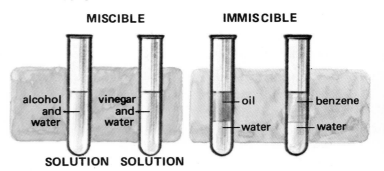

MISCIBLE   IMMISCIBLE

alcohol and water | vinegar and water | oil — water | benzene — water

SOLUTION SOLUTION

Parts of a solution. Mix some sugar with water. The sugar dissolves in the water to form a solution of sugar and water. The sugar dissolved in the water. In a solution, the substance that dissolves is called the <u>solute</u> (SOL-yute). The substance in which the solute dissolves is called the <u>solvent</u> (SOL-vent). In the solution of sugar and water, the sugar is the solute and the water is the solvent.

▶ In a solution of salt and water, which substance is the solute and which is the solvent?

WHAT YOU LEARNED

1. Substances that dissolve in a liquid are soluble in that liquid.
2. Liquids that mix together to form a solution are miscible. Liquids that do not form a solution are immiscible.
3. The substance that dissolves in a solution is called the solute. The substance in which the solute dissolves is called the solvent.

SCIENCE WORDS

soluble (SOL-yuh-bul)
able to dissolve
insoluble (in-SOL-yuh-bul)
not able to dissolve
miscible (MIS-uh-bul) **liquids**
liquids that are able to mix together to form a solution
immiscible (im-MIS-uh-bul) **liquids**
liquids that are not able to mix together to form a solution
solute (SOL-yute)
the substance that is dissolved in a solution
solvent (SOL-vent)
the substance in which a solute dissolves

FINDING OUT MORE

Weathering is the breaking up of rocks and minerals by natural forces, such as wind and water. Water can cause changes in rocks. Many rocks contain minerals that can dissolve in water. As water passes over or through the rocks, the minerals are dissolved and are carried away in the water. This can cause the breaking up of the rocks.

Water may also contain chemicals that react with minerals in rocks. When such reactions occur, new substances are formed. These new substances may be soluble in water. For example, water may have carbon dioxide dissolved in it. This solution can react with minerals containing calcium. The new substance that is formed by the reaction may be soluble in water. The dissolving of soluble minerals can lead to the formation of caves. Oxygen may also be dissolved in water. The dissolved oxygen will rust minerals containing iron. Rocks containing such minerals will crumble away.

ANSWER THESE

1. Which of the following substances are soluble in water?
   a. sugar
   b. iron filings
   c. salt
   d. sulfur
   e. potassium dichromate
2. Which of the following mixtures are miscible?
   a. water and oil
   b. vinegar and oil
   c. water and vinegar
   d. water and alcohol
   e. water and benzene
3. In a solution of carbon dioxide and water, the water is the (**solute, solvent**) and the carbon dioxide is the (**solute, solvent**).

NOW TRY THESE

1. A solid that dissolves in water is _____ .
2. A liquid that is miscible with water is _____ .
3. A gas that dissolves in water is _____ .

Many rocks contain minerals that can dissolve in water. When the minerals dissolve, a cave sometimes forms.

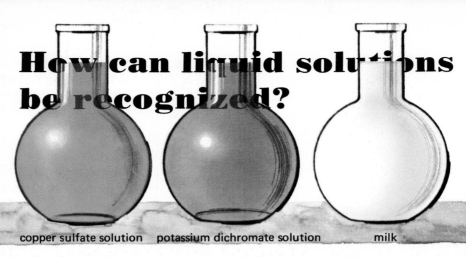

How can liquid solutions be recognized?

copper sulfate solution   potassium dichromate solution   milk

The properties of liquid solutions. Look at the drawing. You can see the lettering behind both solutions. Both solutions are clear. Clearness is one property of a liquid solution. Also, solutions are the same throughout. When something is the same throughout, it is <u>homogeneous</u> (ho-muh-JEE-nee-us). Solutions are homogeneous.

Some liquid mixtures are homogeneous, but they are not solutions. Homogenized (huh-MOJ-uh-nized) milk is milk that has been made the same throughout. It is a homogeneous mixture. But it is not clear. You cannot see through it. Milk is not a solution. Solutions are both clear and homogeneous. A liquid solution is a clear, homogeneous mixture of two or more substances.

▶ **What is a liquid solution?**

cream mixed in   cream on top

homogenized milk   non-homogenized milk

Particles in liquid mixtures. Shake a test tube containing starch and water. Is this a solution? Solutions are clear. This is not a solution because it is not clear. It is cloudy. Examine a drop of the mixture under a microscope. Starch grains can be seen mixed in the water. In liquid mixtures that are not solutions, particles can be seen under a microscope. These particles are microscopic in size.

▶ **How large are the particles in liquid mixtures that are not solutions?**

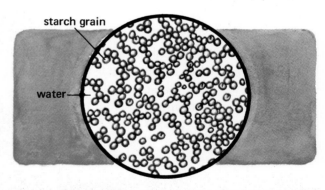

starch grain

water

mixture of starch and water as seen under a microscope

Particles in solutions. Look at some blue copper sulfate with a magnifying lens. Notice the shape of the crystals. Add the copper sulfate to water. It dissolves to form a solution. Examine a drop of the solution with a magnifying lens. Can you see copper sulfate crystals in the water? Examine the solution with a microscope. The copper sulfate has turned the water blue, but no crystals can be seen. The copper

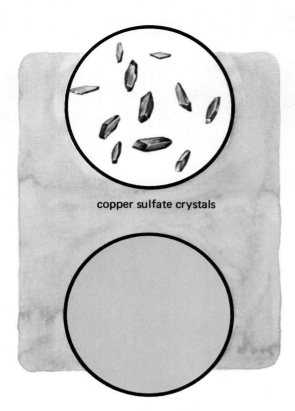

copper sulfate crystals

copper sulfate solution

WHAT YOU LEARNED

1. Liquid solutions are clear, homogeneous mixtures of two or more substances.
2. The particles in a solution are molecular in size.
3. Solvents cause the molecules of a solute to separate when solutions form.

SCIENCE WORD

homogeneous (ho-muh-JEE-nee-us) the same throughout

ANSWER THESE

1. Explain why tomato juice is not a solution.
2. Why can't the particles in a solution be seen with a microscope?
3. Vinegar is a mixture of acetic acid and water. Why is vinegar a solution?

NOW TRY THIS

Which of the following are solutions? Can you explain why?

water	club soda
French dressing	apple juice
noodle soup	coffee

FINDING OUT MORE

Add some copper sulfate to a beaker of water. The mixture is clear. The mixture is the same color blue throughout. This is a solution. It is clear and homogeneous. Fold a piece of filter paper and place it inside a funnel. Place the funnel into a flask. Pour the copper sulfate solution into the funnel. Compare the solution in the flask with the solution in the beaker. They are both exactly the same color. The particles in the solution went through the filter. The particles in a solution are too small to be filtered out.

sulfate cannot be seen with the most powerful microscope. The crystals of copper sulfate have dissolved. They have broken up into very small particles. The particles are the size of molecules. The particles in a solution are molecular (muh-LEC-yuh-ler) in size.

▶ **How large are the particles in a solution?**

How solutions form. Sugar dissolves in water. When sugar dissolves, its molecules mix with the molecules of the water. The water causes the molecules in the crystal of sugar to move away from one another. Solvents separate the molecules of solutes. The molecules of sugar mix with the molecules of water. A solution of sugar and water contains sugar molecules and water molecules. The particles in a solution are molecular in size.

▶ **What happens to the molecules in a crystal of sugar when the sugar dissolves?**

filter paper

Copper sulfate cannot be removed from solution by filtering.

Can solutions be made without water?

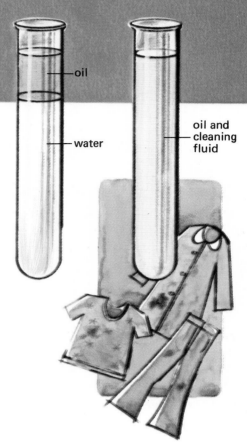

oil

water

oil and cleaning fluid

Cleaning without water. Some kinds of paint cannot be washed off with water. This paint is not soluble in water. The paint is soluble in turpentine (TUR-pen-tine). The paint dissolves in turpentine. It can be removed from skin, brushes, and other things by rubbing it with turpentine. Nail polish is not soluble in water. Nail polish remover contains a chemical called acetone (ASS-uh-tone). Acetone dissolves nail polish. Substances that are not soluble in water may be soluble in other liquids.

▶ **Why can't nail polish be removed with water?**

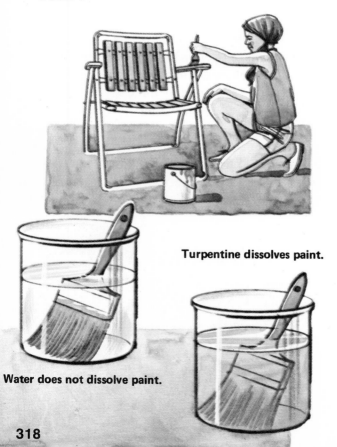

Turpentine dissolves paint.

Water does not dissolve paint.

Dry cleaning. Some stains cannot be removed from clothing by washing with water. Grease and oil are not soluble in water. Water is not a solvent for grease and oil. But other substances will dissolve grease and oil. These substances are solvents for grease and oil. Cleaning fluid is a solvent used by dry cleaners. It is used to remove grease stains from clothing. Cleaning fluid dissolves the grease stains. The dissolved grease is carried away in the cleaning fluid. Oil and water are not miscible. Oil and cleaning fluid are miscible.

▶ **Why is cleaning fluid used to remove grease stains?**

Alcohol solutions. Iodine is a solid element. It does not dissolve in water. But it does dissolve in alcohol. A solution formed when a solid dissolves in alcohol is called a tincture (TINK-chur). Tincture of iodine is used on cuts to prevent infection.

▶ **What is a tincture?**

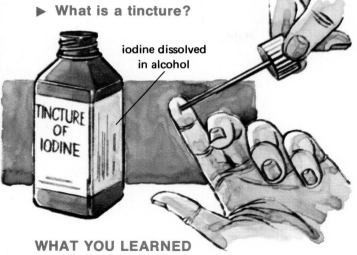

iodine dissolved in alcohol

WHAT YOU LEARNED

1. Substances that do not dissolve in water may dissolve in other solvents.
2. Tinctures are solutions made by dissolving solids in alcohol.

SCIENCE WORD

tincture (TINK-chur)
   a solution of a solid in alcohol

ANSWER THESE

1. Nail polish is soluble in
   a. water
   b. acetone
   c. paint
2. Oil and water are
   a. soluble
   b. miscible
   c. immiscible
3. Tinctures are solutions of solids dissolved in
   a. alcohol
   b. iodine
   c. acetone

NOW TRY THIS

For each substance in column A, find a solvent in column B that the substance will dissolve in.

A	B
Paint	Water
Iodine	Acetone
Sugar	Alcohol
Grease	Cleaning fluid
Nail polish	Turpentine

FINDING OUT MORE

Some solutions become cooler when they form. Measure the temperature of a beaker of water. Add some ammonium nitrate to the water, and stir the mixture. Measure the temperature of the solution. The temperature is lower. Heat is absorbed when ammonium nitrate dissolves in water.

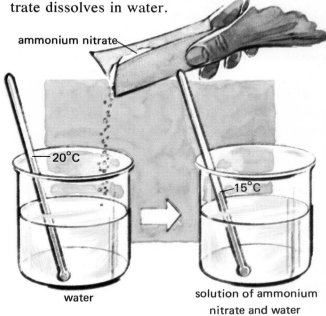

ammonium nitrate

20°C

15°C

water

solution of ammonium nitrate and water

Some solutions become warmer when they form. Measure the temperature of a beaker of water. Carefully add a small amount of concentrated sulfuric acid to the water, and stir the mixture. Measure the temperature of the solution. The temperature is higher. Heat is given off when sulfuric acid dissolves in water.

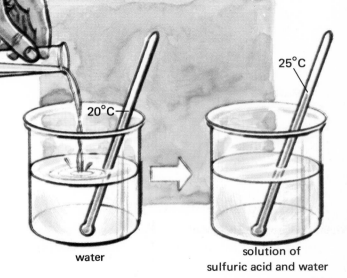

sulfuric acid

20°C

25°C

water

solution of sulfuric acid and water

319

How can we make solutes dissolve faster?

Stirring. Add a teaspoon of sugar to a cup of water. Much of the sugar sinks down to the bottom of the cup. If we let the cup stand, the sugar will finally dissolve. But it takes a very long time for the sugar to dissolve this way. Stir the solution. The sugar begins to dissolve faster. In a short time all the sugar has dissolved. Stirring makes sugar dissolve faster. Stirring is a way of making solutes dissolve faster.

How can sugar be made to dissolve faster in a cup of coffee?

hot water   cold water

Hot water dissolves solutes faster than cold water.

sugar

water

without stirring   with stirring

Stirring makes solutes dissolve faster.

Hot and cold solutions. Place a tea bag in a beaker of hot water. Place a second tea bag in a beaker of cold water. Move both tea bags up and down six times. Remove both tea bags from the water. The hot water is darker than the cold water. More tea has dissolved in the hot water than in the cold water. The hot water dissolves the tea faster than the cold water. Instant coffee dissolves faster in hot water than in cold water. Sugar dissolves faster in hot water than in cold water. Heat makes the solutes dissolve faster.

▶ How does heat help to dissolve a solute?

Particle size. Crush a lump of sugar into small pieces. Add this crushed sugar to a beaker of hot water. Add a whole lump of sugar to a second beaker of hot water. Stir both beakers. In which beaker does the sugar dissolve faster? The sugar that was crushed dissolved faster. Crushing solutes into small pieces makes them dissolve faster. Powdering (POW-duh-ring) is a way

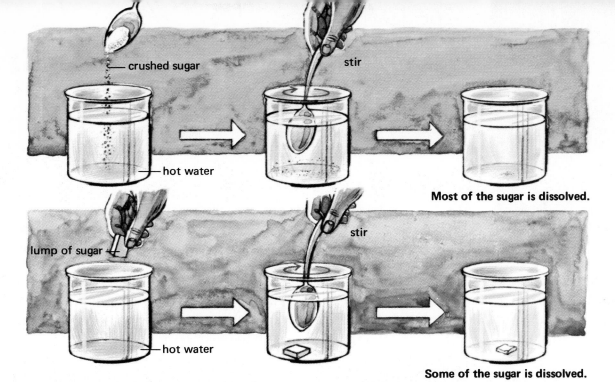

crushed sugar

stir

hot water

Most of the sugar is dissolved.

lump of sugar

stir

hot water

Some of the sugar is dissolved.

of crushing solids into very small pieces. Powdered sugar dissolves even faster than regular sugar. The smaller the solute particles are, the faster they dissolve.

▶ **Why does powdered sugar dissolve faster than regular sugar?**

WHAT YOU LEARNED

1. Solutes dissolve faster when they are stirred.
2. Solutes dissolve faster in hot solutions than in cool solutions.
3. Solutes dissolve faster when they are broken into small particles.

SCIENCE WORD

powdering (POW-duh-ring)
  breaking a solid into very small pieces

ANSWER THESE

1. Sugar dissolves fastest in
   a. hot coffee
   b. cool coffee
   c. iced coffee
2. Powdered sugar dissolves faster than a lump of sugar because
   a. the powdered sugar has larger particles
   b. the powdered sugar has smaller particles
   c. powdering changes the temperature of the solution

3. Stirring will make solids
   a. dissolve faster
   b. dissolve slower
   c. insoluble

NOW TRY THESE

Which of the following methods will make a solute dissolve faster?
1. Placing the solvent in a freezer.
2. Grinding the solute into small pieces.
3. Placing the solvent in a mixing machine.
4. Letting the solvent stand without stirring.
5. Heating the solvent.

FINDING OUT MORE

Some gases, such as oxygen and carbon dioxide, are soluble in water. Oceans, lakes, and rivers contain dissolved oxygen. Soda water contains dissolved carbon dioxide. Solids and liquids dissolve better in warm solvents than in cold ones. Is the same true of gases? Open two bottles of club soda. Let one stand out overnight. Place the other in the refrigerator. The next day, pour a little out of each bottle. Which one has more gas in it? More gas stayed dissolved in the cold liquid. Gases dissolve better in cold solvents. The cold waters surrounding the north and south poles contain more oxygen than the warmer waters at the equator.

How much solute can be dissolved in a solution?

1 g of copper sulfate   5 g of copper sulfate   10 g of copper sulfate

Strong and weak solutions. Put 100 milliliters of water in each of three beakers. To the first beaker add 1 gram of copper sulfate. To the second add 5 grams. To the third add 10 grams. Dissolve the copper sulfate by stirring or heating the mixture. What difference can you see in these solutions? The color of the first solution is light blue. The second solution is medium blue. The third is dark blue. The more solute that is dissolved, the darker the solution. The first solution has the smallest amount of solute. It is the weakest of the three solutions. The third solution has the most solute. It is the strongest. Weak solutions have less solute than strong solutions.

▶ **What is the difference between a weak solution and a strong solution?**

Dilute and concentrated solutions. A weak solution has a small amount of dissolved solute. Weak solutions are also

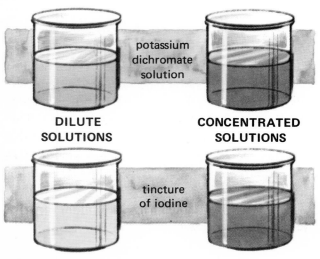

potassium dichromate solution

DILUTE SOLUTIONS   **CONCENTRATED SOLUTIONS**

tincture of iodine

called <u>dilute</u> (die-LOOT) solutions. A strong solution has a large amount of dissolved solute. Strong solutions are also called <u>concentrated</u> (CON-sen-trait-ed) solutions.

▶ **What is a dilute solution?**

Heating a solution. Put 50 ml of water in each of two beakers. Add 10 grams of potassium chloride to each. Stir until the solute dissolves. Keep adding potassium chloride to each beaker, 1 gram at a time, until no more dissolves. Some solute will remain on the bottom. Heat the solution in one of the beakers. The solute on the bottom dissolves. Warm water can hold more potassium chloride than cold water. A warm solvent can usually dissolve more solid solute than a cold solvent.

▶ **How can you make water dissolve more potassium chloride?**

Unsaturated and saturated solutions. Add 1 gram of potassium chloride to 100 ml of water. It dissolves. More solute can be dissolved in this solution. This solution is called an <u>unsaturated</u> (un-SATCH-uh-rate-ed) solution. Unsaturated solutions are solutions that contain less solute than they can hold.

Keep adding potassium chloride to the solution until no more will dissolve. The solution in which no more potassium chloride will dissolve is said to be <u>saturated</u> (SATCH-uh-rate-ed). Saturated solutions contain all the solute they can hold. When saturated solutions are heated, they usually become unsaturated.

▶ **What is a saturated solution?**

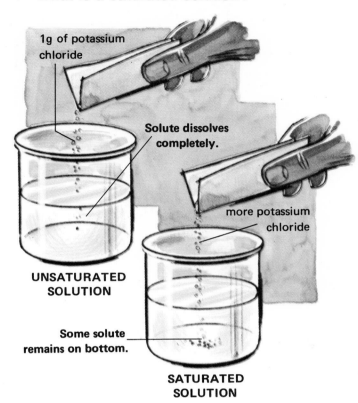

1g of potassium chloride

Solute dissolves completely.

more potassium chloride

UNSATURATED SOLUTION

Some solute remains on bottom.

SATURATED SOLUTION

WHAT YOU LEARNED

1. Weak solutions are also called dilute solutions. Strong solutions are also called concentrated solutions.
2. A warm solvent can usually hold more dissolved solute than a cold solvent.
3. Saturated solutions contain all the dissolved solute they can hold.
4. Unsaturated solutions can dissolve more solute.

SCIENCE WORDS

dilute (die-LOOT) **solution**
a weak solution
concentrated (CON-sen-trait-ed) **solution**
a strong solution
unsaturated (un-SATCH-uh-rate-ed) **solution**
a solution that can dissolve more solute
saturated (SATCH-uh-rate-ed) **solution**
a solution that has all the solute it can dissolve

ANSWER THESE

1. A dilute solution is
   a. weak
   b. strong
   c. saturated

2. When saturated solutions are heated, they become
   a. dilute
   b. unsaturated
   c. concentrated

3. A solution that contains all the solute it can hold is
   a. dilute
   b. unsaturated
   c. saturated

NOW TRY THESE

Tell whether each of the following solutions is dilute, concentrated, saturated, or unsaturated.
1. A light blue solution of copper sulfate.
2. A solution of copper sulfate in which more solute can be dissolved.
3. A solution of copper sulfate in which no more solute can be dissolved.
4. A dark blue solution of copper sulfate.

FINDING OUT MORE

Prepare a saturated solution of ammonium chloride. At room temperature, you can dissolve about 4 grams of this solute in 100 ml of water. Heat the solution. It becomes unsaturated. Add more solute until it becomes saturated again. The solution will hold about 6 grams of solute at 70°C. Let the solution cool back to room temperature. The 6 grams of solute will remain dissolved. At room temperature a saturated solution of ammonium chloride usually holds only 4 grams of solute. Since this solution holds 6 grams, it is called a supersaturated (SOO-per-SATCH-uh-rate-ed) solution. Supersaturated solutions contain more solute than they are usually able to hold at a given temperature.

How can we find the temperature at which liquids freeze?

Removing heat from water. Fill a beaker half full of water. Record the temperature of the water. Place the beaker of water in a freezer. Record the temperature of the water every five minutes. The temperature of the water goes down. The water is losing heat. When water loses heat, its temperature goes down.

▶ What happens to the temperature of the water placed in a freezer?

Changing water to ice. Look at the chart. At what temperature does water begin to freeze? Water begins to freeze at 0° Celsius (SEL-see-us). When water freezes, it turns to ice. The temperature of the water stops going down as the water begins to change to ice. The water is still losing heat. The water changes to ice as more heat is lost. The temperature at which water changes to ice is called its <u>freezing point</u>. The freezing point of water is 0°C.

▶ What is the freezing point of water?

The freezing point of other liquids. When heat is removed from liquids, their temperature goes down. When liquids reach their freezing point, the temperature stops going down. Removing heat from liquids at their freezing points changes them into solids. Every liquid has its own freezing point.

▶ What happens when heat is removed from a liquid at its freezing point?

FREEZING OF WATER

TIME IN FREEZER	TEMPERATURE OF WATER	
0 minutes	22°C	
5 minutes	15°C	
10 minutes	10°C	
15 minutes	6°C	
20 minutes	3°C	
25 minutes	0°C	(ice begins to form)
30 minutes	0°C	
35 minutes	0°C	(water completely frozen)

FREEZING POINTS OF LIQUIDS

LIQUID	FREEZING POINT
water	0°C
ethyl alcohol	−117°C
mercury	−39°C
sea water	−1°C
glycerine	18°C

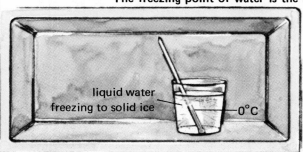

liquid water
freezing to solid ice — 0°C

0°C — solid ice melting
to liquid water

Heating solids. When heat is removed from liquids, they change to solids. When heat is added to solids, they change back to liquids. The temperature at which a solid changes to a liquid is called its <u>melting point</u>. Water freezes at 0°C. Ice melts at 0°C. The freezing and melting points of a substance are the same.

▶ **What happens when a solid is heated to its melting point?**

WHAT YOU LEARNED

1. When heat is removed from a liquid, its temperature goes down.
2. When heat is removed from a liquid at its freezing point, it turns into a solid.
3. Water freezes at 0° Celsius.
4. Different liquids have different freezing points.

SCIENCE WORDS

freeze
  change from a liquid to a solid
freezing point
  the temperature at which a liquid changes to a solid
melting point
  the temperature at which a solid changes to a liquid

ANSWER THESE

1. The freezing point of water is _____ ° Celsius.
2. To change a liquid into a solid, _____ must be removed.
3. The temperature at which a solid changes into a liquid is called its _____ point.
4. The melting point and the freezing point of a substance (are/are not) the same.

5. Most liquids
  a. have the same freezing point
  b. have different freezing points
  c. do not freeze

FINDING OUT MORE

Some chemicals are not found in the liquid state. They change directly from solids into gases or from gases into solids. The process of changing directly from a solid to a gas is called sublimation (sub-luh-MAY-shun). As the temperature of the solid rises, a point is reached at which the solid turns directly to a gas. This point is called the sublimation point. Frozen carbon dioxide is called dry ice. Dry ice changes directly into carbon dioxide gas. It does not melt to form a liquid. Carbon dioxide sublimes (suh-BLIMES) at −78.5°C. Iodine is another substance that changes directly from a solid to a gas. Moth balls are also made of a substance that sublimes. Place a moth ball in a glass. Observe it for several weeks. The moth ball gets smaller. Can you explain why?

Frozen carbon dioxide is used to keep ice cream and ices cold. "Dry ice" is colder than regular ice, and it doesn't make a mess by melting.

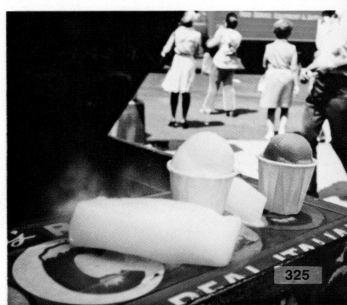

How do solutes affect the freezing point of water?

Freezing salt water. Fill two paper cups with water. Add a teaspoon of salt to one of the cups. Stir the solution. Place a thermometer in each cup. Place the cups in a freezer. Record the temperature of the water in the cups every 5 minutes. Which cup of water freezes first? The water without salt freezes first. Ice begins to form at 0°C. In which cup does the water take longer to freeze? The salt water takes longer to freeze. It freezes several degrees below 0°C. Salt lowers the freezing point of water.

▶ **What happens to the freezing point of water when salt is added to it?**

Adding other solutes to water. Try the same experiment using other solutes, such as sugar or copper sulfate. These solutes also lower the freezing point of the water. Solutes lower the freezing point of solvents in which they are dissolved.

▶ **How do solutes affect the freezing point of solvents?**

Changing the amount of solute in a solution. Put 100 ml of water in each of three beakers. Place 2 grams of salt in the first beaker, 5 grams in the second, and 10 grams in the third. Find the freezing points of the three solutions. Look at the table.

SOLUTION	FREEZING POINT
100 ml of water and 2 g of NaCl	−1°C
100 ml of water and 5 g of NaCl	−3°C
100 ml of water and 10 g of NaCl	−6°C

The more salt we add, the lower the freezing point of the solution. Solutes lower the freezing point of solutions. The more solute in a solution, the lower its freezing point.

▶ **What happens to the freezing point of a solution when more solute is added?**

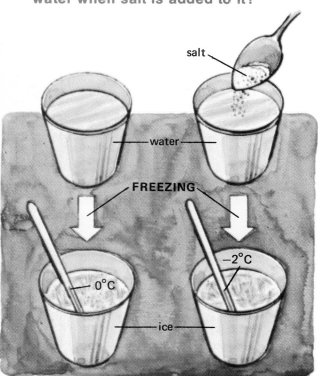

Salt lowers the freezing point of water.

Salt and icy sidewalks. Salt is sprinkled on icy sidewalks. When the ice starts to melt, the salt dissolves in the water and forms salt water. The salt water has a lower freezing point than pure water. Salt water will not freeze at 0°C. The temperature must get lower before salt water freezes. Salt is sprinkled on icy sidewalks because it lowers the freezing point of the water. Ice does not form as fast.

▶ **Why is salt sprinkled on icy sidewalks?**

WHAT YOU LEARNED

1. Solutes lower the freezing point of water.
2. The more solute dissolved in water, the lower its freezing point.

ANSWER THESE

1. Solutes _____ the freezing point of water.
2. The more solute dissolved in water, the lower its _____ point.
3. In the winter, _____ is sprinkled on icy sidewalks.

NOW TRY THIS

Which of the following solutions will have the lowest freezing point?
   a. 2 spoons of salt in 1 liter of water
   b. 2 spoons of salt in 2 liters of water
   c. 4 spoons of salt in 1 liter of water
   d. 4 spoons of salt in 2 liters of water
   e. 6 liters of water

FINDING OUT MORE

Tap water from your sink is not pure water. Tap water does not freeze at exactly 0°C. It freezes at a little lower temperature because it contains dissolved solutes. Some mineral solutes react with soap. Water containing these solutes is called hard water. Soap does not form suds in hard water. Some solutes do not affect the sudsing of soap. Water that has only these solutes in it is called soft water. The table lists some solutes that make water hard. It also shows some dissolved solutes in soft water.

HARD WATER	SOFT WATER
calcium bicarbonate	sodium chloride
calcium sulfate	carbon dioxide
magnesium bicarbonate	oxygen
magnesium sulfate	
calcium chloride	
iron sulfate	

What happens when liquids are heated?

CHANGING WATER TO STEAM

Adding heat to water. Place a thermometer in a beaker of water. Heat the water. The temperature of the water rises. When the temperature reaches 100°C, small bubbles appear in the liquid. These bubbles show that a gas is being formed. As you continue to heat the water, the water bubbles very hard. But the temperature stays at 100°C. The water has reached its <u>boiling point</u>. When water reaches its boiling point, it changes to steam. You can see the bubbles of steam coming out of the water. Steam is water in the gaseous state. Keep heating the water. The temperature of the water will remain at 100°C until all the water has changed to steam.

▶ What is steam?

The boiling point of liquids. When heat is added to water, its temperature rises. The temperature of the water rises until it reaches its boiling point. When water reaches its boiling point, it forms bubbles of steam. The boiling point of a liquid is the temperature at which it forms bubbles of gas. The boiling point of alcohol is 78°C.

At 78°C, alcohol forms bubbles of alcohol gas. Different liquids have different boiling points.

▶ **What happens when a liquid reaches its boiling point?**

LIQUID	BOILING POINT
water	100°C
mercury	357°C
glycerine	290°C
acetic acid	118°C
benzene	80°C
ethyl alcohol	78°C
acetone	39°C

Evaporation. When a liquid is heated to its boiling point, it changes to a gas all through the liquid. Liquids that are allowed to stand at room temperature may also change into gases. But this happens only at the surface of the liquid. Some fast-moving molecules at the surface of the liquid move into the air. The liquid <u>evaporates</u> (eh-VAP-uh-rates). Evaporation slowly changes a liquid

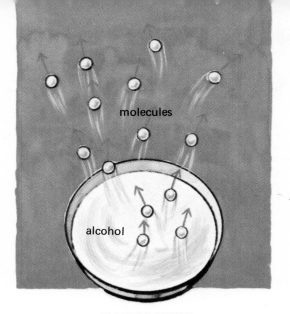

EVAPORATION

to a gas. Leave a small amount of alcohol in an open dish. The alcohol seems to disappear. You can smell the alcohol in the air. Alcohol molecules have escaped into the air and reached your nose. The alcohol has evaporated.

▶ **What is meant by evaporation?**

WHAT YOU LEARNED

1. Heating liquids makes their temperature rise.
2. The temperature at which a liquid forms bubbles of gas is its boiling point.
3. Different liquids have different boiling points.

SCIENCE WORDS

boiling point
   the temperature at which a liquid forms bubbles of gas

evaporate (eh-VAP-uh-rate)
   change from a liquid to a gas

ANSWER THESE

1. The boiling point of water is _____ .
2. If heat is added to a liquid at its boiling point,
   a. the temperature rises
   b. the liquid changes to a gas
   c. the liquid changes to a solid
3. When liquids are allowed to stand, they _____ .
4. Two liquids with boiling points higher than water are _____ and _____ .

5. Two liquids with boiling points lower than water are _____ and _____ .

NOW TRY THESE
Unscramble the following words.

ONARPAVEOTI
ILBOGNI
TEMAS

FINDING OUT MORE

The engine of a car must be kept from getting too hot. Water in the radiator cools the engine. In the winter, plain water would freeze and crack the engine. To prevent this, an antifreeze is mixed with the water in the radiator. The solution of water and antifreeze has a much lower freezing point than water. It also has a much higher boiling point. The antifreeze solution does not evaporate as fast as plain water would in hot weather.

How do solutes affect the boiling point of water?

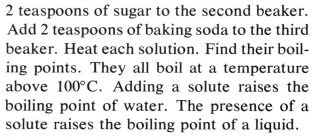

water — 100°C

Boiling water. When heat is added to water, its temperature rises. When the water temperature reaches 100°C, it boils. Adding more heat to boiling water does not raise its temperature. The temperature of the water stays at 100°C. When heat is added to a liquid at its boiling point, the liquid changes to a gas.

▶ What is the boiling point of water?

Solutes and boiling points. Fill three beakers with equal amounts of water. Add 2 teaspoons of salt to the first beaker. Add

— 100°C

salt and water

— 100°C

sugar and water

— 100°C

baking soda and water

2 teaspoons of sugar to the second beaker. Add 2 teaspoons of baking soda to the third beaker. Heat each solution. Find their boiling points. They all boil at a temperature above 100°C. Adding a solute raises the boiling point of water. The presence of a solute raises the boiling point of a liquid.

▶ How do solutes affect the boiling point of water?

Adding more solute. Place 100 ml of water in each of three beakers. Add 5 grams of salt to the first. Add 10 grams of salt to the second. Add 20 grams of salt to the third. Find the boiling point for each of the three solutions. The table shows that

AMOUNT OF SALT IN 100 ml OF WATER	BOILING POINT
5 grams	101°C
10 grams	102°C
20 grams	104°C

the more salt there is dissolved in the water, the higher the boiling point. Solutes raise the boiling point of water. The more solute added to the solution, the higher its boiling point.

▶ **What effect does the amount of solute have on the boiling point of a liquid?**

WHAT YOU LEARNED

1. Solutes raise the boiling points of liquids.
2. The more solute in a solution, the higher its boiling point.

ANSWER THESE

1. If water boils at 102°C, it probably
   a. is not water at all
   b. contains dissolved solutes
   c. has been overheated
2. Solutes **(raise, lower)** the boiling point of water.
3. The more solute in a solution, the _____ its boiling point.

NOW TRY THIS

In each of the following examples, tell whether the temperature goes up, goes down, or remains the same.

a. The boiling point of water when more water is added.
b. The temperature of boiling water when heat is added.
c. The boiling point of water when salt is added.
d. The boiling point of coffee when sugar is added.
e. The boiling point of water when heat is removed.

FINDING OUT MORE

Eggs cook faster when salt is added to the water. Salt raises the boiling point of water. So the eggs are being cooked at a higher temperature. Fats and oils have higher boiling points than water. When foods are cooked in oil, they are really being boiled in oil. The higher temperature of the oil cooks food much faster. The oil gives the food a different taste, too.

How can a solute be separated from a solvent?

Filtering a solution. Filter a solution of copper sulfate and water. The copper sulfate cannot be filtered out of the solution. A solute cannot be separated from its solvent by filtering. Solutions cannot be separated by filtering.

▶ What happens when a solution of copper sulfate is filtered?

Evaporating a solvent. Prepare a solution of copper sulfate and water. Pour a few ml of the solution into a shallow dish. Let it stand for several days. The water evaporates. Crystals of copper sulfate remain in the bottom of the dish. The solvent can be evaporated from a solution to <u>recover</u> (ree-KUV-er), or get back, the solute.

▶ What happens when copper sulfate solution is left for several days?

Boiling solutions. When a solution is boiled, the liquid is changed to a gas very rapidly. Boil a solution of copper sulfate. After all the water has evaporated, the copper sulfate remains behind. Boiling is a faster way of evaporating solvent from a solution.

▶ What happens when a solution of copper sulfate and water is boiled?

Condensation of gases. Hold a dry mirror (face down) above a pot of boiling water. Droplets of water appear on the mirror. When steam is cooled, it changes back to water. You have learned that changing a gas to a liquid is called condensation.

▶ What is condensation?

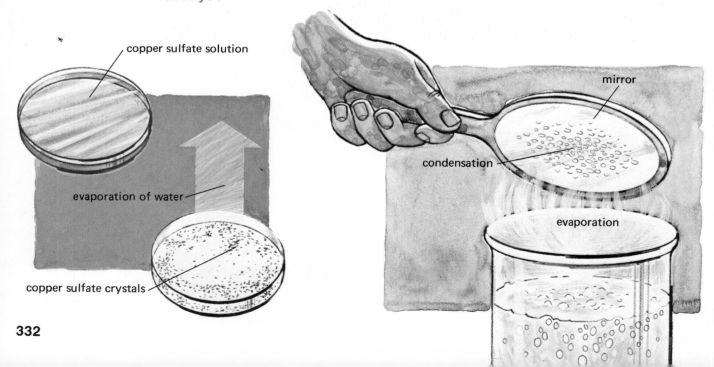

copper sulfate solution

evaporation of water

copper sulfate crystals

mirror

condensation

evaporation

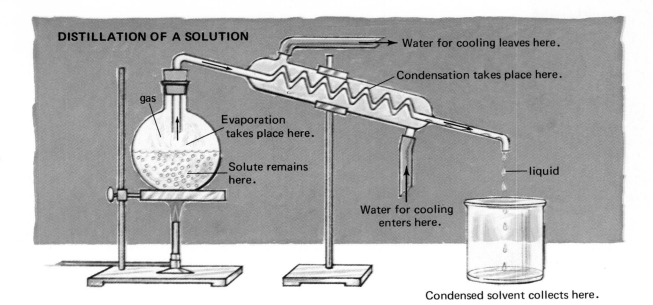

DISTILLATION OF A SOLUTION

gas

Evaporation takes place here.

Solute remains here.

Water for cooling leaves here.

Condensation takes place here.

Water for cooling enters here.

liquid

Condensed solvent collects here.

Distillation. Evaporate the water from a salt solution. The salt is left behind. We have recovered the salt, but the water is gone. <u>Distillation</u> (dis-tuh-LAY-shun) is another way of separating a solvent and a solute. When a solution is distilled (dis-TILLED) we can recover both the solvent and the solute.

In distillation, evaporation and condensation both take place. The solution to be separated is heated. The solvent evaporates and forms a gas. The gas moves through a tube. The tube is called a condenser (cun-DEN-ser). The condenser cools the gas. The gas changes back to a liquid. The liquid drips into a container and can be collected. The solute remains in the heating flask. Both the solute and the solvent have been recovered.

▶ **What happens to the solvent during distillation?**

WHAT YOU LEARNED

1. The solute can be recovered from a solution by evaporating the water.
2. Distillation is a way of separating a solvent and a solute.
3. Evaporation and condensation of the solvent take place during distillation.
4. Both the solute and the solvent can be recovered by distillation.

SCIENCE WORDS

recover (re-KUV-er)
  to get something back the way it was
distillation (dis-tuh-LAY-shun)
  a way of recovering the solute and the solvent from a solution

ANSWER THESE

1. Solutions (can, cannot) be separated by filtering.
2. Evaporating changes
   a. liquids to gases
   b. gases to liquids
   c. liquids to solids
3. When gases are cooled, they _____.
4. Distillation involves both _____ and _____.

FINDING OUT MORE

Fractional Distillation

Solutions of two or more liquids can be separated by fractional (FRAC-shun-ul) distillation. Liquids have different boiling points. When distilled, the liquid with the lower boiling point evaporates first. After most of this liquid evaporates, the liquid with the higher boiling point starts to evaporate. These liquids can be collected separately after condensation. Petroleum products, such as gasoline, kerosene, heating oil, and tar, are separated this way.

What is chromatography?

Absorbing water. If you place the corner of a paper towel in a glass of water, the whole towel becomes wet after a while. The paper has soaked up the water. It has <u>absorbed</u> (ab-SORBED) the water. As the water is absorbed, it slowly moves through the paper.

▶ **What happens if you put the end of a paper towel in a glass of water?**

Moving spots. Place a drop of red food coloring near the corner of a paper towel. Let it dry. Place the corner of the towel in a glass of water. The paper absorbs the water. The water moves through the paper. The spot of food coloring moves also. As the water moves through the paper, the red spot moves along with it. The water dissolves the spot and carries it along.

▶ **What happens to a spot of food coloring on a piece of paper towel when the paper is placed in water?**

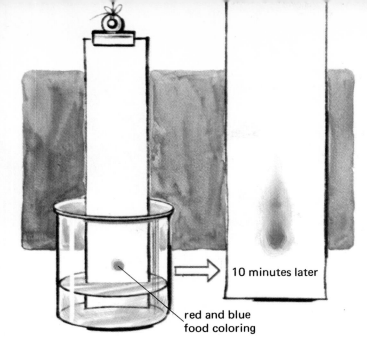

red and blue
food coloring

10 minutes later

Separating substances. Mix red and blue food coloring together. Place a drop of this mixture near the end of a long strip of filter paper. Place the end of the paper strip in water. Allow the paper to remain in the water for 10 minutes. Remove it from the water and let it dry. The two colors have separated from one another on the paper. The water carried the food coloring molecules up through the paper. The different molecules separated because they moved at different rates along the paper. This process for separating mixtures is called paper chromatography (kro-muh-TOG-ruh-fee). Paper chromatography is a way of separating some mixtures. It is used in chemistry to find out what substances are present in a mixture.

▶ What is paper chromatography?

WHAT YOU LEARNED

Paper chromatography is a method of separating some mixtures.

SCIENCE WORDS

absorb (ab-SORB)
 soak up

paper chromatography (kro-muh-TOG-ruh-fee)
 a method of separating a mixture of substances

ANSWER THESE

1. When a paper towel is placed in water, the water is
   a. evaporated
   b. distilled
   c. absorbed
2. A good material for absorbing liquids is
   a. iron
   b. cotton
   c. concrete
3. In chromatography, two colors separate from one another on a piece of paper because the _____ move at different _____.

NOW TRY THIS

How many 3-letter words can you make from the letters in CHROMATOGRAPHY?

FINDING OUT MORE

Chlorophyll is the green substance that gives green plants their color. Chlorophyll can be removed from the leaves of plants with alcohol. Paper chromatography of chlorophyll shows some interesting results. It shows that chlorophyll is made up of three different chemicals. One is green, one is red, and one is yellow. In the fall season in some parts of the country, the green part of the chlorophyll is destroyed. The red and yellow then stand out, giving the leaves beautiful colors.

PAPER CHROMATOGRAPHY OF CHLOROPHYLL

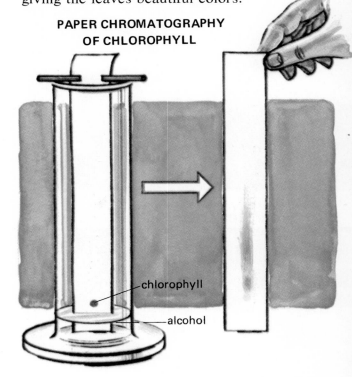

chlorophyll

alcohol

SALT CRYSTALS (magnified)

Making crystals. Evaporate the water from a solution of sodium chloride. Crystals of the solute remain. Examine the crystals with a lens. They all have the shape of cubes. Some of the sodium chloride crystals are larger than others. But they all have the same shape.

▶ What is the shape of a sodium chloride crystal?

Shapes of crystals. Examine some copper sulfate with a magnifying lens. This substance is also made up of crystals. Each copper sulfate crystal has the same shape.

COPPER SULFATE CRYSTALS (magnified)

EPSOM SALT CRYSTALS (magnified)

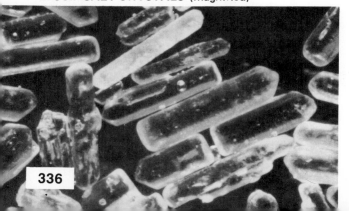

Some may be larger than others, but each has the same shape. Examine some Epsom salts with the magnifying lens. It is also made up of crystals. Each crystal of Epsom salts has the same shape. All crystals of a substance have the same shape.

▶ **How many different shapes can the crystals of one substance have?**

Supersaturated solutions. An unsaturated solution can dissolve more solute. Saturated solutions cannot hold any more solute at that temperature. If more solute is added, it will not dissolve. If a saturated solution is warmed, more solute will dissolve in it. When this solution cools, it contains more dissolved solute than it can usually hold. This is a <u>supersaturated</u> (SOO-per-SATCH-uh-rate-ed) <u>solution.</u>

▶ **What is a supersaturated solution?**

Growing crystals. One way to grow crystals is to evaporate the solvent from a solution. Another way is to use a supersaturated solution. Prepare a supersaturated solution of copper sulfate. Let it cool to room temperature. Add a small copper sulfate crystal to this solution. This extra copper sulfate in the supersaturated solution causes new crystals to form. Copper sulfate comes out of the solution and forms crystals. Crystals can form from supersaturated solutions.

▶ **Describe two ways to grow crystals.**

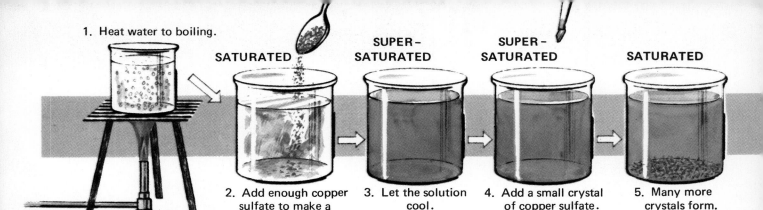

1. Heat water to boiling.

SATURATED 2. Add enough copper sulfate to make a saturated solution.

SUPER-SATURATED 3. Let the solution cool.

SUPER-SATURATED 4. Add a small crystal of copper sulfate.

SATURATED 5. Many more crystals form.

GROWING CRYSTALS FROM A SUPERSATURATED SOLUTION

WHAT YOU LEARNED

1. Crystals form when a solvent is evaporated from a solution.
2. Crystals of the same substance always have the same shape.
3. Supersaturated solutions contain more solute than they can usually hold.
4. Crystals will form when extra solute is added to a supersaturated solution.

SCIENCE WORDS

supersaturated (SOO-per-SATCH-uh-rate-ed) **solution**

a solution containing more dissolved solute than it can usually hold at that temperature

ANSWER THESE

1. Crystals of different substances
   a. usually look alike
   b. usually have the same shape
   c. usually have different shapes
2. All crystals of sodium chloride
   a. are round
   b. have the same shape
   c. have different shapes
3. Below are five steps for growing crystals from supersaturated solutions. Put them in correct order.
   a. Let the solution cool.
   b. Add enough solute to make a saturated solution.
   c. Crystals form.
   d. Heat water.
   e. Add a few crystals of solute.

NOW TRY THIS

Are the following solutions *unsaturated, saturated,* or *supersaturated*?
1. More solute can be dissolved.
2. When crystals of solute are added, they fall to the bottom and do not dissolve.
3. When crystals of solute are added, more crystals begin to form.
4. A saturated solution that has been heated.

DO THIS AT HOME

Making Rock Candy

1. Boil ½ cup of water in a pot.
2. Remove the water from the heat. Add sugar until no more will dissolve. Pour this sugar solution into a glass.
3. Tie a clean piece of wet string to a pencil. Dip the string in sugar.
4. Tie a button to the end of the string. Place the pencil across the top of the glass so that the string hangs in the water.
5. Let the solution stand for several days.

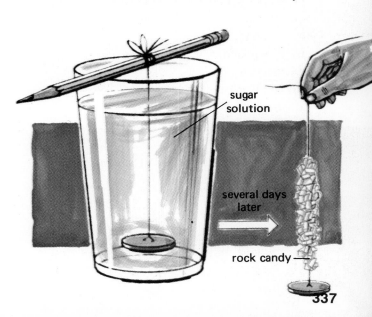

sugar solution

several days later

rock candy

Do the following questions on a separate sheet of paper.

Matching   *Write down each of the statements in Column I, leaving one line of space after each statement, write the word or phrase from Column II that is described by that statement.*

Column I	Column II
1. Can be separated by physical means.	dissolve
2. Can be separated only by chemical means.	mixture
3. Become part of a solution.	insoluble
4. Able to dissolve.	solvent
5. The same throughout.	compound
6. A solution that can dissolve more solute.	unsaturated
7. A solution of a solid in alcohol.	solute
8. Not able to dissolve.	tincture
9. Substance dissolved in a solution.	homogeneous
10. Substance in which a solute dissolves.	

Multiple Choice   *Write the letter of the choice that best completes the statement or answers the question.*

1. The substances in a mixture
   a. have no chemical properties
   b. lose their chemical properties
   c. keep their chemical properties
2. Solutions are a special kind of
   a. element
   b. compound
   c. mixture
3. Oil and water are
   a. miscible
   b. immiscible
   c. soluble
4. A concentrated solution is usually also a
   a. weak solution
   b. strong solution
   c. dilute solution

5. Adding salt to water
   a. lowers its freezing point
   b. lowers its boiling point
   c. raises its melting point
6. Adding more heat to boiling water
   a. raises its temperature
   b. does not raise its temperature
   c. lowers its boiling point
7. One way of separating a solute and a solvent is
   a. filtering
   b. distillation
   c. condensation
8. Paper chromatography is a method of
   a. taking pictures
   b. mixing solutions
   c. separating some mixtures

UNIT 18

Suspensions

Unit Lessons

1. Why are some liquids cloudy?
2. How can we remove the particles from a suspension?
3. What is an emulsion?
4. What is a colloid?

Goals and Objectives

After completing this unit, you should be able to:
- describe the characteristics of a suspension.
- demonstrate several ways of causing a suspension to separate.
- explain why soap is an emulsifying agent.
- explain why colloids cannot be separated by filtering.

UNIT 18
Suspensions
1

Why are some liquids cloudy?

sugar in water

A SOLUTION

starch in water

A SUSPENSION

Cloudy mixtures. Add some sugar to water. The sugar dissolves and forms a solution. Solutions are clear. The sugar particles in the solution are molecular in size. Add some starch to water. Shake the mixture. The water turns cloudy. Starch does not dissolve in water. Starch mixes with the water but does not form a solution. A mixture of this type is called a <u>suspension</u> (suh-SPEN-shun). A suspension is formed when a substance mixes with a liquid but does not dissolve. Suspensions are usually cloudy.

▶ **What is a suspension?**

Mixtures that settle. Mix some clay and water. A cloudy mixture forms. This is a suspension. Allow the suspension to stand overnight. In the morning the water is clear. The clay has <u>settled</u> to the bottom of the container. When suspensions are left standing, solid particles usually settle out.

▶ **What happens to the particles in a suspension when it is left standing?**

Separating suspensions. Solutions cannot be separated by filtering, because the particles in a solution pass through the holes in the filter. Filter a suspension of starch and water. The starch is trapped by the filter. The particles in a suspension are too large to pass through the holes in a filter. Suspensions can be separated by filtering.

▶ **Why can suspensions be separated by filtering?**

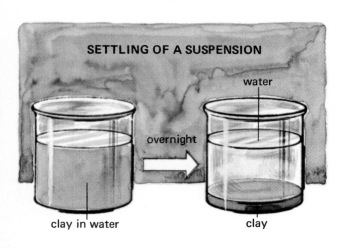

SETTLING OF A SUSPENSION

water

overnight

clay in water

clay

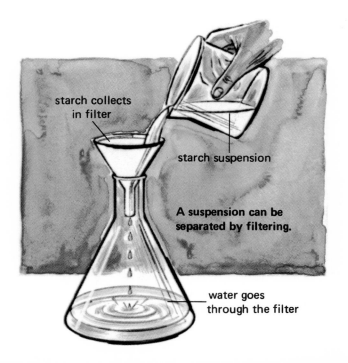

starch collects in filter

starch suspension

A suspension can be separated by filtering.

water goes through the filter

340

COMPARING LIQUID SOLUTIONS AND SUSPENSIONS

SOLUTION	SUSPENSION
1. mixture of two or more substances	1. mixture of two or more substances
2. clear	2. cloudy
3. does not settle	3. usually settles on standing
4. cannot be separated by filtering	4. can be separated by filtering
5. particles are molecular in size	5. particles are larger than molecular in size
6. particles dissolve	6. particles do not dissolve

WHAT YOU LEARNED

1. Suspensions are liquid mixtures that settle on standing.
2. Suspensions are cloudy.
3. The particles in a suspension are larger than those in a solution.
4. Suspensions can be separated by filtering.

SCIENCE WORDS

suspension (suh-SPEN-shun)
   a cloudy mixture of two or more substances that settles on standing
settle
   separate by falling to the bottom

ANSWER THESE

1. Which of the following are examples of suspensions?
   salt water
   milk
   tomato juice
   club soda
   muddy water
2. The particles in a suspension are
   a. molecular
   b. larger than the holes in a filter
   c. smaller than the holes in a filter

FINDING OUT MORE

In a starch suspension, a solid is suspended in a liquid. Suspensions can also be made with other states of matter. In a bar of soap that floats, there is a gas suspended in a solid. Air bubbles suspended in the soap allow it to float. Fog is a suspension of a liquid in a gas. It consists of tiny water droplets suspended in air. Bottles with labels that say "SHAKE WELL BEFORE USING" contain suspensions. They must be shaken before use because they settle on standing.

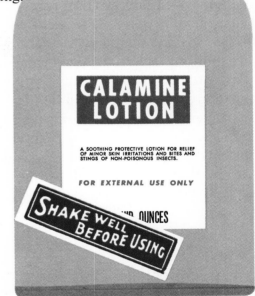

CALAMINE LOTION

A SOOTHING PROTECTIVE LOTION FOR RELIEF OF MINOR SKIN IRRITATIONS AND BITES AND STINGS OF NON-POISONOUS INSECTS.

FOR EXTERNAL USE ONLY

SHAKE WELL BEFORE USING

SUSPENSIONS

How can we remove the particles from a suspension?

Particles in suspension are too big to go through tiny holes in filter paper.

filter paper

Molecules of liquid can go through holes in filter paper.

funnel

How a suspension is separated by a filter.

Suspensions usually separate on standing. Fill a graduated cylinder with water. Add some sand, some clay, and some copper sulfate to the water. Shake the cylinder so that everything mixes together. A cloudy mixture forms. This is a suspension. Allow the suspension to stand. After several minutes, the sand settles to the bottom. By the next morning, the clay has settled to the bottom. The particles of sand are much larger and heavier than the particles of clay. The heavier particles of sand settle faster than the lighter particles of clay. The copper sulfate does not settle at all. It is dissolved in the water.

▶ Why did the sand settle before the clay did?

Suspensions can be separated by filtering. Filters contain holes. Particles that are larger than the holes cannot pass through the filter. The particles in a suspension are large enough to be trapped by most filters.

▶ Why can suspensions be separated with a filter?

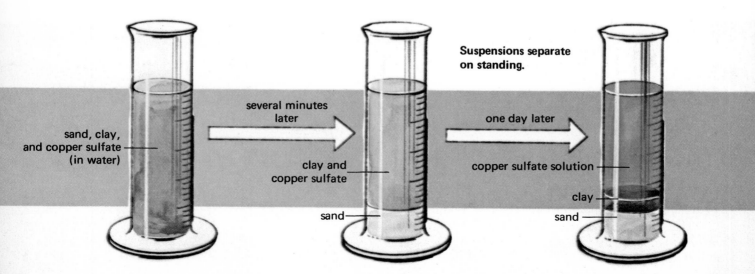

sand, clay, and copper sulfate (in water)

several minutes later

Suspensions separate on standing.

clay and copper sulfate

sand

one day later

copper sulfate solution

clay

sand

Coagulation. Chemicals can be used to make suspensions separate faster. This process is called coagulation (coh-AG-yew-LAY-shun). The chemicals cause the particles in the suspension to clump together. The clumps of particles are heavier than the single particles. The clumps settle faster.

A solution of alum and ammonium hydroxide can be used to coagulate particles in water. Add a small amount of clay to each of two test tubes. Shake both tubes. Add some alum solution to one of the tubes. Let both tubes stand for several minutes. In which tube did the clay settle faster? The alum solution forms a jelly-like material. This jelly causes the particles of clay to stick together. The large lumps of clay settle faster.

▶ What is coagulation?

WHAT YOU LEARNED

1. In suspensions, heavier particles settle faster than lighter particles.
2. Suspensions will separate on standing.
3. Chemicals can be used to make suspensions separate faster.

SCIENCE WORD

coagulation (coh-AG-yew-LAY-shun)
the use of chemicals to make particles clump together

The wiggly line in this photo is the Mississippi River, seen from high up in the air. Can you see where it has formed a delta?

ANSWER THESE

1. Which of the following will be the first to settle out of a suspension?
   a. clay
   b. sand
   c. gravel
2. A mixture is left standing for several days. It does not separate.
   a. It probably is a suspension.
   b. It probably is not a suspension.
3. In coagulation, chemicals are used to
   a. break particles apart
   b. clump particles together
   c. dissolve particles

NOW TRY THIS

Which of the following are properties of a suspension?
   a. Does not settle.
   b. Can be filtered.
   c. Is cloudy.
   d. Is clear.

FINDING OUT MORE

The fast-moving waters of rivers carry particles of different sizes. They carry large particles, such as pebbles. They carry medium-sized particles, such as sand. And they carry tiny particles, such as clay. Where rivers empty into oceans, their waters slow down. Here the particles begin to settle. The heavier pebbles settle first. Then the sand settles. Finally the lightest particles settle. A new piece of land called a delta may form at the mouth of a river.

What is an emulsion?

EMULSIONS

Emulsions. A suspension of two liquids is called an <u>emulsion</u> (eh-MUL-shun). Salad dressing, milk, and many medicines are emulsions. Shake a mixture of oil and water. It forms an emulsion.

▶ What is an emulsion?

Emulsions that do not separate. An emulsion of oil and water will separate on standing. The particles in this emulsion are large. Because of their size, they separate quickly. Add some soap to a mixture of oil and water. Shake the mixture well, and let it stand. It does not separate. The soap keeps the emulsion from settling. The soap makes the particles in the emulsion so small that they do not separate.

▶ How can you keep an emulsion from separating?

Emulsifying agents. Some emulsions contain chemicals that keep them from separating. These chemicals are called <u>emulsifying</u> (eh-MUL-suh-fy-ing) <u>agents.</u> Soap is an emulsifying agent. Soap will keep an emulsion of oil and water from separating. The soap breaks up the oil into very tiny particles. These particles are so small that the emulsion will not separate. Soap is useful in washing grease-stained clothes. The soap breaks up the grease into tiny particles. These particles can then be washed away by the water. The grease and soap form an emulsion with the water. Gelatin and egg yolk are other useful emulsifying agents. Bile, produced by the liver, emulsifies fats in our digestive system.

▶ What is an emulsifying agent?

MAKING A PERMANENT EMULSION

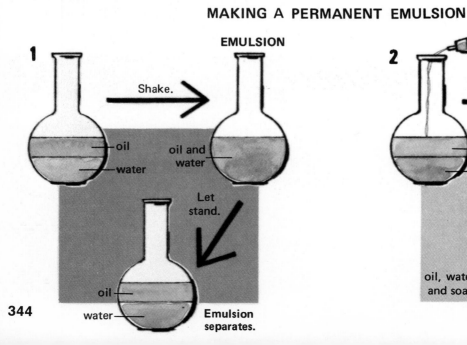

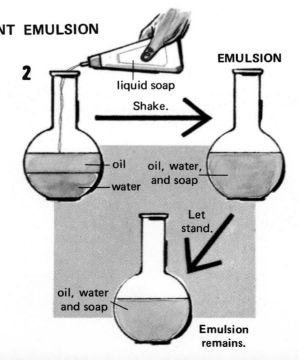

Homogenization. Homogenized milk is an emulsion that does not separate. Milk does not contain emulsifying agents. Milk, right from the cow, will separate into milk and cream. The cream is lighter than the milk and floats to the top. When milk is homogenized, it is spun around rapidly in a machine like a blender. The cream is broken down into very small particles. This is <u>homogenization</u> (huh-moj-uh-nuh-ZAY-shun). The small particles of cream do not separate from the rest of the milk.

▶ How is milk homogenized?

WHAT YOU LEARNED

1. A suspension of two liquids is called an emulsion.
2. Emulsions can be kept from separating by adding emulsifying agents or by homogenization.

SCIENCE WORDS

emulsion (eh-MUL-shun)
a suspension of two liquids
emulsifying (eh-MUL-suh-fy-ing) **agent**
a substance that keeps emulsions from separating
homogenization (huh-moj-uh-nuh-ZAY-shun)
making a permanent emulsion by rapid spinning

ANSWER THESE

1. Emulsions are suspensions of
   a. two liquids
   b. two solids
   c. a liquid and a solid
2. Milk will not separate if it is
   a. pasteurized
   b. heated
   c. homogenized
3. An example of an emulsifying agent is
   a. oil
   b. mayonnaise
   c. soap

NOW TRY THIS

Tell whether each of the following is a *solution*, a *suspension*, or an *emulsion*.

fog	salt water
house paint	coffee
milk	mayonnaise

DO THIS AT HOME

Mayonnaise is an emulsion of oil and vinegar in which egg yolk is the emulsifying agent. You can make your own mayonnaise. You will need:

¾ cup salad oil   1 egg yolk   vinegar

Slowly add 1 tablespoon of vinegar to the egg yolk, stirring constantly.

Add 1 tablespoon of oil, one drop at a time. Beat the mixture thoroughly after each drop.

Add the rest of the oil 1 teaspoon at a time, beating thoroughly each time.

Season to taste with lemon juice.

What is a colloid?

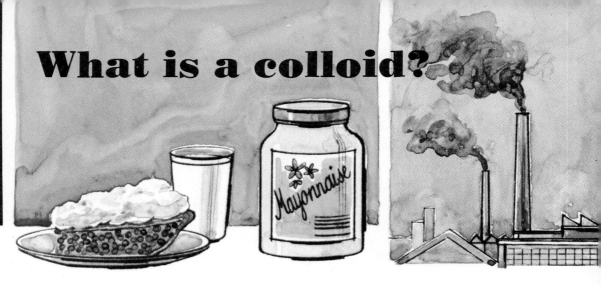

Colloids. Suspensions that do not separate on standing are called <u>colloids</u> (COL-oids). Whipped cream, smoke, and fog are examples of colloids. Emulsions such as homogenized milk and mayonnaise are also colloids.

▶ **What is a colloid?**

Types of colloids. Colloids can be made from almost all states of matter. The chart below shows the different types of colloids.

▶ **What type of colloid is an emulsion?**

Filtering colloids. Try to filter milk. The milk passes through the filter paper. It does not separate. The particles in the milk are small enough to pass through the holes in the filter paper. Colloids cannot be separated by filtering through filter paper.

▶ **Why can't milk be separated by filtering?**

Particles in colloids. A colloid is a suspension that will not separate on standing. Colloids cannot be separated by filtering through filter paper. The particles in a colloid are very small. They are not as small as the particles in a solution. They are smaller than the particles in suspensions that settle. The particles in a colloid are made up of groups of molecules.

▶ **What is the size of particles in a colloid?**

TYPES OF COLLOIDS

gas in liquid	foamy shaving cream, whipped cream
liquid in liquid	emulsions (homogenized milk, mayonnaise)
solid in liquid	dyes in water
gas in solid	floating bars of soap
liquid in solid	jellies and jams
liquid in gas	fog, clouds
solid in gas	smoke in the air

A colloid cannot be separated by filtering through filter paper.

filter paper

homogenized milk

WHAT YOU LEARNED

1. Colloids are suspensions that do not separate on standing.
2. The particles in a colloid are small enough to pass through filter paper.
3. The particles in colloids are made up of groups of molecules.

SCIENCE WORD

colloid (COL-oid)
a type of suspension that does not separate on standing

ANSWER THESE

1. Colloids
   a. separate on standing
   b. do not separate on standing
   c. can be separated by filtering

2. The particles in a colloid
   a. are molecular in size
   b. are atomic in size
   c. consist of groups of molecules

3. A colloid is a type of
   a. solution
   b. suspension
   c. emulsion

NOW TRY THIS

Match the colloids in column A with the states in column B.

A	B
Floating soap (soap plus air)	Gas in liquid
Whipped cream (cream plus air)	Liquid in gas
Mayonnaise (oil plus vinegar)	Liquid in liquid
Clouds (air plus water)	Gas in solid

FINDING OUT MORE

Particles in a colloid are very small. They are composed of groups of molecules. Particles in a colloid are affected by the molecules around them. This causes a dancing, zig-zag motion. The motion is called Brownian (BROW-nee-un) movement. Place a small amount of carmine dye in some water. This forms a colloid. Examine a drop of this mixture through the high power objective of a microscope. Can you see the particles of carmine? How do they move?

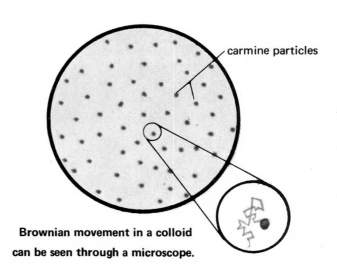

carmine particles

Brownian movement in a colloid can be seen through a microscope.

UNIT 18 Review

Do the following review questions on a separate sheet of paper.

Modified True/False   *Write down each of the following statements, leaving a blank line between each line you write. Before the number for each statement, write T if the statement is true and F if the statement is false. For the false statements, cross out the word written in capital letters and write above it a word that will make the statement true.*

1. Homogenized milk is a COLLOID.
2. Colloids CAN be separated by filtering.
3. An EMULSION is a suspension of two liquids.
4. Coagulation causes suspensions to separate SLOWER.
5. A solution CAN be separated by filtering.

Multiple Choice   *Write the letter of the choice that best completes the statement or answers the question.*

1. A suspension is formed when a substance
   a. mixes with a liquid but doesn't dissolve
   b. dissolves in a liquid
   c. doesn't mix with a liquid
2. Suspensions can be separated
   a. only by chemical means
   b. by filtering
   c. by shaking
3. A solution of alum and ammonium hydroxide causes
   a. evaporation
   b. coagulation
   c. melting
4. Soap is a(n)
   a. coagulating agent
   b. emulsifying agent
   c. pasteurizing agent
5. Mayonnaise is an example of
   a. an emulsifying agent
   b. an unhomogeneous substance
   c. a colloid

UNIT 19

Acids, Bases, and Ions

Unit Lessons

1. How can acids be recognized?
2. How can bases be recognized?
3. How can we identify acids and bases?
4. What happens when an acid is mixed with a base?
5. How can we change the electrical properties of water?
6. Why do some solutions conduct electricity?

Goals and Objectives

After completing this unit, you should be able to:
- give examples of common acids and bases.
- describe the chemical properties of acids and bases.
- use certain indicators to identify acids and bases.
- describe a neutralization reaction.
- explain how ions in solution conduct electricity.

UNIT 19
Acids, Bases, and Ions
1

How can acids be recognized?

SUBSTANCES CONTAINING ACIDS

sour milk

Acids. <u>Acids</u> are a special group of chemical substances. Vinegar, lemons, and sour milk all contain acids. Acids give these foods their sour taste. (Never taste a substance to find out what it is.)

Acids are found in many substances. Citrus fruits, such as oranges and lemons, contain citric acid. Sour milk contains lactic acid. Vinegar contains acetic (uh-SEE-tic) acid. Hydrochloric (HY-dro-CLOR-ic) acid is found in the stomach. It helps digest foods. Soda water contains carbonic acid.

▶ **What acid is found in vinegar?**

Acids react with metals. Add some hydrochloric acid to zinc. Zinc is a metal. What do you see? The bubbles show that a gas is being produced. Collect some of the gas in a bottle. Test the gas with a burning splint. Do you remember the name of the gas that explodes when a flame is placed near it? The gas produced is hydrogen. Acids react with some metals to produce hydrogen.

▶ **What gas is produced when acids react with some metals?**

Acids contain hydrogen. Look at the chart. All acids contain hydrogen. The hydrogen produced when acids react with metals comes from the acid. Acids are chemicals containing nonmetallic elements combined with hydrogen. The properties of acids come from the hydrogen that they contain.

▶ **What do all acids contain?**

COLLECTING HYDROGEN

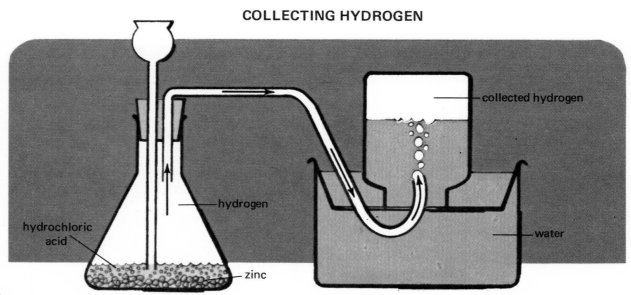

collected hydrogen

hydrogen

hydrochloric acid

zinc

water

350

ACID	CHEMICAL FORMULA	WHERE FOUND, USES
acetic acid	$HC_2H_3O_2$	vinegar
boric acid	H_3BO_3	used as eyewash
carbonic acid	H_2CO_3	soda water
hydrochloric acid	HCl	aids digestion in stomach
nitric acid	HNO_3	used in making explosives
sulfuric acid	H_2SO_4	used in making plastics

WHAT YOU LEARNED

1. Acids are chemical substances that react with metals to release hydrogen.
2. Acids taste sour.

SCIENCE WORD

acid

a chemical substance that reacts with metals to release hydrogen

ANSWER THESE

1. Hydrogen is produced when acids react with
   a. bases
   b. vinegar
   c. metals
2. The acid found in the stomach is
   a. hydrochloric acid
   b. boric acid
   c. acetic acid
3. Sour milk contains
   a. acetic acid
   b. nitric acid
   c. lactic acid

NOW TRY THIS

Which of the following chemical formulas are acids?

HCl $HC_2H_3O_2$
NaCl   KBr
H_3PO_4 CO_2
$CaSO_4$ H_2CO_3

FINDING OUT MORE

Soda water contains dissolved carbon dioxide. The dissolved carbon dioxide reacts in the solution to form carbonic acid. The carbonic acid gives soda water its flavor. Beer and some wines also contain carbonic acid. Bubbles of carbon dioxide can be seen in soda, beer, and sparkling wines.

How can bases be recognized?

BASES

MILK OF MAGNESIA
U.S.P.

Soap. Early settlers in the United States made their own soap. They mixed animal fat and wood ashes in huge pots. The mixture was boiled and stirred for many hours, and it gradually changed to soap. Soaps are made by combining fats or oils with a type of chemical called a base. Wood ash contains potassium hydroxide. Potassium hydroxide is a base. Soaps have some of the properties of bases.

▶ How is soap made?

Properties of bases. Acids taste sour. Bases taste bitter. Milk of magnesia and soap contain bases. This gives them their bitter taste. Soap is slippery. It is the base in the soap that makes it slippery. Bases taste bitter and feel slippery.

▶ What are two properties of bases?

Forming bases. When some metals are placed in water, a chemical reaction takes place. This reaction produces a base and hydrogen. Bases are formed when metals react with water.

▶ How are bases formed?

metal + water ⟶ base + hydrogen

metal		water		base		hydrogen
sodium	+	water	⟶	sodium hydroxide	+	hydrogen
potassium	+	water	⟶	potassium hydroxide	+	hydrogen
calcium	+	water	⟶	calcium hydroxide	+	hydrogen
magnesium	+	water	⟶	magnesium hydroxide	+	hydrogen

BASE	CHEMICAL FORMULA	WHERE FOUND, USES
potassium hydroxide	KOH	soap, glass
magnesium hydroxide	$Mg(OH)_2$	milk of magnesia
calcium hydroxide	$Ca(OH)_2$	mortar
aluminum hydroxide	$Al(OH)_3$	coagulants for water purification
ammonium hydroxide	NH_4OH	ammonia water
sodium hydroxide	NaOH	lye, soap

Bases contain hydroxyl ions. Look at the chart. All the bases contain hydrogen and oxygen. The hydrogen and oxygen are combined in a polyatomic ion called a <u>hydroxyl</u> (hy-DROK-sil) <u>ion</u> (OH^-). Chemical compounds containing a hydroxyl ion are bases. Bases are compounds of metals combined with a hydroxyl ion.

▶ **What base is found in milk of magnesia?**

WHAT YOU LEARNED

1. Bases are substances that have a bitter taste and a slippery feel.
2. Bases are formed when certain metals react with water.
3. Bases contain a hydroxyl ion (OH^-).
4. Bases are compounds made up of metals combined with a hydroxyl ion.

SCIENCE WORDS

base
    a chemical compound made up of a metal combined with an OH^- ion

hydroxyl (hy-DROK-sil) **ion**
    a combination of one hydrogen and one oxygen atom, with an extra electron

ANSWER THESE

1. Bases are formed when
    a. metals react with water
    b. metals react with acids
    c. nonmetals react with water

2. Soap is made by combining a base with
    a. an acid
    b. water
    c. fats or oils
3. Bases
    a. taste sour and feel slippery
    b. taste bitter and feel slippery
    c. taste sour and react with water

NOW TRY THIS

Match the names of the bases in column B with the formulas in column A.

A	B
$Al(OH)_3$	calcium hydroxide
$Ca(OH)_2$	potassium hydroxide
KOH	sodium hydroxide
NH_4OH	aluminum hydroxide
NaOH	ammonium hydroxide

DO THIS AT HOME

Some bases are used as cleaning agents because they dissolve oil and grease. Some bases are used to make cleaning agents such as soap. To compare the strength of several cleaning agents, carry out the following experiment: Rub a small bit of margarine or butter on each of four plates. Wet a sponge with water and try to clean the margarine or butter off one of the plates. On the second plate, use a sponge soaked with ammonia water. Try to clean the third plate with a sponge that has a small amount of soap from a soap bar. On the fourth plate use a sponge that has ammonia water and soap. What happens in each case? Which substances remove the oil most easily? What typical household products contain ammonia?

How can we identify acids and bases?

Chemicals that change color. Dip one end of a piece of blue litmus (LIT-mus) paper into some vinegar. The litmus paper changes color. It turns red. Blue litmus paper turns red in acids. Dip one end of a piece of red litmus paper into some soapy water. The red litmus paper turns blue. Red litmus paper turns blue in bases.

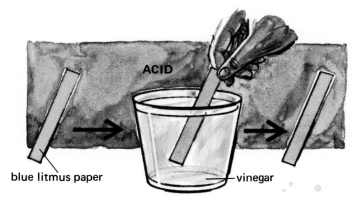
blue litmus paper   ACID   vinegar

▶ **What color does blue litmus paper change to in an acid?**

Acid and base indicators. Chemicals that change color in acids and bases are called indicators (IN-duh-kate-ers). Litmus turns from blue to red in acids and from red to blue in bases. Litmus is an indicator. Phenolphthalein (feen-ul-THAL-een) and methyl (METH-ul) red are also indicators. Phenolphthalein is colorless in acids and pink in bases. Methyl red is red in acids and yellow in bases.

red litmus paper   BASE   soapy water

Identifying acids and bases. Acids and bases have very different properties. We can tell if a substance is an acid or a base by checking the properties shown in the chart on the next page.

▶ **What is an indicator?**

▶ **What are some properties of bases?**

INDICATORS	COLOR IN ACIDS	COLOR IN BASES
litmus	red	blue
phenolphthalein	colorless	pink
methyl red	red	yellow
congo red	blue	red
bromthymol blue	yellow	blue

PROPERTIES OF ACIDS AND BASES	
ACIDS	**BASES**
1. taste sour	1. taste bitter
2. contain hydrogen ions (H⁺) combined with a non-metallic element	2. contain hydroxyl radicals (OH) combined with a metallic element
3. turn blue litmus paper red	3. turn red litmus paper blue
4. react with metals to produce hydrogen	_____
_____	4. feel slippery

WHAT YOU LEARNED

1. Indicators are chemicals that change color in acids and bases.
2. Litmus turns red in acids and blue in bases.

SCIENCE WORD

indicator (IN-duh-kate-er)
 a chemical that changes color in acids and bases

ANSWER THESE

1. Litmus paper turns from red to blue in
   a. acids
   b. bases
   c. water

2. Phenolphthalein turns from pink to color-less in
   a. acids
   b. bases
   c. water

3. A chemical that changes color in acids and bases is called
   a. an indicator
   b. a metal
   c. a non-metal

NOW TRY THIS

Is each of the following a property of an acid or a base?
1. Tastes bitter.
2. Reacts with metals to produce hydrogen.
3. Turns methyl red from red to yellow.
4. Feels slippery.
5. Tastes sour.
6. Turns phenolphthalein pink.

FINDING OUT MORE

pH is a term used to show whether a substance is an acid or a base. Acids have a pH from 0 to 7. Bases have a pH from 7 to 14. Substances that are neither an acid nor a base have a pH of 7. These substances are said to be neutral (NOO-trul). The lower the pH of an acid, the stronger the acid. The higher the pH of a base, the stronger the base.

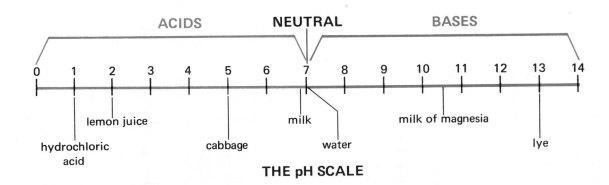

THE pH SCALE

What happens when an acid is mixed with a base?

Neutral substances. Acids turn blue litmus red. Bases turn red litmus blue. Some substances do not cause red or blue litmus paper to change color. These substances are <u>neutral</u> (NOO-trul). Neutral substances are neither acids nor bases.

▶ How do neutral substances affect the color of litmus paper?

Mixing acids and bases. Acids and bases may be dangerous chemicals. Mix them together, and interesting things happen. Look at the chemical equation. Both hydrochloric acid and sodium hydroxide are very dangerous. They both can cause bad burns to the skin. When mixed together, they form sodium chloride and water. Sodium chloride is table salt. The result of mixing the acid and the base is salt water! Salt water is not dangerous. The reaction between hydrochloric acid and sodium hydroxide has formed new chemicals with different properties.

▶ What happens when hydrochloric acid is mixed with sodium hydroxide?

Neutralization. Place a piece of red litmus in salt water. It does not change color. Place a piece of blue litmus in salt water. It does not change color. Salt water is neutral. It is neither acid nor basic (BAY-sic). When acids are mixed with bases, <u>neutralization</u> (noo-truh-luh-ZAY-shun) occurs. Neutralization is a reaction between an acid and a base that forms a salt and water. It is a double replacement reaction.

▶ When does neutralization occur?

Salts. Sodium chloride is called salt, or table salt. But sodium chloride is just one of many different kinds of salts. In chemistry, a <u>salt</u> is a substance formed when an acid reacts with a base. Mixing sulfuric acid with sodium hydroxide produces sodium sulfate and water. Sodium sulfate is a salt. Potassium chloride is a salt formed by mixing hydrochloric acid with potassium hydroxide.

▶ What is a salt?

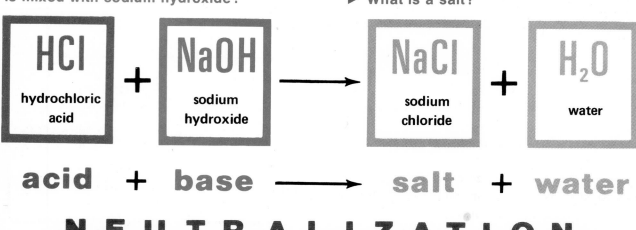

HCl	+	NaOH	→	NaCl	+	H₂O
hydrochloric acid		sodium hydroxide		sodium chloride		water

acid + base ⟶ salt + water

NEUTRALIZATION

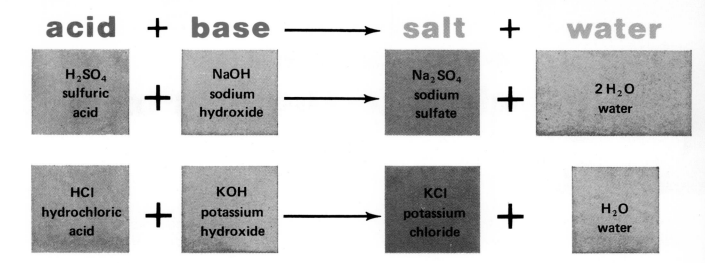

acid + base ⟶ salt + water

| H₂SO₄ sulfuric acid | + | NaOH sodium hydroxide | ⟶ | Na₂SO₄ sodium sulfate | + | 2 H₂O water |

| HCl hydrochloric acid | + | KOH potassium hydroxide | ⟶ | KCl potassium chloride | + | H₂O water |

WHAT YOU LEARNED

1. Neutral substances are neither acid nor basic.
2. Neutralization occurs when an acid is mixed with a base to form a salt and water.
3. Salts are chemicals that are formed when an acid is mixed with a base.

SCIENCE WORDS

neutral (NOO-trul)
neither acid nor basic

neutralization (noo-truh-luh-ZAY-shun)
mixing an acid and a base to produce a salt and water

salt
a chemical produced by the reaction between an acid and a base

ANSWER THESE

1. Neutral substances
   a. change blue litmus to red
   b. change red litmus to blue
   c. do not cause litmus to change color

2. The salt formed from calcium hydroxide and hydrochloric acid is
   a. sodium sulfate
   b. calcium chloride
   c. calcium sulfate
3. Acid + base ⟶ _____ + _____ .

NOW TRY THIS

Match the salts in column C with the acids and bases in columns A and B that formed them. For a start, K_2SO_4 is the salt of KOH and H_2SO_4.

A ACIDS	B BASES	C SALTS
HCl	NaOH	K₂SO₄
H₂SO₄	Ca(OH)₂	Ca(NO₃)₂
HNO₃	NH₄OH	NH₄Cl
H₃PO₄	KOH	K₃PO₄
		CaSO₄
		NaNO₃

FINDING OUT MORE

We can compare the strengths of acids by neutralizing them with a base. Place 10 ml of acid in a beaker. Add a few drops of phenolphthalein. Add a base drop by drop to the mixture. Stop when the phenolphthalein turns light pink. How many drops of base were used? Do the same thing with 10 ml of a different acid. The stronger acid is the one that needs a larger amount of base to be neutralized.

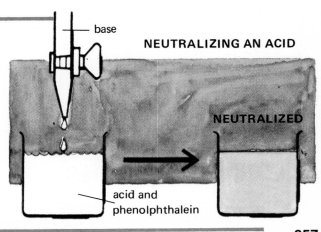

base

NEUTRALIZING AN ACID

NEUTRALIZED

acid and phenolphthalein

How can we change the electrical properties of water?

Distilled water. Distilled water is pure water. It does not contain any dissolved substances. It does not contain any suspended particles. Place some distilled water in a conductivity (con-duc-TIV-uh-tee) tester. The bulb does not light. Electricity does not flow through the circuit. Distilled water is not a good conductor of electricity.

▶ **What is distilled water?**

Acids and bases. Glacial (GLAY-shul) acetic acid is pure acid. Pour some glacial acetic acid into the conductivity tester. The bulb does not light. Pure acetic acid is not a good conductor of electricity. Place some solid sodium hydroxide in the conductivity tester. The bulb does not light. The sodium hydroxide is not a good conductor of electricity. Pure acids and bases are poor conductors of electricity.

▶ **How can we show that pure acids do not conduct electricity?**

TESTING CONDUCTIVITY

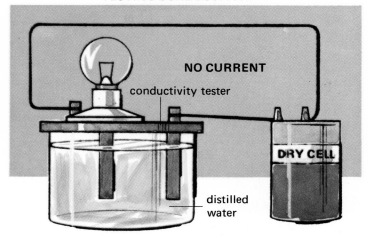

NO CURRENT

conductivity tester

DRY CELL

distilled water

Distilled water is a poor conductor of electricity.

Conductivity of salts. Salts are solids. Place some pure sodium chloride in a conductivity tester. It does not conduct electricity. Test some other salts. They do not conduct electricity either. Salts are poor conductors of electricity.

▶ **How can we show that salts are poor conductors of electricity?**

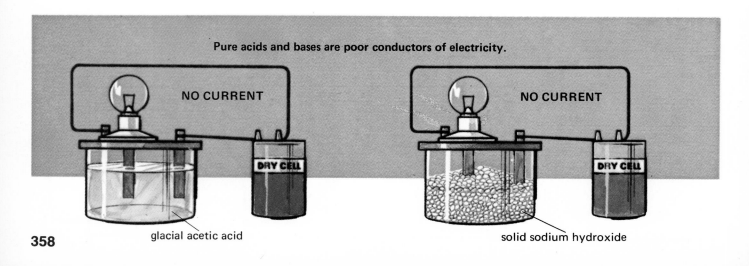

Pure acids and bases are poor conductors of electricity.

NO CURRENT

DRY CELL

glacial acetic acid

NO CURRENT

DRY CELL

solid sodium hydroxide

Making water conduct electricity. Pure water is not a good conductor of electricity. Pure acids and bases are not good conductors of electricity. Pure salts are not good conductors of electricity. Place some distilled water in the conductivity tester. Add some acetic acid. The bulb lights. A solution of acetic acid and water is a good conductor of electricity. Add some sodium hydroxide to distilled water. This solution will also conduct electricity. Add some sodium chloride to distilled water. This solution conducts electricity, too. Solutions of acids, bases, or salts in water are good conductors of electricity.

▶ **What can you add to distilled water to make it a conductor of electricity?**

Conductors and non-conductors. A sodium chloride solution is a good conductor of electricity. Substances that can make water conduct electricity are called electrolytes (eh-LEK-truh-lites). Sodium chloride makes water conduct electricity. Sodium chloride is an electrolyte. Salts are usually electrolytes. Acids and bases are also electrolytes. A sugar solution does not conduct electricity. Sugar is not an electrolyte. It is a non-electrolyte. It cannot make water conduct an electric current. Some electrolyte solutions conduct electricity better than others.

▶ **What is an electrolyte?**

WHAT YOU LEARNED

1. Pure water is a poor conductor of electricity.
2. Pure acids, bases, and salts are poor conductors of electricity.
3. Solutions of acids, bases, and salts will conduct electricity.
4. Electrolytes are substances that make water a conductor of electricity when they are dissolved in the water.
5. Acids, bases, and salts are electrolytes.

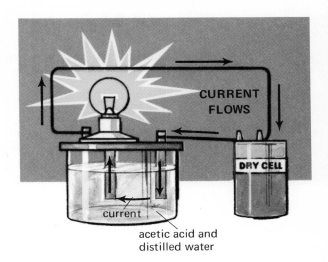

CURRENT FLOWS

DRY CELL

current

acetic acid and distilled water

SCIENCE WORDS

conductivity (con-duc-TIV-uh-tee) **tester**
an instrument used to see if solutions conduct electricity

electrolyte (eh-LEK-truh-lite)
a substance that can make water conduct electricity

non-electrolyte
a substance that will not make water conduct electricity

ANSWER THESE

1. Pure water
   a. is a good conductor of electricity
   b. is a poor conductor of electricity
   c. contains dissolved substances
2. Pure acids and bases
   a. are good conductors of electricity
   b. are poor conductors of electricity
   c. contain distilled water
3. Salts are usually
   a. solids
   b. liquids
   c. gases
4. Substances that make water conduct electricity are called
   a. solutes
   b. electrolytes
   c. non-electrolytes
5. An example of a non-electrolyte is
   a. soldium chloride
   b. copper sulfate
   c. sugar

Why do some solutions conduct electricity?

CRYSTAL OF SODIUM CHLORIDE

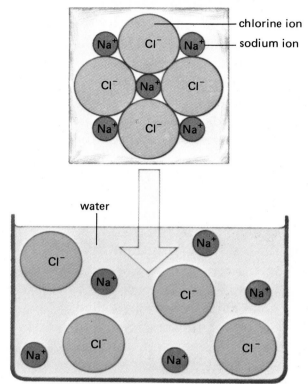

chlorine ion
sodium ion

water

SODIUM CHLORIDE SOLUTION

Salt crystals are made of ions. Sodium combines with chlorine to form crystals of sodium chloride. Each sodium atom lends an electron to a chlorine atom. The sodium atom becomes a sodium ion with a positive electric charge. The chlorine atom becomes a chlorine ion with a negative charge. Opposite electric charges attract each other. The attraction between the sodium ions and the chlorine ions holds the sodium chloride crystal together.

▶ **What holds a sodium chloride crystal together?**

Ions can be separated. Drop a crystal of sodium chloride into a beaker of water. The sodium chloride dissolves in the water. What happens to make sodium chloride dissolve in water? Water molecules act like tiny wedges. They get between the sodium and chlorine ions in the crystal of sodium chloride. The sodium and chlorine ions are split apart by the water molecules. The ions separate and spread through the water. When a salt dissolves in water, it breaks apart into its separate ions. This separation of a salt into its ions is called ionization (EYE-uh-nuh-ZAY-shun).

▶ **What happens to the ions of a salt when it dissolves in water?**

Ions can make an electric current. Ions have an electric charge. Moving ions can form an electric current. A solution that contains ions can conduct an electric current. The ions move and carry the current

through the solution. Electrolytes separate into ions when they dissolve in water. That is why solutions of electrolytes can conduct an electric current.

▶ **What carries an electric current through a solution of an electrolyte?**

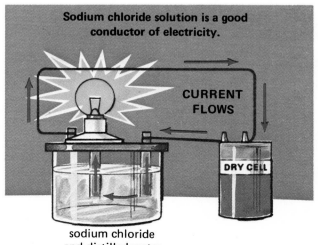

Sodium chloride solution is a good conductor of electricity.

CURRENT FLOWS

DRY CELL

sodium chloride and distilled water

Non-electrolytes have no ions. Many non-electrolytes can dissolve in water. The molecules of non-electrolytes are not made of ions. When a non-electrolyte dissolves, it breaks up into its separate molecules. But the molecules do not separate into ions. Solutions of non-electrolytes do not contain ions. Solutions that have no ions cannot conduct an electric current. A solution of a non-electrolyte cannot conduct an electric current.

▶ **Why can't a solution of a non-electrolyte conduct an electric current?**

Ionization of acids and bases. Acids and bases are good electrolytes. Acids and bases separate into ions in water solutions. When hydrochloric acid (HCl) is placed in water, it separates into hydrogen ions (H^+) and chlorine ions (Cl^-). All acids contain hydrogen. Solutions of acids contain hydrogen ions. Potassium hydroxide (KOH) is a base. In solution it separates into potassium ions (K^+) and hydroxyl ions (OH^-). All bases have an OH^- part and a metallic part. Bases separate into metallic ions and hydroxyl ions. Solutions of bases contain hydroxyl ions.

▶ **What happens to acids in water solutions?**

WHAT YOU LEARNED

1. When electrolytes are placed in water, they separate into ions.
2. Ions can carry an electric current through electrolyte solutions.
3. Acid solutions contain hydrogen ions (H^+).
4. Basic solutions contain hydroxyl ions (OH^-).

SCIENCE WORD

ionization (EYE-uh-nuh-ZAY-shun)
   to separate into ions

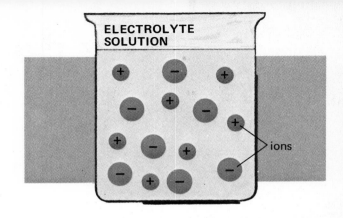

ELECTROLYTE SOLUTION

ions

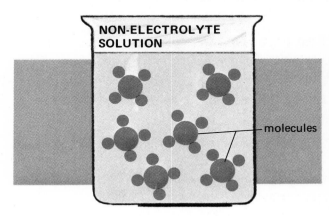

NON-ELECTROLYTE SOLUTION

molecules

ANSWER THESE

1. Electrically charged particles in electrolyte solutions are
   a. molecules
   b. ions
   c. acids
2. Acid solutions contain
   a. H^+ ions
   b. OH^- ions
   c. salts
3. To separate into ions is called
   a. distillation
   b. centrifugation
   c. ionization

NOW TRY THIS

What ions will be found in solutions of the following acids and bases?
Example: $HCl \rightarrow H^+ + Cl^-$

H_2SO_4
NaOH
NH_4OH
HI
$Ca(OH)_2$

19 Review

Do the following review questions on a separate sheet of paper.

Modified True/False   Write down each of the following statements, leaving a blank line between each line you write. Before the number for each statement, write T if the statement is true and F if the statement is false. For the false statements, cross out the word written in capital letters and write above it a word that will make the statement true.

1. ACID solutions contain hydrogen ions (H^+).
2. ACID solutions contain hydroxyl ions (OH^-).
3. Acids, bases, and salts are ELECTROLYTES.
4. Distilled water is a BASIC liquid.
5. Phenolphthalein is an INDICATOR.

Multiple Choice   Write the letter of the choice that best completes the statement or answers the question.

1. Acids are chemical substances that react with metals to
   a. release hydrogen
   b. combine with hydrogen
   c. oxidize hydrogen
2. Chemical compounds containing hydroxyl ions are
   a. acids
   b. bases
   c. neutral
3. Litmus paper turns from blue to red in
   a. lemon juice
   b. salt water
   c. milk of magnesia
4. An acid and a base combine to form a salt and water in a
   a. nuclear reaction
   b. physical reaction
   c. neutralization reaction
5. Ions can carry electricity through
   a. pure water
   b. pure acids and bases
   c. electrolyte solutions

GLOSSARY OF SCIENCE WORDS

On the following pages are the meanings of all the important science words in this book. At the end of each meaning, there are two numbers. These numbers tell you the lesson where you can find out more about the word. The first number is the Unit Number. The second number is the lesson number.

For example, look at the meaning of **absorb**. The numbers 8-13 and 17-13 tell you that you can find out more about the meaning of "absorb" by reading lesson 13 in Unit 8 and lesson 13 in Unit 17.

A

absorb (ab-ZORB): Soak up. (8-13) (17-13)

acceleration: How fast an object changes its velocity. (4-2)

acid: A chemical substance that reacts with metals to release hydrogen. (19-1)

actual M.A.: The M.A. a machine really has. (3-8)

alloy (AL-loy): A mixture of two or more metals. (16-3)

alternating (ALL-ter-NAY-ting) **current:** Electric current that keeps moving back and forth. (10-10)

ammeter (AM-mee-ter): An instrument for measuring electric current. (9-8)

ampere (AM-peer): The unit for measuring electric current. (9-8)

amplitude (AMP-lih-tood): The width of a sound's pattern. (7-2)

angle of incidence (IN-suh-dinse): The angle between the incident ray and the normal line. (8-5)

angle of reflection (ruh-FLEK-shun): The angle between the reflected ray and the normal line. (8-5)

Archimedes' Principle (ar-kuh-MEED-eez PRIN-sih-pull): The fact that the loss of weight of an object in water is equal to the weight of the displaced water. (5-5)

asbestos (as-BES-tus): A material used to make brakes. (3-6)

atom (AT-um): The smallest part of an element that is still that element. (12-1)

atomic mass: The total number of protons and neutrons in the nucleus of an atom; sometimes called "atomic weight." (12-4)

atomic (uh-TOM-ic) **number:** A number used to identify an element and show its place in the periodic table. (11-7)

atomic weight: The total number of protons and neutrons in the nucleus of an atom. (12-4)

axle (AX-ul): A rod that a wheel turns on. (2-5)

B

balance (BAL-uñss): Make the number of atoms of each element the same on both sides of an equation (13-8)

balanced forces: Forces that are equal in size but opposite in direction. (4-3)

base: A compound made up of a metallic element or radical combined with one or more hydroxyl radicals. (19-2)

battery (BAT-uh-ree): Two or more electrical cells connected together. (9-9)

boiling point: The temperature at which a liquid forms bubbles of gas. (17-10)

burning: Fast oxidation. (13-5)

C

calorie (CAL-o-ree): A unit of heat. The amount of heat needed to raise the temperature of 1 gram of water 1°C. (6-8)

Calorie: A large calorie; 1000 calories. (6-8)

Celsius (SEL-see-us) **scale:** The temperature scale in which the freezing point of water is 0° and the boiling point is 100°. (6-7)

centimeter (SEN-tih-mee-ter): 1/100 of a meter. (Page 4)

chemical (KEM-i-kul) **change:** A change that produces new substances. (13-7)

chemical equation (uh-KWAY-zhun): A way of telling about a chemical reaction with symbols and formulas. (13-8)

chemical formula (KEM-i-kul FOR-mew-luh): A shorthand way to write the name of a compound. (13-3)

chemical reaction (ree-AC-shun): A change that produces one or more new substances. (13-8)

chemical symbols (SIM-buls): A short way of writing the names of the elements. (11-6)

chemistry (KEM-iss-tree): The study of matter. (11-1)

chord (CORD): Three or more notes played together. (7-10)

closed circuit: A complete path for electricity to move along. (9-6)

coagulation (coh-AG-yew-LAY-shun): The use of chemicals to make particles clump together. (18-2)

coefficient (COH-uh-FISH-unt): A number that tells how many molecules of a substance are needed or produced in a reaction. (13-8)

colloid (COL-oid): A type of suspension that does not separate on standing. (18-4)

compound (COM-pound): A combination of elements that has different properties from the elements that make it up. (13-1)

compress (kum-PRESS): Squeeze together. (7-4)

concave (CON-CAVE) **lens:** A lens that is curved inward. (8-9)

concentrated (CON-sen-trait-ed) **solution:** A strong solution. (17-7)

condensation (con-den-SAY-shun): Changing from a gas to a liquid. (11-3)

conduction (con-DUCK-shun): Movement of heat energy by molecules bumping into each other. (6-2)

conductivity (con-duc-TIV-uh-tee) **tester:** An instrument used to see if solutions conduct electricity. (19-5)

conductor (con-DUCK-ter): A material that electricity can go through very well. (9-2)

conservation (con-ser-VAY-shun) of energy: The idea that energy cannot be made or destroyed, but only changed in form. (1-4)

contract (con-TRACT): Get smaller; take up less space. (6-5)

convection (con-VEC-shun): The way that heat travels through gases and liquids. (6-3)

convection currents: Up-and-down movements of gases or liquids caused by convection. (6-3)

convex (CON-VEX) **lens:** A lens that is curved outward. (8-9)

core: The material in the center of an electromagnet. (10-7)

cornea (COR-nee-uh): The clear front of the eye. (8-10)

corrosion (cur-ROH-zhun): The wearing away of metals. (16-5)

covalent (coh-VAY-lent) **compound:** A compound in which atoms share electrons. (14-3)

crystal (CRISS-tul): A piece of a solid that is shaped like a jewel. (13-4)

D

deceleration: Negative acceleration; "slowing down." (4-2)

decibel (DESS-uh-bell): A measurement of the loudness of sound. (7-2)

decomposition (DEE-com-puh-ZISH-un) **reaction:** A reaction that breaks down compounds into simpler substances. (15-3)

degree (duh-GREE): A unit of temperature. (6-7)

dense: Heavy for its volume. (5-1)

density (DEN-suh-tee): Mass of a certain volume of a material. (5-1)

diatomic (DY-uh-TOM-ic) **molecule:** A molecule containing two atoms of the same element. (14-5)

diffuse dih-FYOOS) **reflection:** Reflection from a rough surface, reflection that does not give images. (8-6)

dilute (die-LOOT) **solution:** A weak solution. (17-7)

direct current: Electric current that moves in one direction only. (10-10)

displaced (dis-PLACED) **water:** The amount of water pushed out of the way by an object. (5-5)

dissolve (dih-ZOLV): Become part of a solution. (17-2)

distillation (dis-tuh-LAY-shun): A way of recovering the solute and the solvent from a solution. 17-12)

double replacement reaction: A reaction in which elements from two compounds change places, and two new compounds are formed. (15-5)

dry cell: An electrical cell that has a moist electrolyte. (9-5)

E

echo (EK-oh): A sound that is bounced back by an object. (7-8)

efficiency (eh-FISH-un-see): The percent of useful work obtained from a machine. (3-8)

effort (EFF-ert): The force used on a lever. (2-2)

effort arm: The distance from the fulcrum to where the effort is put on a lever. (2-2)

electric (e-LEC-tric) **charge:** A condition produced by electricity. (9-1)

electric circuit (SURK-ut): The path that an electric current follows. (9-6)

electric current (CUR-rent): A flow of electrical charge. (9-1)

electrical (e-LEC-tri-cul) **energy:** The kind of energy that moving charges have. (9-4)

electrocuted (e-LEC-tro-kew-ted): Killed by an electric current. (9-1)

electrode (e-LEC-trode): The negative or positive part of an electric cell. (9-5). A rod that allows an electric current to enter or leave an electrolyte solution. (16-7)

electrolysis (e-lec-TROL-uh-sis): Using an electric current to break down a compound. (15-3)

electrolyte (e-LEC-tro-lite): a liquid or moist substance that can conduct electricity. (9-5) A substance that can make water conduct electricity. (16-7) (19-5)

electromagnet (e-LEC-tro-MAG-net): A coil of wire that uses an electric current to make a strong magnetic field. (10-6)

electromagnetic (e-lec-tro-mag-NET-ic) **spectrum:** The spectrum made up of radio waves, infrared, visible light, ultraviolet, X rays, gamma rays, and cosmic rays. (8-12)

electromotive (e-LEC-troh-MOH-tive) **force:** The push that makes electricity move. (9-9)

electron (e-LEC-tron): A negatively charged atomic particle. (9-4, 12-2)

electron shell: All of an electron's orbits, or paths, put together. (12-5)

electroplating (e-LEC-tro-plate-ing): Using an electric current to plate one metal onto another metal. (16-7)

element (EL-uh-ment): A simple substance that cannot be broken down into simpler substances. (11-4)

emulsifying (eh-MUL-suh-fy-ing) **agent:** A substance that keeps emulsions from separating. (18-3)

emulsion (eh-MUL-shun): A suspension of two liquids. (18-3)

energy: The ability to do work. (1-6)

evaporation (ee-VAP-uh-RAY-shun): Changing from a liquid to a gas when the liquid is left open to the air. (11-3) (17-10)

expand (eck-SPAND): Get larger, take up more space. (6-5) (7-4)

extended (eck-STEN-ded) **source:** A light source made up of many point sources. (8-3)

F

Fahrenheit (FAR-en-hite) **scale:** The temperature scale in which the freezing point of water is 32° and the boiling point is 212°. (6-7)

filter: A material that transmits some colors of light and blocks others. (8-13)

fixed pulley. A pulley that does not move. (2-5)

focal (FOH-kul) **length:** The distance from the focal point to the lens. (8-9)

focal point: The place where light rays from a lens meet. (8-9)

formula mass: The sum of all the atomic masses in a molecule. (14-7)

formula weight: The sum of all the atomic weights in a molecule. (14-7)

freezing: Changing from a liquid to a solid. (11-3)

freezing point: The temperature at which a liquid changes to a solid. (17-8)

frequency (FREE-kwun-see): The number of vibrations per second. (7-3)

friction (FRIC-shun): Rubbing. (6-1) A force that acts against the motion of one surface over another. (3-6)

fuel (FEWL): Material that is burned to produce heat energy. (6-1)

fulcrum (FULL-crum): The point where a lever is supported. (2-2)

G

galvanized (GAL-vuh-nized) **iron:** Iron that is plated with zinc. (16-7)

galvanometer (gal-va-NOM-uh-ter): A tool for measuring very small electric currents. (10-8)

gas (GASS): The form of matter that has no definite shape or volume. (11-2)

gram: A unit of mass in the metric system. (Page 2)

gravity (GRAV-uh-tee): The force that pulls things down toward the center of the earth. (1-5)

group: A family of elements going down the periodic table. (11-7)

H

harmony (HAR-muh-nee): Combining musical notes. (7-10)

heat: A form of energy that we can feel. (6-1)

hertz (HURTS): The unit used for measuring frequency. (7-3)

Hoffman apparatus (HOFF-mum AP-uh-RAT-us): A device that can break water down into its elements. (13-2)

hologram (HOH-luh-gram): A 3-D photograph made with a laser. (8-15)

homogeneous (ho-muh-JEE-nee-us): The same throughout. (17-4).

homogenization (huh-moh-uh-nuh-ZAY-shun): Making a permanent emulsion by rapid spinning. (18-3)

hydroxide (hy-DROK-side) **ion:** An ion containing one oxygen atom and one hydrogen atom. (14-4)

I

ideal (eye-DEEL) **M.A.:** The M.A. a machine would have it there were no friction. (3-8)

identify (eye-DEN-ti-fy): Recognize or find out what something is. (11-5)

illuminated (ih-LOOM-ih-nate-ed) **objects:** Objects that light shines on. (8-3)

image (IM-ij): Reflection in a mirror. (8-6)

immiscible (im-MIS-uh-bul) **liquids:** Liquids that are not able to mix together to form a solution. (17-3)

incident (IN-suh-dint) **ray:** The ray of light that hits something. (8-5)

inclined (in-CLINED) **plane:** A flat furface that is tilted. (2-4)

indicator (IN-duh-kate-er): A chemical that changes color in acids and bases. (19-3)

induced (in-DOOSED) **current:** An electric current made by a moving magnetic field. (10-8)

induced magnetism: Magnetism caused by touching or being near a magnet. (10-2)

induction (in-DUCK-shun) **coil:** A primary and secondary coil working together. (10-9)

inertia: The tendency of an object to keep its same motion. (4-4)

infrared (in-fruh-RED) **light:** Invisible light with wavelengths longer than red. (8-12)

insoluble (in-SOL-yuh-bul): Not able to dissolve. (17-3)

instantaneous speed: Actual speed at any given moment. (4-1)

insulator (IN-suh-lay-ter): A material that electricity cannot go through. (9-2)

ion (EYE-on): An atom that is electrically charged because it has lost or gained electrons. (14-1)

ionic (eye-ON-ic) **compound:** The kind of compound formed when atoms combine by lending and borrowing electrons. (14-2)

ionization (EYE-uh-nuh-ZAY-shun): To separate into ions. (19-6)

iris (EYE-ris): The part that controls the amount of light entering the eye. (8-10)

J

joule (JOOL): One newton-meter of work. (1-7)

K

kilogram (Kill-uh-gram): 1,000 grams. (Page 3)

kilometer (KILL-uh-mee-ter): 1,000 meters. (Page 4)

kinetic (kuh-NET-ic) **energy:** Energy in moving things. (1-5)

knife switch: A kind of switch that is good for doing low voltage experiments. (9-3)

L

laser (LAY-zor): A device that makes one-color, high energy light. (8-15)

lens (LENZ): A curved piece of glass. (8-9)

lever (LEV-er): A simple machine with a fulcrum, an effort arm, and a resistance arm. (2-2)

light-year: The distance that light travels in one year. (8-1)

limewater (LIME-water): A chemical that turns milky-white when it mixes with carbon dioxide. (13-6)

lines of force: The lines that show a magnetic field. (10-3)

liquid (LIK-wid): The form of matter that has a definite volume but no definite shape. (11-2)

liter (LEE-ter): 1,000 cubic centimeters. (Page 5)

longitudinal (lon-jih-TOO-dih-nul) **wave:** A wave that moves back-and-forth. (7-4)

luminous (LOOM-in-us) **objects:** Objects that give off their own light. (8-3)

luster (LUS-ter): The shininess of a material. (11-5)

M

magnetic field (mag-NET-ic FEELD): The pattern of magnetism around a magnet. (10-3)

magnetize (MAG-nuh-tize): Make into a magnet. (10-2)

malleable (MAL-ee-uh-bul): Able to be hammered into different shapes. (11-5)

manometer (muh-NOM-uh-ter): An instrument used to measure pressure. (3-11)

mass: The amount of matter in an object. (3-5)

matter: Anything that has weight and takes up space. (11-1)

mechanical advantage (muh-CAN-i-cul ad-VAN-tij): The number of times a machine multiplies the effort. (2-3)

media (MEE-dee-uh): More than one medium. (8-7)

medium (MEE-dee-um): A material that carries a wave. (7-4)

melody (MEL-uh-dee): The tune of music. (7-10)

melting: Changing from a solid to a liquid. (11-3)

melting point: The temperature at which a solid changes to a liquid. (17-8)

metals (MET-uls): Elements that have certain properties. (11-5)

meter (MEE-ter): The unit of length in the metric system. (Page 4)

metric system (MEH-trick SIS-tem): The units of measurement used by scientists. (Page 2)

millimeter (MILL-ih-mee-ter): 1/1000 of a meter. (Page 4)

miscible (MIS-uh-bul) **liquids:** Liquids that are able to mix together to form a solution. (17-3)

mixture (MIX-chur): Two or more substances that have been put together, but have not been changed chemically. (13-9) (17-1)

molecular (muh-LEK-yuh-ler) **mass:** The same as formula mass. (14-7)

molecular (muh-LEK-yuh-ler) **weight:** The same as formula weight. (14-7)

molecules (MOL-uh-kewls): The tiny bits that make up matter. (11-2)

moment (MOH-ment): The turning effect of a force. (2-6)

more active metal: A metal that replaces another metal from its compounds. (16-4)

movable (MOOV-uh-bul) **pulley:** A pulley that moves. (2-5)

N

negative (NEG-uh-tiv) **charge:** Opposite of positive charge; the kind of charge on an electron. (12-2)

neutral (NEW-trul): Neither positively nor negatively charged. (12-2) Neither acid nor basic. (19-4)

neutralization (noo-truh-luh-ZAY-shun) **reaction:** Mixing an acid and a base to produce a salt and water. (15-5) (19-4)

neutron (NEW-tron): A neutral atomic particle. (12-2)

newton (NOO-tun): A unit of force. (3-5)

newton-meter: A unit of work. (1-7)

nichrome (NY-crome): A high resistance metal used to make wires for toasters. (9-11)

non-electrolyte: A substance that will not make water conduct electricity. (19-5)

non-metals: Elements with properties that are the opposite of metals. (11-5)

normal line: A line drawn at right angles to a surface. (8-5)

notes: Musical sounds of different pitches. (7-9)

nucleus (NEW-clee-us): The center of an atom. (12-4)

O

octave (OK-tiv): A set of eight notes of the musical scale. (7-10)

ohm: The unit of resistance. (9-12)

opaque (oh-PAKE) **materials:** Materials that block all light. (8-3)

open circuit: An incomplete path that electricity cannot move along. (9-6)

optic nerve (OP-tik): The nerve that carries the signals from the eye to the brain. (8-10)

oppose (op-POZE): Try to stop. (9-11)

orbit (OR-bit): A path that electrons follow around the nucleus. (12-4)

ore (OR): A mineral compound from which we can get a useful metal. (16-1)

overtones (Oh-ver-tones): The extra frequencies that give a sound its quality. (7-7)

oxidation (OX-i-DAY-shun): Combining with oxygen. (13-5) Losing electrons in a chemical reaction. (16-8)

P

parallel (PA-ruh-lel) **circuit:** A circuit that has more than one path for the electricity to follow. (9-7)

penumbra (pih-NUM-bruh): A gray, outer shadow around an umbra. (8-4)

percussion (per-CUSH-un) **instruments:** Musical instruments played by hitting. (7-11)

period (PEER-ee-ud): A family of elements going across the periodic table. (11-7)

phase: One of the forms in which matter may be found. (11-2)

photoelectric (foh-toh-uh-LEC-tric) **cell:** A cell that changes light into electricity. (8-14)

photon (FOH-ton): A tiny particle of light. (8-14)

physical (FIZZ-i-cul) **change:** A change that does not produce a new substance. (13-7)

pitch: How high or low a sound is. (7-3)

plating (PLATE-ing): Coating one metal with another metal. (16-7)

point source (SORSS): A tiny point of light. (8-3)

poles: The ends of a magnet. (10-1)

polyatomic (pol-ee-uh-TOM-ic) **ion:** An ion containing one oxygen atom and one hydrogen atom. (14-4)

positive (POS-i-tiv) **charge:** Opposite of negative charge: the kind of charge on a proton. (12-2)

potential (puh-TEN-shul) **energy:** Stored energy. (1-5)

powdering (POW-duh-ring): Breaking a solid into very small pieces. (17-6)

precipitate (pruh-SIP-ih-tate): An undisolved solid that usually sinks to the bottom of a mixture. (15-5)

predict (pree-DICT): Tell what will happen. (9-12)

pressure (PRESH-er): The amount of force on a certain amount of area. (3-10)

primary (PRY-ma-ree) **coil:** A coil that induces a current in another coil. (10-9)

prism (PRIZ-um): A triangular-shaped piece of glass. (8-11)

product (PROD-uct): A substance that is produced in a chemical reaction. (15-1)

properties (PROP-er-teez): Things that help identify something. (11-5)

proton (PROH-ton): A positively charged atomic particle. (12-2)

pulley: A simple machine made of a wheel and an axle. (2-5)

pupil (PYOO-pull): The opening into the eye. (8-10)

pushbutton switch: A kind of switch that opens when you take your finger off the button. (9-3)

Q

quality (KWAL-ih-tee): The difference in sounds due to different overtones. (7-7)

R

radiation (ray-dee-AY-shun): The way that heat energy travels through space. (6-4)

radiometer (ray-dee-OM-uh-ter): A device that turns when sunlight shines on it. (6-4)

ray: A line that shows the direction of a light wave. (8-2)

reactant (ree-ACT-ent): A substance that is changed in a chemical reaction. (15-1)

real image: An image that can be projected. (8-9)

recover (re-KUV-ver): To get something back the way it was. (17-12)

reduction (ree-DUCK-shun): Removing oxygen from an ore to free the metal in the ore. (16-2) Gaining electrons in a chemical reaction. (16-8)

reflected (ruh-FLECK-tid) **light:** Light that has has bounced off something. (8-5)

reflected ray: The ray of light that bounces off something. (8-5)

refraction (ruh-FRAK-shun): The bending of light as it passes from one medium to another medium at an angle. (8-7)

regular reflection: Reflection from a smooth surface; reflection that gives clear images. (8-6)

repel (ree-PEL): Push away. (9-4)

replace: Take the place of. (15-4)

resistance (ree-ZIS-tense): A measure of how easy or hard it is for electric current to move through a material. (9-11) The force that acts against a lever. (2-2)

resistance: The object moved by a lever. (2-2)

resistance arm: The distance from the fulcrum to where the resistance acts on a lever. (2-2)

retina (RET-in-uh): The back part of the eye on which images form. (8-10)

rhythm (RITH-um): The beat of music. (7-10)

roasting: Heating an ore in air to produce an oxide. (16-2)

rusting: The slow oxidation of iron. (13-5)

S

salt: A chemical produced by the reaction between an acid and a base. (19-4)

saturated (SATCH-uh-rate-ed) **solution:** A solution that has all the solute it can dissolve. (17-7)

secondary (SEC-un-DER-ee) **coil:** A coil in which current is induced. (10-9)

series (SEER-eez) **circuit:** A circuit that has just one path for the electric current to follow. (9-6)

settle: Separate by falling to the bottom. (18-1)

short circuit: A short electrical path that has very low resistance. (9-13)

single replacement (ree-PLACE-ment) **reaction:** A chemical reaction in which one element replaces another element in a compound. (15-4)

solar (SOH-ler) **cell:** A device that produces electricity when sunlight shines on it. (6-4)

solid (SOL-id): The form of matter that has a definite shape and volume. (11-2)

soluble (SOL-yuh-bul): Able to dissolve. (17-3)

solute (SOL-yute): The substance that is dissolved in a solution. (17-3)

solution (suh-LEW-shun): A mixture of two or more substances that mix evenly with each other. (17-2)

solvent (SOL-vent): The substance in which a solute dissolves. (17-3)

sonar (SOH-nahr): A way of using underwater echoes to find distances. (7-8)

sound wave: Many compressions and expansions of sound moving through a medium. (7-4)

speed: How long it takes to go a certain distance. (4-1)

spring constant: The amount a spring will stretch for each unit of force added. (3-4)

state: One of the forms in which matter may be found. (11-2)

streamlined (STREEM-lined): Shaped to have little air friction. (3-6)

stringed instruments: Musical instruments that make their sound by means of vibrating strings. (7-11)

subscript (SUB-script): A number in a chemical formula that shows how many atoms of an element are in a molecule. (13-3) (14-7)

superconductor (SOO-per-con-DUCK-ter): A material that loses all its resistance when it is very cold. (9-11)

supersaturated (SOO-per-SATCH-uh-rate-ed) **solution:** A solution containing more dissolved solute than it can usually hold at that temperature. (17-14)

suspension (suh-SPEN-shun): A cloudy mixture of two of more substances that settles on standing. (18-1)

switch: Something used to turn electric current on and off. (9-3)

synthesis (SIN-thuh-sis) **reaction:** A reaction in which two elements combine to form a compound. (15-2)

T

temperature (TEM-pruh-chur): A measure of how hot a material is. (6-6)

tension (TEN-shun): The tightness of a string. (7-9)

terminal (TURM-i-nul): The negative or positive end of an electrical cell. (9-5)

theory (THEE-uh-ree): An idea based on scientific experiments or observations. (1-4)

thermal (THUR-mul) **pollution:** Wasted heat that warms the air and waters of the earth. (1-3)

thermometer (ther-MOM-uh-ter): A tool used to measure temperature. (6-6)

tincture (TINK-chur): A solution of a solid in alcohol. (17-5)

toggle (TOG-gull) **switch:** A kind of switch that is used for lights in a home. (9-3)

transformer (trans-FOR-mer): An induction coil that uses alternating current. (10-10)

translucent (trans-LOOSE-ent) **materials:** Materials that let just some light pass through. (8-3)

transmit (trans-MIT): Allow to pass through. (8-13)

transparent (trans-PAIR-ent) **materials:** Materials that let light pass through them. (8-3)

transverse (TRANZ-VERSE) **wave:** A wave shaped like a water wave. (8-2)

tungsten (TUNG-sten): A high-resistance metal used to make wires for light bulbs. (9-11)

tuning (TOON-ing) **fork:** A Y-shaped metal instrument that vibrates to make musical sounds. (7-1)

U

ultraviolet (ul-truh-VYE-uh-let) **light:** Invisible light with wavelengths shorter than violet. (8-12)

umbra (UM-bruh): A sharp, black shadow. (8-4)

unbalanced force: Any force that changes the motions of the object it acts upon. (4-3)

unit YOU-nit): An amount that is used to measure things. (Page 2)

universal (YEW-ni-VERS-al): Worldwide; the same all over the world. (11-6)

unsaturated (un-SATCH-uh-rate-ed) **solution:** A solution that can dissolve more solute. (17-7)

V

vacuum (VAK-yoom): A space where there is no matter; empty space. (3-3) (7-5)

valence (VAIL-ens): The number of electrons an atom borrow or lends. (14-1)

velocity: Speed and direction of travel. (4-1)

verdigris (VERD-uh-griss): The green coating on corroded copper. (16-5)

vibrate (VY-brate): Move back and forth quickly in a small space. (11-2)

vibration (vy-BRAY-shun): a quickly repeated back-and-forth motion. (7-1)

visible spectrum (VIZ-uh-bul SPEK-trum): The seven colors of the rainbow. (8-11)

volt (VOHLT): The unit for measuring electromotive force. (9-9)

voltage (VOHL-tig): The number of volts. (9-9)

voltmeter (VOHLT-mee-ter): An instrument for measuring force. (9-10)

volume (VOL-yoom): The amount of space matter takes up. (11-1)

W

weight: The force of gravity on an object. (3-5)

wet cell: An electrical cell that has a liquid electrolyte. (9-5)

wind instruments: Musical instruments played by blowing. (7-11)

Y

yield (YEELD): Produce. (13-8)

INDEX

PHOTOGRAPH CREDITS

Photographs of the following pages by George A. Bakacs:

8, 9 (top left, right center), 16, 18 (bottom right), 19, 24, 28, 34, 38, 49, 53, 54, 56, 57, 88, 98, 99, 100, 162, 163, 166, 184, 185, 216, 218, 222, 252, 282, 291, 298, 300, 302, 303, 310, 312, 323, 327, 329, 334, 339, 349

PAGE

9 (Top right) N.Y. Daily News
12 Wide World Photos
15 General Public Utilities
18 N.Y. Daily News
25 Copyright Rube Goldenberg, by permission of King Features Syndicate
106 Edward P. Diehl
107 Edward P. Diehl
113 Bettmann Archive
117 Armstrong Cork Company
122-123 Edward P. Diehl
124 Moss from Black Star
142 Edward P. Diehl
143 Edward P. Diehl
155 (Top) AIP Niehls Bohr Library; (Bottom) AP/Wide World Photos
159 Edward P. Diehl
160 Bell Labs Photo
161 Bell Labs Photo
166 A Devaney, Inc.
167 Con Edison
199 Grant White from F.P.G.
207 Paul Johnson
208 Ford Parts Division
214 Tzvoras/Editorial Photocolor Archives
233 Lawrence Radiation Laboratory, Berkeley
239 (Top) Columbia University; (Bottom) Courtesy of AT&T Bell Laboratories
292 Kennecot Copper Corp.
315 National Park Service
343 NASA, ERTS
352 Proctor & Gamble Company